Howard's Fourth Government

AUSTRALIAN COMMONWEALTH
ADMINISTRATION 2004–2007

Howard's Fourth Government

Edited by Chris Aulich and Roger Wettenhall

UNSW PRESS

A UNSW Press book

Published by
University of New South Wales Press Ltd
University of New South Wales
Sydney NSW 2052
AUSTRALIA
www.unswpress.com.au

© UNSW Press 2008
First published 2008

This book is copyright. Apart from any fair dealing for the purpose of private study, research, criticism or review, as permitted under the Copyright Act, no part may be reproduced by any process without written permission. While copyright of the work as a whole is vested in UNSW Press, copyright of individual chapters is retained by the chapter authors. Inquiries should be addressed to the publisher.

National Library of Australia
Cataloguing-in-Publication entry

> Howard's fourth government: Australian commonwealth administration, 2004–2007/editors, Chris Aulich and Roger Wettenhall.
> Sydney: University of New South Wales Press, 2008.
> ISBN: 978 086840 982 5 (pbk.)
> Includes index.
> Howard, John, 1939–. – Political and social views.
> Public administration – Australia.
> Australia – Politics and government – 2001–
> Other Authors/Contributors: Aulich, Chris, 1947– ,
>   Wettenhall, R.L. (Roger Llewellyn), 1931–.

324.29405

Design Josephine Pajor-Markus
Cover Newspix
Cartoons Nicholson from *The Australian* www.nicholsoncartoons.com.au
Printer Ligare

This book is printed on paper using fibre supplied from plantation or sustainably managed forests.

Contents

	Preface	*vii*
	Contributors	*viii*
1	Introduction Chris Aulich and Roger Wettenhall	*1*

Part I GOVERNANCE ISSUES

2	The search for balance and effectiveness in the Australian Public Service John Halligan	*13*
3	Non-departmental public bodies as a focus for machinery-of-government change Roger Wettenhall	*31*
4	Continuing Howard's privatisation agenda Chris Aulich	*57*
5	The Senate a paper tiger? Gwynneth Singleton	*75*
6	Reconfiguring the Federation? Andrew Parkin and Geoff Anderson	*95*
7	Reshaping public integrity John Uhr	*114*

Part II POLICY ISSUES

8	The economy Anne Garnett and Phil Lewis	*135*
9	Rural policy issues Linda Courtenay Botterill	*152*
10	Industrial relations and the labour market Phil Lewis	*169*
11	In the name of failure: A generational revolution in Indigenous affairs Will Sanders	*187*
12	Discovering the environment Jenny Stewart and Carolyn Hendriks	*206*
13	From multiculturalism to citizenship Heba Batainah and Mary Walsh	*227*
14	Searching for the national interest Daniel Baldino	*244*

Part III JOHN HOWARD, PRIME MINISTER

15	Staying on David Adams	*263*
	Index	*286*

Preface

This is the ninth volume in the Australian Commonwealth Administration series initiated from the University of Canberra and its predecessor Canberra College of Advanced Education. Each volume has mapped events and issues which have characterised the administration and policy of successive governments since Hawke's first government. The evolution of the series is explained briefly in chapter 1.

In this book we again have invited scholars from a number of universities to contribute their views on those elements which have defined the fourth Howard government. The editors are grateful to these scholars, for their insights and their capacity to deliver a manuscript so soon after the election, when the focus of most Australians was more likely to be on what was to come rather than on what has been.

Assembling this book took more than a year and the editors are most appreciative of the efforts of all of the authors involved to meet deadlines and offer their analysis of the performance of Howard's fourth government in their own field of research interest. Our thanks go to them and to the public agencies and departments and funding bodies which supported and assisted them to bring their work to fruition. We would also like to specifically acknowledge the research assistance provided to some authors by Toby Halligan (chapter 2), Andrew Carr (chapter 4), Kim Pham and Stefan Kraus (chapter 12), Alex Karolis (chapter 13) and Judy Aulich for her assistance with several chapters. We are also grateful to Carla Taines for her incredibly thorough editing of the manuscript and to Michael Harrington for compiling the index.

We are delighted that Peter Nicholson has kindly consented to allow us to use his cartoons to illustrate our chapters. Peter's insights typically say much more than our many words!

Finally, we want to offer our sincere thanks to John Elliott and the staff of UNSW Press who obviously share our enthusiasm for maintaining the integrity of this important series – we can only hope that they will again agree to work with us in compiling the tenth volume in the series, *Rudd's First Government*!

Chris Aulich and Roger Wettenhall

Contributors

Editors

Chris Aulich is Associate Professor in Public Administration, University of Canberra, and formerly Director of the University's Centre for Research in Public Sector Management.

Roger Wettenhall is Emeritus Professor and Visiting Professor in the Centre for Research in Public Sector Management, University of Canberra.

Authors

David Adams is an Adjunct Fellow in Political Science and International Relations, Australian National University.

Geoff Anderson is a Senior Research Associate and Lecturer in the School of Political and International Studies, Flinders University.

Daniel Baldino is a Lecturer in Politics in the Faculty of Business & Government, University of Canberra.

Heba Batainah is a PhD Candidate in Politics, University of Canberra.

Linda Courtenay Botterill is a Fellow in the Political Science Program, Research School of Social Sciences, Australian National University.

Anne Garnett is a Senior Lecturer in Economics at Murdoch University and a Research Associate of the Centre for Labour Market Research.

John Halligan is Research Professor in Government and Public Administration in the Faculty of Business & Government, University of Canberra.

Carolyn Hendriks is a Lecturer, Crawford School of Economics and Government, Australian National University.

Phil Lewis is the Canberra Director of the Centre for Labour Market Research and Professor of Economics, University of Canberra.

Andrew Parkin is Deputy Vice Chancellor (Academic) and Professor of Political and International Studies, Flinders University.

Will Sanders is Senior Fellow at the Centre for Aboriginal Economic Policy Research, Australian National University.

Gwynneth Singleton is an Adjunct Associate Professor in Politics, University of Canberra.

Jenny Stewart is Associate Professor in Public Policy in the Faculty of Business & Government, University of Canberra.

John Uhr is Professor, Crawford School of Economics and Government, Australian National University.

Mary Walsh is a Senior Lecturer in Politics in the Faculty of Business & Government, University of Canberra.

1 Introduction

Chris Aulich and Roger Wettenhall

Any change in government excites interest, whether it involves anticipation, apprehension or some other strong feeling. Given that Australia has only changed its government 11 times since Federation, the promise of a new government carries a particularly high level of emotion, and so it proved with the election victory of Kevin Rudd's Labor Party on 24 November 2007. Popular columnist Peter FitzSimons (2007) reflected this heightened sense of change when he commented on remarks made by Mungo MacCallum (2007):

> **MacCallum:** If you have any doubt that the election of the Rudd Labor Government has changed the country, consider this: a year ago, did you imagine that the Prime Minister would be sending an openly gay woman of Chinese ancestry to Bali to ratify the Kyoto protocol on Australia's behalf?
>
> **FitzSimons:** Exactly! And, of course, it goes far beyond Senator Wong's trip to Bali to sign us up to sanity. Everywhere else, it seems, so many of the things that John Howard stood for – WorkChoices, our engagement in Iraq, limiting gay rights, no 'sorry' to Aborigines – have been so completely swept away, it seems extraordinary now that they were holy writ of the political establishment as recently as *last month*.

This level of emotion was further underlined with the 'real' election period stretching over more than a year leading up to the actual election date, and the possibility of a new government occupying many commentators, perhaps displacing some of the focus on Howard's fourth term in office. Discussion of the election campaign, the demise of the Howard government, the dramatic loss of the Prime Minister's own seat and reflections on the entire 11½ years of coalition government have quite naturally become the subjects of innumerable television, newspaper and journal pieces. The lead story in *The Canberra Times* the morning after the election said it all: 'Rudd buries Howard era' (Fraser 2007). What runs the risk of being lost amid this excitement is the specific performance of Howard's fourth government, which has yet to attract serious reflection and commentary, beyond its impact on the final election result. This book aims to make a contribution to filling this gap – to map Howard's fourth term, identify key issues and reflect both on key policy debates and on changes to the machinery of government, and to place these on record.

When we began this Australian Commonwealth Administration series in the 1980s (for a complete list of publications in this series, see appendix 1.1) the focus was mostly on the organisational and structural arrangements that underpinned the activities of the commonwealth government. That was appropriate for a university school whose interests related to the administrative rather than the political side of governing. However, through the early volumes, there were some extensions into policy areas where there was a strong connection with the major cross-governmental structural issues, notably 'great spy dramas' (1983), employment, education and training reform (1992), corporations law reform (1992), microeconomic reform (1995) and science and technology policy-making (1995).

Authorship throughout the series has mixed researchers drawn from relevant teaching sections of CCAE/University of Canberra (hereafter UC) with others from other Australian universities and occasionally the bureaucracy, but the planning, co-ordinating and editing has always centred on UC, with support (until we went to a commercial publisher) from the ACT Division of the Institute of Public Administration Australia and its forerunners. It was inevitable that, in a rapidly developing institution of higher education, there would be teaching and research movement into a broader range of social science policy areas. So it was inevitable too that this movement would be reflected in later volumes in this series. More chapters came to be devoted to policy areas that loomed large in the considerations of the governments being reported on. Thus issues like Indigenous affairs, international relations, waterfront reform, welfare reform and tax reform gained chapter-length treatment (2000, 2005).

This account of the fourth Howard government has been organised in three sections: it begins with a group of essays which reflect on changes during the period of review to the institutions of governance covering both the core public service and the outer public sector with its non-departmental bodies. This first section also deals with key governance issues such as privatisation, the management of the Howard government's Senate majority, intergovernment relations and issues relating to accountability and ethics. The second section examines those policy issues that dominated this fourth term such as management of the economy, rural policies (particularly wheat and drought), industrial relations, Indigenous policy, the environment, multiculturalism and citizenship, and foreign affairs: all played a role in defining the fourth term and some, in particular industrial relations and the environment, were sufficiently influential to contribute to the electoral loss of the Howard government. As with the previous two volumes in this series, the third section containing the final chapter has been written by David Adams and focuses on John Howard in his role as prime minister.

Matters of governance: structural and functional arrangements

In chapter 2 John Halligan looks at developments in the Australian Public Service over the fourth government period. He gives attention to a number of themes in management reform which in part demonstrate considerable continuity over a longer reform period beginning in the 1980s, but which in part also reflect new emphases and new tensions arising in the period being reported on. The new emphases come primarily from the heightened security environment following the al-Qaeda attacks on New York and Washington in September 2001 and the associated push towards whole-of-government solutions to administrative problems, a push Australia has shared with many other countries. In tracing these developments, this chapter shows how the dramatic downsizing of the public service characteristic of the earlier Howard period came to be reversed, with the service again increasing in size and beginning to demonstrate 'big government' characteristics. The government was giving more attention to central co-ordination and monitoring and to performance measurement, all orchestrated by the core agencies (the 'central agencies'). This centralising tendency is consistent with the rise of 'prime ministerial government' memorialised in an important address by Paul Kelly, editor of *The Australian* newspaper, early in the fourth government period (Kelly 2006). Additionally, in noting some significant failures of the period,

Halligan is also documenting rising signs of tension between ministers and their public service advisers.

The whole-of-government theme gets further attention in chapter 3. Roger Wettenhall deals with developments affecting the large complement of 'non-departmental public bodies' (NDPBs) within the government system. In particular, the 'principles' outlined in the Uhrig Report, submitted during the third government period but implemented during the fourth, had a major effect on the style of government. This implementation process removed some NDPBs, but more importantly it enhanced ministerial authority over the whole public sector by reducing the autonomy of many agencies, large and small, within it. This chapter records the general effect of these changes, alongside the creation of some new NDPBs to serve new policy initiatives of the period.

Chris Aulich traces ongoing movements in the area of privatisation in chapter 4. He focuses his chapter on the key privatisation technologies of divestment, outsourcing and user-pays. While the pace of divestment activity may have slowed during the period under review, the general effect has been to continue the process of placing greater reliance on the private sector to satisfy the needs of the community, reflecting a fundamental neo-liberal distrust of government action and capacity (Brett 2007). As Aulich demonstrates, Howard's 'small government' stance has continued through the fourth government period notwithstanding the growth in the core public service as recorded in chapter 2.

In chapter 5, Gwynneth Singleton looks at what surely became the main issue in government–parliament relations during the fourth government period: the effect of the Howard government gaining a majority in the Senate. She explores the impact of this change in terms of its influence on parliamentary procedures (notably time allowed for debates, question time, committee hearings and reports, production of documents) and what it has meant for the 'balance of power'. This issue too clearly contributed to the strengthening of the Prime Minister's hand within the system.

The fourth government period was marked by dramatic changes in the balance of relations between the commonwealth and the states and territories within the federal system. These changes are explored in chapter 6 by Andrew Parkin and Geoff Anderson, who look particularly on the seeming 'grab' for more power by the commonwealth in areas like industrial relations, education, health and water management, and note the important role of the High Court in furthering these federal ambitions. The authors trace John Howard's increasing articulation of 'aspirational nationalism', marking him as a great centraliser, a prime minister prepared to break with a long Liberal Party tradition of defending 'states' rights'.

Finally in this first group of chapters, John Uhr (chapter 7) investigates the debates of the period about the public integrity of the government, with particular attention to the matters of truth, honesty and accountability. He looks at competing claims over the integrity of the Howard government, and argues that the standards of public integrity are themselves controversial, and that new models are required for proper understanding.

It is likely that the main gaps in our treatment of the structural and functional arrangements in this part of the book relate to issues of public finance and procurement, to matters relating to judicial and administrative review, and to the question of the way in which public inquiries are conducted. All are touched on in various ways in the chapters we have just introduced, but it is unfortunate that considerations of time, space and resources have prevented us from dealing with them more fully. In the finance and procurement area, readers will find some references to budget-making in chapter 2 and 8; and, while the specific case is not noted in chapter 3, we point out that serious problems in procurement within the defence portfolio led to the creation of a distinct Defence Materiel Organisation as a 'prescribed agency' of the kind discussed in that chapter. The role of the judiciary gains recognition especially in chapter 6, which deals with the High Court's extension of the application of the corporations power under the constitution, a decision which significantly extends the commonwealth's strength within the federal system. And the role played by formally established inquiries in the processes of government, however public or private they may seem, is noted in several places in the book, notably chapters 3, 9 and 12. As editors we note further that, during the term of the fourth Howard government, Scott Prasser, a contributor to earlier volumes in this series, has published a comprehensive review of the role of such inquiries in Australia (Prasser 2006).

Matters of policy

It is clear from the analysis in many of the chapters that the fourth term was not John Howard's best especially in relation to policy-making: concerns raised by the authors in this volume relate to the lack of investment by his government into ensuring that all policy decisions were soundly based. These criticisms often refer to his government's tendency to make policy on the run without undertaking what Judith Brett describes as 'knowledge-gathering' (Brett 2007). This knowledge-gathering related to matters such as embedding the new policies into strategic policy and programs already being undertaken, capitalising on established expertise in government organisations, or even providing a forum where policy issues can be worked through in detail before being committed to law. In respect of the last, perhaps the control Howard secured over the Senate during this period and the consequent changes to the parliamentary committee system and to the exercise of gags and guillotines in the Senate (see chapter 5) may have worked for decisive decision-making but against sustainable policy-making. Perhaps the readiness to proceed without adequate consultation related to a perceived need on the part of the government to give an appearance of activity and freshness in policy in an attempt to stave off an increasingly popular opposition.

In relation to harmonisation with current policies and their knowledge bases, for example, we witnessed the intervention into the Mersey hospital (chapter 6) without strategic links being established with the Tasmanian government and its expert advisory group to ensure that the Mersey proposals were consistent with state plans to provide health services on a regional basis. Similarly, the interventions in the Northern Territory Aboriginal communities (chapter 11) were undertaken without care to harmonise with territory policies relating to issues such as health care, policing or child welfare, or indeed with the Indigenous community itself. Howard's water initiative targeted a major environmental crisis yet did not include substantial discussion with the Murray-Darling Basin Commission and its cadre of experts in the field (chapter 12). In other policy areas, few attempts were made by the Howard government to initiate wide-ranging debate on issues such as proposals to establish nuclear power stations in many regions of the country, the shift from multiculturalism to citizenship (chapter 13), and the sale of the remaining government-owned enterprises beyond Telstra (chapter 4). In these cases, policy-making was typically incremental, often with the end-goal obscured.

In chapter 8, Anne Garnett and Phil Lewis focus on one of John Howard's strengths – his governments' management of the economy. Lewis and Garnett argue that, while the foundations for reform of the economy were laid down by their predecessors, successive Howard governments introduced a range of economic policies which capitalised on those foundations, and the authors provide evidence of 'exceptional economic growth and prosperity' during the period of review. In particular, they cite the Australian economy's capacity to adjust to economic shocks without reducing economic growth as a strong performance indicator of the four Howard governments.

Similarly, Linda Botterill takes a longer term view of rural policies in chapter 9, in tracing agricultural industry policies and related policies aimed at farmers by past governments. She argues that such policies have moved incrementally over time but have still retained the overarching goals of productivity improvement and assistance for structural adjustment. Botterill notes that this policy continuity has often meant that rural policies have been developed without strong reference to overall government direction. She follows this general discussion with a focus on two key issues which emerged during the period of review – wheat and drought. They were potent issues for the Howard government to manage but, perhaps surprisingly, the government emerged from the period relatively undamaged by them.

In contrast, the issues of industrial relations reform created a major policy problem for Howard's fourth government. In chapter 10 Phil Lewis argues that while the new industrial relations changes followed a fairly continuous trajectory of labour market reform stretching back to the 1980s, the fourth Howard government mishandled the politics of the changes, in the process losing the support of both employers and employees. This proved to be one of the key issues in determining the outcome of the 2007 election.

Will Sanders continues the discussion of Indigenous policies that he began in the last volume (Sanders 2005), but locates discussion of contemporary policy-making in this area as part of a wider analysis of Indigenous policy over the past 50 or so years. Sanders argues that much policy change over time has been predicated on perceptions of, and an attempt to distance from, past policy failures. He asks the question of whether Indigenous affairs deserve better than the 'generational revolutions' which have marked approaches by past governments, and specifically by Howard's fourth government.

As a counter-balance to this cycle of failure and subsequent revolution, Jenny Stewart and Carolyn Hendriks argue in chapter 12 that Howard managed to keep environmental issues off the political agenda for much of his period in office. However, public action on environment issues, especially water and climate change, eventually overwhelmed the government so that it was forced to include them as part of the institutional agenda. Like industrial relations policy, the electoral consequences of environment issues for Howard's fourth government were profound especially as many criticisms were being voiced by those whose interests the coalition sought to represent and protect.

Heba Batainah and Mary Walsh return us to the issue of incremental policy-making in chapter 13. They map the gradual dismantling of longstanding multicultural policies and their replacement with a new focus on Australian citizenship as a primary force for social cohesion. The authors discuss changes to immigration and citizenship policies, including the introduction of a new citizenship test, all designed to make Australian citizenship more 'precious' than previously. These new policies have provided a more insular focus which they describe as an 'Australia first' approach.

This more insular focus resonates in Daniel Baldino's chapter 14 on foreign policy. Eschewing multilateral arrangements in favour of bilateral ones, Australia continued to strengthen its ties with the United States, identifying its interests more closely with those of Australia's premier ally. Baldino describes Australia's reaction to the 'war on terror' and details some of the issues relating to the David Hicks case and to the introduction of new anti-terrorist laws. He concludes that Howard's preoccupation with the war on terror and the US alliance may well have undercut a more balanced approach to foreign policy-making by reducing Australia's capacity for flexible and independent action in some arenas.

A key characteristic of administrative arrangements and of policy-making during the period of review has been the increasing centralisation and control of government activity, not only vertically with commonwealth incursions into areas traditionally dominated by the states and territories (for example, education, health and water policies), but also horizontally with the divestment of the more autonomous public enterprises, rearrangement of NDPBs and the strengthening of co-ordination arrangements across agencies. Despite this trend, however, during the period there has been little evidence of major new policy in a number of areas of national significance such as industry policy, trade, tourism, arts and culture, and even transport and communications. Certainly, debate has occurred on infrastructure issues like those involving the possible establishment of new broadband arrangements, and large grants were provided by Howard governments to improve roads, but addressing infrastructure renewal more generally remains a much needed policy focus for the new government.

John Howard, Prime Minister

As he has so capably done in the previous two volumes in this series, David Adams writes the final chapter of this book. He provides an analysis of John Howard's leadership, particularly during this fourth term, linking this to the key issues and events which characterised the period. Adams portrays Howard as a complex individual, so that it is difficult for us to appreciate what exactly he stood for. While valuing Howard's political skills Adams presents a picture of a leader who may have been past his best and who stayed on too long. However, Adams concludes that while retirement would have been better for John Howard, it might not have been any better for his party.

In the previous volume, we noted that many Australian social scientists had been alienated by the policy stances of Howard as prime minister and by the style of 'wedge politics' he was often considered to employ. This sense of alienation – or at least strong disagreement – could be observed in some of the chapters of that volume, but all contributors were virtually united in their respect for John Howard as 'a master craftsman of the politician's art, and as an effective party leader' (Aulich & Wettenhall 2005: ix–x).

Reflecting the events of late 2007, many commentators are no longer prepared to grant Howard that sort of respect: David Adams is in effect asking 'Why did he not have the wit to go earlier, and at a time of his own choosing?' It is worth remembering, however, that respect for John Howard was earned over a long period of prime ministerial government. And we note John Uhr's argument that much of the comment about the alleged lack of honesty and accountability of the Howard government itself 'lacks a degree of analytical integrity'. It behoves us all to be cautious about rushing to judgment in what we write and what we say, and to be aware that, if former Liberal Prime Minister Malcolm Fraser was quoted correctly in saying that 'Life was never meant to be easy', so too we can all say 'Governing was never meant to be easy'.

References

Aulich, C & Wettenhall, R (2005) Preface. In C Aulich & R Wettenhall (eds) *Howard's Second and Third Governments: Australian Commonwealth Administration 1998–2004*, UNSW Press, Sydney: vii–xi.

Brett, J (2007) Exit right: The unravelling of John Howard, *Quarterly Essay*, 28: 1–96.

FitzSimons, P (2007) Sign o' the times: The Fitz Files, *Sun-Herald*, 9 December.

Fraser, A (2007) Rudd buries Howard era, *Sunday Canberra Times*, 25 November.

Kelly, P (2006) Re-thinking Australian governance: The Howard legacy, *Australian Journal of Public Administration*, 65(1): 7–24.

McCallum, M (2007) Thank you and goodnight, John Howard, *Crikey*, 3 December, at <www.crikey.com.au/Search.html>.

Prasser, S (2006) *Royal Commissions and Public Inquiries in Australia*, LexisNexis Butterworths, Sydney.

Sanders, W (2005) Never even adequate: Reconciliation and Indigenous affairs. In C Aulich & R Wettenhall (eds) *Howard's Second and Third Governments: Australian Commonwealth Administration 1998–2004*, UNSW Press, Sydney: 152–72.

Appendix 1.1
Australian Commonwealth Administration Series

Australian Commonwealth Administration 1983: Essays in Review, Alexander Kouzmin, JR Nethercote & Roger Wettenhall (eds), School of Administrative Studies, Canberra College of Advanced Education in association with ACT Division, Royal Australian Institute of Public Administration, 1984.

Australian Commonwealth Administration 1984: Essays in Review, J R Nethercote, Alexander Kouzmin & Roger Wettenhall (eds), School of Administrative Studies, Canberra College of Advanced Education in association with ACT Division, Royal Australian Institute of Public Administration, 1986.

Hawke's Second Government: Australian Commonwealth Administration 1984–1987, Roger Wettenhall & J R Nethercote (eds), School of Management, Canberra College of Advanced Education, and Royal Australian Institute of Public Administration (ACT Division), 1988.

Hawke's Third Government: Australian Commonwealth Administration 1987–1990, John Halligan & Roger Wettenhall (eds), School of Management, Canberra College of Advanced Education, and Royal Australian Institute of Public Administration (ACT Division), 1992.

From Hawke to Keating: Australian Commonwealth Administration 1990–1993, Jenny Stewart (ed.), Centre for Research in Public Sector Management, University of Canberra, and Royal Institute of Public Administration Australia, 1995.

The Second Keating Government: Australian Commonwealth Administration 1993–1996, Gwynneth Singleton (ed.), Centre for Research in Public Sector Management, University of Canberra, and Royal Institute of Public Administration Australia, 1997.

The Howard Government: Australian Commonwealth Administration 1996–1998, Gwynneth Singleton (ed.), UNSW Press, Sydney, 2000.

Howard's Second and Third Governments: Australian Commonwealth Administration 1998–2004, Chris Aulich & Roger Wettenhall (eds), UNSW Press, Sydney, 2005.

PART I

Governance issues

2
The search for balance and effectiveness in the Australian Public Service

John Halligan

Howard's fourth term was notable for a continuation of trends that emerged in the previous term (Halligan 2005), and for new issues that arose directly or indirectly from political agendas. It is not unusual for a duality to be apparent in public service agendas for the public service pursues management improvement, while the government of the day seeks greater responsiveness and effectiveness. Usually these agendas are convergent and relatively seamless, but when extraneous issues of public administration surface publicly and tensions about values and fundamentals of governance and the state of the public service are manifest, the divergences are apparent.

The signs of tensions between politicians and their public service advisers increased towards the latter half of the term as party government became disengaged from the public service and pragmatic decision-making became a feature of the election year. There were clear indications that Howard's mode of governing in this term was producing discontent at senior levels, and more generally within the nation, the government was being widely castigated for decision-making in 2007 that was ad hoc, capricious and populist.

This chapter gives attention to several continuing themes in management reform, which are drawn together under a discussion of the move towards integrated governance. The focus is on the implications of questions, such as co-ordination and performance management, that predate this term, but have continued to be salient because of discussion about their efficacy. Finally, the fourth term raised questions about the long-term impact of and judgments about the Howard government's 11 years.

State of the service and the return of big government

The trends reported on in the last Howard government volume continued (Halligan 2005), reflecting often a move away from a 'new public management' (NPM) agenda. The size of the public service provides a good example.

Earlier in the reform era structural adjustments in Australia had reversed the long-term process of extending and maintaining the role of the state. The Howard government, driven by the size of the budget deficit, downsized the public service, but the long-term trend was a result of actions by successive governments (from 173 444 in 1985 to 118 644 in 2001 with predictions that the figure of 100 000 would be achieved). By the mid-2000s a reversal was clear with 146 234 APS staff for 2006 and a further hike to 155 482 by 30 June 2007. The numbers for the senior executive service were now well above the old rule of thumb of 2000 to 2509 for mid-2007, an increase of over 11 per cent on the previous year (APSC 2007b).

The return of big government has been attributed to increased spending on welfare, health and education and other services (Norton 2006–07), as well as the expansion of staff employed to implement the government's agendas in specific areas such as taxation, policing, welfare and security (Dobbin 2007).

There is some irony in this apparent expansion, if not systematic renewal, of public service capacity in some areas. By this decade, the public service had become less self-sufficient and more integrated with other industry sectors with regard to sharing personnel and practices. The range of options open to governments expanded greatly as they increasingly utilised external contractors and partners from the private sector.

Questions have been raised about public service capability that had been dismantled in the reform era, particularly with regard to loss of core capacity to handle policy, to operate strategically and to retain and enhance knowledge.

Courtesy of Peter Nicholson, *The Australian*, 4 February 2006

By the middle of the decade, the public service was seen to be in crisis because of the difficulties of attracting staff in a competitive market.

Moving towards integrating governance

The Australian model that has emerged in the 2000s represents a significant redesign with at least four dimensions, each aiming to draw together fundamental aspects of governance: resurrection of the central agency as a major actor with more direct influence over departments; whole-of-government as the new expression for co-ordination; central monitoring of agency implementation and delivery; and departmentalisation through rationalising the non-departmental sector. At the same time, the commitment to performance management remained an important element. A centralising trend within the federal system has also been identified, which stretches across policy sectors (Wiltshire 2005). In combination these offer formidable potential for integrated governance (Halligan 2006, 2007b).

These trends have shifted the focus to some extent from the vertical towards the horizontal. A greater emphasis was now put on cross-agency programs and relationships and with driving agendas and monitoring by central agencies, yet at the same time there was a reinforcement of, and significant extension to, vertical relationships. The result has been the tempering of devolution through strategic steering and management from the centre and a rebalancing of the positions of centre and line agencies.

Underlying each of these dimensions of change, discussed below, has been a political control dimension: these include improved financial information on a program basis for ministers; strategic co-ordination under cabinet; control of major policy agendas; organisational integration through abolition of bodies and features of autonomy; and monitoring the implementation of government policy down to the delivery level. The overall result has been greater potential for policy and program control and integration using the conventional machinery of cabinet, central agencies and departments.

An overriding trend to devolve responsibilities to agencies[1] remains a feature of the Australian system, but it has been modified in two respects involving central agencies: first, through the whole-of-government agenda driven by the Department of the Prime Minister and Cabinet (DPM&C); and second, through a more prominent role for central agencies in espousing and enforcing principles, and monitoring and guiding in the areas of budgeting, performance and values. The Department of Finance and Administration's (DoFA) role and capacity to oversight financial management and information was enhanced, with a greater focus on departmental programs and an expansion of staff capacity to provide the necessary advice for government. With regard to monitoring, the Australian Public Service Commission (APSC) invested in improvements to its capacity for evaluation. The devolved environment was being balanced by greater public accountability through the legislative requirement of an annual report by the Public Service Commissioner on the 'State of the Service'. The evaluations in the report now included surveying employees and agencies, and scrutinising more closely public service values and practice as part of a greater focus on evaluation and quality assurance (APSC 2005, 2006).

The new prominence of co-ordination reflects in part a rebalancing following the emphasis on NPM in the 1990s but its forms seem to have acquired some fresh characteristics. Australia came relatively late to new wave co-ordination, variously termed joined up, horizontal, integrated government and whole-of-government. Traditional co-ordination has of course been an integral layer of the governmental machinery, but the new whole-of-government conception was ambitious with high-level commitment to a multi-layered approach that had at its core a focus on cultural change. Horizontal governance was located alongside vertical relationships and hierarchy. The Secretary of DPM&C, effectively the head of the public service, saw building a culture of collegiality and creativity as his primary objective (Shergold 2004b, 2005).

Whole-of-government approaches attempt to promote inter-agency collaboration and co-operation in the pursuit of government policies, and reflect both traditional co-ordination and new forms of organising, structuring, and co-ordinating that seek to connect distinct parts of the public sector. The whole-of-government approach has been officially defined as 'agencies working across portfolio boundaries to achieve a shared goal and an integrated governance response to particular issues'. The conception is fairly inclusive for approaches may operate formally and informally, range from policy development through program management to service delivery and cover the activities of co-ordinating departments (i.e. central agencies), integration (reducing the number of departments) and co-operative federalism (MAC 2004: 1, 6–7).

A core principle of the 1980s was to require departments to manage as well as to provide policy advice. Under the market agenda of NPM, outsourcing, agents and specialised agencies were favoured for service delivery. The language and aim during the mid-2000s became to enforce effective delivery as well as policy advice with the latter defined in terms of outcomes. A Cabinet Implementation Unit (CIU) was established to seek effectiveness in program delivery by ensuring government policies and services are delivered on a timely and responsive basis. It has been depicted as a partnership with government agencies in producing systematic reform to the implementation of government policies, and to ensuring effective delivery. The monitoring of implementation involves testing against reality the logic underlying policy decisions, the policy instruments and the resources allocated during the policy formulation (Halligan 2005).

The authority of cabinet was drawn on both as a 'gateway' and a 'checkpoint'. New proposals required appropriate details regarding implementation. Cabinet submissions with a risk element had to address a delivery framework including milestones, impacts and governance. As well, adopted policy proposals required formal, detailed implementation plans. On the basis of these plans, progress was reported to the Prime Minister and cabinet against milestones in 'traffic light' format, which was regarded as a powerful incentive for organisational learning for public servants. The CIU reviews of policy initiatives that cross portfolio boundaries were seen to be requiring agency reflection on how to improve co-ordination.

Around 200 policy implementations have been monitored. Cultural change is being promoted around a project management approach employing a methodology designed to codify and think through the connections between policy objectives, inputs, outputs and outcomes, to expose underlying assumptions to questioning and to clarify risks and results (Shergold 2004b; Wanna 2006).

Broadly similar movements have been underway in countries internationally reflecting a mood to review and tighten oversight through reviewing and rationalisation of public bodies. An agenda for resurrecting a more comprehensive ministerial department through absorbing bodies or extending controls was given formal recognition through the Uhrig (2003) review into the corporate governance of statutory authorities and office holders (see chapter 3 for details of the Uhrig reviews). The post-Uhrig agenda has been for ministerial departments to have tighter and more direct control over public agencies because of concern about the extent of and governance of non-departmental organisations. The array of commonwealth public bodies had been mapped by the DoFA. The dangers of 'bureaucratic proliferation' were proclaimed with departments of state employing only 22 per cent of public sector employees – most of them were in approximately 180 agencies, many with statutory independence. The official concern was with different legislative bases, constitutions (boards or not) and opaque governance:

> If implementation is to be driven hard it is important that there be clarity of purpose, powers and relationships between ministers, public servants and boards. Good governance depends upon transparency of authority, accountability and disclosure. There should be no doubts, no ambiguities. (Shergold 2004a)

The new departmentalisation could be expressed through absorbing statutory authorities and reclaiming control of agencies with hybrid boards that did not accord with Uhrig's corporate (and therefore private sector) governance prescriptions.

Impact of horizontal and integrated governance

The model the new integration allows is a combination of devolved dimensions with a reactivated centre. The relational basis retains a strong hierarchical dimension underpinned by political authority but with a reliance on performance management and the employment of project management for some purposes. The elements that emerge are the search for coherence, strengthening of internal capacity and performance improvement. Organising for coherence has been occurring within and across portfolios and organisations with the whole-of-government agenda. The reliance is less on legislation, the management framework and values for sustaining organisational operations – although each remains prominent – and more on bureaucratic structures and formal centres of influence such as the ministerial department.

There is also a strengthening of internal capacity, through the whole-of-government agenda, enhancing central agencies' roles in co-ordination, and improving implementation and capability. While the previous agenda was to shed responsibilities, and devolution continues to be a cornerstone because it has produced improved performance and productivity, now there is a preference to reincorporate, to clarify, to establish better accountability, and to improve performance. In response to the challenges of complexity and through attentiveness to maintaining system attributes, in the new construction horizontal governance ranks equal with vertical relationships and hierarchy (Shergold 2004b, 2005). There has been a reconfirmation of the three organisational components of the traditional system: cabinet, central agency and the department.

MULTI-AGENCY CASE: CENTRELINK

Designed as a one-stop-shop, multi-purpose delivery agency to provide services to several purchasing departments, Centrelink represents an ambitious and complex case of horizontal co-ordination that is politically salient and budget-significant, and operating in an 'ambiguous environment' (Halligan 2007c). The ambiguity derives from how the functions were originally divided up, the scope for differing interpretations of relationships between the agency and departments, and the multiple models that entered into the calculations for the new agency. In essence a horizontal question (inter-agency failures in collaboration) was converted into a vertical question (defining the relationship in terms of purchaser and provider). The basis for subsequent debates about the roles of purchasing department and provider agency were laid by embedding several models in its organisational imperatives.

The tensions between models also provided opportunities for advocacy of a distinctive agenda and employing smart practices in pursuit of public management innovation and interagency collaboration. Centrelink developed a new service delivery model and reformulated external relationships despite obstacles and the need to balance the several imperatives of customers, clients, competitors and politicians. Importantly, Centrelink was able to transcend relying on its own capacity within a competitive environment to develop inter-agency collaborative capacity. There remained issues about the separation of policy formation and implementation and how best to constitute a multi-purpose service delivery agency, and the limitations of basic purchaser–provider as the means for handling relationships were apparent. The advantages of the horizontal integration of welfare delivery can be realised more effectively through partnerships and alliances for delivering services for a range of clients (Halligan 2007c).

The position of Centrelink changed in 2004 under the integrated governance agenda discussed earlier. The changes included agency governance and ministerial accountability, centralising impulses designed to temper high levels of devolution, and Centrelink-specific matters regarding relationship issues such as the operation of a purchase–provider within the same portfolio, governance by board and minister, and interdepartmental tensions. Centrelink came under a new parent department and within a new portfolio under a central agency. The Department of Human Services was created within the Finance portfolio with responsibility for six delivery agencies that now operated under direct ministerial control and one advisory board (discussed also in chapter 3). The rationale was to improve the delivery of services within a whole-of-government approach. The CEO of Centrelink, and five other agencies, 'retain responsibility for day-to-day operations in their agencies, the department provides assurance to the minister on cross-agency issues, the quality of outcomes, and the achievements of the government's objectives' (DoHS 2005: 13).

CO-ORDINATING STRUCTURES AND CULTURE

Much of modern co-ordination is similar to traditional arrangements, but there was now a greater intensity and commitment to horizontal co-ordination and embedding inter-agency collaboration in the public service. The official literature was inclined to regard all cross-service and interdepartmental activity as 'whole-of-government'.

The interdepartmental committee (IDC) was a central component of traditional machinery, but was less valued now as the main mode of cross-departmental co-ordination for program design, review and management with new structural innovations emerging for strengthening collective and cross-portfolio co-ordination (MAC 2004). Taskforces originally rose to prominence as a means of avoiding the defects of IDCs and as short-term vehicles for giving focus to government agendas. Whereas once taskforces were distinguished informally from other cross-agency structures, the understanding was now entrenched of the taskforce as 'a discrete, time-and-purpose limited unit responsible for producing a result in its own right'. Their capacity for operating independently from policy departments was strengthened by the DPM&C being assigned administrative responsibility for them in many cases (Hamburger 2007).

Taskforces have become relatively institutionalised and have addressed significant issues, but they only affect a relatively small proportion of senior executive service/executive level public servants (13 per cent). Joint teams (regarded as longer lasting structures that blend functions across portfolios) accounted for 16 per cent. Membership of IDCs continues to be the most significant activity (22 per cent) (APSC 2006).

The key issue with the whole-of-government approach is about refocusing agencies constituted around functional hierarchies into ones that routinely incorporate horizontal collaboration and integration in their modes of operating. Long-term change is unlikely without cultural change because pressures from functional established systems are too intense.

How do public servants incorporate whole-of-government operating principles into underlying assumptions that shape day-to-day work; and how do agencies substantiate claims about cultural change? The evidence to date is uneven. Most senior executive service/executive level public servants have some form of direct dealings with other agencies, but 61 per cent of those surveyed for 2005–06 had no structured engagement. The remainder were involved in taskforces and IDCs and joint teams. Figures for the previous two years indicate a marginal decrease across the categories for structured activity (APSC 2006: 214). Agency support for collaboration was quite strong according to public servants' perceptions of whether their agency encouraged a constructive approach to collaboration with public organisations. However, some slippage was apparent suggesting that the level of support might be waning as the intensity of commitment to a new initiative fades. Multi-agency forums had been represented as an indicator of change and commitment. Yet public servants saw such forums as more focused on solving agency objectives compared to whole-of-government priorities. Of the indicators, high support for a cross-boundary focus on outcomes was the more promising.

The whole-of-government agenda raises intriguing issues in organisation design and behavioural challenges. This Australian agenda is fairly ambitious in international terms. There has been sustained political and bureaucratic drive and support. The obstacles to inculcating cultural change however remain substantial. The imperative of the functional principle and the rigidity of organisational boundaries still loom prominently. The horizontal agenda requires a combination of leadership and incentives. Leadership at the public service level has been clear, but more attention needs to be provided to the incentives for agencies to engage systematically in horizontal collaborations.

Performance management

A performance focus has been prominent in Australia for two decades. As the Secretary of the DPM&C announced: 'The next challenge is to ensure that the performance of the Australian Public Service (APS) – as a coherent whole – is lifted; and to ensure that the implementation of delivery is viewed as just as important as the development of policy'. The concept of the 'performing state' was used for a system 'that is continuously open to, and reading its environment, and learning and changing in response: a state "inherently in transition"' (Shergold 2004a: 6).

Australia's official framework for performance management is among the more developed internationally (Bouckaert & Halligan 2008; Halligan 2007a). The framework introduced in 1999 changed financial management and reporting through budgeting on a full accrual basis, implementation of outputs and outcomes reporting, and extended agency devolution to inter alia budget estimates and financial management. However, the limitations of the framework in practice produced reincorporation of departmental programs, a renewed emphasis on cash accounting and other changes that enhanced the DoFA role and capacity to oversee financial management and information, and to provide appropriate advice to government.

The outcomes and outputs approach has been central to the management framework. There are three main dimensions to using performance information: internal use by agencies and individuals, budget decisions and process, and reporting. With internal use by agencies, the quality of financial information has improved as a result of the Australian outcomes/output framework in registering government preferences (intentions and results) and by allowing performance indicators to be explicitly identified (DoFA 2006b). Output performance measures are generally more appropriate and measurement more reliable than outcome measures. The Auditor-General reported that performance information was being used by decision-makers for policy development and allocating resources, but the actual 'influence of outcomes and outputs information on decision-making was mixed' (McPhee 2005: 3, 4).

The second dimension is performance and budgeting. Performance information is meant to inform the budget process. For Australia, budget information is now 'more comprehensive, based on external reporting standards, and provides better alignment between appropriation Acts, Performance Budgeting Statements and agency annual reports' (DoFA 2006b: 11)[2]. The Australian outcomes policy provides for agencies to use performance information in budget decision-making, but the potential has not been achieved because of the variable influence of this information on decisions and resource allocation during the process. DoFA has explored means for improving the use of performance information by revising the information required for new policy proposals and making greater use of reviews, regarded as an instrument through which performance information can best feed into budget decision-making (for example, through the automatic review of lapsing programs). Reviews have not registered much impact because only a minute proportion of total expenditure is affected (DoFA 2006a).

The third dimension is reporting. The quality of performance reporting is argued to have improved since the introduction of accrual-based budgeting (DoFA 2006b: 9). Nevertheless, improvements in annual reporting frameworks have been urged to enhance accountability and transparency to stakeholders, particularly parliamentarians, because the presentation and analysis of performance information does not allow them to properly understand results. Specific issues have been the need to analyse and assess performance; review trends in financial and non-financial performance; use evaluations for acquiring performance information on effectiveness; and comply with mandatory requirements for reporting (ANAO 2003, 2007; DoFA 2006b).

The impact of performance management at both the individual (i.e. public servant) and organisational (agency) levels has raised issues. There is considerable variation among agencies in how they engage and show up on performance management. This reflects in part the nature of agencies, with some more able to demonstrate effective use of performance information. Significant variation existed with the development of performance indicator regimes, quality of and information used in annual reports, and in the alignment between goals and organisational priorities of many agencies and their performance management systems. Many agencies lacked systems for supporting performance management, and were not assessing its internal impact and use. As a result, performance management was not contributing to effective business outcomes (ANAO 2004, 2007).

The credibility of performance management systems as they affect individual public servants, particularly performance pay, has been exposed by several inquiries, with the proportions of employees judging pay systems positively being relatively low and declining (ANAO 2004; APSC 2005). The Auditor-General concluded that the significant investment in performance-linked remuneration was 'delivering only patchy results and uncertain benefit' (ANAO 2004: 22). Performance management has been officially depicted during the 2000s as a 'work in progress' with major challenges, particularly on the issues of credibility and staff engagement. APS employees have continued to perceive a gap between their experience and the rhetoric (ANAO 2004).

Australia has been highly committed to performance management over two decades and has substantially refined the measurement and performance framework and increased capacity to monitor performance. Yet practice falls short of aspirations and significant questions remain about the quality and use of performance information, particularly in budget decision-making and external reporting, and the variable engagement of agencies. Performance management remains a 'work in progress' as governments continue to seek improvements in managing performance. Evaluating performance improvement has been neglected since the centrally-driven approach of mandatory, systematic evaluation was abandoned. There is now understanding that review and evaluation is required on a more systematic basis (DoFA 2006b; ANAO 2007).

Reality checks through failures in oversight and governance

Two extraordinary cases during the fourth term revealed fundamental weaknesses in the internal operations of a major department and lack of oversight of a privatised body that was critical for public policy. Together they raised a gamut of issues ranging from ministerial responsibility through to basic management.

INTERNAL GOVERNANCE FAILURE: THE CASE OF IMMIGRATION

The Department of Immigration and Multicultural Affairs (DIMA) was found during 2005 and 2006 to have experienced an internal breakdown of basic operating procedures, culture and leadership.[3] The department had acquired a high profile because of the government focus on keeping illegal immigrants out and locating and deporting those already in Australia. The failure of governance in DIMA was revealed through a succession of inquiries into the handling of the detention of citizens. As head of the public service, Shergold is reported as describing 'the cases as the worse thing that has happened in the public service in recent years' and blaming the failures on public service deficiencies. He is quoted as saying that in addition to failures in IT systems and record keeping: 'It was a failure of public administration ... it was failure in some ways of executive leadership' (ABC 2006).

The first investigation was the Inquiry into the Circumstances of the Immigration Detention of Cornelia Rau (Palmer 2005), which arose out of the illegal detention and efforts to secure the deportation of an Australian citizen. The second involved the unlawful detention and removal from Australia of another citizen, Vivian Alvarez (Commonwealth Ombudsman 2005). Palmer reported an astounding range of weaknesses, flaws, and disconnects within an overall managerial approach that was 'process rich' and 'outcome poor' and an 'assumptive culture' (2005: x, 164–68).

In light of the Rau and Alvarez affairs the government referred 247 immigration matters to the Ombudsman for investigation. In other reports he examined how and where the department made mistakes, and in a synoptic report (2007) discussed ten lessons of public administration, including maintaining quality records, adequate controls on exercise of coercive powers, active management of difficult cases, removing obstacles to inter-agency exchange of information, managing complexity in decision-making, checking for warning signs of bigger problems and control of administrative drift.

The case had broader implications for other departments (see the APSC 2007a response), and produced a major reform agenda to correct the litany of deficiencies in the department, which was regarded as being back on track under new leadership (Metcalfe 2007).

OVERSIGHT OF PRIVATISED PUBLIC POLICY: AWB

The Australian Wheat Board (AWB) paid kickbacks to the Iraqi government in the form of a transport surcharge. The Department of Foreign Affairs and Trade (DFAT) claimed to have been unaware of the nature of the AWB's actions. Both DFAT and the Wheat Export Authority (WEA) were unable to demand documents from the AWB, inhibiting their capacity to confirm or certify the AWBs claims. The AWB lied on numerous occasions to inter alia the United Nations, DFAT, and WEA, a statutory body responsible for monitoring the export activities of AWB.

The government was either unwilling or unable to exercise oversight of the illegal activity, but did initiate an investigation. The Cole inquiry (2006) was restricted to the activities of the AWB and did not extend to scrutiny of executive responsibility for the scandal, or to the level of governmental knowledge at each step of the process. Cole's findings were that AWB, AWB International (its global arm) and a dozen or so AWB employees *may* have committed various offences. It recommended that, since the AWB faked several documents it provided to DFAT (which were then forwarded to the UN), there be requirements for certification of such documents; since no government agency was able to compel the AWB to provide it with documents regarding compliance with sanctions, Cole proposed that agencies be so empowered.

Two issues stood out. First, the unwillingness of senior officials and ministers to acknowledge awareness or responsibility, in particular the failure of the Prime Minister to require his minsters to accept ministerial responsibility, was depicted as symptomatic of arrogance and being out of touch (*Australian* 2007). Second, the capacity of DFAT and the WEA to oversee the AWB actions was limited. DFAT and WEA could not demand documents from AWB, nor could they force AWB to co-operate with the UN investigation. Given the functions of AWB to represent Australian farmers there appeared to be serious gaps in the regulatory framework (for further details of the AWB case, see chapter 9, and for a longer discussion of accountability, see chapter 7).

Politicians and bureaucrats

The nexus between the political executive and senior officials became frayed and there continued to be public debate about the character of the relationship. A particular focus was the impact of ministerial advisers on public servants (Barker 2007), their lack of accountability when involved in major public policy issues (Walter 2006) and the lack of a governance framework for the staffers (Tiernan 2007).

There was private discussion among senior officials about the short-term focus of politicians, and eventually strident public comment about ad hoc decision-making by the government in an election year. Traditional formulations of Westminster principles were restated. Treasury Secretary Ken Henry (2007: 13–14) observed that:

> 2007 will test our mettle as apolitical public servants ... This is a key feature of our system of government. The legislated APS values

make it clear that the public service is apolitical, yet responsive to the government of the day ... Our capacity to ensure that our work is 'responsible', and not just 'responsive', will be put to the test. How successful we are will impact on our integrity as public servants and our long-term effectiveness.

The press continued to accept some degree of 'politicisation' as a given (e.g. Grattan (2007) on how public servants have been constrained under the Howard government), and the debate surfaced again in the exchange that followed former Public Service Commissioner Andrew Podger's (2007) reflections on the handling of senior appointments, which produced a defence of the record from Shergold as head of the public service (Shergold 2007).

The most riveting public disclosure was arguably the declaration that one of the key agencies of government was bypassed by the government. Treasury Secretary Henry (2007: 6) reported to an internal staff function that the department had worked to:

> develop frameworks for the consideration of water reform and climate change policy. All of us would wish that we had been listened to more attentively over the past several years in both of these areas. There is no doubt that policy outcomes would have been far superior had our views been more influential. That is not just my view; I know that it is increasingly widely shared around this town.

Conclusion

The fourth term needs to be considered in the context of all four Howard terms. The initial years were overshadowed by a government which was estranged from the public service and took more than a term to engage with its official support. At the same time, the government pursued a neo-liberal agenda of NPM, which eventually lost impetus once core programs such as outsourcing failed, and environmental threat and a focus on improving effectiveness produced new directions. The fourth term reinforced the fine-tuning of the system but flaws were exposed in portfolio management and eventually in governing by the political executive.

The new Rudd government is promising to respond to the excesses of its predecessor both with explicit objectives and a raft of options. The accountability agenda covers ministerial staff involved in decision-making being expected to have to account to parliamentary committees; ministers will be subject to a new code of conduct; and the parliamentary committee system will be strengthened. In contrast to the Howard government's inaugural years, Rudd intends to engage the public service more directly while placing pressures on it to perform and maintaining a commitment to longstanding conventions including continuity for senior officials (apart from changes in responsibilities where departments are abolished). Other proposals are for cuts to the size of the public service (including a smaller senior executive service), an increase in the efficiency dividend, and a reduction in consultancies. It will take some time to work through the agendas, and to clarify the impact on the public service.

Notes

1. The term 'agencies' here is used in its broadest sense, and includes mainstream departments.
2. But note that most of the annual appropriations do not relate to outcomes: only 9 per cent are appropriated by outcomes. Departmental outputs (18 per cent) and administered programs (73 per cent) appropriated outside annual appropriations (i.e. by special or annual appropriations) are not appropriated against outcomes, leaving 9 per cent that is (DoFA 2006b: 13).
3. For a full treatment of the case, see Tony Tucker's (2007) analysis.

References

ABC (2006) 'Public service' to blame for immigration failures, *ABC Online*, 8 September.
ANAO (Australian National Audit Office) (2003) *Annual Performance Reporting*, Audit Report No. 11 2003–04, ANAO, Canberra.
—— (2004) *Performance Management in the Australian Public Service*, Audit Report No. 6 2004–05, ANAO, Canberra.
—— (2007) *Application of the Outcomes and Outputs Framework*, Audit Report No. 23 2006–07, ANAO, Canberra.
APSC (Australian Public Service Commission) (2005) *State of the Service Report 2004–05*, APSC, Canberra.
—— (2006) *State of the Service Report 2005–06*, APSC, Canberra.
—— (2007a) *Agency Health: Monitoring Agency Health and Improving Performance*, Commonwealth of Australia, Canberra.
—— (2007b) *Australian Public Service Statistical Bulletin 2006–07*, Commonwealth of Australia, Canberra.
Australian (2007) Editorial, 22 November.
Barker, G (2007) The public service. In C Hamilton & S Maddison (eds) *Silencing Dissent*, Allen & Unwin, Sydney: 124–27.
Bouckaert, G & Halligan, J (2008) *Managing Performance: International Comparisons*, Routledge, London.
Cole, T (2006) Report of the Inquiry into certain Australian companies in relation to the UN Oil-for-Food Programme, Canberra.

Commonwealth Ombudsman (2005) *Inquiry into the Circumstances of the Vivian Alvarez Matter*, Report 031, Commonwealth Ombudsman, Canberra.
—— (2007) *Lessons for Public Administration: Ombudsman Investigation of Referred Immigration Cases*, Commonwealth Ombudsman, Canberra.
Dobbin, M (2007) AFP dumps new $70m HQ, *Canberra Times*, 14 August.
DoFA (Department of Finance and Administration) (2006a) *Australia's Experience in Utilising Performance Information in Budget and Management Processes*, Report for the 3rd Annual Meeting of the OECD Senior Budget Officials Network on Performance and Results, DoFA, Canberra.
—— (2006b) Submission to the Senate Finance and Public Administration References Committee, Inquiry into the Transparency and Accountability of Commonwealth Public Funding and Expenditure, 4 August.
DoHS (Department of Human Services) (2005) *Annual Report 2004–05*, DoHS, Canberra.
Grattan, M (2007) Silence of the service, *Age*, 31 August.
Halligan, J (2005) Public sector reform. In C Aulich & R Wettenhall (eds) *Howard's Second and Third Governments: Australian Commonwealth Administration 1998–2004*, UNSW Press: 21–41.
—— (2006) The reassertion of the centre in a first generation NPM system. In T Christensen & P Lægreid (eds) *Autonomy and Regulation: Coping with Agencies in the Modern State*, Edward Elgar, Cheltenham: 162–180.
—— (2007a) Reform design and performance in Australia and New Zealand. In T Christensen & P Laegreid (eds) *Transcending New Public Management*, Ashgate, Aldershot: 43–64.
—— (2007b) Reintegrating government in third generation reforms of Australia and New Zealand, *Public Policy and Administration*, 22(2): 217–38.
—— (2007c) Advocacy and innovation in interagency management: The case of Centrelink, *Governance*, 20(3): 445–67.
Hamburger, P (2007) Coordination and leadership at the centre of the Australia Public Service. In R Koch (ed.) *Public Governance and Leadership*, Deutscher Universitats-Verlag, Wiesbaden: 207–31.
Henry, K (2007) Secretary's speech to staff, 17 March, at <www.treasury.gov.au>.
McPhee, I (2005) Outcomes and outputs: Are we managing better as a result?, Paper presented to CPA National Public Sector Convention, 20 May.
MAC (Management Advisory Committee) (2004) *Connecting Government: Whole of Government Responses to Australia's Priority Challenges*, Public Service Commission, Canberra.
Metcalfe, A (2007) Post-Palmer reform of DIAC and regulation of the migration advice industry, Address to the Inaugural CPD Immigration Law Conference, 9 February.
Norton, A (2006–07) The rise of big government conservatism, *Policy*, 22(4): 15–22.
Palmer, M (2005) *Report of the Inquiry into the Circumstances of the Immigration Detention of Cornelia Rau*, DIMIA, Canberra.
Podger, A (2007) What really happens: Departmental secretary appointments, contracts and performance pay in the Australian Public Service, *Australian Journal of Public Administration*, 66(2): 131–47.
Shergold, P (2004a) Connecting government: Whole-of-government responses to Australia's priority challenges, Speech at launch of Connecting Government: Whole-of-Government Responses to Australia's Priority Challenges,Canberra, 20 April.
—— (2004b) Plan and deliver: Avoiding bureaucratic hold-up, Speech to Australian Graduate School of Management/Harvard Club of Australia, 17 November, Canberra.

—— (2005) Foundations of governance in the Australian Public Service, Speech delivered at launch of *Foundations of Governance in the Australian Public Service*, 1 June, Canberra.
—— (2006) Implementation matters, Speech given at Implementation Matters: the best Practice Guide to Implementation of Programme and Policy Initiatives, Old Parliament House, Canberra.
—— (2007) What really happens in the Australian Public Service: An alternative view, *Australian Journal of Public Administration*, 66(3): 367–70.
Tiernan, A (2007) *Power without Responsibility? Ministerial Staffers in Australian Governments from Whitlam to Howard*, UNSW Press, Sydney.
Tucker, T (2007) Corporate governance, Unpublished paper, University of Canberra.
Uhrig, J (2003) *Review of Corporate Governance of Statutory Authorities and Office Holders*, DoFA, Canberra.
Wanna, J (2006) From afterthought to afterburner: Australia's Cabinet Implementation Unit, *Journal of Comparative Policy Analysis*, 8(4): 347–69.
Walter, J (2006) Ministers, minders and public servants: Changing parameters of responsibility in Australia, *Australian Journal of Public Administration*, 65(3): 22–27.
Wiltshire, K (2005) Political overview. In *Economic and Political Overview*. CEDA White Paper Number 25, February, Melbourne.

3

Non-departmental public bodies as a focus for machinery-of-government change

Roger Wettenhall

This chapter continues the exploration of developments in the use of non-departmental public bodies (NDPBs) that has run through previous volumes in the Australian Commonwealth Administration series. A consideration of what has been happening in this area in the fourth Howard government period must necessarily focus largely on showing how Uhrig-influenced changes have led to the absorbing of some functions previously performed by NDPBs within departments, the eliminating of boards in some NDPBs, and the enhancement of ministerial control over NDPBs generally. Such movement reflects the hardening of the whole-of-government perspective, and thus connects closely with the strengthening of core government processes discussed in chapter 2 of this volume. This chapter also includes a brief consideration of argument about the need to insulate integrity agencies (ombudsman, audit office, human rights and electoral commissions and the like) against these more general changes.

The Governor-General's speech opening the 41st Parliament on 16 November 2004 actually downplayed the reform aspects of the government's intended program. It focused instead on how that program would implement the various policy commitments the government made during the election campaign. In terms of structural adjustment, the only mention of the core framework of ministries and departments was that relating to the creation of the new Department of Human Services – but that was immediately relevant to the main concern of this chapter because it involved a restructuring of a group of important NDPBs. In dealing with the policy commitments, however, the Governor-General's speech foreshadowed several other developments likely to affect the non-departmental arrangements, notably the establishment of a Future Fund 'with the aim of fully funding Commonwealth superannuation liabilities by 2020' and a National Water Commission as 'an independent statutory authority in the Prime Minister's portfolio' (Jeffery 2004).

The portfolio and departmental arrangements are shown in appendix 3.1, which lists Human Services as an 'outlier department' (that is, lacking a full portfolio in its own right) along with the longstanding Veterans Affairs. It also shows mid-term realignments within and between portfolios. These realignments reflect the government's changing policy priorities, concerning especially immigration/citizenship/Indigenous/multicultural affairs, and environment/heritage/water resources, and they connect with discussion in other chapters in this book. In the Australian commonwealth system, changes in the departmental alignments are effected by Orders-in-Council (that is, the Executive Council) recorded in the Administrative Arrangements Orders that are gazetted after each of the relevant changes; unlike changes in the major NDPB group, the statutory bodies, they do not require parliamentary approval and often do not attract much debate.

Re-examining the NDPB sector

In respect of the organisational arrangements for the outer part of the commonwealth public sector, the period of Howard's second and third governments was marked particularly by a continuation of the trend towards using the form of the government-owned company in preference to the more traditional form of the statutory authority (statutory corporation when incorporated), and by the introduction of what was a new form for Australia, the executive agency (Wettenhall 1998, 2003a, 2003b). The basic framework laws established in the period of the first Howard government – the Commonwealth Authorities and Companies (CAC) Act and the Financial

Management and Accountability (FMA) Act, both 1997– seemed well settled, and they were supplemented by provisions of the revised Public Service Act of 1999 that not only introduced the new 'executive agency' category but also established a new term – 'statutory agency' – to cover those statutory authorities that were staffed under the provisions of that legislation.[1] Of course, many statutory bodies, and all except one of the government-owned companies, were staffed independently of it. Another overlapping term, 'prescribed agency', was introduced by the FMA Act to cover:

- statutory authorities, including all the statutory agencies and some others, except those covered by the CAC Act (virtually all of which are statutory corporations);
- the executive agencies; and
- some specified branches of departments with a higher degree of separation than most, such as AusAID, Geoscience Australia and the Royal Australian Mint.

These developments were described more fully in chapter 5 of the preceding volume in this series (Wettenhall 2005a; see also Wettenhall 2000).

As also discussed in that chapter, it had never been easy to track all the NDPBs operating within the commonwealth public sector.[2] Towards the end of the period of the third Howard government, however, it seemed that an initiative of the Department of Finance and Administration (DoFA) was likely to go some way towards alleviating that problem. The first DoFA *List of Australian Government Bodies* (2004; also Wettenhall 2005a: 78–79) was followed by another soon after the opening of the fourth government period (DoFA 2005a). The *Lists* were organised around the 18 ministerial portfolios and departments (as shown in appendix 3.1),[3] but the additional entries under each of them raised the 'bodies' total to 1153, increased from the 955 of the first list. The availability of this guide was of significant benefit to all those wanting to understand the structures of federal administration; arguably, however, the total was unnecessarily inflated, giving support to forces pushing the view that the structural arrangements were excessively convoluted, that simplification was required for its own sake, and that consolidation was necessary in order to advance those whole-of-government imperatives.

On any objective consideration, many of the listed bodies are not part of the administrative establishment that warrants such a judgment. As well as the usually recognised NDPBs, the list includes parliamentary committees (which are political, not administrative), commonwealth–state structures including ministerial councils (again political, not administrative), international agencies with Australian representation, advisory committees, departmental functions 'with distinct branding', and 'business operations' lacking clear organisational identity.[4] So it provides good ammunition for those wanting to streamline and simplify the system, but it is deceptive because it includes those political and intergovernmental items and many others that lack significant autonomy and would be required in any well-run system of government. Of course ministers and senior officials have been careful to say that there were only 170 or 180 of the statutory authorities that constituted the main category in their sights, but the broader collation stood by their side to suggest incoherence and capacity to obstruct (for discussion, see Bartos 2005b; Wettenhall 2006a).

Indeed, this listing exercise was associated with a controversial inquiry, with its report released just before the election that returned the fourth Howard government, that demonstrated to the full the tensions involved in the effort to assimilate the population of NDPBs to the whole-of-government drive on which the government was now focused.

A new verb emerges: To be 'uhriged'

One of Howard's early actions as Prime Minister was to urge his ministers to curb the use of statutory authorities and to be watchful over those they had inherited (Brough 1997, and see Wettenhall 2007a: 68; Macintosh 2007: 159–54). Then, in the lead-up to the 2001 election which returned the third Howard government, the coalition parties indicated that they regarded the reform of the public service as one of their major achievements and now saw the need to focus their reform efforts on 'statutory authorities and office holders' (LNP 2001: 15–16).[5] The Prime Minister announced at an Australian Chamber of Commerce and Industry function in November 2002 the appointment of respected businessman John Uhrig to lead an inquiry. Uhrig's mission was to review the corporate governance of the commonwealth's statutory authorities and office holders with a particular focus on a select group of agencies with critical business relationships (Howard 2002). He conducted his inquiry over the next six months and submitted his report in June 2003 (Uhrig 2003), but it was not released by the government until August 2004 (Minchin 2004), close to the election which resulted in the formation of the fourth Howard government.

Uhrig worked with a small secretariat housed in DoFA. His inquiry was a closed one, not calling for public submissions; and his findings were clearly well in line with the government's own thinking. Essentially he proposed that statutory authorities should be sorted into two categories, with governance arrangements designed accordingly. First was the 'board template', appropriate where it had been determined that the governing board should have 'full power to act', including power to appoint and remove the chief executive, most likely to apply where the function is commercial. Second was the 'executive management template', where an 'executive management group ... is governed directly by the Minister with departmental support and advice', most likely to apply to authorities undertaking regulatory or service provision functions. The implication was that it was not appropriate for authorities in the second category to have boards at all; rather their executives would stand face-to-face with ministers. Even in the first group, however, the minister would set strategic directions and, effectively as owner, hold the board responsible for performance; and for both groups the portfolio secretary would be installed as a much more important link than had previously been recognised. A second set of recommendations was designed to improve the functioning of boards where they did exist.[6]

Uhrig's concern was always that it is the minister who may be disadvantaged in these relationships, and his recommendations were all designed to strengthen his governance role; indeed, Uhrig urged caution in creating statutory authorities at all. His subsequent reflections indicate that he had a unilinear appreciation of what governance is about. Thus, 'governments must govern'; you cannot 'let ... government itself off the hook'. Thus again, 'governance can't exist successfully if those with the responsibility for governance don't have all the power necessary to carry it out, and carry it out under all circumstances'. He understood that others may have 'more complex views', but was unrepentant. On the business analogy, 'the purpose of government is to secure the success of the enterprise' – so, 'if you're going to reach the right conclusions you must see all of the issues from the point of view of the owners', and 'the framework of governance [therefore] has to give support to ministers' (Uhrig 2005: 6–7).

There were many criticisms from outside government, variously about the lack of public input to the inquiry; its failure to think critically about the relevance of private sector models; its readiness to apply its findings to all authorities after a close look at only eight of them; its lack of interest in previous inquiries and reports into the governance of statutory authorities or in how they were arranged in other jurisdictions; its neglect of the issue of the parliamentary relationship; and its failure to see that statutory bodies were sometimes in need of protection against excessive ministerial interventions as they go about the tasks allocated to them (e.g. Fels & Brenchley 2004; Gourley 2004; Holland 2004; Bartos 2005a; Macintosh 2007; Wettenhall 2004a, 2005b, 2006b, 2007a: 69–71). In its broadest expression, the critique suggested that Uhrig was part of the Howard campaign 'to concentrate power, stamp out dissenters and reshape Australian society in accordance with conservative ideals' (Macintosh 2007: 154; see also Clark 2002).

Within the authorities themselves there was much concern to understand the Uhrig 'principles' and to push protective views, and through 2005 and 2006 there were many seminars, workshops and conferences to explore the implications of the report. But the government was not much interested, and was determined to proceed in line with the Uhrig proposals. As Halligan and Horrigan (2005: 6) reported, mainstream organisational attention was being shifted to the design of whole portfolios, marked by 'the resurrection of a more comprehensive ministerial department'; and the government was now likely to view argument focusing on particular agencies at sub-portfolio level, either individually or collectively, as an unwanted diversion.

In releasing the Uhrig Report, the Minister for Finance had indicated that 'the statutory authorities and similar bodies' would be assessed 'against the governance templates' (Minchin 2004), and many ministers were engaged in these reviews. As indicated in the next section, action followed fairly quickly in relation to many authorities. Some changes were announced on the formation of the fourth Howard government, soon after release of the report, and the assessments went on through the remainder of the fourth government period (Minchin 2006a; see also Briggs 2005). Bartos (2006) reported that there was now a new verb in the public service lexicon: 'to uhrig', as in 'have you been uhriged yet?' Many NDPBs were indeed being 'uhriged'.

DoFA issued further reports (notably DoFA 2005b, 2005c) explaining the procedures, and one rather surprising outcome was the reappearance of a stated preference for the form of the statutory authority over that of the company even for CAC bodies. Reversing what has been fairly normal practice over the previous decade, it was now proposed that use of the company form should be restricted to 'exceptional circumstances', for example 'where the body is going to operate for profit in a commercial environment, is on path to privatisation or will implement a joint enterprise between the Commonwealth and State governments and/or the private/not-for-profit sectors' (DoFA 2005b, Overview: 1).

Changes to particular authorities

That Uhrig would have a significant impact on the structures of government was immediately clear when Howard announced the formation of his fourth ministry. Six service delivery agencies were brought within the new sub-portfolio of Human Services, all to have their own boards disbanded and replaced by a single portfolio advisory board,[7] and several other NDPBs in both statutory authority and executive agency forms were abolished (Howard 2004). In these changes, the Uhrig principles clearly interacted with and supported a view within government that some of the agencies concerned, notably Centrelink, the Child Support Agency and the Health Insurance Commission (HIC), had been slack in their work and needed tighter control (Hockey 2005; Fraser 2005). Reflecting the tensions involved, Centrelink CEO Sue Vardon resigned almost immediately and was replaced by former HIC CEO Jeff Whalan, and HIC was significantly reduced in size and status.

As foreshadowed in the Governor-General's speech and in documents preceding formation of the fourth government, forward policy development would bring into existence new NDPBs, and it was now inevitable that their design would also be affected by the Uhrig principles. So any account of NDPB development in this period – closures, mergers, reductions in autonomy, new creations – needs to take into account both 'the Uhrig factor' and new policy development. Taken together, the adaptations to existing NDPBs and the provisions for new NDPBs in part based on that factor reveal some quite significant systemic changes (some related innovations are summarised in appendix 3.2):

- conforming to Uhrig's executive management template, some statutory authorities retired their governing boards and moved to executive management under chief executive officers (CEOs), most of them now described as 'statutory agencies';
- some agencies under executive management were brought under the Public Service Act for the first time, and/or within the terms of the FMA Act;
- for some 'bodies that suit the board template' (DoFA 2007), the board's 'power to act' was strengthened as they were given the power to appoint CEOs, though that may be subject to ministerial approval;
- the size of some boards was varied (usually a reduction) and others had members removed who represented particular interests (for example, designated departments, other NDPBs, or staff constituencies);

- there were several mergers, in one case leading to a merged administrative support service even as the separate decision-making bodies remained;
- responsible ministers agreed to issue Statements of Expectations to over 120 NDPBs within their portfolios (many authorities and several companies), and to receive Statements of Intent from them;
- some NDPBs were abolished, their functions mostly returning to ministerial departments.

Occasional progress reports pointed to the changes that were taking place in existing bodies (Minchin 2006a; Ioannou 2006; DoFA 2006, 2007), and there was a steady stream of new legislation through to the middle months of 2007 as ministers raced to complete the task before the close of the fourth government period. It is not likely that members of parliament took much interest in what was happening. Over 160 bodies had been reviewed, and often the actual tasks being performed did not seem to matter much. Thus, demonstrating that this was the outcome of a new dominating fashion, the legislation removing the Australian Trade Commission's executive board was justified *only* by reference to the Uhrig principles – no consideration was given to the functions the board had previously performed or to the (good!) reasons why it had been established in the first place (Vaile 2006). The legislation removing the council from the Australian Research Council was processed in the same way, though in that case opposition spokesman Peter Garrett pointed out that the Uhrig-instigated changes would enhance the already-controversial ministerial power to intervene in research grant decisions (Garrett 2006).

There were some 'reprieves', notably for the few remaining NDPBs classified as 'government business enterprises' (which were already required to prepare comparable documents), for some 'highly independent bodies' such as the Audit Office, Ombudsman, Public Service Commission and Reserve Bank, and for 'prescribed agencies' such as AusAID and Geoscience Australia which remained components of the relevant departments.

In the fourth government period, the focus has been so heavily on the restructuring of the commonwealth's own machinery of government that there has been less development of joint commonwealth–state authorities than experienced under the earlier Howard governments. No doubt the commonwealth's increasing isolation within the Australian family of governments – in which all eight subnational units currently had Labor governments – was a contributing factor.

Impact of ongoing policy development

While the new NDPBs reflect the operation of the Uhrig principles, the circumstances leading to their establishment are as distinctive as the agencies themselves, and in several cases these circumstances have produced considerable political debate. In accordance with the new DoFA guidelines, they are mostly statutory authorities. In several cases ministers have used the word 'independent' in describing the new creations (for example, Andrews 2005: 7; Andrews 2006; Minchin 2006b; Turnbull 2007: 6). In the Uhrig context, however, it has to be seen as a very qualified form of independence, the Uhrig principles reinforcing a tendency apparent over a longer period to grant ministers extensive directive powers over most NDPBs.

Of the new statutory authorities, the Future Fund and the National Water Commission reflect priorities announced in the Governor-General's speech. The first, intended to be funded out of government surpluses, was to cover the future costs of the commonwealth's previously unfunded superannuation liabilities, but it was soon extended as a repository of the Telstra shares remaining in public hands after the third tranche sale (for further details see chapters 4 and 8 in this volume), and later it became the manager of the new Higher Education Endowment Fund. There is both a 'management agency' as a statutory agency and a 'board of guardians' as a body corporate to handle all the investment decisions, the two linked by the provision that the board chair will double as the agency CEO. The second, which is subject to a sunset clause, is charged with spearheading funding and program measures to cope with what is increasingly seen as one of the nation's most critical policy problems – the commission includes members nominated by all signatories to the intergovernmental National Water Initiative agreements, while the CEO and staff constitute the statutory agency.

The government's highly controversial efforts to reform the industrial relations system produced several waves of adjustments to relevant NDPBs. The Fair Pay Commission emerged in the first wave, associated with a reduction in the powers of the older Industrial Relations Commission and creation of a new executive agency, the Office of Workplace Services (OWS), to monitor workplace changes under the new system. In the second wave, OWS was itself displaced by the Workplace Ombudsman, while a new Workplace Authority, with most of its statutory powers centred in the Workplace Authority Director, replaced the older Office of the Employment Advocate.

The new Building and Construction Industry Commission and the associated Federal Safety Commissioner (though that office is within the minister's department) are also IR-related, involving a special application of the workplace reforms in an industry shown by a royal commission inquiry to have a 'deplorable' industrial relations record (Andrews 2005: 5; Cole 2003). Among other new authorities, Cancer Australia delivered on a special health policy election commitment; the Australian Commission for Law Enforcement Integrity, headed by an Integrity Commissioner, was foreshadowed early in 2004, but the creating legislation and the recruitment of commissioner and staff were processed through the period of the fourth government;[8] the Australian Communications and Media Authority (ACMA), a merger of earlier communications and broadcasting regulators, similarly reflected decisions already taken by the previous Howard government; and the picturesquely named Australian Reward Investment Alliance (ARIA) resulted from another merger, that of two earlier public sector superannuation funds. In this case, explanatory documents made it clear that the changes were developed in accordance with the Uhrig principles but also that they were needed to achieve the modernisation of the relevant funds in line with major changes occurring in the national superannuation environment. Reform of the military justice system, following a Senate Committee (SFADTRC 2005) and earlier reports, saw the creation of several new statutory bodies and officials, but they were financed and staffed within the Australian Defence Force and so not much affected by the 'Uhrig factor'; while the Wheat Marketing Commission emerged from pressures coming quite late in the period under review as a result of the demonstrated weakness of the earlier Wheat Marketing Authority in the AWB Iraqi sanctions-busting affair. Also, emerging from a late policy initiative and relying in part on its external affairs power under the constitution, the commonwealth established the Murray-Darling Basin Authority as a 'basin-wide institution' to plan and regulate the relevant water resources 'in the interests of the basin as a whole and not along state lines' (Turnbull 2007: 6).[9]

Reflecting DoFA's new advice that use of the company form should be restricted to exceptional circumstances (DoFA 2005b), there have been fewer company formations than under the earlier Howard governments. Indeed, the education portfolio has been the only significant generator of new companies. Notices under the CAC Act tabled in parliament show limited movement in other commonwealth shareholdings, with several of these transactions involving streamlining action which may or may not be directly Uhrig-related.[10]

Probably the most significant of the abolitions was that of the Aboriginal and Torres Strait Islander Commission (ATSIC) and its regional councils (see Sanders 2005: 161–66 and chapter 11 in this volume). The general plan was to return services for Indigenous people to mainline departments and agencies in accordance with the new whole-of-government approach, although some ATSIC functions went to other dedicated NDPBs (notably the Indigenous Land Corporation and Indigenous Business Australia); a new non-statutory advisory National Indigenous Council was established, and the ATSIC abolition legislation provided for an Office of Evaluation and Audit (Indigenous Programs) as a sort of half-way house with statutorily prescribed functions but within the supervising minister's department. The Torres Strait Regional Authority was left in place.

While the so-called Uhrig process was virtually complete at the close of the period under review, a few residual matters remained to be attended to and would be the subject of further legislation. A DoFA tally at the close of the period indicated the numerical impact of the changes already made. There were now 90 CAC bodies, 18 fewer than at the commencement of the fourth Howard government; and 77 FMA bodies other than departments, 13 more than at the commencement of the period, illustrating the trend away from the more autonomous to the less autonomous category. Appendix 3.3 provides a breakdown of these figures.

Among other NDPB changes that do not appear to be primarily Uhrig-related, the office of the Commonwealth Ombudsman has been expanded to embrace the supplementary roles of Migration Ombudsman and Postal Industry Ombudsman, while fresh legislation containing measures to improve the working of the Administrative Appeals Tribunal has steered clear of the draconian attempts to muzzle the appeals bodies under the earlier Howard governments (see Wettenhall 2005a: 81).[11]

While many NDPBs are not much noticed as they go about their tasks, a few attract considerable controversy. In this respect the ABC is probably unmatched: its efforts to give some coverage to all mainstream views and opinions ensured that it was always 'destined ... to be a field of contest', as well illustrated in a significant organisational history published during the period under review (Inglis 2006: backcover).

In the heightened security environment in the period under review, ASIO and the Australian Federal Police, virtually ignored by Uhrig, have also never been far from the cut-and-thrust of political debate. Late in the fourth government term, AFP Commissioner Keelty seemed quite unable to separate himself from the politics of the case of Indian doctor Haneef, which led a state premier to describe the authority Keelty headed as 'a bunch of keystone cops' and a multitude of writers to newspapers to assert that it had lost their respect (see e.g. Waterford 2007a, 2007b).[12]

A very different sort of example is provided by the Reserve Bank, specifically exempted from Uhrig-style treatment, whose independence in fixing the interest rates which so heavily affect the state of the national economy is frequently and publicly analysed, in the context of not-so-subtle prime ministerial messages that it should *not* raise rates (see discussion of the Reserve Bank's position in Wettenhall 2004a: 68–69). As yet another example, soon after its establishment the Workplace Authority's Director was appearing controversially, in TV advertisements and elsewhere, as an enthusiastic advocate of the government's second-wave IR policies, and earning criticism that she was thus showing poor judgment in breaching Australian Public Service guidelines about always behaving in an apolitical manner (Podger 2007) – guidelines that surely have added significance when applied to statutory officers. Again, CSIRO regularly attracts controversy.

A generic issue that runs much beyond the matter of the Uhrig Report and its applications concerns the question of how appointments are made to senior NDPB positions, both board chairs and members and chief executives. Uhrig proposed that, where there were boards, they should appoint the CEOs. But the issue is broader than that and, as remarked in the previous volume in this series, it is one 'that will not go away' (Wettenhall 2005a: 87). In the period under review it has again been widely discussed. Researchers in an ARC-funded project on corporate governance in the public sector have given it much attention, including examination of new provisions in Britain and Canada aimed at elevating merit over partisanship in the appointment process. It has been suggested that there might be useful models here for Australia to follow; and there has been much interviewing in Canberra to discover what actually happens in the commonwealth system. Clearly there is still much to be done, as a poker-faced comment from the chair of one authority with a board indicates: 'We are totally independent. We are absolutely independent despite the fact that board members are all mates with the PM' (cited in Edwards 2006a: 10; see also Wettenhall 2004b; Gourley 2005, 2006; Edwards 2006b).

The special case of 'integrity agencies'

An unintended consequence of the desire of Uhrig and his backers to enhance ministerial authority over NDPBs is that the attention of others has been focused on a special group of agencies that must necessarily, if they are to perform their allocated tasks satisfactorily, be in conflict with ministers from time to time. This group includes ombudsmen, audit offices, and human rights, anti-corruption, electoral and data protection commissions. They are sometimes described as 'integrity agencies', and were the subject of a large ARC-assisted project reported in *Australian Journal of Public Administration* (Brown & Head 2005).

The problem is that they are funded by the governments they will inevitably be criticising when, in the performance of their tasks, they find the performance of some part of the government system improper or inadequate. Governments like to show that they work with such bodies, but they have a variety of ways of weakening them or neutralising their effects: for example, they can keep funding to unrealistically low levels, or fail to appoint commissioners even though the posts are statutorily available. Commentators urge that the legislatures that have created these bodies must protect them against such weakening efforts by governments, but often the legislatures themselves are dominated by the governments and so unable or unwilling to provide the required protections. For this reason, a movement has developed in some legislatures to establish a new category of 'officers of parliament' to embrace agencies in this position. Within our region, New Zealand has been a leader in this development, and Victoria and Western Australia have taken significant action – special parliamentary committees are created to watch the interests of these 'officers', and the parliaments assume a bigger role than before in making appointments and providing funding. Where this movement is well advanced, the agencies concerned come to be seen as part of the parliamentary establishment and not part of executive government at all (see Beattie 2006; PAECV 2006; Wettenhall 2005b, 2007b). For the commonwealth, however, it seems that the National Audit Office is currently the only NDPB to approach this sort of treatment.

It is a paradox that, because of its failure to pay attention to issues of parliamentary accountability and democratic process, the Uhrig Report may actually increase discussion of such issues.

Final word: always NDPBs, but also trends and cycles

The Uhrig Report and the resulting changes to the NDPB sector can all be seen as feeding into the whole-of-government strategy pursued through the period of the later Howard governments, discussed in more detail in chapter 2. Portfolios focused around 'comprehensive ministerial departments'

(Halligan & Horrigan 2005: 6) now dominate machinery-of-government considerations, arguably as never before, with NDPBs mostly reduced to the role of service providers in areas not caught up in the privatising drives of the late 20th and early 21st centuries, or regulators in areas that have been privatised.

For a decade or more, 'agencificationists' have been asserting that there has been a large increase in the number of 'agencies' or 'quangos' (my NDPBs) around the world as governments have embraced the teachings of so-called 'new public management' and moved to decentralising and disaggregating arrangements in their administrative systems. These claims have always been controversial, and they never made much sense in the Australian context (discussed in Wettenhall 2005c). Now, however, there is fairly broad agreement that, if that was indeed a strong trend, it is being reversed – the call for 'joined-up government' is often heard, Britain is reducing its large crop of executive agencies, New Zealand is witnessing an anti-fragmentationist return to the centre (see Gregory 2003), and so on. Australia's Uhrig-style changes can be seen as part of this movement.

Nonetheless NDPBs continue to exist. Uhrig and whole-of-government notwithstanding, they allow for a degree of flexible devolution not possible within the departments themselves, and they are unlikely ever to disappear. A longer term view of the field suggests that it is one that is particularly subject to cyclical fashions. Many years ago, drawing on some contemporary political science literature (see Macmahon 1961; Freidrich 1963; Fesler 1964) and some remarkable student insights, I expressed this view (1968: 352–53):

> there has always been, and always will be, rivalry between forces seeking greater standardisation, closer integration in the activities of government, on the one hand, and forces seeking greater flexibility, more independence for the various parts, on the other. Sometimes one set of forces gains the upper hand and sometimes the other, so that the real shape of the machinery of government is likely to be determined in pendulum fashion as the focus shifts back and forth between the unification pole and the diversity pole. Each pole contains within itself the seeds of counter-movement. The scattered system has its disorderliness and the standardised system its rigidity. Any final solution at one extreme or the other is impossible; and no single point of compromise can be expected to win general acceptance.

Forty years later, I see no reason to change this view. Governments will go on creating NDPBs, though they will sometimes do it more freely, sometimes less freely. Functions will continue to move in and out of departments depending on the current state of the cycle, and there will always be half-way house compromises. Sometimes the cycle will favour granting more autonomy to the various constituents of the sector, at other times less. And the movement will not necessarily be uniform over a total government system – as a recent Dutch study has indicated, it is possible that some policy areas (and related ministries) within a particular system will be more amenable to significant devolution and grants of autonomy than others (van Thiel 2006).

This is not a static field (Wettenhall & Aulich 2007), and it is inevitable that there will be further changes. In the lead-up to the election that concluded the term of the fourth Howard government there were already many pointers to changes to come.[13] It was entirely safe to predict that, whoever won that election, the very useful NDPB arrangement would continue to be utilised in the service of public policy and public management, but also that the field would be subject to further changes of fashion as the arguments about centralising and decentralising go on.

Notes

1   Previously, lacking such a sub-category of statutory authority, NDPBs in this position were sometimes referred to as 'as if' departments – they were staffed under the Public Service Act 'as if' they were separate departments (see e.g. Wettenhall 1975: 316; 1988: 258).

2   It was, of course, by no means the only public sector to exhibit this problem. Since many NDPBs exist on the margins of the public sector, questions sometimes arise as to whether they are really a part of that sector or not. But there are also problems of classification and of visibility. For a discussion of the British situation which uses the word 'quango' as synonymous with NDPB, see Flinders 1999: 3–8. Other class names or field descriptions are also in use, and are similarly fairly elastic in what they cover: e.g. 'distributed public governance' gained considerable traction after an OECD review which used that term (OECD 2002; Flinders 2004), and 'non-majoritarian institutions' has come into use in Europe as away of referring to public institutions not headed by elected officials such as ministers (Thatcher & Sweet 2002).

3   An additional section dealt with 'parliamentary bodies'.

4   The business operations and distinctly branded functions are reminiscent of what Flinders (2004: 893) described as 'the non-statutory "soft-law" governance framework which surrounds certain types of autonomous public bodies' in Britain. An Australian case which became controversial during the fourth government period was that of the Therapeutic Goods Administration (TGA), a longstanding departmental 'outrider'. It was the subject of bitter political debate through early 2006 over the question whether the minister's approval was necessary before the abortion drug RU486 could be listed as a therapeutic good able to be subsidised under the Pharmaceutical Benefits Scheme. The TGA itself is simply a 'division' or 'unit' of the Department of Health and Ageing; a statute regulates the listing procedure and makes the departmental secretary the

regulating authority. During these debates, however, the general public perception was to see it as an autonomous or even 'independent' body (for a brief discussion, see Wettenhall 2007a: 72).

5   The term 'statutory office holder' has related traditionally to arrangements where a statutory body is headed by a single official such as an ombudsman, auditor-general or commissioner of taxation rather than a board or commission.

6   The only proposal specifically rejected by the government was that an Inspector-General of Regulation be established.

7   In the event, not all received this drastic treatment: though they were included in the new portfolio, Hearing Services Australia (a statutory authority) and Health Services Australia (a company) retained their boards and their CAC Act status.

8   Its jurisdiction is limited to official agencies of government, but there has been considerable press comment suggesting that there is a need for an independent body with a wider remit to investigate corruption and misconduct by politicians as well as officials, as now exists in some states: see for example Bartos 2007.

9   It did not, however, replace the already-existing intergovernmental Murray-Darling Basin Commission, leaving difficult relationship questions still to be worked out.

10 An episode which revealed some of the uncertainties surrounding the government's ownership of many of these companies occurred when, during Senate committee estimates hearings in May 2007, Minister for Human Services Chris Ellison denied that he was a shareholding minister for Health Services Australia, a GBE in company form – he was then informed that he was, and had to correct the record (*CT* 2007). The biggest company transaction of the period came with the sale of third-tranche Telstra shares (further details on the sale of Telstra can be found in chapter 4).

11 Indicative of other such changes, the Australian Community Pharmacy Authority twice had its life extended as consultations with the Pharmacy Guild of Australia relating to budget measures to support the Pharmaceutical Benefits Scheme dragged on. And the establishment of a new, more comprehensive regulatory regime for the private health insurance sector saw the Private Health Industry Administration Council, a statutory authority, reconstituted under its own legislation, retaining its CAC Act and non-Public Service Act status.

12 On the security agencies, like ASIO, see also Wilkie 2006.

13 Indications of changes to come were available in the government's 2007 budget documents and in a mass of pre-election policy announcements by government and opposition and by others seeking to exert influence. To give just a few examples: If the government were returned and kept to its budget plans, there would be a new Australian Screen Authority to absorb several existing agencies operating in the film and television industry. Labor policy plans announced around mid-2007 included creation of a dedicated Petrol Commissioner to regulate fuel pricing and a Small Business Advisory Council, greater independence for the Building and Construction Industry Commissioner, conversion of the Fair Pay Commission into a Fair Work Commission, and another new statutory body to advise government on the future skills needs of the nation. Indeed, a Liberal Party spokesman asserted that 'Labor was already promising 75 new commissions and bureaucracies' (reported in Price 2007). Families Australia, an NGO, urged on both main political groups the establishment of an Australian Families Commission, the Australian Health Care Reform Alliance wanted an independent multi-jurisdictional National Health Commission, ANU academic Professor Clive Williams called for a body independent of the government to 'manage' all the security agencies, and controversies surrounding the pre-election debate between the Prime

Minister and Leader of the Opposition led to a proposal that there should be another independent authority to regulate such events, based on a US model.

References

Andrews, K (Minister for Employment and Workplace Relations) (2005) Second reading speech on Building and Construction Industry Improvement Bill 2005, *Com. Parl. Debs HoR*, 9 March.

—— (2006) Establishment of the Office of Workplace Services as an independent agency (Media release), 30 March.

Bartos, S (2005a) The Uhrig Report: Damp squib or ticking timebomb? *Australian Journal of Public Administration*, 64(1): 95–99.

—— (2005b) Shock! Horror! Departments find bodies under the carpet, *Public Sector Informant*, December.

—— (2006) All quiet on the review front in the long wait to be uhriged, *Public Sector Informant*, September.

—— (2007) Weighing up the case for a standing commission against corruption, *Public Sector Informant*, April.

Beattie, A (2006) Officers of Parliament: The New Zealand model, *Australasian Parliamentary Review*, 21(1): 143–56.

Briggs, L (2005) Bringing agencies into the APS fold: The Uhrig reforms and the APS, *Public Sector Informant*, June.

Brough, J (1997) Howard to rein in statutory bodies, *Sydney Morning Herald*, 6 March.

Brown, AJ & Head, B (2005) Assessing integrity systems: Introduction to a symposium, *Australian Journal of Public Administration*, 64(2): 42–47.

CT (*Canberra Times*) (2007) ALP queries health contracts, 29 July.

Clark, A (2002) Untold power, *Australian Financial Review*, 23 March.

Cole, TRH (Commissioner) (2003) *Final Report of the Royal Commission into the Building and Construction Industry: Summary of Findings and Recommendations*, DoFA Information Services, Canberra.

DoFA (Department of Finance and Administration) (2004) *List of Australian Government Bodies 2002–2003*, DoFA, Canberra.

—— (2005a) *List of Australian Government Bodies and Governance Relationships as at 31 December 2004*, DoFA, Canberra.

—— (2005b) *Governance Arrangements for Australian Government Bodies*, DoFA, Canberra.

—— (2005c) *Governance Implementation Update (Uhrig Review): The Implementation Process, Guidance Material and the Timeline for Assessments*, DoFA, Canberra.

—— (2006) *Governance Implementation Update (Uhrig Review): How is the Assessment Process Progressing?*, DoFA, Canberra.

—— (2007) *Governance Implementation Update (Uhrig Review): Outcomes of the Uhrig Review Process*, DoFA, Canberra.

Edwards, M (2006a) Appointment processes raise worries on transparency and accountability, *Public Sector Informant*, April.

—— (2006b) *Appointments to Public Sector Boards in Australia: A Comparative Assessment*, University of Canberra Corporate Governance ARC Project, Issues Paper Series No. 3.

Fels, A & Brenchley, F (2004) Chance missed to give regulators more teeth, *Australian Financial Review*, 16 August.

Fesler, JS (1964) Approaches to the understanding of decentralisation, *Journal of Politics*, 27: 536–66.
Flinders, MV (1999) Setting the scene: Quangos in context. In MV Flinders & MJ Smith (eds), *Quangos, Accountability and Reform*, Palgrave Macmillan, Basingstoke: 3–16.
—— (2004) Distributed public governance in Britain, *Public Administration*, 82(4): 883–909.
Fraser, A (2005) Not so jolly as Hockey sticks it to the other side, *Canberra Times*, 29 October.
Friedrich, CJ (1963) *Man and His Government*, McGraw-Hill, New York.
Garrett, P (2006) Speech on second reading of Australian Research Council Amendment Bill 2006, *Com. Parl. Debs HoR*, 14 June.
Gourley, P (2004) Recommendations not worth the wait: The Uhrig Report, *Public Sector Informant*, September.
—— (2005) Easy as ABC: A proper process for being above board, *Public Sector Informant*, May.
—— (2006) Jobs for the girls and boys, *Public Sector Informant*, August.
Gregory, R (2003) All the King's horses and all the King's men: Putting New Zealand's public sector back together again, *International Public Management Review*, (2): 41–58.
Halligan, J & Horrigan, B (2005) *Reforming Corporate Governance in the Australian Federal Public Sector: From Uhrig to Implementation*, University of Canberra Corporate Governance ARC Project, Issues Paper Series No. 2.
Hockey, J (Minister for Human Services) (2005) Making life easier: The role of Human Services in improving Commonwealth service delivery, Speech to National Press Club, Canberra, 20 April.
Holland, I (2004) The review of the corporate governance of statutory authorities and office holders, *Public Administration Today* (formerly *Canberra Bulletin of Public Administration*), issue 1: 64–66.
Howard, J (Prime Minister) (2002) Address to the Australian Chamber of Commerce and Industry, The Great Hall, Parliament House, Canberra, 14 November.
—— (2004) Fourth Howard Ministry (Prime Minister of Australia Media release), 22 October.
Inglis, K S (2006) *Whose ABC? The Australian Broadcasting Commission 1983–2006*, Black Inc., Melbourne.
Ioannou, T (Branch Manager, Government Structures Branch, DoFA) (2006) Paper presented at National Institute for Governance (University of Canberra) Uhrig Implementation Seminar, Australian War Memorial, 27 September.
Jeffery, M (Governor-General) (2004). Governor-General's Speech, *Com. Parl. Debs S*, 16 November.
LNP (Liberal and National Parties) (2001) *The Howard Government: Putting Australia's Interests First*, Liberal and National Parties, Canberra.
Macintosh, A (2007) Statutory authorities. In C Hamilton & S Maddison (eds), *Silencing Dissent*, Allen & Unwin, Sydney: 148–74.
Macmahon, A W (1961) *Delegation and Autonomy*, Asia Publishing House, Bombay.
Minchin, N (Minister for Finance and Administration) (2004) Australian Government response to Uhrig Report (Media release), 12 August.
—— (2006a) Uhrig Review: Progress with implementation (Media release), 5 January.
—— (2006b) Second reading speech on National Health and Medical Research Council Amendment Bill 2006, *Com. Parl. Debs S*, 29 March.
OECD (Organization for Economic Cooperation and Development) (2002) *Distributed*

Public Governance: Agencies, Authorities and Other Public Bodies, OECD, Paris.
PAECV (Public Accounts and Estimates Committee, Victorian Parliament) (2006) *Report on a Legislative Framework for Independent Officers of Parliament*, Government Printer for the State of Victoria, Melbourne.
Podger, A (2007) Pride and prejudice: Ms Bennett as the face of a very public service, *Public Sector Informant*, August.
Price, J (2007) Calls for debate shake-up, *Canberra Times*, 24 October.
Sanders, W (2005) Not even adequate: Reconciliation and Indigenous affairs. In C Aulich & R Wettenhall (eds), *Howard's Second and Third Governments: Australian Commonwealth Administration 1998–2004*, UNSW Press, Sydney: 77–102.
SFADTRC (Senate Foreign Affairs, Defence and Trade References Committee) (2005) *The Effectiveness of the Australian Military Justice System*, Department of the Senate, Canberra.
Thatcher, M & Sweet, AS (eds) (2002) The politics of delegation: Non-majoritarian institutions in Europe, Special Issue of *Western European Politics*, 25(1).
Turnbull, M (Minister for Environment and Water Resources) (2007) Second reading speech on Water Bill 2007, *Com. Parl. Debs HoR*, 8 August.
Uhrig, J (2003) *Review of the Corporate Governance of Statutory Authorities and Office Holders*, DoFA, Canberra.
—— (2005) Transcript of comments to a Governance Network Workshop on *The Uhrig Report: Its Implications for the Australian Government*, Canberra, 18 May.
Vaile, M (Minister for Trade) (2006) Explanatory Memorandum on Australian Trade Commission Legislation Amendment Bill 2006, Parliament of the Commonwealth of Australia, Canberra.
van Thiel, S (2006) Styles of reform: Differences in quango creation between policy sectors in the Netherlands, *Journal of Public Policy*, 26(2): 115–39.
Waterford, J (2007a) The damaged repute of an AFP acting as judge and jury too, *Canberra Times*, 21 July.
—— (2007b) Deep harm in Haneef wreck, *Canberra Times*, 1 August.
Wettenhall, R (1968) Government department or statutory authority?, *Public Administration* (Sydney), 27(4): 350–59.
—— (1975) Report on statutory authorities. In *Royal Commission on Australian Government Administration, Appendix*, vol. 1, AGPS, Canberra: 312–64.
—— (1998) The rising popularity of the government-owned company in Australia: Problems and issues, *Public Administration and Development*, 18(3): 243–55.
—— (2000) Reshaping the Commonwealth public sector. In G Singleton (ed.), *The Howard Government: Australian Commonwealth Administration 1996–1998*, UNSW Press, Sydney: 65–95.
—— (2003a) These executive agencies!, *Canberra Bulletin of Public Administration*, No. 106: 9–14.
—— (2003b) Kaleidoscope, or 'Now we see them, now we don't!': Commonwealth public sector involvement in company formation, *Canberra Bulletin of Public Administration*, No. 110: 29–44.
—— (2004a) Statutory authorities, the Uhrig Report and the trouble with internal inquiries, *Public Administration Today*, Issue 2: 62–76.
—— (2004b) Jobs for the mates not the way to go, *Public Sector Informant*, February.
—— (2005a) Non-departmental public bodies. In C Aulich & R Wettenhall (eds), *Howard's Second and Third Governments: Australian Commonwealth Administration 1998–2004*, UNSW Press, Sydney: 152–72.

—— (2005b) Parliamentary oversight of statutory bodies: A post-Uhrig perspective, *Australasian Parliamentary Review*, 20(2): 39–63.
—— (2005c) Agencies and non-departmental public bodies: The hard and soft lenses of agencification theory, *Public Management Review*, 7(4): 615–35.
—— (2006a) Good ammunition for killing off bodies, *Public Sector Informant*, February.
—— (2006b) Understanding public sector boards: Before Uhrig, Uhrig, and afterwards?, at <www.canberra.edu.au/corpgov-aps> (Originally presented at Conference on Corporate Governance in the Public Sector: From Theory to Practice, Old Parliament House, Canberra, 8–10 March 2006)
—— (2007a) Non-departmental public bodies under the Howard governments, *Australian Journal of Public Administration*, 66(1): 62–82.
—— (2007b) Parliaments, executives and integrity agencies: Reporting on an international conference on transparency for better governance, *Australasian Parliamentary Review*, 22(1): 115–36.
Wettenhall, R & Aulich, C (2007) The public sector's use of agencies: A dynamic rather than static scene, Paper for meeting of EGPA Study Group on Governance of Public Sector Organizations on 'The governance, control and autonomy of public sector organizations in a multi-level and multi-actor setting', Madrid, 19–22 September.
Wilkie, A (2006) *All Quiet in the Ranks: An Exploration of Dissent in Australia's Security Agencies*, The Australia Institute, Canberra.

Appendix 3.1

Departments during the period of the fourth Howard government

I. MINISTERIAL (PORTFOLIO) DEPARTMENTS

	Revisions	
From 26 October 2004*	*26 January 2006*	*24 January 2007*
Agriculture, Fisheries and Forestry	+	+
Attorney-General's	+	+
Communications, Information Technology and the Arts	+	+
Defence (with Veterans' Affairs as separate outlier department)	+	+
Education, Science and Training	+	+
Employment and Workplace Relations	+	+
Environment and Heritage	+	Environment and Water Resources
Family and Community Services	Families, Community Services and Indigenous Affairs	+
Finance and Administration (with Human Services as separate outlier department)	+	+
Foreign Affairs and Trade	+	+
Health and Ageing	+	+
Immigration and Multicultural and Indigenous Affairs	Immigration and Multicultural Affairs	Immigration and Citizenship
Industry, Tourism and Resources	+	+
Prime Minister and Cabinet	+	+
Transport and Regional Services	+	+
Treasury	+	+

II. PARLIAMENTARY DEPARTMENTS

Dept of the House of Representatives

Dept of the Senate

Dept of Parliamentary Services

Notes:
* Unchanged from the final dispositions in the third Howard government except for the addition of Human Services as a new outlier department within the Finance portfolio.
+ Unchanged.

Appendix 3.2

Innovations related to systemic changes

The term 'statutory agency' is now often built into the creating legislation. As noted above, it is a new category introduced by the 1999 changes to the Public Service Act, and refers to statutory authorities staffed under that legislation.

A related new practice is to separate some collective decision-making bodies such as the Fair Pay Commission and the Guardians of the Future Fund from the associated management services by declaring that only the CEO (or the chair if those offices are combined) and associated staff constitute the statutory agency. It would seem, therefore, that the statutory agency can be something less than the full statutory authority.

Another effect that confronts earlier linguistic understandings is the formal statutory entrenchment of the notion that a 'commission' or 'council', previously widely regarded as a multi-member organ heading an authority, can consist of a single chief officer together with supporting staff. There also appears to be an emerging view that a 'commission', where it remains a multi-member device, can exist within an executive management-template authority; it is thus differentiated from the sort of 'board' that heads a board-template authority.

A tendency to eliminate familiar class-names such as board, commission, council or authority from the formal titles of NDPBs, first noted for the second/third government period, has continued.

Similarly, there has been more use of what was described for the second/third government period as 'the intermediate position' whereby an office or section within a department is given statutory recognition and statutory functions and powers in its own right, while still being regarded as part of the department.

Appendix 3.3
Impact of Uhrig-process changes

Total numbers of NDPBs

NUMBERS AT BEGINNING OF FOURTH GOVERNMENT PERIOD
CAC Act: 108 (81 statutory bodies; 27 companies)
FMA Act (other than departments): 64 bodies
Total: 172

NUMBERS AT END OF FOURTH GOVERNMENT PERIOD
CAC Act: 90 (64 statutory bodies; 26 companies)
FMA Act (other than departments): 77 bodies
Total: 167

NOTES
1   The FMA numbers include some branches of departments classified as 'prescribed agencies' – Biosecurity Australia and Defence Materiel Organisation were additions in this category.
2   Since the introduction of the CAC and FMA categories, there have always been a few NDPBs that have not been so classified, the most obvious ones being those with an intergovernmental character such as the Murray-Darling Basin Commission.
3   Thanks to Marc Mowbray-d'Arbela, John Kalikerinos, John Cassidy and Lillian Patterson of DoFA's Legislative Review Branch for assistance with these tables.

NDPBs that have been abolished

STATUTORY AUTHORITIES AND CORPORATIONS
Aboriginal and Torres Strait Islander Commission
Australia-Japan Foundation
Australian Maritime College (transferred to University of Tasmania)
Australian National Training Authority
Classification Board/Classification Review Board (films etc)
Employment Services Regulatory Authority
Forest and Wood Products R & D Corporation (converted to industry services company)
National Occupational Health and Safety Commission
Stevedoring Industry Finance Committee
Tobacco Research and Development Corporation

EXECUTIVE AGENCIES
Aboriginal and Torres Strait Islander Service
Australian Government Information Management Office
Australian Greenhouse Office
National Oceans Office

GOVERNMENT-OWNED COMPANIES
Employment National Ltd
Enterprise and Career Education Foundation Ltd
Health eSignature Authority Pty Ltd
National Institute of Clinical Studies Ltd (absorbed in NHMRC)
Telstra Corporation Ltd
Telstra Instalment Receipt Trustee Ltd

New creations

STATUTORY AUTHORITIES AND CORPORATIONS
Auditing and Assurance Standards Board
Australian Building and Construction Commission (ABBC) (here the commission and staff together constitute a 'statutory agency')
Australian Commission for Law Enforcement Integrity
Australian Communication and Media Authority (merger of earlier Australian Broadcasting and Communications Authorities)
Australian Fair Pay Commission (with its Secretariat classified as a 'statutory agency')
Australian Reward Investment Alliance (merger of earlier Commonwealth Service and Public Service Superannuation Boards)
Australian Sports Anti-Doping Authority (replacing Australian Sports Drugs Agency)
Cancer Australia
Export Wheat Commission (replacing Wheat Export Authority)
Future Fund Management Agency with its associated Board of Guardians
Higher Education Endowment Fund Advisory Board
Medicare Australia (replacing Health Insurance Commission)
Military justice agencies (Australian Military Court, Registrar of Military Justice, Director of Military Prosecutions, Inspector-General of Australian Defence Force)
National Water Commission
Workplace Authority (replacing Employment Advocate)
Workplace Ombudsman

EXECUTIVE AGENCY
Office of Workplace Services (short-lived)

GOVERNMENT-OWNED COMPANIES
The Carrick Institute for Learning and Training in Higher Education Ltd
HIH Claims Support Ltd (becomes a solely owned commonwealth company)
Teaching Australia – Australian Institute for Teaching and School Leadership Ltd
Telstra Sale Company Ltd, to act as trustee for shares sold as instalment receipts in the third-tranche sale prior to payment of second instalment

Other already-existing NDPBs affected by this reform process[1]

STATUTORY AUTHORITIES AND CORPORATIONS
Australian Broadcasting Corporation
Australian Centre for International Agricultural Research
Australian Institute of Family Studies
Australian Institute of Marine Science
Australian Nuclear Science and Technology Organisation
Australian Pesticides and Veterinary Medicines Authority
Australian Prudential Regulation Authority
Australian Research Council
Australian Securities and Investment Commission
Australian Trade Commission
Centrelink
Child Support Agency
Commonwealth Scientific and Industrial Research Organisation
Corporations and Markets Advisory Committee
Defence Housing Authority (renamed Defence Housing Australia)
Export Finance Insurance Corporation
National Health and Medical Research Council (NHMRC)
National Offshore Petroleum Safety Authority
Primary Industries and Energy R & D Corporations generally
Private Health Industry Ombudsman
Royal Australian Navy Central Canteens Board
Tourism Australia

NOTE
1   This listing does not include bodies affected only by the requirement that ministers should issue them with Statements of Expectations and receive from them Statements of Intent.

4
Continuing Howard's privatisation agenda

Chris Aulich

Since early European settlement, Australia had a longstanding affection with public enterprise and with the notion of 'public' more broadly. The Hawke–Keating governments first challenged this affection with their privatisation of a number of public enterprises through a series of divestments. The election of the Howard government in 1996, however, ushered in a period of fierce privatisation, which has gone far beyond public enterprise divestment, expanding the range and the impact of privatisation technologies. The privatisation agenda of both major parties has, however, resulted from a re-examination of the role of government and the part to be played by the public sector in providing collective or public services. In this sense, there has been policy continuity, although differences are evident in intensity and application.

This chapter continues the privatisation story discussed in previous volumes in this series by mapping further development of Howard's privatisation agenda and by considering the impact of this agenda after a decade of implementation.

During the period of review, the Howard government has focused particular attention on the divestment of three iconic Australian public organisations: Telstra, Medibank Private and the Snowy Hydro scheme. The efforts to divest these public enterprises well illustrate Howard's approach to privatisation throughout the past decade, based on strong ideological commitment to private over public enterprise, but an approach which can easily be shifted to accommodate political exigencies of the time. What has also been noteworthy during this period has been the subtle, incremental use of other privatising technologies, such as outsourcing and user-pays, which have probably contributed more than divestment to the impact of privatisation during the watch of the fourth Howard government.

Privatisation under Howard governments

In this analysis of the Australian privatisation story, I use the term 'privatisation' in its broadest sense: an array of ways in which there are substitutions for government-*owned*, government-*funded* and government-*provided* services by non-government agencies and private funding mechanisms (Aulich 2005). The net impact of these substitutions is the greater reliance on private institutions and less on government to satisfy people's needs (Savas 1993: 40). Typically governments have available to them a number of broad technologies with which to privatise (Aulich & O'Flynn 2007a), but this chapter focuses on three – divestment, outsourcing and user-pays – which have dominated the Howard privatisation agenda.

The Howard approach has been driven by his and his governments' philosophical preference for the notion of 'private' over 'public' or collective activity. As Leader of the Opposition, Howard argued that privatisation would act as an important protection against the erosion of basic rights and would assist in fostering incentives, choice, competition and customer-oriented public services (LNP 1988). He advocated small government on the basis that public activity was often able to crowd out private enterprise (Howard 1981a, 1981b) and was convinced of the 'innate capacity of individuals to make better decisions about their future than the ... government' (Howard 1981c). As he stressed in one of his 'headland' speeches, 'Australians may not want government out of their lives, but they do want it off their back' (Howard 1995).

As Leader of the Opposition he promised to implement 'the most vigorous privatisation program undertaken by any national government' (Howard 1989), a promise he has surely kept. However, in giving effect to his ideological commitment to privatisation, Howard has also shown a keen sense of pragmatism, being able to identify what is politically possible. Concerned that Labor was misrepresenting and distorting his party's commitment to privatisation (Howard 1985), he adopted a highly pragmatic communication strategy in which issues of privatisation were not discussed either as a set of guiding principles or as a political ideology. In the last decade he refrained from any major speeches on the issue, instead only discussing privatisation on a case-by-case basis. He followed a clear communication strategy with respect to his governments' privatisation policy, a strategy that he had enunciated in the late 1980s:

> We're not walking away from privatisation, but we've learned something about marketing it. The way to handle it is portfolio by portfolio. When you talk about communication you say what you are going to do with Telecom, and so on. If it is put up as a general thing it can get kicked around. (in Randall 1986)

Despite his championing of private over public activity, he persisted in assuring the public that he was no ideologue: 'this isn't and never has been a question of ideology but of the best and fairest way to deliver services to the Australian people' (Howard 2001).

Divestment: substitutions of public ownership

Divestment activity during the period represents the end game after more than $85 billion of public enterprises and assets were divested over the past decade (Aulich & O'Flynn 2007a, 2007b). The following three cases illuminate the interplay between pragmatism and political ideology and illustrate Howard's deftness in shifting between them while maintaining a clear focus on his vision of a state where individual activity trumps collective or public activity.

TELSTRA

The biggest and most well-known divestment in Australia has been that of Telstra. In his first term Howard's attempts to obtain the full sale of the company were checked by his coalition partners and independents in the Senate, but he managed to reap $14.2 billion from the partial sale of one-third of the company, plus a $3 billion payment to the commonwealth from retained earnings (Aulich 2005).

In the lead up to the 1998 election, the first Howard government announced that it would not divest its remaining government stake in Telstra.

However, on just the second day of the new parliament, the newly elected government introduced enabling legislation for a full sale of Telstra. Again Howard's intentions were thwarted by the Senate, and in a compromise, he agreed in October 1999 to sell a further 16.6 per cent of the company, leaving public ownership at 50.1 per cent. Independent Senators Colson and Harradine were able to exploit their critical votes by negotiating enhancements for their constituents (Aulich & O'Flynn 2007a). This second tranche of Telstra shares represented the largest share offer in Australian history. More than 1.48 million individual buyers were involved in the sale, a very satisfying result for a political party that had long championed the growth of a 'capital-owning democracy' (LNP 1988).

During the 2001 election campaign, the Prime Minister again repeated the government's desire to divest the remaining public share in Telstra, even planning for its proceeds in the 2002–03 budget. However, he was again to be frustrated both by a Senate rejection of his sale plans and by a fall in the value of Telstra shares from over $9 in 1999 to $4.60 by 2002.

As the 2004 election approached, the ALP under both Crean and Latham campaigned to 'once and for all stop the full sale of Telstra' (Chaudri & Kerin 2004). However, winning control of the Senate in 2004 offered new opportunities for Howard to advance the full sale of Telstra. Not only was this a longstanding ideological position of the government, but the mixed public–private ownership of Telstra 'rest[ed] uncomfortably with many government ministers, many in the business sector and with the board of Telstra itself' (Aulich 2005: 63). The Prime Minister described Telstra as 'neither fish nor fowl' (Chaudri & Kerin 2004) and expressed concern that 'the Government ... had a massive conflict of interest, as the owner and seller of Australia's largest telco and as the industry regulator' (Grattan & Murphy 2006).

However, majority control of the Senate did not immediately grant the Howard government the sale it wanted. Howard found his coalition partners (and even some Liberal backbenchers) were still concerned about the impact of the full sale of Telstra.

Unlike its past three terms where the job was to make the argument for sale, Howard's fourth term agenda was to overcome public concerns and problems, while engaging in the last negotiations and planning for the sale of Telstra. No longer did the Prime Minister need to make the public argument for the sale, instead he had to deal with dissent in the Senate, and implement a policy for which he believed he had a mandate. While the government began counting Senate numbers and planning the sale, it also had to endure other challenges such as an increasingly independent Telstra board, a stock market that was not very eager to buy Telstra shares and a public wary and tired of the ideas of privatisation and the 'share-holder democracy' Howard had promoted.

This change in focus was underlined by the Prime Minister passing off most of the announcements about Telstra to the Treasurer and Finance Minister. Howard would continue to respond to the daily news cycle, and to ALP attacks, but the sale of Telstra was now seen as a budgetary decision, not a major piece of government policy.

After conceding further guarantees on customer service and re-direction of some of the proceeds to rural areas, the Howard government's bill enabling the full sale of Telstra finally passed the Senate on the 14 September 2005, nearly a year after the government gained majority control of the senate (*SMH* 2005). The Telstra 3 Share Offer was completed on 20 November 2006 resulting in the sale of 4.25 million shares with a total value of $15.4 billion (DoFA 2007). On 28 February 2007, the government transferred the remaining 17 per cent of its holding in Telstra to the Future Fund (for further details, see chapter 8). According to Finance Minister Nick Minchin, 'this is the final step in the full privatisation of this great Australian company' (Reuters 2007) and it was with great publicity that the government announced in 2006 that the national debt was zero, down from $96 billion when it assumed office (*Australian* 2006). This was due largely to the application of the proceeds of the sale of Telstra to public debt.

In March 2007, the ALP declared that, when in government, it would not attempt to nationalise Telstra, and Lindsay Tanner, the opposition spokesman on communications was reported as saying that: 'We accept we've lost that battle ... We accept that we can no longer defend the idea of a 17 per cent shareholding in Telstra being in the public interest' (Grattan et al. 2007).

Despite its victory, the Howard government did not appear to have benefited politically from the divestment of Telstra. This was due to the persistence of low share prices, especially the failure of the Telstra 2 share offer to return to its sale price, and a continuing battle with the new Telstra board over issues of broadband, regulation and the quality of telecommunications in the bush.

What at first glance might have appeared a relatively simple divestment of a publicly-owned, commercial enterprise, consistent with the political intentions of a conservative government, proved to be a long and arduous process; one which probably exhausted and alienated many of the public who would initially have been positive. The sale amplified tensions within the Coalition parties, forced the government to make compromises with

MEDIBANK PRIVATE

While government-owned, Medibank Private has operated as a 'government controlled, not-for-profit entity' (DPS 2006), designed to promote competition in the health insurance sector. It is currently the largest health insurer in Australia with around 1.3 million members, and an average market share of 28 per cent from 1999–2005 (PHI 2005).

In March 2006, the Howard government announced its intention to sell Medibank Private, Finance Minister Minchin declaring that there was 'no good public policy reason' for continued government ownership. Further, he said:

> Floating the company will give all Australians an opportunity to own part of Medibank Private and will also allow existing members to be recognised by way of an entitlement in the public offer ... A

Courtesy of Peter Nicholson, *The Australian*, 14 May 2002

> privatised Medibank can deliver lower management expenses and can look to expand into new business areas, lowering its average costs across the business. (AAP 2006b)

The opposition opposed the sale, arguing that the floating of Medibank Private would raise premiums in the market. Queensland's Senator Joyce also voiced his concern about the sale, particularly the role of foreign ownership, and the need to delay the sale until after the Telstra float had occurred (*Age* 2006). Joyce, however, was not opposed to the sale, and suggested his constituents didn't care either way. As he remarked, 'you don't find people walking down the street wanting to talk to you about Medibank Private' (ABC 2006b).

Despite it 'remaining the policy of the government to privatise Medibank Private' (AAP 2006a) the decision was taken in mid-September 2006 to delay the sale of Medibank Private until after the 2007 election. The decision was influenced by the Senate's passing of the Telstra privatisation legislation, amid concern from investment advisors and some sections of government that a $1–2 billion dollar float could affect demand for Telstra shares. Unsurprisingly, the opposition suggested that polls showing that a majority of Australians were opposed to the sale underpinned the decision to postpone the sale (ABC 2006b).

There were, however, unresolved issues about the ownership of the enterprise which needed resolution before this divestment could proceed at some future time. A September 2006 Parliamentary Library report found that:

> Medibank Private … is the vehicle used to hold the legal interest in the Medibank Private fund and its assets, but neither the company nor the Commonwealth can be described … as the true owner of the funds and associated assets. (DPS 2006: 20)

Finance Minister Senator Minchin responded to the Parliamentary Library's report with legal advice supporting the government's claim to ownership of Medibank Private, but this has not clarified all of the relevant issues. Even if the government is correct in claiming ownership, some have argued Medibank Private's members could have claim to either ownership of Medibank's $653 million dollar asset base (enough to prevent their sale) or compensation should the government sell the fund (Schubert 2006).

Unlike discussions about the divestment of Telstra and the Snowy Hydro scheme, the debate over Medibank saw significant public disagreement within the government about how the divestment should be managed. While the

Prime Minister, Treasurer, Health Minister and Finance Minister supported a public float, some members in the government had argued for it to be sold in a trade sale, or even broken up. The government sought independent private advice as well as from the Australian Competition and Consumer Commission about the valuation and competition implications for various methods of sale (Bartholomeusz 2006). While a float would have been the easiest political option, particularly if the existing membership were seen to benefit, many of Medibank Private's competitors and international investors were keen to see a break up or trade sale. Some competitors, such as MBF, had even indicated they might need to look towards consolidation with some of the other 40 private health insurers to try and guard against an unleashed Medibank Private.

With so much uncertainty, and with the ongoing issues related to a post-privatised Telstra, the government decided to postpone the divestment until after the election. With Labor in government, it remains to be seen whether or not it will continue with the sale, even though it meets the principles for divestment set during the last Labor period in office: a fully commercial entity with few community service obligations, operating in a contestable environment (Aulich & O'Flynn 2007a).

SNOWY HYDRO SCHEME

The Snowy Mountains Hydro-Electric Scheme was established in October 1949 and represents one of the great engineering and iconic nation building achievements in Australian history. Finished in 1974, it cost more than $820 million and was built by nearly 100 000 mainly post-war migrant workers. It includes seven power stations, 16 major dams, 145 km of tunnels, 80km of aqueducts, and a lake seven times the capacity of Sydney Harbour (Hannan & Wallace 2006). While the Snowy Hydro scheme is often seen as a water storage facility, its main source of income and national importance is in hydro-electricity production. It is the single largest supplier in the national energy market although it only provides around one-tenth of its potential electricity supply, but its ability to rapidly increase supply (within 90 seconds) has allowed it to operate as an electricity insurer for energy providers (Hannan & Wallace 2006).

In 1993 the Council of Australian Governments (COAG) agreed to begin the process of reform and corporatisation of the Snowy Hydro scheme. In October 1997, as part of that agreement, the NSW and Victorian governments established the Snowy Hydro Trading Pty Ltd as a joint venture with the simultaneous federal passage of the *Snowy Hydro Corporatisation Act 1997* (DPL 2003).

This legislation provided for the corporatisation of the Snowy Mountains Hydro-Electric Authority, and the establishment of the Snowy Hydro Limited (SHL) to assume control of the assets of the scheme. At the time, federal Minister for Industry, Science and Resources, Senator Minchin argued that 'corporatisation is an integral part of the Council of Australian Governments electricity reform agenda' (M2 Communications 2001). The NSW government became the majority shareholder with 58 per cent of the shares, Victoria holding 29 per cent and the commonwealth the remaining 13 per cent.

On 16 December 2005, the NSW government announced that it was planning to divest its SHL shareholdings. The initial public response was positive with over 150,000 people registering for a prospectus. In February 2006, the federal ministers for Finance, Public Administration, Industry, Tourism and Resources announced that the federal government would support the sale:

> The Australian Government views the sale of its minority 13 per cent share as being in the interests of Australian taxpayers, and consistent with our strong support for the privatisation of government-owned electricity generators and increased competition in the electricity market, particularly in NSW. (Macfarlane & Minchin 2006)

Following the decision of the NSW and Australian governments to divest their shares, the Victorian government quickly embraced the idea, and began planning in its budget for the use of the estimated $600 million that would flow to it from the sale. When the sale was announced debate centred around three key issues: the ability of the scheme to maintain itself, the impact of a privatised scheme on the waterways and environment, and the sale of a national icon.

The Managing Director of SHL, Terry Charlton, argued at the time of the proposed sale that the system's 40-year old assets required a high level of maintenance which governments were not willing to provide: 'Whilst we can handle much of that with cash flow, which is strong, we can't handle all of it, and we can't handle the additional demands to grow to meet society's need for peak power'. (Hannan & Wallace 2006) The governments of NSW, Victoria and the commonwealth joined with SHL to argue that the sale was necessary, fearing that SHL would 'lose its important role in the electricity market' (Della Bosca 2006). However, some proponents of the sale were critical of the management performance of SHL accusing them of not being sensitive to the needs of irrigators in managing water releases (Hannan & Wallace 2006).

Opposition to the sale came from a number of quarters. Federal Labor argued for government to maintain a role in investment in national infrastructure (Kirk 2006). Labor spokesman Peter Garrett also raised concerns about the robustness of the agreement to ensure water flows if ownership were vested in a private company (Garrett 2006). There was also a growing public perception that the asset was being sold mainly to enable state governments to receive the estimated $3 billion in revenues (Kohler 2006). Other opponents of the sale, such as Independent MP Tony Windsor, raised concerns about the scheme falling into foreign ownership (Windsor 2006).

When the Snowy scheme was first announced in 1949, Prime Minister Chifley claimed it as 'the greatest single project in our history ... a plan for the whole nation, belonging to no one state' (Ramsey 2006). In similar vein, Independent MP Peter Andren later described the Snowy scheme as the 'vegemite of national infrastructure' (Hannan & Wallace 2006). It became clear in discussions about the proposed sale that the scheme's iconic status surpassed even that of other public enterprises which had already been privatised, such as the Commonwealth Bank, Qantas and Telstra. As journalist Paul Kelly noted, the federal government was most vulnerable to community arguments based on this special status, as it would receive only 13 per cent of the revenue, but 100 per cent of the pressure to withdraw from the sale (ABC 2006a).

Indeed the Prime Minister, in announcing the federal government's withdrawal from the sale, said he had come to recognise the 'overwhelming feeling in the community that the Snowy is an icon, [that] it's part of the great saga of post-World War II development in Australia' (Ramsey 2006). Howard said he had been taken aback by public feeling but blamed the states for initiating the divestment:

> The only reason [the commonwealth] decided to sell its 13 per cent was in consequence of the unilateral decision of the NSW Government to sell its 58 per cent, followed by the decision of the Victorian Government to sell its [29 per cent]. We felt at the time it would make sense to add our 13 per cent. (Ramsey 2006)

This position followed just one week after he had argued strongly in parliament for the sale, assuring stakeholders that 'the water needs of downstream users and the environment are fully protected by the current water-licensing regime' and reasserting his ideological position that 'we believe that the private sector is better at running private businesses than the government' (Howard 2006a).

At the press conference announcing his withdrawal from the sale, Howard defended his position, arguing that the government needed to always have the support of '50 plus 1'. He claimed that the rejection of the sale was consistent with his past approach to privatisation: 'I am not such a zealot about privatisation that you sell everything under the sun, irrespective of the circumstances ... Let me say to the Australian public, we do listen' (Howard 2006b).

Howard also sought to downplay comparisons with the unpopular sale of Telstra:

> Well there's a big difference. There's a long-term public benefit [from selling Telstra]. It's the major telecommunications company in the nation and it has been our policy for each election. It was our policy in 1996, it was our policy in 1998, it was our policy in 2001, it was our policy in 2004. The Snowy has never been an election commitment. (Howard 2006b)

The NSW government initially declared that it would continue with the sale, then 23 minutes later declared that the commonwealth had 'pulled the rug from under the sale' and decided not proceed (*SMH* 2006). Victoria soon announced that it, too, had withdrawn from the sale. Following the collapse of the sale the NSW government sought to blame and demand payment from the federal government for up to $12 million in bills for the bankers, lawyers and advertising agencies it had hired to proceed with the sale (*SMH* 2006). In total the two states and the federal government had by the collapse of the sale spent over $9.75 million on fees for financial advisors, so often the winners from these divestments (see Collyer et al. 2001).

Outsourcing: substitution for public delivery of services

Outsourcing is probably one of the most common yet most complex forms of privatisation utilised by modern governments. The Howard government has embraced the outsourcing technology with vigour, applying two key decision tests to services: is it appropriate for government to continue providing this service? If so, how can it be exposed to greater market pressures?

The failure of the ambitious IT outsourcing initiative which had been driven by strong ideological convictions led to a rethink of the implementation of its outsourcing policy by embracing a 'market testing' regime where more pragmatic, agency-based approaches would test the efficiency of government-provided services against competitors in the market place (Aulich & Hein 2005). Current approaches now integrate market testing, decentralisation of decision-making to agencies, joint initiatives with other providers, and include in-house providers where appropriate. Indeed, government agencies more usually refer to this approach as 'sourcing', leaving open the scale and type of arrangement agencies choose (Aulich & O'Flynn 2007b).

Outsourcing has led to a steady transfer of service provision to the private sector, with significant public funds now financing private providers of public services. For example, in the period 1999 to 2004 the value of outsourced business services for central agencies alone rose from $3.7 billion to $5.7 billion (AusTender 2006). In particular, the most recent round of contracts for the provision of contracts to employment providers totalled $1.8 billion, with only 8 per cent of contracts being let through competitive tendering (DEWR 2007).

There has been criticism of the failure to fully and formally evaluate these policies (Aulich 2005) and their current operations are more opaque given the decentralization of decision-making to agencies. While the Humphry Review did make an assessment of the savings in relation to the IT initiative and there has been a thorough evaluation of the Jobs Network program, there is little analysis or publication of projected whole-of-government savings for the current corporate services and IT initiatives to date. What is clear is that there are motives beyond costs savings that have driven the outsourcing and market testing initiatives. While cost and efficiency concerns are typically the most important considerations in outsourcing decisions by governments, political factors such as the importance of special interest groups, community political sentiments, and the power of trade unions have also been significant in the Australian context (Argy 2003; Bisman 2003).

During the period under review, tensions emerged between the government and providers of some services, especially with regard to welfare-to-work programs. A number of NGOs expressed their concerns that these welfare programs were too punitive and some of the biggest charities refused to continue their involvement in the program to financially case-manage the most vulnerable unemployed (Karvelas 2006). Others were concerned that being critical of government policy might negatively impact on their capacity to 'win' contracts (Hamilton & Maddison 2007: 89). Further, the National Welfare Rights Network raised the issue of contracting to some religious groups, especially the evangelical ones, as many people 'would be reluctant to deal with [them]' raising concerns 'about the blurring of an organisation's religious pursuits and its relationship with their welfare services' (Karvelas 2006). Tensions erupted between St Vincent de Paul's Queensland branch and a private company which they established to manage their welfare services, Ozcare. With more than 2000 staff and 8300 clients Ozcare's net assets were reported to be at least $118 million and members of St Vincent de Paul raised concerns that their primary purposes may be being eroded (McKinnon 2006). St Vincent de Paul joined Catholic Services Australia in distancing itself from the welfare-to-work programs arguing that they were 'not in the interests of social justice' (Naylor 2006).

The issues of independence of contractors from government policy and the potential impacts that delivering government programs have on the values and core business of NGOs need further analysis than is possible here. What is clear is that, while the Howard governments had replaced their initial ideological drive with a more pragmatic one, they had still to take stock of the overall impacts of their policies in this area.

User pays: substitutions for public funding

Under successive Howard governments individual users were required to make higher contributions to many of the public services they received. These services were also less likely to be delivered by public sector providers and non-payers were more easily excluded. This market exchange steadily supplanted traditional notions of subsidised or free government services, which have been cornerstones of the Australian welfare state. In such arrangements non-cash government outlays on education, health, child care, public housing, home ownership and government business enterprises have been considered part of the social wage and used as an instrument of redistribution (Argy 2003).

The revamping of the Higher Education Contribution Scheme was one of many examples of user pays privatisation ensuring that university students make a higher private contribution to their own education. Similarly, the tightening of qualifications for social welfare payments; and the option for universities to set aside places for full fee-paying Australian students, all shift the costs burden for some services from public to private. As a result families and non-government agencies are accepting a more significant role in the provision of public services as the government shifts further away from universal provision.

In the years from 1996 to 2000, cost recovery procedures under the Howard government increased by 20 per cent in real terms, exceeding $3.2 billion raised in 1999–2000 (PC 2001). Out-of-pocket expenses by individuals for health services, for example, amounted to more than $16.5 billion annually, an increase of $9 billion since 1996, and patient contributions to medicines rose in real terms by 6.7 per cent annually (AIHW 2006: 37–38, 26).

The introduction of new cost recovery programs in 2002 aimed at increasing the extent to which agencies can fund services through user charging. Under these new guidelines:

> Agencies should set charges to recover all the costs of products and services where it is efficient to do so, with partial CR to apply only where new arrangements are phased in, where there are government endorsed community service obligations, or for explicit government policy purposes. (DoFA 2005)

Almost all agencies, whether government departments, industry regulators or information agencies have attempted to recover some of their costs via this process. This has reduced the number and extent of 'services by right or entitlement' available to citizens, in favour of the purchase of public services by customers undertaking regular market transactions.

The Australian community appears to increasingly accept the superiority of private provision especially as successive Howard governments provided incentives to assist the move from public to private services in health and education. During the Howard decade around 200 000 students shifted from the public to the private education sector (increasing enrolments in private schools by 22 per cent) and spending on private schools doubled to $4.7 billion by 2005 (Maiden 2006). The Howard government also used a complex mixture of tax penalties and subsidies to 'encourage' Australians to purchase private health insurance. The cost of such programs has been substantial, estimated at $2.3 billion for private health insurance (Morrissey 2006), $5.5 billion for private education and $1.4 billion for private child care (Commonwealth of Australia 2005) during the period 2001–05.

It is possible that the goal for this privatisation technology was to have private provision dominate health, education and like services, based on user-pays principles, with public provision limited to a safety net role for those unable or unwilling to pay.

Conclusions

The past two decades have seen a substantive shift in the ways Australian governments deliver their public services. This chapter has mapped the final three years of a decade-long policy of privatisation conducted by successive Howard governments, utilising a range of privatisation technologies to achieve their policy goals. Privatisation has been one of the critical facilitators of a historic transition from government primarily focused on nation building and its affection with public enterprise. No longer does government of either persuasion see a primary role for government in directly providing services such as banking, transport, insurance, telecommunications, utilities and the like; rather, it prefers to 'enable' services to be delivered by private institutions, regulates private provision, rations some services to users on the basis of willingness and capacity to pay, and provides incentives as well as sanctions to encourage citizens to take up privately provided services. This signals a cultural shift from Australia's earlier strong state traditions towards one which places a higher value on private over collective activity.

The Australian public sector is now smaller as a result of 'significant functional cuts, efficiency improvements and contracting out of functions' (APSC 2003: 53–54). The national government has lost employment share and there has been a decline by 40 per cent in absolute public sector job numbers from 422 000 in 1984 to 251 000 in 2005 (Kryger 2005). However, the size of the core public service is approximately the same ten years on from the election of the first Howard government. This means that the decrease in public sector activity and employment has been borne largely by the 'outer' public service, public enterprises and non-departmental agencies. Inevitably, this will make tighter central control more possible than when there was a larger more autonomous outer public sector (this theme of increasing centralisation is taken up in chapter 2).

Privatisation has the capacity to erode the welfare state as it disproportionately affects those on the margins. There is a risk of developing a 'two-tiered' state where public provision of services is considered 'residual', only providing a safety net for those unable to purchase services. This possibility, however, raises issues about the need for future governments to consider the implications of this for the basic values that have hitherto sustained Australian society. As Argy notes:

> Australians have always viewed themselves as egalitarians ...
> faith in democratic egalitarianism and in the state as a vehicle for

> social change was ingrained in the so-called Australian settlement and was gradually translated into an impressive array of socially progressive policies. (Argy 2003: 134)

This is not to argue that the status quo is preferable to changes that might follow further development and application of privatisation technologies. Rather, it is an appropriate point at which to take stock of those ideals which the Australian community has traditionally valued and to decide whether or not they are appropriate for the next generations of Australians. Howard's preferences have been clear during his decade, the challenge is for the incoming government to decide whether or not to continue the direction of current policy.

References

AAP (2006a) Voters get say on Medibank Private sale, *Age,* 12 September.
—— (2006b) Medibank sale on hold until 2008, *Herald Sun,* 12 September.
ABC (Australian Broadcasting Corporation) (2006a) Scrapping of Snowy sale a win for backbenchers, 4 June.
—— (2006b) Government trying to bury Medibank sale issue: Beazley, 12 September.
Age (2006) Premiums 'will rise' if Medibank sold, 6 September.
Australian (2006) Government eliminates national debt, 20 April.
AIHW (Australian Institute of Health and Welfare) (2006) *Health Expenditure Australia 2004–05,* AIHW, Canberra.
APSC (Australian Public Service Commission) (2003) *The Australian Experience of Public Sector Reform,* APSC, Canberra.
Argy, F (2003) *Where to From Here? Australian Egalitarianism Under Threat,* Allen & Unwin, Sydney.
Aulich, C (2005) Privatisation and outsourcing. In C Aulich & R Wettenhall (eds) *Howard's Second and Third Governments: Australian Commonwealth Administration 1998–2004,* UNSW Press, Sydney: 57–76.
Aulich, C & Hein, J (2005) Whole of government approaches to outsourcing at the commonwealth level, *Australian Journal of Public Administration,* 64(3): 35–45.
Aulich, C & O'Flynn, J (2007a) John Howard: The great privatiser? *Australian Journal of Political Science,* 42(2): 1–18.
—— (2007b) From public to private: The Australian experience of privatisation, *Asia Pacific Journal of Public Administration,* 29(2): 153–71.
AusTender (2006) Contracts database, at <www.contracts.gov.au/OutputReachContract.asp>.
Bartholomeusz, S (2006) There's more to Medibank sale than the dollar figure, *Sydney Morning Herald,* 5 September.
Bisman, J (2003) *The Hidden Costs of Politics in Australian Public Sector Outsourcing,* Working Paper 8/03, Faculty of Commerce Working Paper Series, Charles Sturt University: Wagga Wagga.
Chaudri, V & Kerin, R (2004) Not fish nor fowl: Why Telstra model stinks, *Australian Financial Review,* 21 February.

Collyer, F, McMaster, J & Wettenhall, R (2001) Privatization and public enterprise reform in Australia. In Farazmand, A (ed.) *Privatization or Public Enterprise Reform?*, Greenwood Press, Westport, CT: 141–71.

Commonwealth of Australia (2005) *Budget Paper* No. 1, at <www.budget.gov.au/2005-06>.

Della Bosca, J (2006) NSW Legislative Council, Hansard in Committee, The Snowy Hydro Corporatisation (Parliamentary Scrutiny of Sale) Bill, 27 June, p. 746.

DEWR (Department of Employment and Workplace Relations) (2007) *Job Network Services: Rolling Tender Outcomes 2007*, at <www.workplace.gov.au/NR/rdonlyres/2B2E69B0-F79C-4E1D-9F67-A6E40FAEBB90/0/07243_JN_tender_factsheet_aw.pdf>.

DoFA (Department of Finance and Administration) (2005) Australian government cost recovery guidelines (Finance Circular 2005/09), at <www.finance.gov.au/finframework/docs/FC_2005.09.pdf>.

—— (2007) *Annual Report*, at <www.finance.gov.au/publications/annualreport06-07/chapter_05/government_business_enterprises_ownership.html>.

DPL (Department of Parliamentary Library) (2003) *Bills Digest No. 97 2002–03 Snowy Hydro Corporatisation Amendment Bill 2002*.

DPS (Department of Parliamentary Services) (2006) *The Proposed sale of Medibank Private: Historical, Legal and Policy Perspectives*, 1 September, No. 2.

Garrett, P (2006) *Com. Parl. Debs HoR*, 30 March, at <www.petergarrett.com.au/c.asp?id=160>

Grattan, M & Murphy, K (2006) Now you're talking ... T3 is on, *Age*, 26 August.

Grattan, M, Schubert, M & Doherty, B (2007) Rudd axes Telstra sale policy, *Age*, 22 March.

Hamilton, C & Maddison, S (2007) *Silencing Dissent*, Allen & Unwin, Sydney.

Hannan, E & Wallace, R (2006) Against the flow, *Australian,* 1 June.

Howard, J (Prime Minister) (1981a) *Com. Parl. Debs HoR*, 26 February.

—— (1981b) *Com. Parl. Debs HoR*, 24 March.

—— (1981c) *Com. Parl. Debs HoR*, 30 April.

—— (1985) Address by the Hon. John Howard MP, Shadow Treasurer and Leader of the Opposition to the National Press Club, Canberra, 28 August.

—— (1989) *Com. Parl. Debs HoR*, 13 April.

—— (1995) The role of government: A modern liberal approach, The Menzies Research Centre 1995 National Lecture Series, at <www.australianpolitics.com/executive/howard/pre-2002/95-06-06role-of-government.shtml>.

—— (2001) Centenary of the public service, Oration to the centenary conference of the Institute of Public Administration Australia, 19 June, at <www.pm.gov.au/news/speeches/2001/speech1163.htm>

—— (2006a) *Com. Parl. Debs HoR*, 30 May.

—— (2006b) Transcript of the Prime Minister, the Hon. John Howard MP (Joint press conference with the Special Minister of State, The Hon. Gary Nairn MP), Parliament House Canberra, at <www.pm.gov.au/news/interviews/Interview1960.html>

Karvelas, P (2006) Catholics quit 'immoral' program, *Australian*, 18 August.

Kirk, A (2006) Andren wants Snowy-Hydro sale revisited – Independent MP to move to debate Snowy-Hydro sale, Australian Broadcasting Corporation Transcripts, 30 May.

Kohler, A (2006) Inside business: Bidding to start on Snowy Hydro, Australian Broadcasting Corporation Transcripts, 21 May, at <www.abc.net.au/insidebusiness/content/2006/s1643618.htm>.

Kryger, T (2005) The incredible shrinking public sector (Research Note No. 29), Parliamentary Library, at <www.aph.gov.au/library/pubs/RN/2005-06/06rn29.htm>.

LNP (Liberal Party and National Party) (1988) Future directions: It's time for plain thinking (Election Programme), Liberal Party of Australia, Canberra.

M2 Communications (2001) Minchin announces incorporation of the Snowy Hydro Limited, 27 June.

Macfarlane, I & Minchin, N (2006) Sale of Snowy Hydro shareholding (Joint press release), at <http://minister.industry.gov.au/index.cfm?event=object.showContent&objectID=6B837721-DD07-0694-CC4AC3F9DCEB4DB1>.

Maiden, S (2006) Teenagers flocking to private schools, *Australian*, 24 February.

McKinnon, M (2006) Vinnies sues aged-care firm for return of $130m, *Australian*, 29 June.

Morrissey, J (2006) Health policy under the Howard government – A review, Conference Paper for John Howard's Decade, Museum of Australia, 3 March.

Naylor, C (2006) Charities refuse to take part in 'harsh punitive' welfare programs, *Canberra Times*, 19 August.

PHI (Private Health Insurance) Ombudsman (2005) *Annual Report 1999–2005*, at <www.phio.org.au>

PC (Productivity Commission) (2001) *Cost Recovery by Government Agencies* (Inquiry Report No. 15), Productivity Commission, Melbourne.

Ramsey, A (2006) Forced to retreat make no mistake, *Sydney Morning Herald*, 3 June.

Randall, K (1986) Howard takes the baton, *Business Review Weekly*, 23 May.

Reuters (2007) Australia government says complete Telstra sale, 28 February.

Savas, E (1993) It's time to privatize, *Government Union Review*, 14(1).

Schubert, M (2006) Medibank members could have case for compo, *Sydney Morning Herald*, 8 September.

SMH (*The Sydney Morning Herald*) (2005) Senate votes in favour of Telstra sale, 14 September.

—— (2006) Iemma shifts Snowy blame, 26 August.

Windsor, T (2006) *Com. Parl. Debs HoR*, 30 March.

5
The Senate a paper tiger?

Gwynneth Singleton

Since the introduction of proportional representation for the Senate in 1949 it has been difficult for either of the major parties to gain a majority in that house. For 24 years, between 1 July 1981 and 30 June 2005, successive Australian governments operated under the constraints imposed by the lack of a Senate majority. Governments over this period had to gain the support of either the opposition or the minor parties and/or independents who held

Table 5.1   Composition of the Senate

1 July 2002 – 30 June 2005		From 1 July 2005	
Coalition	35	Coalition	39
Labor	28	Labor	28
Greens	2	Greens	4
Democrats	8	Democrats	4
One Nation	1	Family First	1
Harradine Group	1		
Independent	1		

the balance of power, which often required compromise and modification to legislation to ensure its passage through the parliament.

From 1 July 2005, when senators elected at the 2004 federal election took their seats in the chamber, the fourth Howard government with a majority of one in the Senate had the numbers to pass its legislation through both houses of parliament (see table 5.1).

Prime Minister Howard said his government would take advantage of its majority to deliver government policy previously blocked by the Senate, but would use its power in a responsible manner. He said he had 'no intention of riding roughshod over the parliamentary processes, or of letting the government's new power go to its head' (*CT* 2005).

> I want to assure the Australian people that the Government will use its majority in the new Senate very carefully, very wisely and not provocatively. We intend to do the things we've promised the Australian people we would do but we don't intend to allow this unexpected but welcome majority in the Senate to go to our heads. (Prime Minister John Howard 2004)

Critics argued that this promise was not upheld. They claim that the coalition has used its majority to restrict the capacity of the opposition and minor parties to question and challenge the government by gagging and guillotining debate in the chamber and by changing the structure of the Senate committee system. The government was accused of ruthlessly using the Senate 'as an instrument of its authority' (Lewis 2006a), and picking 'away at the elements of the Senate's claim to be a house of genuine review' (Humphries 2006a). The validity of these assertions is examined below.

Parliamentary procedures

CONTESTED LEGISLATION

Table 5.2 reveals that the government used its majority after 1 July 2005 to override opposition and minor party amendments to its legislation. There is nothing surprising about this because any government with a majority would have done the same. At its most basic, it is a function of having the power and using it.

Table 5.2   Impact of the government's Senate majority on the passage of contested legislation

	2004	2006
Bills on which there was disagreement between the Houses	23	1
Successful amendments in committee of the whole moved by the opposition	130 of 161	2 of 299
Successful amendments in committee of the whole moved by the Australian Democrats	71 of 199	0 of 248

SOURCES Dept of the Senate 2004a, 2006a.

QUESTION TIME: CHANGE TO THE ALLOCATION OF QUESTIONS

In 1995 it was agreed by the Senate Procedure Committee that, in principle, questions should be allocated between the parties and independents in proportion to their numbers in the Senate, although this is not set down in Senate rules (Evans H 2004: chapter 19). The quotas determined by this process were then notified to the President of the Senate.

On 9 August 2005, the first sitting day of the Senate with the coalition parties in the majority, the President of the Senate circulated an allocation for questions without consulting the other parties. Senate Labor leader Chris Evans (2005) accused the Howard government of unilaterally changing the allocation to give the coalition extra questions at the expense of non-government senators.

Responding to these criticisms, the government leader in the Senate, Robert Hill (2005), stated that the President made 'the choice as to whom he calls for questions' and that the order was at the President's discretion. He said the new allocation was a fair reflection of the changes to the party representation in the new Senate. The impact of the changes is shown in table 5.3.

The data reveal that the ALP had fewer questions, but the major impact was on the three minor parties who had to share two questions. This situation was called 'an outrage' that would 'take the teeth out of the Senate' and make 'a mockery' of the institution (Schubert 2005). It is debatable whether the situation was as bleak as these comments suggest because, according to table 5.3, the opposition and minor parties systematically asked 'double-barrelled' questions by the use of supplementary questions (Evans H 2004: 489), thus enhancing their capacity to pursue an issue in greater depth.

Table 5.3   Sample numbers of questions without notice asked before and after 1 July 2005

Pre 1 July 2005	Coalition	ALP	Minor parties
8 February 2005	3	6 (plus 5 supplementaries)	3 (plus 3 supplementaries)
7 March 2005	3	7 (plus 7 supplementaries)	3 (plus 3 supplementaries)
Post 1 July 2005			
4 September 2006	5	5 (plus 5 supplementaries)	2 (plus 2 supplementaries)
10 May 2007	5	5 (plus 5 supplementaries)	2 (plus 2 supplementaries)

sources Com. Parl. Debs S, 2005a, 2005b, 2006, 2007.

QUESTIONS ON NOTICE

Questions on Notice potentially are a useful tool for accountability by providing opposition and minor party senators with the opportunity to seek detailed information from ministers. However, their effectiveness is diminished by the fact that many questions are not answered in a timely manner and some are

Table 5.4   Number of unanswered Questions on Notice

Parliamentary period	Number of questions placed on notice*	Number (%) of questions that remained unanswered at the end of the parliament
37th Parliament – 4 May 1993 – 29 Jan. 1996 (Keating)	2710	78 (2.9%)
39th Parliament – 10 Nov. 1998 – 8 Oct. 2001 (Howard)	3913	209 (5.3%)
40th Parliament – 12 Feb. 2002 – 31 Aug. 2004 (Howard)	3184	326 (10.3%)
41st Parliament – 6 Nov. 2004 – 30 June 2007 (Howard)	3399	522 (15.5%)

* Does not include questions which were withdrawn or lapsed.

sources Dept of the Senate 1996, 2001, 2004b, 2007a.

Table 5.5: Questions on Notice that remained unanswered on the last day of sittings and had been on the Notice Paper for more than 30 days

Parliament	Number of questions on notice remaining unanswered on the last day of sittings*	Number (%) of questions on notice remaining unanswered that had been on the notice paper for more than 30 days
37th Parliament: Notice Paper No. 210, 30 Nov. 1995 (Keating)	124	82 (66%)
39th Parliament: Notice Paper No. 216, 27 Sept. 2001 (Howard)	383	335 (87%)
40th Parliament: Notice Paper No. 161, 30 Aug. 2004 (Howard)	457	402 (88%)
41st Parliament: Notice Paper No. 145, 13 June 2007 (Howard)	556	537 (96%)

* This number relates to the number of questions on notice outstanding on the last day of the parliamentary sitting. The figures given in table 5.4 are for the total number of questions that remained unanswered for the duration of the parliament and include questions answered after the last sitting day.

SOURCES *Senate Notice Paper* 1995, 2001, 2004, 2007.

not answered at all, a trend that has accelerated since the Howard government came to office (see table 5.4).

Under Senate rules, senators who have not received an answer to their Question on Notice within 30 days may seek an explanation from the minister. Table 5.5 reveals a large number of questions remain unanswered after 30 days and the incidence has increased under the Howard government. The average time taken to answer a question by the fourth Howard government across all ministries between 16 November 2004 and 30 June 2007 was 103.11 days (Dept of the Senate 2007a).

USE OF GAG AND GUILLOTINE TO LIMIT DEBATE

The 'gag' is the colloquial term used to describe a motion put before the Senate, usually by a minister or the government Whip, to close down debate. If carried, the question under discussion is then put to the vote without further debate. The term 'guillotine' is commonly used to describe the motion, moved by a minister, to apply a time limit to debate on the stages of bills declared urgent by the government. In other words, debate on the bill is limited, or can be cut off, to permit the bill to pass quickly through the house (Jaensch & Teichmann 1992: 97, 103; Evans H 2004: 215, 263). In the eight years between 1996 and 2004 the guillotine was applied nine times, but it was used seven times in the 17 months between 1 July 2005 and 31 December 2006 (Dept of the Senate 2006b). Between 1 January 2004 and 30 June 2005 the Howard government's use of the gag and the guillotine was limited by the fact that it had to get the support of other parties and/or independents to pass the motion (Evans H 2007) and as a result there were no gag motions moved by the government in the Senate during that period. Between 1 July 2005 and 20 June 2006, however, the government successfully used the gag and the guillotine to curtail debate. The gag was used 16 times, thus reducing the time available for critical scrutiny of government business by the opposition and minor party senators (Evans H 2007: 205).

Labor's Senate Leader Chris Evans (2005) summarised the impact of these strategies on the passage of legislation in the Senate between 1 July 2005 and 16 December 2005:

- Telstra bills: guillotine applied and the gag used three times and Family First Senator Steve Fielding was denied the opportunity to speak;
- 11 October 2005: debate over variation of routine of business and sitting hours gagged twice;
- 3 November 2005: debate gagged on hours and routine of business;
- 8 November: gag used over Labor's proposed amendments to the reference of the Work Choices inquiry;
- 1 December: Work Choices legislation guillotined and debate gagged;
- 5 December: Anti-terror bill and two welfare bills guillotined and gagged.

The Clerk of the Senate, Harry Evans, argued that the time for debate was reduced on bills, especially controversial ones such as the Australian Security Intelligence Legislation (Terrorism) Bill and the Workplace Relations and other Legislation Amendment Bill (Evans H 2007). The government's actions caused debate on some bills to be labelled 'a sham' (Lewis 2006a). For example, Australian Democrats Senator Andrew Bartlett had to debate Telstra legislation he had not seen and comment on the minister's second reading speech that had not been read to the parliament and had been tabled only 30 seconds before, a situation he described as 'contempt for parliamentary process and contempt for democracy' (Bartlett 2005: 35); Work Choices legislation was given to non-government senators only half an hour before debate began and consideration of the 1252-page bill was compressed into a five-day committee inquiry and five days of Senate debate (*SMH* 2005), while 337 amendments were introduced by the government just 35 minutes before the government guillotined debate (Humphries 2005). According to Democrat Senator Lyn Allison, senators had no idea what they were being asked to vote on and 'parliament was effectively redundant in the process' (Humphries 2006b). The government's desire to get the legislation passed before parliament rose at the end of the year explained the haste, but the government's majority made it possible.

SITTING HOURS

The government was also accused of limiting the opportunity for debate and scrutiny of government business by reducing parliamentary sitting hours. Table 5.6 reveals that, compared to the Keating government, the number of sitting days and the total number of sitting hours declined substantially. However, despite this decline, more bills were passed in fewer sitting days in 2006–07 (table 5.7), suggesting that less time was devoted to each bill than in previous periods of government.

Table 5.6   Sitting days and hours before and after 1 July 2005 (excluding election years)

	Number of sitting days	Hours of sitting
Keating government		
1994	80	628
1995	78	637
Howard government		
2002	60	539
2003	64	481
2005	57	543
2006	58	572

SOURCE Dept of the Senate 2007b.

Table 5.7 Number of sitting days and number of bills passed in the Senate (excluding election years)

	Number of sitting days	Number of bills passed in the Senate
Keating 1994–95	158	351
Howard 2002–03	124	309
Howard 2005–06	115	340

SOURCES Dept of the Senate 2005a, 2005b.

ORDERS FOR THE PRODUCTION OF DOCUMENTS

Orders for the production of documents are a tool of accountability because they are the means whereby senators are able to seek information from ministers. Table 5.8 reveals that the Howard government's record prior to 1 July 2005 was poor (Evans H 2007: 207), but after that it has deteriorated dramatically, with only one order for the production of documents passing the Senate (Dept of the Senate 2007c).

Table 5.8: Orders for the production of documents

Period of government	Number of orders agreed to
Keating 1993–96	53
Howard 1996–98	48
Howard 1998–2001	56
Howard 2002–04	91
Howard 2005	18
Howard 2006	1
Howard 2007	0

SOURCES Dept of the Senate 2007c.

Senate committees

SELECT INQUIRIES

Senate select inquiries provide an opportunity for senators to question and scrutinise government activity and thus enhance the accountability function of the Senate. Prior to 1 July 2005, the ALP, Democrats, Greens and independents, who between them held the majority in the Senate, used their numbers to instigate Senate inquiries into matters such as the children overboard affair. Once the government gained control of the Senate that situation changed dramatically. In 2004–05 there were five Senate select inquiries; in 2005–06 the government exercised its majority to negate motions for new inquiries and none was initiated, the first time that this has occurred since 1996–97 (Dept of the Senate 2006c). The government argued that by blocking calls for inquiries from the opposition and minor parties it was 'stopping expensive fishing expeditions' (Brenchley & Morris 2006), but the blocking function can also be used to avoid scrutiny and inquiries into matters that may have caused it political embarrassment.

RESTRUCTURING THE COMMITTEE SYSTEM

On 11 September 2006, the government restructured the Senate committee system by combining the functions of legislation and reference committees which had the effect of reducing the number of legislation and general purpose standing committees from 16 to eight. Each of the new committees has eight members, four nominated by the Leader of the Government in the Senate, three nominated by the Leader of the Opposition in the Senate and one nominated by minority groups and independent senators. The chair of each committee is a government senator.

The government argued that the new system would avoid duplication and be more efficient, the number of portfolios covered would be expanded so that greater attention would be paid 'to the issues that matter to Australian people', and the membership and chairmanship of the committees would reflect the composition of the Senate (Minchin & Coonan 2006). The changes were, in fact, a return to the structure that existed under Labor prior to 1994 when most committees had government majorities and were chaired by a government senator (Dept of the Senate 2006c).

Critics argued that the government would not allow inquiries that might embarrass it and it was now better able to control how inquiries were conducted, for example, through 'the selection of witnesses and the arrangement of hearings' (Evans H 2006a: 3). Even though Labor had been the instigator and beneficiary of a similar system before 1994, it attacked the government's actions as 'an arrogant and contemptuous' use of government power (Hart 2006), and 'a nail in the coffin of the Senate's capacity to hold this government accountable' (Humphries 2006b). The government was accused of 'arrogant administration' and being 'drunk on its power and unwilling to subject its performances to the usual checks and balances our parliamentary system demands' (Lewis 2006b). Family First Senator Fielding argued that the restructuring of the Senate committee system was 'another step in seeing the Senate move from a house of review to a house of one view' (Fielding 2006).

The government defended the new system, saying it had acted responsibly and 'on a clear mandate' (Lewis 2006a), the number of bills and issues referred to committees would be unaffected and the function of the Senate estimates committees would be enhanced by the addition of two portfolio committees (Minchin 2006a). There would be more references to Senate committees and more opportunities for Senate inquiries into significant issues, 'but reflecting the fact that the government has a majority in the Senate' (Minchin 2006b).

During the year 2005–06 under the previous system, there were 61 references to legislation committees (Dept of the Senate 2006c). Under the new system 68 bills were referred to Senate committees over the six-month period 1 January to 14 June 2007 (Dept of the Senate 2007d). However, there was a decline in the government's response rate, which went from 39 reports in 2005 to 29 in 2006 (Dept of the Senate 2007c).

The time allotted for scheduled sittings and reporting times of committees was also reduced. Between 1 January 2004 and 30 June 2005 the average time for a bills inquiry was 39 days. Between 1 July 2005 and 30 June 2006 it had fallen to 27 days. As a result, the time available for hearing witnesses was also reduced. For example, in the final sitting week before the autumn 2006 break, the Senate referred 13 bills to legislation committees and sought feedback on all of them from stakeholders before the end of the parliamentary session (Brenchley & Morris 2006).

The government set a very tight schedule on the time allowed for committees to consider significant and contentious bills. The workplace relations inquiry was allocated only five days to question 105 witnesses and to read 5000 submissions, and had only one day to report (Humphries 2006a). The Senate committee examining the complex Telstra legislation was given only one day of hearings scheduled to take place 24 hours after the bill was tabled in the parliament, a timeframe described as 'unfair and unreasonable' for witnesses and people providing submissions to the inquiry (Lundy 2005: 81).

Senate estimates committees provide senators with the opportunity to question ministers and departmental officers about government expenditure and performance (Evans H 2004: 365). The committees established in September 2006 continued to perform that function, but there were accusations they became 'a paper tiger' because of government limitations on their operations (Allison 2006).

The opposition complained that the government's 'fine-tuning' of estimates proceedings to focus on appropriations, rather than incidental issues (Schubert 2006), was an extreme use of the government's total control in the Senate that would deny proper scrutiny of government action (Fraser 2005). The government denied this would be the case (Schubert 2006), but there were examples of government using the process to its political advantage, including removing two days from estimates committee schedules in May 2006, which, it was claimed, would reduce time for scrutiny (Bartlett 2006).

The Labor opposition complained about 'a pattern of contempt, non-co-operation, obfuscation and just plain lack of corporate memory' in the responses of public service officials to questioning (Evans C 2006). Public servants were directed by cabinet minute not to answer questions in Senate estimates on the Australian Wheat Board's (AWB) dealings in Iraq (SRRATLC 2006: 6). The government declared its decision was in the public interest because to do otherwise would impinge on the Cole Royal Commission hearings into the affair. However, Clerk of the Senate Harry Evans argued the directive was unprecedented 'in the sense that an inquiry by a government-appointed commission had not previously been given as a reason for refusing to answer questions' (Evans H 2006b). Coalition Senator Eric Abetz argued that the directive was 'not a banning' but 'a deferral of the issues' (SRRATLC 2006: 5), but because public service officials were prevented from answering questions from the committee, it still is deemed to be 'a refusal to answer' (Evans H 2007: 212).

Government majorities and government chairs mean that Senate committees are likely to deliver reports that support government policy. But there are avenues for dissent, including minority reports – for example, National Senator Barnaby Joyce lodged a dissenting report with the Senate Economics Committee report on Petrol Prices in Australia (2006) – as well as the option of crossing the floor.

Dissent in the Senate

Some coalition senators have taken advantage of the government's slim majority to pressure the government for amendments to legislation and some have crossed the floor to vote against a bill.

On 9 February 2006, a private members' bill (Therapeutic Goods Amendment (Repeal of Ministerial Responsibility for Approval of RU486)

Bill 2005) to remove the power of approval for the abortion drug RU486 from the Minister for Health, sponsored by the Nationals' Fiona Nash, Liberal Judith Troeth, Labor's Claire Moore and the Democrats' Lyn Allison, passed the Senate. The government allowed a conscience vote on the issue because of the strength of support within coalition ranks, even though it was opposed by the Prime Minister and the Minister for Health. This vote was significant because it introduced gender-based voting into the Senate built around a cross-party coalition of women senators.

On 7 November 2006 the Senate voted to legalise therapeutic cloning for stem cell research using human and animal eggs (Prohibition of Human Cloning for Reproduction and the Regulation of Human Embryo Research Amendment Bill 2006). The bill was introduced by Liberal Senator Kay

Courtesy of Peter Nicholson, *The Australian*, 9 August 2005

Patterson and supported by the Senate Community Affairs Committee on which the government had a majority, despite strong opposition from the Minister for Health (Franklin 2006). The threat of a coalition backbench Senate revolt influenced the Prime Minister's decision to permit a conscience vote on the bill (Franklin & Maiden 2006).

The Senate Legal and Constitutional Legislation Committee chaired by Liberal Senator Marise Payne, and with a government majority, recommended on 13 June 2006 that the government abandon the provisions of the Migration Amendment (Designated Unauthorised Arrivals Bill) 2006 that would require offshore processing of all asylum seekers (SLCLC 2006: ix). When two coalition senators threatened to cross the floor to vote against the bill, demanding changes to ensure that genuine refugees could come to Australia, the Prime Minister withdrew the legislation (*ABC Online* 2006).

On 15 June 2006, Liberal ACT Senator Gary Humphries crossed the floor to vote with opposition and minority party senators against the federal government's disallowance of the ACT Civil Unions Act. As a previous chief minister of the ACT, he supported the rights of the citizens of the ACT to determine their own laws without interference from the commonwealth. The motion was lost when National's Senator Barnaby Joyce and Family First Senator Steve Fielding voted with the government.

In March 2007 the Senate's Finance and Public Administration Committee, including government members, called for a delay and reconsideration of the government's Access Card legislation, because of fears the card could become a 'de facto national ID card' (Hart 2007). The legislation was deferred.

The strategic position of the Nationals within the coalition partnership was enhanced when the election of National's Senator Barnaby Joyce for Queensland gave the coalition a majority of one in the Senate, effectively handing control of the balance of power to the Nationals (Ward 2005: 202). If Joyce were to vote with the opposition and the minor parties against the government in the Senate, the vote would have been tied and decided in the negative, thus defeating government motions, including legislation.

Joyce exercised the balance of power by negotiating changes to some government policies, such as voting for the sale of Telstra only after the government agreed to spend $3.1 billion on rural phone services. On 11 October 2005 Joyce became the first government senator in 19 years to cross the floor when he voted with the opposition and minor parties against the government to remove a schedule from the Trade Practices Legislation Amendment Bill (No. 1) 2005 and block the government's plans to water down the way large mergers are regulated (*Com. Parl. Debs S* 2005c: 140).

He crossed the floor on other occasions to vote against bills with which he disagreed. His reasons for doing so included extant hostility between the Queensland Liberals and the Nationals that caused each to run their own Senate ticket and Joyce's view that he was not in John Howard's team (Cheshire 2007: 83). He considers that his role under the Australian Constitution is to represent his state (Joyce 2005) and support the issues on which the Nationals gave a commitment to the people of Queensland and he has voted in the Senate accordingly. Being called 'a maverick' because of his independent opinions does not concern him because in Queensland that would be 'a badge of honour' (Cheshire 2007: 84).

Joyce's power plays were only successful, however, when his Senate vote decided the outcome of the motion. His vote was not significant when the opposition and/or Family First Senator Steve Fielding voted with the government.

When Joyce defected, the balance of power moved to Family First Senator Steve Fielding. It was presumed that, as a right-wing conservative, he would support the government (Milne 2006), but his record was not that predictable. His core belief that 'the family is the foundation upon which all societies are built and sustained' (Fielding 2005: 125) caused him to vote against the government on some issues.

Conclusion

The fourth Howard government enjoyed a Senate majority from 1 July 2005, but did this translate into the untrammelled power that the critics feared? Did the government's majority extinguish the Senate's capacity to act as 'watchdog' over executive power? There is evidence to answer these questions in the affirmative when we look at the way the government controlled procedural matters such as the allocation of questions, sitting hours, the use of the gag and the guillotine to curtail debate on significant pieces of legislation, and the use of its majority to prevent Senate inquiries into matters that may have caused it political embarrassment. The government did not comply with orders for the production of documents, it directed public servants not to answer questions on the AWB issue, its response rate to Senate committee reports was poor and it was particularly lax in providing answers to Questions on Notice in a timely manner.

These issues by themselves, however, may not be sufficient to warrant labelling the Senate a 'paper tiger' during the period under review, nor did they render the Senate totally impotent as a mechanism for holding the government accountable. There are several reasons for this. The reallocation of questions without notice to reflect the state of the parties in the Senate after 1 July 2005 was in keeping with the operating procedures which applied between 1995 and 2005. The opposition and, in particular, minor party senators lost some questions, but they took full advantage of supplementary questions to expand their opportunity to quiz ministers. The government continued to refer legislation to Senate committees for detailed assessment. Even though tight time limits were placed on the consideration of some bills, public submissions and dissenting minority reports placed alternative views that might not otherwise have been published on the public record.

The Senate estimates committee system remains a useful forum for obtaining information about government activities and departmental performance that is placed on the public record. For example, 2006 estimates hearings by the Senate Community Affairs Legislation Committee (SCALC 2006) into the Health and Ageing portfolio were attended by senior executive officers and senior officers from each of the 13 outcome groups administered by the department. Questions were asked, among many others, about structure and staffing, reasons for delay in answering Questions on Notice, arrangements for the introduction of the Smartcard and the PBS generics policy. Questioning at the 2007 estimates hearings was just as intensive (SSCCA 2007) and there is little obvious evidence in the transcripts of either of these hearings of obfuscation and lack of co-operation from officials. As at 26 June 2007, Senate committees were inquiring into a broad range of issues, including the cost-of-living pressures on older Australians, private equity investment and its effects on capital markets and the Australian economy, academic standards of school education, Australia's involvement in peacekeeping, and additional water supplies for south-east Queensland related to Traveston Crossing Dam. Many inquiries were conducted in a bipartisan and co-operative manner and produced informed and useful outcomes (Holland et al. 2006: 53).

Lack of government co-operation with Senate committees is ongoing and is a function of governments being reluctant to cede power to the upper house, particularly when they lack a Senate majority. Ministers in the Whitlam government directed departmental secretaries not to answer questions (Holland 2002: 15). In 1993, under Keating, public servants giving evidence before the Senate Select Committee on Print Media complied with directions from the Treasurer limiting what they could say in response to questions (Holland 2002: 16–17). In 2002, the Howard government refused to allow departments to make submissions to the Senate Select Committee Inquiry into a Certain Maritime Incident and the committee was also denied access 'by a whole-of-government decision' to ministerial staff they wanted to question (SSCICMI 2002: 20). In 2003 Treasury officials refused to answer questions about currency derivatives trading (Davidson 2007).

Of particular interest has been the way in which backbench coalition senators have exercised their strategic hold on the balance of power to pressure the government to achieve concessions on contentious legislation. Some even crossed the floor when that strategy proved unsuccessful, despite Prime Minister Howard telling coalition members that their first loyalty is to the party room (Grattan 2005). This situation was not unique to the fourth Howard government, however. Between 1950 and August 2004 government senators, most of whom were Liberals, crossed the floor 297 times, 7.87 per cent when the government controlled the Senate (McKeown & Lundie 2005). Malcolm Fraser's majority of six afforded him no protection from internal dissent when his overbearing attitude to the Senate created bitter critics among Liberal senators to the extent that he could not be sure of their total support for his legislative program (Schneider 1980: 1–2; *ABC News* 2005). Indeed, up to 12 coalition senators were prepared to cross the floor under Fraser on issues of accountability (Evans H 2006b).

Opinion that the Liberal Party is less disciplined than Labor when it comes to exercising a conscience vote is one possible explanation for the expression of dissent within the Senate coalition backbench (*ABC Insiders* 2006). It could also be a function of the development of 'a culture of assertiveness' within all parties in relation to the role of the Senate vis-à-vis the executive arising from the continual exercise of the balance of power between 1981 and 2005 when no government held a majority (Brandis 2005). This assertiveness might explain the emergence of a gender-based cross-party voting coalition on issues of particular importance to women and it provides a valid explanation for the actions of Barnaby Joyce who does not believe the government should control individual coalition senators (NIG 2005). Another explanation must be the opportunity to exercise effective political power from the backbench that was facilitated by the government's Senate majority of one. The threat to cross the floor can be more effective from coalition senators, as Michelle Grattan (2006) pointed out, because 'it is much more embarrassing to be held account by your own'.

Politicians see the Senate 'through the prism of power' (Gordon 2003). Opposition parties complain about a threat to democratic process and accountability when a government has a majority in the Senate, but typically use the power themselves when they have the opportunity. We have seen how the Howard government took full advantage of its majority in the Senate to drive through its legislative program. However, political power can be fleeting. The Rudd Labor government elected on 24 November 2007 will have to work with a 'hostile' Senate until 30 June 2008, with coalition senators holding the majority which may make it difficult to pass its legislation through the parliament. After 1 July 2008 it will be faced with a Senate where it will need the support of the five Green senators as well as Family First Senator Stephen Fielding and South Australian Independent Senator Nick Xenophon to pass its legislation. This means it will be back to 'business as usual', with the government having to negotiate with minor party and independent senators and possibly compromise on contested legislation, no doubt extracting criticism from the government about 'Senate obstruction'.

References

ABC Insiders (2006) Transcript, 25 June, at <www.abc.net.au/insiders/content/2006/s1671214.htm>.
ABC News (2005) Fraser defends Senate majority actions, at <www.abc.net.au/news/stories/2005/06/09/1403158.htm>.
ABC Online (2006) PM pulls migration bill, 14 August, at <www.abc.net.au/newsnewsitems/200608/s1714296.htm>.
Allison, L (2006) Democrats support Evans and Senate accountability (Press release number vsgknew), Canberra, 12 April.
Bartlett, A (2005) *Com. Parl. Debs S*, 8 September.
—— (2006) *The Bartlett Diaries*, 14 May, at <www.andrewbartlett.com/blog/?p=223>.
Brandis, G (2005) *The Australian Senate and Responsible Government*, 2005 Constitutional Law Conference, Sydney, 18 February.
Brenchley, F & Morris, S (2006) Canberra keeps tight lid on Senate inquiries, *Australian Financial Review*, 20 April.
Cheshire, B (2007) Barnaby rubble goes to Canberra, *Reader's Digest*, January: 78–85.
Com. Parl. Debs S (2005a) Questions Without Notice, 8 February.
Com. Parl. Debs S (2005b) Questions Without Notice, 7 March.
Com. Parl. Debs S (2005c), 11 October.
Com. Parl. Debs S (2006) Questions Without Notice, 4 September.
Com. Parl. Debs S (2007) Questions Without Notice, 10 May.
CT (Canberra Times) (2005) Expect scrutiny in stacked Senate, 9 August.
Davidson, K (2007) Treasury spins $1.1bn loss into 'gain', *Business Day*, at <www.theage.com.au/articles2007/06/17/1182018934304.html>.
Department of the Senate (1996) *Questions On Notice Summary for the Period 4 May 1993 to 29 January 1996*, Senate Table Office, Canberra.
—— (2001) *Questions on Notice Summary for the Period 10 November 1998 to 8 October 2001*, Senate Table Office, Canberra.
—— (2004a) *Legislation Statistics 2004*, Canberra, at <www.aph.gov.au/Senate/work/statistics/bus_senate/2004/legislation/legis_stats.html>.

—— (2004b) *Questions on Notice Summary for the Period 12 February 2002 to 31 August 2004*, Senate Table Office, Canberra, at <www.aph.gov.au/Senate/work/statistics/bus_senate/2004/legislation/legis_stats.html>.
—— (2005a) *Statistics by Parliament – 37th Parliament*, at <www.aph.gov.au/Senate/work/statistics/parliaments/37.htm>.
—— (2005b) *Legislation Statistics 2005*, at <www.aph.gov.au/Senate/work/statistics/bus_senate/2005/legislation/legis_stats.html> .
—— (2006a) *Legislation Statistics 2006*, Canberra, at <www.aph.gov.au/Senate/work/statistics/bus_senate/2006/legislation/legis_stats.html>.
—— (2006b) *Statistics, government bills considered under a limitation of time ('guillotine') 1983–2006*, at <www.aph.gov.au/senate/work/statistics/consid_legis/urgent_bills.htm>.
—— (2006c) *Annual Report 2005–2006*, Canberra, at <www.aph.gov.au/Senate/dept/annual06/performance/output_group4.htm>.
—— (2007a) *Questions on Notice Summary for the Period 16 November 2004 to 30 June 2007*, Senate Table Office, Canberra, at <www.aph.gov.au/Senate/work/qonsumary/index.htm> .
—— (2007b) *Days and Hours of Sitting 2001–2010 (to 10 May 2007)*, Canberra, at <www.aph.gov.au/Senate/work/statistics/bus_senate_Consolidations/2001-2010>.
—— (2007c) *General Statistics 1991–2000, 2001–2010 (to 10 May 2007)*, Canberra, at <http://www.aph.gov.au/Senate/work/statistics/bus_senate/Consolidations/1991-2000/general.html>, <www.aph.gov.au/Senate/work/statistics/bus_senate/Consolidations/2001-2010/general.html>.
—— (2007d) *Bills List as at 14 June 2007*, Senate Table Office, Canberra, at <www.aph.gov.au/parlinfo/billsnet/billslst.pdf>.
Evans, C (2005) John Howard's Senate abuses – Process, procedure and convention – The story since 1 July (Media release), 16 December, Canberra, at <www.chrisevans.alp.org.au/news/1205senate16-01.php>.
—— (2006) Senate estimates – The Howard outrages escalate (Media release), 16 February, at <http://www.chrisevans.alp.org.au/news/0206/senate16-01.php>.
Evans, H (2004) (ed.) *Odgers' Senate Practice*, 11th edition, Department of the Senate, Canberra.
—— (2006a) The government majority in the Senate: A nail in the coffin of responsible government? Paper presented to Australasian Study of Parliament Group Victorian Chapter, 3 October, at <www.aph.gov.au/Senate/pubs/evans/031006/031006.htm>.
—— (2006b) The Senate: Estimates hearings and government control of the Senate, Australian Policy Online, 12 April, at <www.apo.org.au/webboard/print-version.chtml?filename_num=73481>.
—— (2007) The Senate. In C Hamilton & S Maddison (eds) *Silencing Dissent*, Allen & Unwin, Sydney: 199–221.
Fielding, S (2005) *Com. Parl. Debs S*, 10 August.
—— (2006) *Com. Parl. Debs S*, 14 August.
Franklin, M (2006) Senate report backs cloning, *Australian*, 31 October.
Franklin, M & Maiden, S (2006) PM grants free vote on cloning, *Australian*, 16 August.
Fraser, A (2005) Estimates committees in sights as government reigns supreme in Senate, *Canberra Times*, 27 June.
Gordon, M (2003) Rebuilding the Senate, Howard's way, *Age*, 11 October.
Grattan, M (2005) Be loyal PM tells newcomers, *Age*, 10 August.

—— (2006) Majorities aside, the Senate is still a house with a mind of its own, *Age*, 21 June.
Hart, C (2006) Beazley condemns Senate 'power grab', *Australian*, 26 June
—— (2007) Access Card scheme stalls, *Australian*, 16 March
Hill, R (2005) *Com. Parl. Debs S*, 9 August.
Holland, I (2002) Accountability of ministerial staff, Research Paper No. 19 2001–02, Department of the Parliamentary Library, Canberra, at <www.aph.gov.au/library/pubs/rp/2001-02/02rp19.pdf>.
Holland, I, Dermody K & Humphery, E (2006) Parliamentary committees and neglected voices in society, *Table*, 74: 45–55.
Howard, J (Prime Minister) (2004) Doorstop interview, Sydney 28 October, at <www.pm.gov.au/media/interview/2004/Interview1137.cfm>.
Humphries, D. (2005) Work laws forced through Senate, *Sydney Morning Herald*, 2 December.
—— (2006a) Howard's power house, *Sydney Morning Herald*, 24–25 June.
—— (2006b) Coalition reshapes Senate scrutiny, *Sydney Morning Herald*, 21 June.
Jaensch, D & Teichmann, M (1992) *The Macmillan Dictionary of Australian Politics*, 4th edition, Macmillan, Melbourne.
Joyce, B (2005) Inteview with Laurie Oakes, *Sunday*, Channel Nine, 31 July, at <www.sunday.ninemsn.com.au/sunday>.
Lewis, S (2006a) Sidelined watchdog, *Weekend Australian*, 1–2 July.
—— (2006b) Gutted house, broken system, *Australian*, 27 June.
Lundy, K (2005) *Com. Parl. Debs S*, 12 September.
McKeown, D & Lundie, R (2005) Crossing the floor in the federal parliament 1950 – August 2004, Research Note no. 11, 2005–06, 10 October, Parliamentary Library, Canberra.
Milne, G (2006) Family First finds its wings, *Australian*, 26 June.
Minchin, N (2006a) Letter to the editor, *Australian Financial Review*, 26 June.
—— (2006b) Transcript of interview with ABC Radio *PM*, 20 June, at <www.financeminister.gov.au/transcripts/2006/tr_060620.html>.
Minchin, N & Coonan H (2006), Proposal to reform the Senate committee system (Joint media release), 40/2006, 20 June, at <www.financeminister.gov.au/media/2006/mr_402006_joint.html>.
NIG (National Institute for Governance, University of Canberra) (2005) Notes on a speech by Barnaby Joyce to seminar on Public Sector Governance and the Senate, Seminar series, Canberra, 9 November, at <http://governance.canberra.edu.au>.
SCALC (Senate Community Affairs Legislation Committee) (2006), Estimates hearings, transcript, Wednesday, 31 May.
Schneider, R (1980) *War Without Blood: Malcolm Fraser in Power*, Angus & Robertson, Sydney.
Schubert, M (2005) Coalition cuts opposition questions, *Age*, 10 August.
—— (2006) Liberals to curb probes by Senate, *Age*, 8 August.
Senate Economics Committee (2006), Petrol Prices in Australia Report, 7 December.
Senate Notice Paper (1995) No. 210, 30 November.
—— (2001) No. 216, 27 September.
—— (2004) No. 161, 30 August.
—— (2007) No. 145, 13 June.
SLCLC (Senate Legal and Constitutional Legislation Committee) (2006), Provisions of the Migration Amendment (Designated Unauthorised Arrivals) Bill 2006 Report, 13 June.

SMH (Sydney Morning Herald) (2005) Surrender of the Senate (Editorial), 7 December.
SRRATLC (Senate Rural and Regional Affairs and Transport Legislation Committee), Estimates, (2006) 14 February.
SSCCA (Senate Standing Committee on Community Affairs) (2007), Estimates hearings, transcript, Thursday 30 May.
SSCICMI (Senate Select Committee for an Inquiry into a Certain Maritime Incident) (2002), Report, at <www.aph.gov.au/Senate/Committee/maritime_incident_ctte/report/c07.htm>.
Ward, I (2005) Queensland. In M Simms & J Warhurst (eds) *Mortgage Nation: The 2004 Australian Election*, API Network, Perth: 195–203.

6
Reconfiguring the Federation?

Andrew Parkin and Geoff Anderson

The first three terms of the Howard government had produced a somewhat mixed record in relation to commonwealth–state relations. The implementation of the 'new tax system' in July 2000, with the entire yield from the new goods and services tax thereafter dispatched to the states as untied revenue, had effected a landmark shift in fiscal federalism in favour of substantially greater state-level financial flexibility and autonomy. On the other hand, the first three terms had also provided insights into and rehearsals for what was to become, in the fourth term, a clear centralist orientation (see Parkin & Anderson 2007).

A key contextual factor was the extraordinarily polarised and extraordinarily stable intergovernmental partisan balance: for its entire fourth term (as indeed it had been for nearly all of its third term), the Howard Liberal–National coalition faced entrenched Labor governments in every state and territory. This can, however, only be a partial explanation for the notable centralist shift. A deeper explanation also needs to take seriously Prime Minister Howard's understanding of and commitment to a new conceptualisation of conservative nationalism.

In April 2005, six months into his fourth term, Howard evidently thought it timely to set out the parameters of this new conceptualisation, through a historical and philosophical interpretation of Australian federalism. 'I am', he said, 'first and last, an Australian nationalist', somebody who has 'never been one to genuflect uncritically at the altar of states' rights'. Some form of federalism, he conceded, was an entrenched Australian reality – 'the federal structure of our nation will remain' – but that entrenchment seemed to be its principal claim to legitimacy: 'if we had had our time again, we might have organised ourselves differently' (Howard 2005a).

This argument – both its vocabulary and its intent – was to become a familiar one. Here is Howard explaining in late July 2007 his decision to proceed to seek an imposed commonwealth regime on the Murray-Darling Basin:

> You'll only solve this problem if you effectively obliterate the state borders. This is something that transcends the parochial interests of the states. ... I mean, we are [a] nation, we are not a collection of states and the Australian people are tired, sick and tired of state parochialism on issues like this. (Howard 2007a)

A month later, he took the argument a stage further. 'Aspirational nationalism' was his proclaimed goal, and a re-elected fifth-term Howard government would be 'applying this spirit to the governance of the Federation'. While this would sometimes involve leaving policy areas entirely to the states, and sometimes would involve co-operative federalism, it would also on other occasions 'require the commonwealth bypassing the states altogether and dealing directly with local communities' (Howard 2007b).

This articulation of 'aspirational nationalism' served at the time as a justification for the provocative intervention by the commonwealth into Tasmania's health system to ensure that Devonport's Mersey Hospital (in the marginal electorate of Braddon) remained open. To dismiss it as an expedient piece of rhetoric for short-term political purposes would, however, overlook its resonance with the kind of commonwealth-led reconfigured federation that has been emerging during John Howard's decade in prime ministerial office. It was not the 'nationalism' element that was new in the 2007 version; this had been foreshadowed in the 2005 speech and elsewhere. Rather it was the complementary endorsement of 'localism' – the commitment to 'town and team, neighbourhood and network' – as, with 'nationalism', one of the 'two powerful trends in Australian society today'. There was apparently not much room for the middling level of the states in this world of 'nationalism' and 'localism': 'the old rigid state monopoly models for health, education, employment and welfare services have become increasingly obsolete' (Howard 2007b).

Issues and controversies

Several key headline issues and controversies were important markers of the Howard government's fourth term. Four of these issues and controversies – industrial relations, education, health and the management of the Murray-Darling system – are worth describing for the clear pattern that they provided of an increasingly interventionist commonwealth government in the final stanza of the Howard era.

INDUSTRIAL RELATIONS

The Australian Constitution (Section 51(xxxv)) ostensibly limits the industrial relations powers of the commonwealth parliament to 'conciliation and arbitration for the prevention and settlement of industrial disputes extending beyond the limits of any one State'. In practice, this meant that the Australian system had evolved via a two-level system of national regulation (via, most recently, the Australian Industrial Relations Commission) covering certain national awards paralleled by separate state-based systems covering a raft of separate state awards. The single exception to this was Victoria, where the former Kennett government had unilaterally referred most (though not all) of its industrial relations powers to the commonwealth from November 1996 (Gahan 2005).

The Howard government emerged from the election of October 2004 with the pleasing prospect of a Senate majority by July 2005. Initiatives otherwise likely to be blocked by a non-government Senate majority thus became more thinkable, and prime among these was industrial relations reform. '[W]ith the favourable outcome in the Senate', Howard noted, 'we are now in a position to drive the industrial relations reform process further in ways consistent with liberal philosophy' (Howard 2005a). The substantive arguments about the direction of this reform – further towards a deregulated system with weakening trade union influence – are not the concern here except insofar as the substantive coalition/Labor partisan conflict over this issue helps to explain why state and territory Labor governments opposed the initiative. Rather, the concern here is with the rebalancing of commonwealth–state relations that the initiative entailed. For Prime Minister Howard, a 'single set of national laws on industrial relations' was 'an idea whose time has come':

> [T]his is not about empowering Canberra. It is about liberating workplaces from Colac to Cooktown. ... The current system of

> overlapping federal and state awards is too complex, costly and inefficient. ... [I]n the absence of referrals from the states, the [commonwealth] government will do what it reasonably can to move towards a more streamlined, unified and efficient system. (Howard 2005a)

The new commonwealth industrial relations legislation passed through parliament in December 2005 (for further details, see chapter 10). The states challenged the act on constitutional grounds in the High Court. By a 5–2 majority, the court ruled for the commonwealth in November 2006. The High Court majority's determination in this NSW v Commonwealth of Australia case, essentially finding that the commonwealth's constitutional power over 'corporations' (Section 51(xx)) gives it a capacity to regulate a wide range of industrial relations matters, constituted not just a significant confirmation but arguably also a significant amplification of the legal predominance of the commonwealth within the federal system. The concerns of alarmed defenders of federalism were encapsulated in the pointed dissenting judgment from Justice Kirby, for whom it:

> would be completely contrary to the text, structure and design of the Constitution for the states to be reduced, in effect, to service agencies of the commonwealth, by a sleight of hand deployed in the interpretation by this Court of specified legislative powers of the Federal Parliament. ... Such an outcome would be so alien to the place envisaged for the states by the Constitution that the rational mind will reject it as lying outside the true construction of the constitutional provisions, read as a whole, as they were intended to operate in harmony with one another and consistently with a basic law that creates a federal system of government for Australia. ... Why, for instance, bother to have state Parliaments, with significant federal functions to perform, if by dint of an interpretation of s 51(xx) of the Constitution [i.e. the corporations power] the legislative powers of such Parliaments could effectively be reduced unilaterally by federal law to minor, or even trivial and continually disappearing functions? (HCA 2006: 52 at paras 543 and 549)

The Prime Minister greeted the decision with a characteristic mixture of reassuring calmness and unequivocal 'national interest' insistence:

> We will not interpret this decision as being any kind of constitutional green light to legislate to the hilt. We have no desire

to extend commonwealth power, except in the national interest. I have no desire for takeover's sake to take over the role of the states. (Howard 2006)

EDUCATION

The commonwealth has no direct constitutional jurisdiction over education and the public schooling sector has long been at the core of the business of state governments. Via indirect means such as conditional grants, however, the commonwealth has over the past 40 years increased its influence over aspects of the delivery of schooling (Lingard 1993; Dudley & Vidovich 1995). While the commonwealth remains, in comparison with the states, a minor direct provider of funds to public schools (Harrington 2004a), this funding provides potential leverage to influence the content and management of the schooling services notwithstanding that the schools are ostensibly created by and owned by state governments. This became a particularly contentious theme during the Howard government's fourth term, initially under Brendan Nelson's continuing tenure as education minister and then, from January 2006, under his successor Julie Bishop.

The Howard government's education initiatives ranged from the symbolic to the substantive. The common thread was a growing insistence about greater national consistency (to address what Minister Nelson (2003) had earlier described as 'the national rail gauge problem' across the separate state-level education systems); better reporting by schools to parents about student achievement; greater transparency about measuring and publicising school performance; greater autonomy to school principals (and by implication less authority both to state education bureaucracies and to professional teachers); and making the explicit recognition and teaching of appropriate 'values' a core part of schooling (Harrington 2004b).

At the symbolic end of the interventionist continuum was a requirement that all schools possess a functioning flagpole as a condition of receiving commonwealth funding (DEST 2005). Later came an insistence that the teaching of Australian history – and specifically a sequential notion of Australian history emphasising key dates and events – should be given more emphasis, an idea that escalated from another values-infused symbolic incursion to a 2007 announcement that history should become a compulsory component of the curriculum (Howard 2007c). Other interventions included requirements for public schools to specify performance targets and performance measures, to ensure that student reports were plain English in composition and reveal where a student ranked in his/her class, and to publish school performance information (DEST 2005). As explained by the Prime Minister, 'the incentives need to be right to ensure our schools perform at their best with high academic standards, good teachers, principals with real power and proper accountability' (Howard 2007d).

The adoption of effective nationwide curriculum standards was again placed on the agenda, framed from the commonwealth perspective as a critique of the inadequacies of state-level educational governance (e.g. Ferrari 2006) despite manifest intergovernmental progress over recent decades in agreeing to national schooling goals and collaborative curriculum frameworks (e.g. Curriculum Corporation 2006; MCEETYA 2006). Minister Bishop claimed a 'victory' when the Ministerial Council comprising commonwealth and state education ministers agreed in April 2007 to 'work together ... to develop nationally consistent curricula' (MCEETYA 2007). The same meeting, however, refused to endorse Bishop's push for performance-based pay for teachers or a common school starting age, confirming that considerable residual power – not least the power of inertia – remained in the hands of the state negotiators in these intergovernmental forums.

Doubtless in recognition of this, the schooling sector became a venue for more direct commonwealth action, via a process described elsewhere as 'parallel federalism' (Parkin & Anderson 2007) that bypasses the states altogether. In his 2004 election campaign speech, Prime Minister Howard announced the establishment of 24 'technical colleges'. These were, according to Howard, to be 'the centrepiece of our drive to tackle skills shortages and to revolutionise vocational education and training throughout Australia' (Howard 2004). They were, tellingly, to operate independently of the state education systems, notwithstanding their explicit overlap with the business of state high schools and TAFE campuses. These Australian Technical Colleges proved to be more difficult to get established than first envisaged, but a number (well short of the targets) had become operational by the end of the fourth term (Lebihan 2007; DEST 2007a).

Prime Minister Howard also used the 2004 campaign speech to announce additional funding to an existing program to maintain and upgrade school facilities. However, he added, 'we're going to do things a little differently this time. We're not going to pay the money to the state governments. We're going to deal directly with the parent bodies' (Howard 2004). Thus was set in train the Investing in Our Schools Program, in which projects were to be proposed not by, or even in consultation with, state governments but rather by direct application to the commonwealth by 'school communities' (DEST 2007b).

Nearly all Australian universities are statutory creatures of the states, yet the significance of commonwealth financial contributions, conditional upon university compliance in relation to matters as detailed as course profiles and student service fees, means that even staunch federalists tend to concede the commonwealth's de facto dominance (Craven 2006a, 2006b; Norton 2005). Minister Julie Bishop sought to formalise this situation by proposing that the vestiges of university financial accountability to the states be removed, either by agreement or perhaps even by commonwealth fiat through the same corporations power ascribed to the commonwealth via the High Court's industrial relations decision (Bishop 2007; Garnaut & Crawshaw 2007). The states were not impressed (Healy 2007) and no progress in this direction was made.

HEALTH

The commonwealth has a firmer constitutional foothold in the health domain by virtue of its powers (arising from the 1946 constitutional amendment that produced Section 51(xxiiiA) of the constitution) over the 'provision of ... pharmaceutical, sickness and hospital benefits [and] medical and dental services'. The intergovernmental regime that has evolved in practice sees a major commonwealth role in the regulation of general practice primary health care through the Medicare system and in partial funding of the public hospital system, while the public hospital systems themselves remain under state administration. This regime operates under the rubric of the Australian Healthcare Agreement, a formal commonwealth–state compact that had most recently been renewed for a further five-year period in 2003.

There is widespread recognition that the current cross-governmental arrangements can be problematic (Duckett 1999; Hancock 2002; Buckmaster & Pratt 2005) and various proposals for clarifying and rationalising the respective roles of the commonwealth and the states have been promulgated over the years. On the other hand, many of the well-publicised troubles afflicting public hospitals – such as escalating costs, heightened public expectations and service demands, and the management of the health workforce – are likely to be inherent rather than necessarily affected by the intergovernmental regime.

Tony Abbott as Minister for Health publicly contemplated a total commonwealth takeover of the public hospital sector on a number of occasions (for example, see Saunders and Schubert 2004; Stafford 2005). A commonwealth taskforce headed by Andrew Podger, former Public Service

Commissioner and head of the Department of Health and Ageing, lent some support to this vision (Metherell 2005; see also Podger 2006a, 2006b). But, until 2007, Prime Minister Howard – seemingly aware of the inherent difficulties of health-sector management – consistently signalled that he did not envisage the commonwealth assuming responsibility for public hospitals. He envisaged instead 'incremental change' towards 'finding practical options to improve the delivery of health services' (Howard 2005a).

At least that was the position until August 2007, when the pressure of an impending election and the need to defend the coalition's hold on the marginal Tasmanian seat of Braddon induced a dramatic change of tack. Taking advantage of local community opposition to the plans by Tasmania's Labor government to rationalise hospital services, Prime Minister Howard pledged a takeover of Devonport's Mersey Hospital through a commonwealth-funded local hospital board. While the election pressures influencing the intervention were obvious, Howard was careful to justify it within the new

Courtesy of Peter Nicholson, *The Australian*, 6 April 2005

narrative of federalism – localism and nationalism, minus the states – that he was developing:

> [T]here are certain responsibilities for the States, certain responsibilities for the Federal Government but the public increasingly looks to the national government to plug the gaps and to respond where State and Territory Governments aren't doing a good enough job. ... [T]he public in Australia want services and they don't really care which level of government delivers those services and if they can be effectively delivered by the Federal Government going direct to a local community all well and good. (Howard 2007e)

Health-sector stakeholders were generally unimpressed by the implications of a commonwealth government overturning carefully devised, though politically difficult, regional health management plans. The Tasmanian president of the Australian Medical Association was reported as describing the intervention as a 'disaster' (Denholm 2007). Conservatives previously accustomed to a coalition government defending rather than subverting federalism seemed particularly appalled by the Mersey Hospital episode. A 'betrayal of conservatism' is how Nahan (2007) characterised it, declaring that the commonwealth's 'lack of service delivery expertise and sloppy preparation of the ... takeover to date' meant that 'better outcomes will be difficult to achieve'.

Prime Minister Howard was undeterred: 'Let's see how it works', he mused, 'and if it does, it can represent something of a model for other parts of the country' (Breusch 2007). Within a month or so, it was no longer necessary even to wait for the evidence: 'aspirational nationalism' linked with 'localism' was now the way forward (Howard 2007b).

The new orientation inevitably intruded itself into the ongoing, and unresolved, commonwealth–state negotiations over the next Australian Healthcare Agreement (AHA) due to come into effect in 2008. Until that point, the main sticking point had been money. According to the states, the commonwealth's financial contribution to public hospitals had fallen since 2000 from 50 to 45 per cent of costs, representing a shortfall of over $1 billion (Health Ministers 2007). Minister Tony Abbott had dismissed the claim as ruse by the Labor states to 'give Kevin Rudd a leg up' (AAP 2007), though later – in the middle of the election campaign – the Australian Institute of Health and Welfare (AIHW) essentially confirmed the states' interpretation (AIHW 2007). Meanwhile, however, the new 'localism' and 'aspirational nationalism' themes now provided Abbott and Howard with an additional point of attack. The next AHA, they declared, would require the states to establish community boards to directly administer each of the nation's public hospitals, bypassing state-level administrative and political control, or face the loss of commonwealth funding (Coorey 2007; Tingle 2007).

MANAGING THE MURRAY-DARLING

The Australian Constitution is generally silent about state powers, relying instead on authorising the states to exercise powers not allocated to the commonwealth. This silence, however, does not apply to the power to manage rivers; section 100 states explicitly that 'the Commonwealth shall not, by any law or regulation of trade or commerce, abridge the right of a state or of the residents therein to the reasonable use of the waters of rivers for conservation or irrigation'.

The Murray-Darling river system – comprising Australia's premier river catchment area not just in terms of geographical magnitude but also in relation to economic, social and environmental impact – impinges on four states (Queensland, New South Wales, Victoria and South Australia) and on the Australian Capital Territory. The state-based governance and management of this system, in which upstream decisions have consequential downstream effects, has long been portrayed as an iconic example of the difficulties encountered by federalist arrangements in producing appropriately integrated, co-ordinated, effective and sustainable results (Kellow 1991, 1992). Various intergovernmental arrangements have been instituted over the years (from the creation of the River Murray Commission in 1917 to the Murray-Darling Basin Ministerial Council and associated Commission in 1985), but they have never managed to impose a satisfactory catchment-wide governance and management regime. There had been longstanding complaints about alleged over-allocation to irrigators, inefficient and wasteful irrigation practices, deteriorating water quality and unsustainable environmental flows, and by the term of the fourth Howard government these had escalated markedly during what had become extended drought conditions.

In June 2004, the Council of Australian Governments (COAG) agreed to a new National Water Initiative. This established the National Water Commission (NWC) to oversee another of the national intergovernmental regulatory regimes that has characterised the 'regulatory federalism' of recent decades (Parkin & Anderson 2007). The goal was the creation of a 'nationally-compatible market, regulatory and planning based system of managing surface and groundwater resources for rural and urban use that optimises economic, social and environmental outcomes' (NWI 2004: 3). But progress was slow. In June 2006, the NWC reported to COAG that 'there is still considerable distance to go to achieve sustainability of water management in practice', that 'water markets are still in their infancy' and that 'there is a need for governments to increase their commitment to the National Water Initiative' (NWC 2006).

Progress was predictably particularly slow in relation to the Murray-Darling, with all the continuing complexities and political sensitivities encompassing the multiple governments and multiple stakeholders. In his 2007 Australia Day address, Prime Minister Howard took on this issue via another dramatic intervention. He called on the four Murray-Darling states to refer their powers over water management to the commonwealth, in return for which the commonwealth would commit to a $10 billion expenditure program aimed at producing a more efficient irrigation infrastructure and a reduction in water allocations. The Prime Minister had in mind a reconstituted Murray-Darling Basin Commission (MDBC) reporting, in effect, only to the commonwealth government:

> Rivers do not recognise those lines on the map that we call state borders. ... In the final analysis ... the core problem is that the different states have competing interests. ... We must think and act as Australians and not as Queenslanders, Victorians or New South Welshmen. (Howard 2007f)

By late February, after obtaining assurances that the proposed water management regime would be sufficiently based on scientific principles to insulate it from political pressure, three of the four affected states – New South Wales, Queensland and South Australia – had agreed in principle to refer their powers to the commonwealth. Victoria, however, refused to agree, eventually declaring the idea 'dead in the water' (Mitchell & Marris 2007). Victoria claimed to have in place a sustainable water allocation system for its portion of the Murray-Darling system, and it was not sufficiently assured of the superiority of the foreshadowed national regime, especially since most of the funds to be expended on buying back over-allocated water entitlements would necessarily be spent in New South Wales.

The Victorian position forced the Howard government to pursue an alternative strategy not dependent on the constitutional referral of state powers. Via legislation that passed the Senate in August 2007 with bipartisan support, a new Murray-Darling Basin Authority was established, alongside the ongoing MDBC, with authority to set an overall cap on water allocation but without power to determine allocations to individual irrigators. The commonwealth's $10 billion expenditure proposal remained in place, though there was some doubt about how much of it would be spent in Victoria. The Prime Minister conceded that this was a suboptimal strategy: it did not produce 'the same level of commonwealth power that would have been achieved by a referral of power. ... I would have preferred an alternative course but I'm left with no alternative' (Tingle et al. 2007). He accused the recalcitrant Victorians of 'selfish state parochialism' (Morris 2007).

The evolution of fiscal and regulatory federalism

These issues and controversies over the years of the fourth Howard government relating to industrial relations, education, health and the Murray-Darling reveal the strategies and tactics of a government increasingly comfortable with a more interventionist commonwealth role and increasingly willing to articulate a rationale for it. It is worth reflecting upon what this has meant for the longer term evolution of the Australian federal system.

The first Howard government inherited in March 1996 a system of commonwealth–state relations with two important features. The first was a striking 'vertical fiscal imbalance' in relation to financial relations. The second has been described elsewhere as emergent 'regulatory federalism' in relation to policies and programs (Parkin & Anderson 2007).

After July 2000, the fiscal story revolved around the advent of the goods and services tax (GST) with all revenues flowing unconditionally to the states. Though technically (as a new commonwealth tax replacing some state taxes) this reform exacerbated vertical fiscal imbalance, the GST revenues are directly harvested from national economic activity rather than being dependent on commonwealth fiscal policy decisions, making this a genuinely pro-federalist initiative. The Howard government claimed that the financial transfer to the states was substantially greater than would have otherwise prevailed had the previous system been continued. This was disputed – with contrary contentions pointing to these funds representing a lower proportion of GDP than under the pre-GST system (Robertson 2007; Twomey & Withers 2007: 26) – but the positive impact on state-level fiscal autonomy seems undeniable.

It is telling that, during the fourth term of the Howard government, Treasurer Peter Costello expressed retrospective regret about the GST initiative: 'I think this is one area, the most generous and one of the most fundamental changes, the allocation of a growth tax to the states, which has not proved successful' (Shanahan 2006). Costello alarmed state treasurers at the March 2005 Treasury Ministers Conference by demanding the abolition of a further tranche of state-imposed duties under the implicit threat of some sort of reneging of the GST deal. All states in due course (New South Wales and Western Australian most reluctantly) proceeded to announce an abolition or phase-down of the kind of duties to which Costello was referring.

The evolution of the 'regulatory federalism' story under the Howard government was more complicated. The story here really begins in the early 1990s when COAG began to oversee the development of new collaborative arrangements – that is, the creation of new regulatory regimes – to provide co-ordinated national governance over a range of transportation, financial and professional domains (Parkin 2007). The COAG-negotiated National Competition Policy, instituted in 1995, played a key role in forcing competitive or contested regimes on to monopoly state government utilities and other state-level policy domains. The COAG-centred process went somewhat into recess in the Howard government's first two terms, but it was vigorously resurrected in the third and fourth terms, debating and in some cases resolving a number of crucial national issues.

At times, COAG meetings seemed to be elevated to the status of esteemed national summits, with all leaders – both the prime minister and the bevy of Labor state and territory premiers and chief ministers – keen to be seen to collaborate to advance the national interest. The politics behind this was probably a factor. For the Prime Minister, COAG meetings may have been a means (subliminal or otherwise) to marginalise both the national Labor opposition and his own within-party occasional putative challenger, Treasurer Costello. For the premiers, it was an opportunity for national prominence and favourable media exposure.

International events also served to elevate the role of COAG and the necessity, at least in some areas, for co-operation. The bombs set off in the London transport system in July 2005 dramatically changed attitudes in Australia to the prevention of terrorism. All governments recognised that a national strategy was an essential basis for an effective response. A special September 2005 COAG meeting agreed, after confidential security briefings, to grant increased detention and interrogation powers to police and intelligence services, though state and territory leaders successfully insisted upon various safeguards and limitations. On this matter, the commonwealth needed the states and so, to some extent, the states could flex some political muscle. As Prime Minister Howard explained:

> we cannot pass this legislation credibly without the support of the States, because we do not have the constitutional power. And that's why I approached the states ... In this country we have a written constitution that gives particular powers to the Federal Government and the residue of the powers stay with the States; that's the way the constitution works. And in some of these areas, particularly in the area of preventive detention, there's no constitutional power for us at a Commonwealth level acting unilaterally to detain somebody effectively for more than 48 hours. So if you're going to retain them for 14 days you need the States involved. (Howard 2005b)

This was one of five COAG meetings that took place during the Howard government's fourth term. Earlier, a June 2005 meeting had sidestepped anticipated conflict on industrial relations to reach cordial agreements on exploring a national apprenticeship system, mutual recognition of trade qualifications, a renewal of national competition policy, and some policy aspects of climate change. Later, the February 2006, July 2006 and April 2007 COAG meetings were principally focused on a new National Reform Agenda with three broad components – labelled as human capital, competition and regulatory reform (COAG 2006) – to replace the expiring National Competition Policy (NCP) agreement. Pointedly, the commonwealth successfully deflected state demands for a continuation under the National Reform Agenda of NCP-style compensation payments (COAG 2006).

'Regulatory federalism' also operates at a more micro scale at the program level. Across a raft of policy and program areas, there is evidence that, with a dogged insistence that it legitimately represents some sort of 'national interest' perspective and with some interesting managerial adroitness, the Howard government went further than probably any previous commonwealth administration in more tightly binding the states with conditional grants. The strategies included tightening up on program compliance, insisting on more serious state contributions via matching funds, and insisting on specific attribution of credit to the commonwealth for program outcomes. The changes in the education domain described above illustrate these tendencies.

Particularly controversial were commonwealth-imposed grant conditions unrelated to the immediate policy or program at hand, especially conditions promoting the Howard government's preferred position on industrial relations. The so-called National Construction Code specified that state government agencies must not accept tenders and/or expressions of interest from contractors for commonwealth-funded projects unless they are code-compliant, that is, unless they 'facilitate greater flexibility and productivity' in workplace relations (DEWR 2006).

Conclusion

Prime Minister Howard's articulation of a new conservative nationalism, particularly in its later guise of an 'aspirational nationalism' linked to a notion of 'localism', was a notable innovation both conceptually and pragmatically. Had the Howard government been re-elected for a fifth term, this could have proved to be its most enduring legacy. NSW Premer Bob Carr was reported in March 2005 as claiming that 'John Howard and Costello are turning the states into implementation agencies of a very powerful commonwealth' (Clark 2005). Tony Abbott in July 2006 anticipated 'the withering away of the states … [to become] less like sovereign governments and more like branch offices of Canberra' (Lewis & Price 2006), and a week later Peter Costello likewise envisaged the states as 'moving towards the role of service delivery more on the model of divisional offices than sovereign independent governments' (Costello 2006). The explicit references to the notion of sovereignty – surely fundamental to the basic definition of an authentic federal system (Parkin 1996: 4–7) – are telling.

It is, however, a feature of Australian federalism that challenges from the centre tend to produce counterbalancing thrusts from elsewhere. The Whitlam government of 1972–75 – the regime that, in this respect at least, the later Howard governments most closely resembled – stimulated a resistance from, and indeed a notable policy renaissance among, the states that in many ways left the states stronger and more vibrant than in the pre-Whitlam period. The states remain, even after four terms of the Howard government, entrenched political institutions with crucial policy and service delivery responsibilities. The COAG process, notwithstanding its effect of potentially shifting key state powers to collaboratively endorsed national bodies and protocols, continued under the Howard government to legitimise the states, and especially their leaders, as key actors.

The states also undertook some interesting moves to institute collaborative intergovernmental arrangements that bypass the commonwealth. A new state-constituted Council for the Australian Federation – envisaged as a COAG without the commonwealth – met in October 2006. Some promising proposals for genuine intergovernmental reform produced under its auspices (Twomey & Withers 2007; RSC 2007), plus some others emerging elsewhere (Allen

Consulting Group 2006), were key influences in shaping the noticeably pro-federalist stance adopted by the Rudd Labor opposition in the lead-up to the November 2007 election.

It will be fascinating to observe whether the Rudd government, led as it is by a prime minister with unprecedented experience at the state level in observing and managing commonwealth–state relations, will turn out to be receptive to this pro-federalist stance. If instead it embarks on a more centralist course, it will be one of the ironies of Australian political history that its capacity to do so was enhanced by the nominally conservative Howard government that preceded it.

References

AAP (Australian Associated Press) (2007) Abbott dismisses hospital claim, *Sydney Morning Herald*, 24 June.

AIHW (Australian Institute of Health and Welfare) (2007) *Health Expenditure Australia 2005–06*, Health and Welfare Expenditure Series No. 30. Cat. no. HWE 37, AIHW, Canberra.

Allen Consulting Group (2006) *Governments Working Together? Assessing Specific Purpose Payment Arrangements*, Report to the Government of Victoria, Melbourne.

Bishop, J (Minister for Education and Planning) (2007) Reducing red tape for universities (Media release), 8 May, at <www.dest.gov.au/ministers/bishop/budget07/bud10_07.htm>.

Breusch, J (2007) More takeovers on cards: PM, *Australian Financial Review*, 2 August.

Buckmaster, L & Pratt, A (2005) Not on my account! Cost-shifting in the Australian health system, *Parliamentary Library Research Note*, No. 6 2005–06, Canberra, at <www.aph.gov.au/library/pubs/rn/2005-06/06rn06.htm>.

Clark, A (2005) Carr's big test: getting back on track, *Australian Financial Review*, 17 March.

COAG (Council of Australian Governments) (2006) Council of Australian Governments meeting 14 July 2006, Communique, Canberra, at <www.coag.gov.au/meetings/140706/index.htm>.

Coorey, P (2007) State bypass a lifeline for hospitals, *Sydney Morning Herald*, 2 October.

Costello, P (Treasurer) (2006) The Machiavelli speech: Treasurer Peter Costello outlines his agenda for The Bulletin's most influential Australians, *The Bulletin*, 5 July.

Craven, G (2006a) A lighter hand on the leading rein, *Australian*, 14 June.

—— (2006b) Commonwealth power over higher education: Implications and realities, *Public Policy*, 1(1): 1–13.

Curriculum Corporation (2006) *About Us*, at <www.curriculum.edu.au/who_are_we/whoarewe.php>.

Denholm, M (2007) Mersey plan a 'disaster', *Australian*, 9 August.

DEST (Department of Education, Science and Training) (2005) Schools Assistance Regulations 2005, at <www.dest.gov.au/sectors/school_education/publications_resources/profiles/Schools_Assistance_Regulations_2005.htm>.

—— (2007a) Australian Technical Colleges, at <www.australiantechnicalcolleges.gov.au/>.

—— (2007b) Investing in Our Schools Program, 28 August, at <www.investinginourschools.dest.gov.au/>.

DEWR (Department of Employment and Workplace Relations) (2006) National Code and Revised Guidelines Home, at <www.workplace.gov.au/workplace/Category/PolicyReviews/BuildingConstruction/NationalCodeRevisedGuidlines/>.

Duckett, S (1999) Commonwealth/state relations in health. In L Hancock (ed.) *Health Policy in a Market State*, Allen & Unwin, Sydney: 71–86.

Dudley, J & Vidovich, L (1995) The politics of education: Commonwealth schools policy 1973–95, *Australian Education Review*, No. 36, Australian Council for Educational Research, Melbourne.

Ferrari, J (2006) Canberra to seize syllabus, *Australian*, 6 October.

Gahan, P (2005) The future of state industrial regulation: What can we learn from Victoria, *Australian Review of Public Affairs*, 14 November, at <www.australianreview.net/digest/2005/11/gahan.html>.

Garnaut, J & Crawshaw, D (2007) PM to seize uni control from states, *Sydney Morning Herald*, 10 May.

Hancock, L (2002) Australian federalism, politics and health. In H Gardner & S Barraclough (eds) *Health Policy in Australia*, Oxford University Press, Melbourne: 49–78.

Harrington, M (2004a) Commonwealth funding for schools since 1996: An update, *Research Note no. 41 2003–04*, Parliament of Australia Parliamentary Library, at <www.aph.gov.au/library/pubs/rn/2003-04/04rn41.htm>.

—— (2004b) Schools Assistance (Learning Together – Achievement Through Choice and Opportunity) Bill 2004, *Bills Digest 50 2004–05*, Parliament of Australia Parliamentary Library, at <www.aph.gov.au/library/pubs/bd/2004-05/05bd050.pdf>.

Health Ministers (Governments of the Australian Capital Territory, New South Wales, Northern Territory, Queensland, South Australia, Tasmania, Victoria and Western Australia) (2007) *Caring for our Health: A report card on the Australian Government's performance on public health. A report by state and territory health ministers*, at <www.health.qld.gov.au/news/caringforourhealth/contents.pdf>.

Healy, G (2007) Multiple assault on single body, *Australian*, 24 October.

HCA (High Court of Australia) (2006) New South Wales v Commonwealth [2006] HCA 52; 81 ALJR 34; 231 ALR 1 (14 November 2006) paragraphs 549 & 550, at <www.austlii.edu.au/au/cases/cth/HCA/2006/52.html> .

Howard, J (Prime Minister) (2004) Address at the Coalition Campaign Launch, Brisbane 26 October, at <http://pandora.nla.gov.au/pan/22107/20041008-0000/www.liberal.org.au/ defaultcc00 .html?action=2004_policy>.

—— (2005a) Reflections on Australian federalism, Speech by the Prime Minister to the Menzies Research Centre, Melbourne, 11 April, at <www.mrcltd.org.au/uploaded_documents /australian_federalism_final.pdf >.

—— (2005b) Transcript of interview with Laurie Oaks, *Channel 9: Sunday*, 30 October, at <http://sunday.ninemsn.com.au/sunday/political_transcripts/article_1901.asp>.

—— (2006) Press conference transcript, Sydney, 14 November, at <http://pandora.nla.gov.au/pan/10052/20061221-0000/www.pm.gov.au/news /interviews/Interview2248.html>.

—— (2007a) Press conference, Perth, 24 July, at <http://pandora.nla.gov.au/pan/10052/20070823-732/www.pm.gov.au/media/Interview/2007/Interview 24458.html >.

—— (2007b) Australia rising to a better future, Address to the Millennium Forum, Sydney, 20 August, at <http://pandora.nla.gov.au/pan/10052/20070823-732/www.pm.gov.au/media /Speech/007/Speech24507.html>.

—— (2007c) The teaching of Australian history in schools (Media release), 11 October, at <http://pandora.nla.gov.au/pan/10052/20071016-1104/www.pm.gov.au/media/Release/2007/MediaRelease24615.html>.

—— (2007d) Australia Rising to the Education Challenge, Address to the Centre for Independent Studies, Sydney, 14 May, at <http://pandora.nla.gov.au/apps/PandasDelivery/WebObjects/PandasDelivery.woa/wa/tep?pi=10052 >.

—— (2007e) Interview with Tim Cox, ABC Radio Hobart, 1 August, at <http://pandora.nla.gov.au/pan/10052/20071016-1104/www.pm.gov.au/media/Interview/2007/Interview24473.html>.

—— (2007f) Address to the National Press Club, Parliament House, Canberra, 25 January, at <http://pandora.nla.gov.au/pan/10052/20070321-0000/www.pm.gov.au/media/Speech/2007/speech2341.html>.

Kellow, A (1991) The Murray-Darling Basin. In B Galligan, O Hughes & C Walsh (eds) *Intergovernmental Relations and Public Policy*, Allen & Unwin, Sydney: 129–45

—— (1992) *Saline Solutions: Policy Dynamics in the Murray Darling Basin*, Deakin University, Geelong.

Lebihan, R (2007) Tech colleges: Three years, $550m, no graduates, *Australian Financial Review*, 14 August.

Lewis, S & Price, M (2006) Canberra threat to rewrite GST deal, *Australian*, 4 July.

Lingard, B (1993) Corporate federalism: The emerging approach to policy-making for Australian schools. In B Lingard, J Knight & P Porter (eds) *Schooling Reform in Hard Times*, Falmer Press, London: 24–35.

MCEETYA (Ministerial Council on Education, Employment, Training and Youth Affairs) (2006) The Adelaide Declaration on National Goals for Schooling in the Twenty-First Century, Document endorsed by State, Territory and Commonwealth Ministers of Education in April 1999, at <www.mceetya.edu.au/mceetya/default.asp?id=11576>.

—— (2007) Information statement, 21st MCEETYA meeting, Darwin 12–13 April, at <www.mceetya.edu.au/mceetya/21st_mceetya_meeting,18933.html>.

Metherell, M (2005) PM's taskforce backs takeover of hospitals, *Sydney Morning Herald*, 12 March.

Mitchell, S & Marris, S (2007) PM's $10bn water plan unravelling, *Australian*, 24 May.

Morris, S (2007) PM fishes for water votes, *Australian Financial Review*, 21 September.

Nahan, M (2007) Liberal Party has lost its soul, *Australian*, 3 August.

Nelson, B (Minister for Education, Science and Training) (2003) Nationally consistent schools (Interview transcript), 26 June, at <www.dest.gov.au/ministers/nelson/jun_03/transcript_260603.htm>.

Norton, A (2005) Universities in a state: The federal case against commonwealth control of universities, *Issues Analysis*, 56, Centre for Independent Studies, Sydney.

NWC (National Water Commission) (2006) *Progress on the National Water Initiative: A Report to the Council of Australian Governments*, Canberra, 1 June, at <http://svc044.wic032p.server-web.com/publications/docs/COAG_report_2006.pdf>.

NWI (National Water Initiative) (2004) *Intergovernmental Agreement on a National Water Initiative Between the Commonwealth of Australia and the Governments of New South Wales, Victoria, Queensland, South Australia, the Australian Capital Territory and the Northern Territory*, at <http://svc044.wic032p.server-web.com/nwi/docs/iga_national_water_initiative.pdf>.

Parkin, A (1996) The significance of federalism: A South Australian perspective. In A Parkin (ed.) *South Australia, Federalism and Public Policy*, Federalism Research Centre,

Australian National University, Canberra: 1–23.
—— (2007) COAG. In B Galligan & W Roberts (eds) *The Oxford Companion to Australian Politics,* Oxford University Press, Melbourne: 108–10.
Parkin, A & Anderson, G (2007) The Howard government, regulatory federalism and the transformation of commonwealth–state relations, *Australian Journal of Political Science*, 42(2): 295–314.
Podger, A (2006a) Directions for health reform in Australia. In *Productive Reform in a Federal System: Roundtable Proceedings*, Roundtable 27–28 October, Productivity Commission, Canberra, at <www.pc.gov.au/research/confproc/productivereform/productivereform.pdf>.
—— (2006b) A model health system for Australia, Inaugural Menzies Health Policy Lecture, Australian National University, Canberra, 3 March, at <www.ahpi.health.usyd.edu.au/pdfs/events2006/apodgerlecture.pdf>.
RSC (Review Steering Committee) (2007) *The Future of Schooling in Australia: A Report by the States and Territories*, Federalist Paper 2, Council for the Australian Federation, at <http://education.qld.gov.au/publication/production /reports/pdfs/2007/federalist-paper.pdf>.
Robertson, R (2007) Canberra's tax/GDP ratio at all-time highs, Macquarie Bank, reproduced on 24 April, at <www.crikey.com.au/Politics/20070426-Moneybags-Costello-and-the-poor-state-relations.html>.
Saunders, M & Schubert, M (2004) Give us health, Abbott taunts, *Australian*, 25 February.
Shanahan, D (2006) The boom we had to have, *Weekend Australian*, 25–26 February.
Stafford, A (2005) Abbott stirs states over control of health system, *Australian Financial Review*, 5 September.
Tingle, L (2007) PM to up ante on health funding, *Australian Financial Review*, 2 October.
Tingle, L, Burrell, A & Hughes, D (2007) Powers invoked to break water stalemate, *Australian Financial Review*, 25 July.
Twomey, A & Withers, G (2007) Australia's federalist future, Federalist Paper 1, Council for the Australian Federation, at <www.crawford.anu.edu.au/pdf/staff/glenn_withers/federalist_paper.pdf>.

7
Reshaping public integrity

John Uhr

In this chapter I investigate debates over the Howard government's public integrity. Howard critics fear that public integrity has been reshaped or distorted by the Howard government. Three integrity standards I apply here are quite traditional: truth; honesty; and accountability. Each is an important (if debatable) measure of integrity in democratic regimes (Dobel 1999; Montefiore & Vines 1999). While examining the story of integrity under the Howard government, my larger aim is to reshape the intellectual framework for examining debates over any government's public integrity. I assess the details of government performance in the context of the institutional settings that are distinctive to the evolving Australian story of responsible parliamentary government (Uhr 2002). I evaluate competing claims over the government's compliance with standards of truth, honesty and accountability in the context of the Australian setting and the institutional powers and also the institutional constraints facing the fourth Howard government.

Most commentary on Howard and integrity takes integrity as unproblematic and the Howard government as cleverly dishonest, even when talking about the importance of honest government (see for example Gaita 2004; Kelly 2005, 2006; Walter & Strangio 2007: 13–26). In many cases, such a perspective presupposes that conventional standards of public integrity are themselves uncontroversial. I disagree: democratic theory is not quite

Courtesy of Peter Nicholson, *The Australian*, 18 October 2003

as simple as that. To help anchor this analysis, I use 'insider' justifications from prominent Howard minister Tony Abbott whose 'case for the defence' is usually overlooked in assessments by Howard's critics (Abbott 2004, 2007). Although I am not trying to save the Howard government from its many accusers, I am trying to save the accusation itself from some of the worst excesses of the accusers (Kelly 2007). Although one short chapter is not the place for a comprehensive testing of all the relevant evidence, I will draw on the experience of the fourth Howard government to open up a wider debate over appropriate standards of public integrity in contemporary democratic government, internationally as well as in Australia.

Standards of public integrity

This chapter provides a framework which can bring greater discipline, academic and political, to the multiple layers of dispute over the credentials of the fourth Howard government. Many other commentators have marked their scorecards and told their tales about what went right and what went wrong under the watch of this government (Gaita 2004, 2007). To some extent I have already shown my hand in *Terms of Trust: Arguments over Ethics in Australian Government* which was published early in the life of this term of the Howard government (Uhr 2005). This chapter looks back on that early assessment from the luxury of hindsight, taking account of what came to pass rather than what I or others might have feared or suspected would come to pass.

There are two important things that I find missing from much of the debate over the state of public integrity under this and indeed most other Australian governments. The first is adequately dispassionate treatment of the strengths and weaknesses of Australian structures of national governance relating to institutions of integrity, along the lines of Mulgan (2007). The second is close attention to the government's own defence of its performance in relation to the demands of public integrity, as best we can establish its internal conviction and justification of its own successes and failures. These two issues are closely related. It is possible, for instance, that when we take proper account of the institutional limitations on the free action of an Australian national government that we might begin to pay more credit to governments for the positive things they have done and, just as importantly, impose a lesser penalty on them for the things they have failed to do. Sometimes governments simply do not have the power at their disposal to act as well as they might profess or indeed as badly as they might be tempted to try (Kelly 2005). In conventional social science terms: the degree of *agency* available to a government is dependent on the environment of *structure* around them, parts of which in turn reflect the agency of earlier governments. Indeed, the structures in place at the end of Howard's fourth government include many established through the deliberate agency of that government which provides the institutional environment for the successor government.

When dealing with debates over public integrity, it helps to draw back and try to see things in a larger comparative perspective (Uhr 1998a; Saint-Martin & Thompson 2006; Donovan et al. 2007; Mulgan 2007). I will highlight this situation in three stages, dealing in succession with the three aspects of public integrity conveyed in the title: truth; honesty; and accountability. Each is held to be a fundamental principle or benchmark challenging the best efforts of every democratic government (Dobel 1999). To find that the fourth Howard government 'does not measure up' to the most exacting standards of public integrity might tell us more about the feasibility of our standards than about the performance of the Howard government. But even if we take a strict-compliance line and find worrying shortfalls between international democratic standards and Australian practical performance, it still makes sense to pay attention to the government's own account of its own performance, and to keep ourselves open to persuasion that there were 'good reasons' which explain that performance.

During the period under review, Tony Abbott was the Howard government's Minister for Health and Aging. He was also one of the most spirited defenders of the integrity of the Howard government. Abbott's role in national politics makes him a prominent participant in three important spheres of public integrity. First, as Minister for Health, Abbott weighed into many health policy debates from the perspective of someone with a commitment to strong ethical convictions. He won some and he lost some: the most notable loss being his parliamentary defeat over his attempt to ban medical use of an abortion drug he regarded as socially undesirable. Typical of his resilience was his sponsorship of a fresh national debate over medical ethics, illustrated by his release of the June 2007 report on *Challenging Ethical Issues in Contemporary Research on Human Beings* from the National Health and Medical Research Council. Second, in his role as Leader of the House or Manager of Government Business in the House of Representatives, Abbott orchestrated the government's approach to the tactical side of political ethics, reflected in decisions over the agenda of parliamentary business and the opportunities for non-government participation in the legislative process. This sphere is the world of conventional politics: sharing power and policy responsibility among friends and denying it to one's enemies. Third, and more personally, Abbott carved out a role as public advocate or chief defence counsel for the Howard government, with sustained contributions as a media commentator and speech-maker, reflecting his pre-parliamentary career as a political journalist.

In this third sphere of public advocacy, Abbott provided the classic defence of what he termed 'the moral case for the Howard government' (Abbott 2004). Several features of that defence deserve comment. First, the argument about what he termed 'moral seriousness' is realistic and hard-headed. Abbott used the experience of the Howard government to demonstrate the nature of what he identified as 'moral courage', defined as 'doing what's right when people who should know better declare you're wrong'. Arguing that the Howard government had the courage to take hard decisions across many policy areas (from welfare reform to international security), Abbott defended the honour of his government by noting that 'there is a moral quality to success in a good cause'. Honour is Abbott's standard: the high principle of honour or respect, which can be distinguished from the lesser standard of honesty or honest-dealing. Although this sense of public honour cannot be reduced to the claim that ends justify the means, it does imply that actions, including hard decisions, speak louder than words, particularly moral clichés like 'doing the right thing'. The first lesson is that Abbott's defence of the integrity of the Howard government lifts the bar from everyday honesty (telling the truth) to exceptional honour (deserving public respect).

Second, Abbott contrasts the public honour of his government with the questionable private honour of those he terms 'the moral guardians' who think that 'the proper role of government is to play the Good Samaritan on an epic scale' (Abbott 2007). The argument here is that the Howard government has been a good government precisely because it has risen above moralism. The Howard government has put orthodoxy (right thinking) to one side and overcome the temptation to apply standardised solutions based on established pieties (such as international norms of good governance). Implied in this defence is the belief that political leadership demands decisiveness rather than dogma, which will eventually be appreciated by a public grateful for a government that takes hard decisions.

Third, Abbott contends that good governments are open- rather than closed-minded: unlike doctrinaire governments, prudent governments are prepared for 'the complexities of command'. They are prepared even to break promises 'if circumstances change in ways that make keeping a commitment wrong'. This train of reflection leads to a series of contrasts between the difficult path of decent government, exercising its flexibilities of command, and the alternative paths advocated by Howard's opponents: variously called 'sanctimonious moral guardians', 'professional fault-finders', and 'the politically correct establishment' (Abbott 2007). Abbott's defence of the morality of the Howard government comes down to this justification of prudence over moralism, of practical political reasoning over abstract theory, and of the ultimate judgment of voters over the sermonising judgment of virtuous commentators. Some might see in Abbott's principled account of the vocation of politics reflections of Max Weber's defence of an 'ethic of responsibility' that celebrates hard decisions to overturn conventional orthodoxy in the gamble that the results will vindicate public support for a government prepared to do 'whatever it takes' under compelling circumstances (Uhr 2006). The record tends to support Abbott: over many elections, Australian voters opted for Howard, consistent with the international standing of Australians as a people prone to give authority the benefit of the doubt and to take the government's word that it can be trusted (Donovan et al. 2007: 102–103).

I will return to Tony Abbott's pleading in the conclusion. In what follows, I engage more with the proposed standards of public integrity than with the alleged performance of the Howard government. I argue that Australian political analysis is weak and misdirected when dealing with debates over public integrity. My solution is to reconstruct the three core concepts of truth, honesty and accountability by reconnecting them to the discipline of political theory which barely features in Australian political commentary (Uhr 1998b).

Truth

Where better to begin than with the value of truth? Well, possibly quite a few values, including the value of politics (Mulgan 2007: 573–76). I contend that there is something unrealistic about expecting truth in politics. Politics is adversarial, not consensual; political success is manipulated, not peer-reviewed; the determination of party political leadership and the determination of who gets the power to govern are not evidence-based processes. In fact, truth is a comparatively late addition to the standards expected of democratic governments. Classical norms of the best regime like Plato's *Republic* presumed a permanent gulf between the two worlds of truth and politics. Plato's model republic was built on the noble lie between rulers and the ruled, and this lie reflects a fundamental belief that politics can never really be practised on the basis of the open truth. The basic reason is that politics operates in the sphere of loosely informed public opinion which is limited in its epistemic or knowledge-processing capacities.

Can there be truths about political opinion? Sure enough, political theory investigates knowledge about the effective management of public opinion (see Aristotle's *Rhetoric*); but the craft of politics is one of opinion-management, not knowledge-management (see Thucydides' *History*). The public realm is characterised by the reign of opinion which, according to the traditional view found in classical democratic theory, can never really be enlightened by truthfulness. Only approximating the truth are salutary prejudices from below and well-intentioned lies from on high. In ancient political practice as well as in classical political theory, even the best-regulated democracy distinguished between the requirements of truth and politics, with the former belonging to realms of evidence and knowledge and the latter to realms of credibility and trust. Political rulers might indeed owe an account of the justice of their rule to those over whom they ruled, but the classical view of democracy was that political trust and public credibility rather than 'truth' were the real tests of democratic integrity (Uhr 2005: 68–73).

One of the traditional complaints about democracy was that democratic politics was inherently factional, with a wealth of competing sectional or narrow interests threatening to diminish the wider public interest. Those advocating the revival of republican government in the early modern era had to contend with the prevailing prejudice that classical democracy was at its weakest when tested against its very own republican standards. That is, the 'res publica' was all very well in high theory but the low practice of ancient democracy was more about the power of sectional interests to take turns dominating political life. Factions might proclaim that they were motivated by the public interest but their everyday practice showed that they were not telling the truth but using fancy political rhetoric to disguise their deeper partisan intentions and commitments. Democratic or popular governments are, in effect, governments by the unknowledgeable: but to their credit, the people at least know what they do not know and this explains their willing deference to popular leaders claiming to know the arts of government.

Machiavelli is one of the leading modern revivers of classical republicanism. In his hard-headed realism we get a good glimpse of the perilous place of truth in all governments. *The Prince* has one classic exposition of truth in politics and importantly that is in the context of the problem of flattery (*The Prince*, ch. 23). The situation is not simply that rulers protect their own interests by flattering and appeasing their followers: followers and advisers to rulers also flatter rulers in ways that deny rulers the truth they need to hear if they are to rule effectively. Machiavelli suggests that all rulers, popular and princely, need among their followers a band of frank and fearless advisers prepared to 'speak truth to power' as we have come to call this Machiavellian exception to the rule of protective flattery. Machiavelli sketches an institutional design along the lines of a divide-and-rule model that rulers can use to promote frank and fearless advice among their closest followers. By extension, we can see that Machiavelli's confidence in the modern revival of republicanism rests on the innovation of devices to protect truthfulness, which is one of the first casualties in the war that is politics (Machiavelli 1998).

The original generation of political modernisers, represented by the English theorist Thomas Hobbes, argued in effect that modern political development had to choose between democracy and truth. Hobbes contributed effectively to the case against democracy by drawing attention to the duplicity of ancient democrats and their reliance on forms of political rhetoric that disguised the truth about whose interests were holding sway in the parade of factional cliques featured in the unstable periods of classical democratic rule (Hobbes 1968; Uhr 1998b: 43–47). If truth were a primary requirement of government, then Hobbes' advice was to follow his support for regimes of enlightened despotism where a powerful sovereign could promote the cause of truth by keeping democrats at a distance and enlisting the growing powers of a modern nation-state, including its truth-discovering instruments of modern science (Hobbes 1968).

Thus one of the great barriers to the revival of the democratic prospect in the modern era was the reputation that ancient democracy had as a forum for liars. Hobbes' contempt for democracy was eventually overtaken by the political philosophy of liberal constitutionalism which recovered truth as an important political standard for public integrity. The model of this more contemporary stance is Immanuel Kant whose refurbishment of republican theory marks the beginnings of the modern liberal-democratic approach to public integrity. Kant sketches an influential model of ethical politics complete with the very model of a modern moral politician: and this normative framework has been explicitly relied on by the most philosophically informed of critics of the Howard government (Kant 1991; Gaita 2004).

In the context of politics, truthfulness refers to disclosure of all that one knows about a subject under question. Open disclosure might or might not be wise, depending on the circumstances. The extent to which one should be truthful in specific circumstances is a matter for judgment. Kant tended to believe that everyone should be truthful at all times, and that only a faulty sense of judgment would give one the confidence or excuse to lie. Kant's classic distinction between the expediency of the 'political moralist' and the integrity of the 'moral politician' turns on this issue of lying (Kant 1991: 116–25). The political moralist acts on the principles that we now know as 'all politics is local', in that success implies truck and trade with local notables. The political moralist complies with the conventional ways of the world, including lying and dishonesty as reliable means to the desirable ends of political success. By contrast, the moral politician adopts Kant's cosmopolitan principles associated with the famous categorical imperative of universal right, based on a model of public integrity that treats all citizens as autonomous legislators in their own right. The ethical obligation that flows from Kant's approach is that public integrity requires, above all else, government commitment to 'the transcendental principle of publicness': in other words, transparent government. Political warfare will begin to cease within and across nations only with the adoption of Kant's modernised republicanism with its fences against the 'despicable tricks' of 'world-wise politicians' with their deceptive 'skill in being all things to all men' (Kant 1991: 125–27).

Where does all of this leave us when examining the public integrity of the fourth Howard government? My analysis shows that truthfulness is not intrinsic to democratic politics and that the requirement for truthfulness is an external constraint or imposition on democratic politics. Truthfulness is a requirement of external accountability, demanded of executive officials by those politicians (typically non-government politicians, particularly the official opposition) and public institutions (such as the state audit agency and the ombudsman) with distinctive ethical obligations of public scrutiny and accountability. Truthfulness does not come naturally to democratic politics. Democratic integrity demands that executive government comply with standards of truthfulness when responding to demands made by legitimate public agencies in the name of public accountability. Thus truthfulness features in democratic politics as a responsive quality extracted from government when called on to account publicly for their conduct. Truth runs against the grain of democratic, perhaps all, politics. Public integrity therefore requires the imposition of external checks to test government claims against the truth as revealed in government practices (Uhr 1998a: 52–55).

Honesty

Often confused with truthfulness, honesty refers to a separate dimension of integrity (see e.g. Greene & Shugarman 1997). Usually, *truthfulness* becomes an issue of individual ministerial responsibility investigated through accountability mechanisms explicitly established to test the credibility of a suspect minister or ministers or high officials. Typically, *honesty* becomes a general issue of collective ministerial responsibility, investigated at large by a loose coalition of public scrutineers, including many self-appointed scrutineers in the media and civil society. We can make an important distinction: if truthfulness relates closely to the ethics of accountability, then honesty relates closely to the ethics of responsibility. By 'the ethics of responsibility', I mean the ethical standards expected of government when exercising its proactive agenda of policy and program initiative. The concept of 'responsible government' refers to the necessity for initiative and discretion in executive government: that is, executive government that takes responsibility for making decisions about policy and program priorities. Responsible government means that executive officials are expected to exercise their judgment about the relative priority of their governing responsibilities (Uhr 2005: 119–37).

Where does the standard of honesty fit into this picture? Honesty refers to the quality of responsible judgment that governments are expected to exercise when governing. Honesty deals with the *proactive* side of government; accountability deals with the *reactive* world of government. Honesty supplements 'truthfulness' as a measure of public integrity: where truthfulness highlights the ethics of full disclosure under external scrutiny (by the opposition, by dedicated accountability agencies, by the courts or by media), honesty highlights the ethics of fair play and decency in evidence in the proactive world of responsible discretion required of executive government.

A good example from the fourth Howard government about how honesty played out relates government to the 2007 Haneef affair involving the allegations of terrorism levelled against Dr Mohamed Haneef, the Indian medical doctor who lost his work permit and immigration status (Waterford 2007a). The legal processes of accountability effectively tested the alleged truths conveyed in the government charges, revealing important gaps between the government prosecution and the truth of Haneef's conduct. The case is a good one because it also reveals a disturbing story about government dishonesty. Former prime ministers Whitlam and Fraser used this incident to urge all political parties to comply with stricter standards of ministerial responsibility, even calling for the resignation of Immigration Minister Kevin Andrews (Maley 2007). While the courts and the legal process were sufficient to hold the government accountable for its lack of truthfulness, it took a vigorous media to ferret out the deeper dishonesty revealed in, for example, the minister's justifications for the suspension of Haneef's work visa, and the Attorney-General's justifications for bringing the case in the first place. The standard of dishonesty captures important aspects of defective government integrity that the standard of truthfulness, and its associated accountability agencies, cannot be expected to capture.

Democratic integrity works along both dimensions of democratic government, with the *accountability dimension* dealing with the 'reporting back' by rulers to the ruled; and the *responsibility dimension* dealing with the delegation and exercise of powers by those given governing responsibilities. Democratic integrity refers to the strength of the ethic of accountability as measured by the truthfulness of those providing public accounts, and the strength of the ethic of responsibility as measured by the honesty of those exercising the responsibilities of rule. The truth standard is breached if one holds back or fails to disclose relevant knowledge; truth thus lends itself to a strict-compliance regime of integrity. Honesty brings with it a more subtle and perhaps more tolerant standard. Dishonest conduct captures forms of deceit and manipulation that might be unrelated to outright lying.

In my framework, dishonest government involves the irresponsible use of government powers and this standard has less of a narrow legal character than the truthfulness standard. Both standards, of course, call for careful political judgment about the conduct of government. The honesty standard is more permissive by giving the government considerable latitude to exercise its discretion and make responsible use of the powers of government, as illustrated by the broad discretionary power on display by the immigration minister in the Haneef case. Whether a government can defend its claims to responsibility depends on its ability to maintain public confidence, which explains why governments spend so much time and energy in persuading the public about the merits of government action: including, one must note, the use of suspect means to promote or advance desirable ends, as with so many domestic episodes in the Howard government's 'war on terror' (Walter & Strangio 2007).

With a lineage as ancient as 'truth', the standard of honesty can be traced back to classical Roman concepts of *honour* and related concepts of decency and fair-dealing. Honesty in government refers to that dimension of public integrity associated with the capacity of public officials for 'being genuine': acting as they should when exercising the powers of government, and therefore complying with their obligations as public servants separate and distinct from their private or partisan interests. If honesty is taken in the conventional sense to mean 'telling the honest truth', then we can expect a repeat of the tensions seen in the place of truth in democratic integrity. But if honesty is taken, as I think it should, to refer to 'acting the honest part' in government, then we begin to see that the standard of honesty has more to do with fulfilling a public role of 'honest broker' rather than complying with abstract standards of full and total truthfulness or transparency or disclosure.

Accountability

Accountability is the testing ground for both truth and honesty (Cohen 2006). For our purposes, we can investigate the ways that various accountability processes have dealt with debates over the truth and honesty of the fourth Howard government. I argue that each of these two integrity standards lends itself to a distinctive form of accountability: truth to narrowly focused legal-institutional processes; and honesty to loosely focused media-political processes. Failures of truthfulness are exposed through disciplined cross-examination before legal and administrative judges; failures of honesty are exposed through the intensity of unwanted scrutiny and publicity. But precisely because the fate of governments depends on sustained public confidence, all governments have an interest in curbing the potential power of accountability agencies. This interest opens up another line of investigation into the ways that the Howard government has managed institutions of accountability to protect vulnerable interests of the government threatened by opponents.

My approach to public integrity reveals the dual expectations of accountability. Truthfulness and honesty are two of the core standards of democratic integrity, each tested through distinctive processes of accountability. Truthfulness tends to be tested reactively, as for example when government officials are called to account for suspect things they have done. An outstanding example under Howard's fourth government is the Cole inquiry with the rare example of a Prime Minister in the witness box. This mode of accountability displays the strengths and limitations of a legalistic model of accountability. By contrast, honesty tends to be tested proactively, often by the media hunting for scalps on the merest of hints of wrongdoing, as for example when government officials are scrutinised for suspect things they have said or are saying, even though there might not yet be sufficient evidence to marshal legalistic forms of accountability. The political party in opposition tends to favour this mode of accountability because success depends more on securing 'moral convictions' relating to abuse of public trust rather than 'legal convictions' relating to criminal offences. The two modes of accountability often merge. A classic example is when the opposition moves against government ministers for misleading parliament. The rationale for the opposition is not really that ministers have lied (that is, broken the rules) but that ministers have acted in ways that suggest a larger pattern of conduct that is dishonest (that is, broken the trust).

One demanding test of a government's accountability relates to its management of the public account. Two examples of this quite fundamental issue of public accountability increasingly haunted the fourth Howard government. The first example related to the role of the budget bureaucracy in bringing a degree of internal accountability to ministerial decision-making. A flashpoint was the role of Treasury head Dr Ken Henry as a manager of government accountability (Gourley 2007). Frequently over the final months of the fourth Howard government, critics of the government taunted ministers by asking whether this or that policy expenditure initiative, such as the 2007 drought package or the 2007 Northern Territory intervention, had passed 'the Ken Henry test', implying that responsible policy-making required public evidence of prior Treasury approval. Flattering as this might be to professional public servants, Howard government ministers including Treasurer Peter Costello responded that the elected government was delegated with the responsibilities of office and also with the primary burden of public accountability. Readers of Dr Henry's publicly available speeches could see what some of the critics were getting at: that any government can be tempted to use its powers of the purse in less than fully responsible ways and, further, tempted to ease some of their accountability obligations, especially over public expenditure (see e.g. Henry 2007).

A second example deals with relationships between the Howard government and the Reserve Bank of Australia (RBA). The government went to the 2004 election with promises that it would keep interests rate 'low'. By the time of the 2007 election, the official interest rate had been increased six times by the RBA, including a few weeks before the election. In public debate, the issue became that of the government's accountability for this indicator of alleged economic mismanagement. The government found itself in an accountability dilemma: when rates remained low, the government claimed that it bore primary responsibility for good economic performance because of its commitment to 'taking the hard decisions' (but of course not on interest rates) and so should be rewarded with re-election through the processes of electoral accountability. But as interests rates rose, the government distanced itself from this aspect of accountability by claiming that the rightly independent RBA was responsible for taking the decisions to increase the official rate, which was unwarranted (because electorally unwelcome) in the eyes of the government. So far, so good: but when during the 2007 election campaign Prime Minister Howard said 'sorry' for the final rate increase, critics took this not simply as an acknowledgment of the public pain at rising interest rates. Howard denied that saying 'sorry' amounted to an apology: that would be to concede that the government was accountable for decisions over interest rates. But the 'sorry' did suggest that Howard was reluctantly conceding that the RBA was holding the government accountable for its expansive election-year public expenditure. This accountability dilemma repeated the theme of the Treasury story about the Howard government's uneasiness with the core institutions of financial accountability.

I mentioned at the outset that critics must take into account the institutional setting experienced by Australian governments, which in some ways might raise our expectations of their decency and in other ways might excuse or at least explain their lapses from decency. Time now for an example relating to *political* rather than *financial* accountability. The Howard government's remarkable Senate majority won at the 2004 election paved the way for a fundamental alteration of the institutional management of government accountability. The standard default position since the early 1980s is that elected governments do not win Senate majorities. Small as this limitation on power might seem, it helps explain some of the limited ambition of many Australian national governments, which knew that they would never have the total parliamentary power required to transform Australian politics and public policy. Federalism sits in the background of the Senate scene and provides much of the institutional logic behind the system of Australian governance. But this same set of 'veto powers' wielded by non-government interests in either the Senate or by state governments also helps explain another limitation: the limited capacity for irresponsible government decision-making. Under standard conditions, not experienced for much of the fourth Howard government, Australian national governments cannot be as good or as bad as their inclinations might suggest (Uhr 2005; Walter & Strangio 2007).

The default position of limited parliamentary power might soon return. But the window of rare opportunity of total parliamentary power won by the Howard government at the 2004 election redrew the map of public accountability. Truth and honesty faced their severest tests: truth found itself untested by the scrutiny of non-government mechanisms of parliamentary accountability; and honesty found itself tested by the temptations to use, or to misuse or even to abuse, the new parliamentary powers with irresponsible ease. To repeat earlier qualifications: not all commentators are convinced that the fourth Howard government failed the fundamental tests of truth and honesty (Kelly 2005, 2006). But many commentators provide credible evidence that is not easily rebutted. For example, the case for the Howard government's evasion of parliamentary accountability is made by Harry Evans (Evans 2006, 2007). The case about the Howard government's dishonest misuse and abuse of its governing responsibilities is made with vigour by Gaita (2007) and is also canvassed in chapter 5 in this volume.

Conclusion

I have argued that the fourth Howard government strayed too far from desirable standards of truth, honesty and accountability. But I have also argued that Australian political debate over issues of public integrity itself lacks a degree of analytical integrity. I have used Tony Abbott's defence of the Howard government as a useful way of opening up the governance narrative preferred by Howard ministers. Like many of the Howard critics, I do not find Abbott's advocacy convincing. Unlike many of those critics, however, I find Abbott's advocacy useful in forcing us to rethink the standards of public integrity relevant to debates over truth, honesty and accountability in democratic government. The important lesson is that critics, no less than governments, must measure up to standards of integrity, and that we analysts and commentators still have some learning to do in relation to the nature of those standards.

Public judgments about a government's truth, honesty and accountability all turn on access to relevant information, particularly government information. The non-government organisation known as Australia's Right to Know drove home the policy limitations on freedom of information in Australia in a major report released during the 2007 election campaign (Moss 2007). Described as 'an independent audit of the state of free speech in Australia', this report identified significant structural defects in the access-to-information regime. For example, the report found 'mounting evidence that the lure of political advantage increasingly trumps principles of democratic transparency when governments decide to withhold or bias the release of information' (Moss 2007; Mulgan 2007: 581–83). This situation relates not only to ministerial control over the bureaucracy but also to the ministry's own management of media conferences, which have 'become worse under the Howard Government ' (Moss 2007: ii; Walter & Strangio 2007: 61–62). And what of those government employees attempting to use 'public-interest disclosures' to get around rigidities in the access system? The report singled out the commonwealth government for its 'dogged refusal to provide substantial legislative protections to whistleblowers' (Moss 2007 iv; Waterford 2007b). Without access to government information, accountability agencies have to take the government on trust, which has steadily proven to be a very weak accountability option.

What of the view from within government, again taking Tony Abbott as our representative voice? In the months leading up to the 2007 election, Abbott spoke about the disconnect between what he termed 'good government' under Howard and the increasingly disenchanted electorate (Abbott 2007). He offered this trend as one provocative defence of the Howard government: that under its reign Morgan poll ratings for politicians' ethics and honesty had doubled, from a low base of 9 per cent to nearly 20 per cent. The implication was that the former Hawke and Keating governments had driven down public respect for the ethics of politicians, and that the Howard government had restored honour to what he interestingly termed 'the vocation of politics'. Of course, Abbott's political opponents could just as easily explain this rise in ratings by reference to the steady spread of Labor governments across the federation (see Bean & Denemark 2007). But Abbott seemed to sense a low ceiling in public respect for political ethics. Contrasting the hard grind of ministerial life with 'the Truman Show confections' of Rudd's early leadership, Abbott recorded his dismay at 'the popular impression that most politicians are essentially fakes'. This is a revealing line from a governing minister operating in a political culture that has historically deferred to authority and taken the government's own 'terms of trust' as agreeable terms on which to do business (Uhr 2005: 27–31; Donovan et al. 2007).

Admittedly, even political fakes pay attention to the appearance of ethics. Trying to overcome sustained public cynicism about politics, Abbott reiterated his theme of the moral case for the Howard government reflecting that government's history of 'making hard choices between unpalatable alternatives' (Abbott 2007). A trustworthy government is not necessarily one that professes its purity or harps on its honesty; instead, it is one that uses public power for worthy public ends, even if this means adapting to changing circumstances rather than adhering to outmoded promises. Over many elections, Australian voters seemed to have understood this nice ethical distinction between decent and dogmatic government. But in the approach of the 2007 election, Abbott drew attention to the spreading public distrust of politics generally by opinion leaders in civil society. To Abbott, what was wrong with this impression was 'the tendency to assume the moral equivalence of both sides of politics without any careful study of the evidence' (Abbott 2007).

In this chapter, I have tried to do as Abbott suggests and carefully study the evidence, especially the evidence about appropriate standards of ethics and integrity in Australian politics. Of course, Australian politics are not so dissimilar from politics in other parliamentary democracies and we can learn much from the experience of political analysts in many other comparable countries. For instance, Greene and Shugarman provide a valuable Canadian model of how to investigate and also promote public integrity (Greene & Shugarman 1997). By comparison, Australian political analysis is rudimentary in much of its investigation of public integrity. This chapter has tried to illustrate a more demanding approach that blends appropriate political theory with case analysis. The purpose here has not been limited to assessing the integrity of the Howard government. The larger purpose has been to reshape conventional models of public integrity in light of neglected aspects of democratic theory (Uhr 1998a, 1998b). The fact that my examination rests on allegations of clever political deception by the Howard government is not the most important matter, when we see that these allegations stimulate us to step outside the conventional debate and try to identify more robust criteria for evaluating democratic integrity.

References

Abbott, T (Minister for Health and Ageing) (2004) The moral case for the Howard government, Speech to Young Liberals, 23 January, at <www.tonyabbott.com.au/news/article>.

—— (2007) The reflections of voters on politicians and vice versa, Speech to Sydney Institute, 5 June, at <www.tonyabbott.com.au/news/article>.

Bean, C & Denemark, D (2007) Citizenship, participation, efficacy and trust. In S Wilson, G Meagher, R Gibson, D Denemark & M Western (eds) *Australian Social Attitudes: Citizenship, Work and Aspirations*, UNSW Press, Sydney: 58–80.

Cohen, S (2006) Management ethics, accountability and responsibility. In SR Clegg & C Rhodes (eds) *Management Ethics: Contemporary Contexts*, Routledge, London: 113–34.

Dobel, J (1999) *Public Integrity*, Johns Hopkins University Press, Baltimore.

Donovan, T, Denemark, D & Bowler (2007) Trust, citizenship and participation: Australia in comparative perspective. In S Wilson, G Meagher, R Gibson, D Denemark & M Western (eds) *Australian Social Attitudes: Citizenship, Work and Aspirations*, UNSW Press, Sydney: 81–106.

Evans, H (2006) The government majority in the Senate, at <www.aph.gov.au/Senate/pubs/evans>.

—— (2007) Getup! seminar on the Senate, at < www.aph.gov.au/Senate/pubs/evans>.

Gaita, R (2004 Breach of trust: Truth, morality and politics, *Quarterly Essay*, 16, 1–67.

—— (2007) Sorry state of affairs, *The Australian Literary Review*, November.

Gourley, P (2007) Caution, election ahead, *Public Service Informant,* June.

Greene, I & Shugarman, D (1997) *Honest Politics: Seeking Integrity in Canadian Public Life*, Lorimer, Toronto.

Henry, K (2007) Secretary's speech to staff, 17 March, at <www.treasury.gov.au>.

Hobbes, T (1968) *Leviathan*, ed. CB Macpherson, Penguin Books, Harmondsworth [first published 1657].

Kant, E (1991) *Political Writings*, ed. H Reiss), 2nd edn, Cambridge University Press, Cambridge.

Kelly, P (2005) Breach of trust, *Quarterly Essay*, 17: 86–90.

—— (2006) Re-thinking Australian governance: The Howard legacy, *Australian Journal of Public Administration*, 65(1): 7–24.

—— (2007) The lucky country (but not why you think), *The Australian Literary Review*, October.

Machiavelli, N (1998) *The Prince*, trans. HC Mansfield, University of Chicago Press, Chicago [first published 1513].

Maley, M (2007) Ex-PMs urge Andrews resignation, *Australian*, 12 November.

Montefiore, A & Vines, D (eds) (1999) *Integrity in the Public and Private Domains*, Routledge, London.

Moss, I (2007) *Report of the independent audit into the state of free speech in Australia*, Australia's Right to Know, at <www.abc.net.au/news/opinion/documents/files/20071105_righttoknow.pdf>.

Mulgan, R (2007) Truth in government and the politicization of public service advice, *Public Administration*, 85(3): 569–86.

Saint-Martin, D & Thompson, F (eds) (2006) *Public Ethics and Governance*, Elsevier, Amsterdam.

Uhr, J (1998a) Democracy and the ethics of representation. In N Preston & C Sampford

with C-A Bois (eds) *Ethics and Political Practice*, Routledge, London: 11–24.
—— (1998b) *Deliberative Democracy in Australia: the Changing Place of Parliament*, Cambridge University Press, Cambridge.
—— (2002) What's so responsible about responsible government? In D Burchell & A Leigh (eds) *The Prince's New Clothes: Why do Australians Dislike their Politicians?*, UNSW Press, Sydney: 155–66.
—— (2005) *Terms of Trust: Arguments Over Ethics in Australian Government*, UNSW Press, Sydney.
—— (2006) Professional ethics for politicians? In D Saint-Martin & F Thompson (eds) *Public Ethics and Governance*, Elsevier, Amsterdam: 207–25.
Walter, J & Strangio, P (2007) *No, Prime Minister: Reclaiming Politics from Leaders*, UNSW Press, Sydney.
Waterford, J (2007a) The Haneef affair, *Public Sector Informant*, August.
—— (2007b) Juries to look into leaks – and leakages, *Public Service Informant*, November.

PART II
Policy issues

8
The economy

Anne Garnett and Phil Lewis

John Howard's fourth government has been a period of exceptional economic growth and prosperity. During this term over 855 000 net new jobs were created, unemployment, at just over 4 per cent, hit the lowest rate since 1975, while inflation largely remained within the Reserve Bank of Australia's target rate of 2–3 per cent (ABS 2007a; RBA 2007a). The Howard government stands among the few governments in the world with budget surpluses and among the very few with no net government debt, having inherited a $96 billion debt with annual interest repayments of close to $8 billion when it first came to office in 1996 (Australian Treasury 1998). The total debt was repaid during its fourth term, with the commonwealth now a net lender to the financial sector.

Policy and growth

The fourth term has, in many economic policy areas, been largely a continuation of the policies that were introduced by the Howard government in its previous three terms. Perhaps the most publicised new policy has involved its labour market reforms, and in particular, the Work Choices legislation. Howard's fourth term has also seen taxation reform together with significant changes to Australia's superannuation system. However, the 16 years of continuous economic growth that the Australian economy has achieved, even during times when other countries' economies experienced recessions, span not just the period of office of the Howard government but also the latter years of the Keating government. This suggests that the economic reform process carried out during Howard's term in office can be thought of as a mix of new policy together with a continuation of the reform processes which commenced under previous ALP governments.

There is a nagging question as to what extent Australia's economic success is due to good policy or good luck! For example, was the prosperity achieved under Howard's governments due to good economic policy, or due to growth in the world economy, particularly development in China and India and the corresponding minerals and energy boom in Australia? This is a difficult question to answer but several pieces of evidence suggest that external factors may not have been as important as some commentators suggest. For instance, the Australian economy was more or less untouched by the 'Asian financial crisis' of 1996–97 and the recession in the United States (US) in 2001. During the fourth Howard government, the US also experienced economic slowdown, rising unemployment and financial turmoil due to the crippling bad debts resulting from the meltdown of the subprime mortgage market. Despite these factors, the Australian economy continued to grow, with the rate of economic growth rising and unemployment falling during the most recent US slowdown.

The Australian economy has been growing continuously for over 16 years whereas the mining boom has only been running for five years (ABS 2007b). Also, in the June quarter of 2007, exports grew at 2 per cent on an annual basis, which is only half the rate of growth of the economy as a whole. Simulation modelling of the Australian economy by the Melbourne Institute of Applied Economic and Social Research indicates that, although the initial impact of the change in terms of trade (prices received for exports relative to prices paid for imports) had a dramatic positive effect on real gross domestic product (GDP), the economy would have achieved the same rate of growth by 2006 without the improved terms of trade, and the rate of inflation would have been 0.5 per cent lower that it was (Lim et al. 2007). Therefore the evidence indicates that good economic management and economic reform has been paramount to the economic prosperity achieved, with some good luck thrown in for good measure!

The Howard government has also continued the microeconomic reform policies which began in the 1980s with some reduction in the rates of tariffs on imported goods and the deregulation of the financial sector. The release of the National Competition Policy Report (Hilmer et al. 1993), commissioned by the former Labor government, provided the framework for many of

Australia participates in China's economic growth
Courtesy of Peter Nicholson, *The Australian*, 31 December 2005

the microeconomic reforms that the Howard government implemented. Recommended microeconomic reform policies included deregulation, continued tariff reduction, the reform or privatisation of public monopolies, reducing anti-competitive behaviour of firms, and working with the states and territories to enhance free market competition. Economists see the increased productivity levels of the second half of the 1990s and early 2000s as resulting from microeconomic reform and the adoption of new technology.

However, growth in productivity slowed considerably during the fourth term of the Howard government. Many areas of Australia's infrastructure were showing signs of much needed reform to enable the continuation of productivity growth and economic prosperity. Rail and road transport, ports, broadband speed, water and energy emerged as needing quite urgent reform. But the ability of the Howard government to address infrastructure problems has been hindered by the lack of a working relationship between state and commonwealth governments.

The labour market

Media attention and commentary has strongly focused on the labour market policies of the fourth Howard government. The most notable and controversial labour market policy has been the introduction of Work Choices under the

Workplace Relations Amendment (Work Choices) Act 2005, which enacted significant changes to the workplace relations system. These changes involved further deregulation of the labour market, which began under the Keating government in 1991, and are discussed in chapter 10.

Although there is not universal acceptance of the role of industrial relations reform, the majority of economists and commentators point to increased labour market flexibility as being a key element in Australia's economic success. Coupled with the industrial relations reform, the Howard government also introduced new measures to make it more difficult for social security recipients to receive benefits without satisfying a 'work test'. For instance, under the Welfare to Work policy, sole parents with the youngest child over eight years of age (originally over six years of age) must now accept job offers and work a minimum of 15 hours per week in order to continue receiving their Newstart Allowance. This measure was estimated to have put over 230 000 people back into the workforce, and yet the unemployment rate continued to drop.

The rapid growth in employment during Howard's fourth term perhaps has not received the attention it deserved. The changing structure of the economy, new technology, and changes in consumer demand mean that in the normal workings of the labour market, thousands of jobs become redundant each year but thousands more are created in new businesses or industries. However, between November 2004 and October 2007, the creation of new jobs far outstripped the loss of 'old' jobs. The net growth in jobs during this period was around 855 000, or an annual growth rate of just over 3 per cent. This compares to 1 441 700 or an annual jobs growth rate of around 2 per cent for the first, second and third terms of the Howard government as a whole. The rate of unemployment in 2007 had fallen to 4.2 per cent – a 32-year low (ABS 2007a).[1] John Howard claimed this success for his government, stating that 'Jobs have become our holy grail' (Hartcher & Coorey 2007).

There is evidence of growing labour market participation, with the participation rate – those of the population aged between 15 and 65 years of age who are working or looking for work – at 63.7 per cent at the commencement of the Howard government in 1996, at 63.3 per cent at the start of Howard's fourth term, and rising to 65 per cent by October 2007 (ABS 2007a).

In examining the labour market during Howard's fourth term, one of the biggest issues facing the Australian economy was *shortages* of labour. Shortages arose in both the private and public sectors, ranging from skilled to unskilled labour. Professions affected included medical practitioners, nurses, school teachers, pilots, economists, trades and engineers, through to agricultural workers and shop assistants. As an economy nears full-employment, bottlenecks in certain parts of the economy are expected, as economic growth and structural change are not evenly spread throughout the economy, and some industries can adjust quicker than others. One attempt to alleviate the shortages was to increase the intake of migrants and temporary residents. In 2006 the net inflow of new migrants was 134 600, up 23 per cent from the first Howard government period and there was a net addition of over 200 000 long-stay arrivals over departures (ABS 2007d).

Budgets and debt

The Howard government has operated with budget surpluses since 1997–98 in every year except one (2001–02), with surpluses reaching around 1 per cent of GDP during its fourth term (Australian Treasury 2007); see figure 8.1. The record economic growth led to huge windfalls in receipts from company income tax. Falls in unemployment, jobs growth and wages growth have greatly increased personal income tax receipts. While government expenditure as a proportion of GDP has been fairly stable, although rising slightly, this expenditure pattern has to be seen in the context of a switch from public provision of services to private provision.

Figure 8.1   Commonwealth government budget – surpluses and deficits, 1976–77 to 2007–08

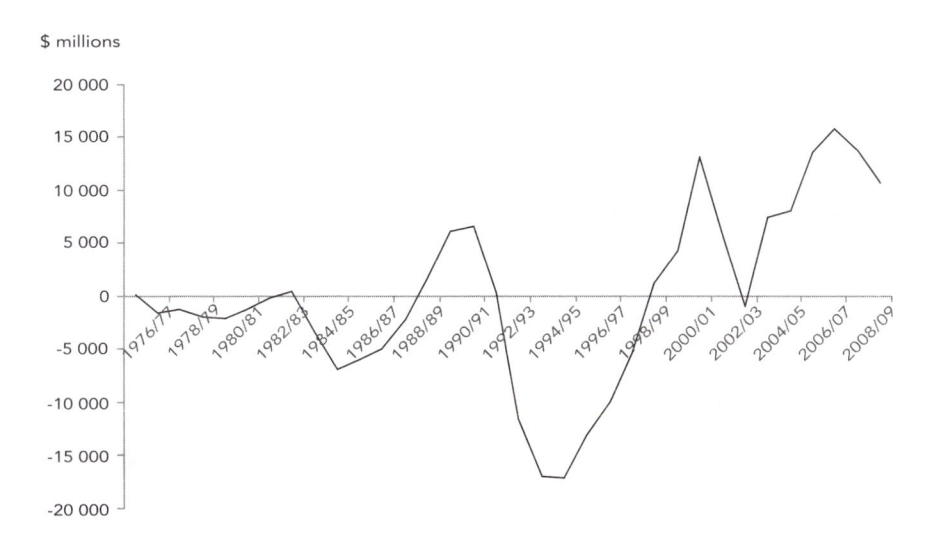

SOURCE Australian Treasury 2007.

Howard's fourth government also saw the historic paying-off of commonwealth debt, with net debt levels reaching zero in 2005–06. It was the first time since 1976 that a commonwealth government has not had debt, achieved at a time when state and territory governments continued to run up substantial debt. The release of the government from interest repayments has meant that the net drain on the budget has been eliminated and Australia is now one of the very few countries in the world with a government that has net savings.

The balanced budget and net saving position enabled the government to establish specific-purpose funds for superannuation. The Future Fund was established by legislation to help future Australian governments meet the cost of public sector superannuation liabilities. In 2007, this liability was $103 billion and is estimated to rise to $148 billion by the year 2020 – also a time when the ageing of the population may see lower tax revenues. The Future Fund began with a balance of $16 billion, and by late 2007 contained approximately $60 billion, including 2.1 billion Telstra shares (Future Fund 2007) (see chapter 4 for details of the sale of Telstra). The fund is under the management of the Chicago-based Northern Trust Corporation. The appointment of a foreign-based financial institution was, at the time, criticised by the media and some Australian financial institutions.

Accumulating budget surpluses into the Future Fund will reduce the need for tax revenue in the future which will allow the allocation of future revenues to priority areas. This tactic makes sense if there will be relatively fewer taxpayers in the future, as will be the case if the scenario of an ageing population materialises. The amounts directed into the Future Fund now are not available for government spending or tax reductions – in essence, the Future Fund means foregoing consumption now for consumption in the future. Thus, the standard of living of the current generation of taxpayers is reduced. One aspect of redirecting the surpluses into the Future Fund is that the current generation of taxpayers will face a double burden in that they will finance both the current and future generations of public service superannuants.

The Future Fund poses an interesting issue for any future government as it has been accumulating at a fast rate, with returns to investment at record high levels. With a clear government commitment to budget surpluses by both major political parties, the question becomes: what will the government do with the surpluses which, at current levels of accumulation, will exceed superannuation requirements?

A second fund was established during the fourth term of the Howard government, with some of the proceeds from budget surpluses used to provide investment returns for higher education institutions. The Higher Education Endowment Fund (HEEF) was announced in the 2006–07 Budget with an initial investment of $5 billion, and an additional $1 billion added in August 2007 (DEST 2007). The dividends from HEEF can be used by universities and other higher education institutions for infrastructure and research.

Taxation reform

Perhaps the biggest reform, together with industrial relations, carried out by the Howard government was in the area of taxation (Daly 2005). While the introduction of the goods and services tax (GST) was the main reform of Howard's second term (July 2000), the third and fourth terms have seen some notable further changes to income tax, capital gains tax and superannuation contributions. Table 8.1 shows the personal income tax rates applicable in 2007–08 compared to 2003–04. The marginal and average tax rates have been reduced for all income groups but the biggest impacts have been for those in the highest income bracket, with the top marginal rate dropping from 47 per cent to 45 per cent and the top threshold lifted from $62 500 to $150 000.

Table 8.1   Tax scales, 2003–04, 2007–08

	2003–04		2007–08
Taxable income	Tax payable	Taxable income	Tax payable
$0–6 000	Nil	$0–6 000	Nil
$6 001–21 600	17c for each $1 over $6 000	$6 001–30 000	15c for each $1 over $6 000
$21 601–52 000	$2 652 plus 30c for each $1 over $21 600	$30 001–75 000	$3 600 plus 30c for each $1 over $30 000
$52 001–62 500	$11 772 plus 42c for each $1 over $52 000	$75 001–150 000	$17 100 plus 40c for each $1 over $75 000
Over $62 500	$16 182 plus 47c for each $1 over $62 500	Over $150 000	$47 100 plus 45c for each $1 over $150 000

SOURCES Australian Government 2004; ATO 2007.

In the 2004–05 federal budget, Treasurer Peter Costello announced the 'baby bonus', a lump sum payment of $3000 to the parents, receivable after the birth of each child. It has since risen from $3000 on commencement on 1 July 2004 to $4000 in 2005 and to $5000 on 1 July 2008, and is indexed to inflation, as measured by the Consumer Price Index (CPI). With 259 800 registered births in Australia in 2005, that amounted to eligible payments of around $780 million. The Treasurer urged Australian couples to have babies, saying: 'you should have, if you can ... one for your husband and one for your wife and one for the country' (Costello 2004). In the same budget there were other significant increases in benefits to families with children as well as tax cuts for all Australians. As more than one commentator has pointed out, there has been an incredible degree of giving with one hand and taking away with the other with inevitable administrative cost and waste. The biggest single item of government expenditure is on social welfare – approximately 41 per cent in 2007 – and the majority of the recipients are middle-income households due to the generosity of family payments. In 2007, even families with $100 000 in income were eligible for child support. In effect, what the Howard government has built up is a system of massive transfers from middle-income taxpayers back to middle-income consumers. It might well have been more efficient to let these middle-class households keep the money instead of paying extra tax.

In 2007, during the election campaign, further planned personal income tax cuts of $34 billion over five years were promised by the Howard government and matched by the ALP, with the ALP firmly in its policy-copying 'me too' mode. Peter Costello claimed that the ALP leader, Kevin Rudd, had copied 91.5 per cent of the coalition's tax policy, stating that: 'if he'd have brought his exam paper in after copying 91.5 per cent of the answers from the student sitting next to him, he would have got an F for fail' (Costello 2007).

The result of policy-matching has meant that the Howard government has effectively locked the Labor government into their tax reforms. The tax-free threshold would be raised to $14 000 in 2008–09, and raised each year after that until it reached $16 000, with the intention to raise it to $20 000 by 2012. The lowest tax level of 15 cents per dollar is to be raised to apply to incomes of up to $37 000, with all other tax thresholds to be increased, and the top tax rate of 45 cents per dollar ultimately lowered to 40 cents per dollar.

Significant changes were made to superannuation policy in 2007, referred to as 'Better Super'. The majority of workers can now withdraw their superannuation tax-free after they reach the age of 60. Most self-employed can claim their superannuation contributions as a tax deduction. In addition, semi-retired people can continue to work part-time, and use part of their tax-free superannuation to top up their pay.

The outcomes of the 'Better Super' reforms have been significant and varied. Since retirees with relatively low superannuation payouts paid little tax before, the new tax rules have led to a considerable redistribution of income of retirees toward the wealthier retirees. Part of the aim of the new superannuation arrangements was to encourage people to stay at work longer; however, the effect of the changes so far appear to be mixed. While there is now an incentive to stay at work longer and continue contributing to superannuation, there is also an incentive to leave work at age 60, since the tax-free treatment of superannuation after age 60 means that people can achieve their retirement income goal earlier than before.

Another interesting effect of the superannuation tax reform is that it has radically changed the distribution of assets in Australia as the generosity of the tax treatment of superannuation has meant that many tax avoidance schemes became largely redundant. A further effect is that despite the relatively generous tax treatment of capital gains, the new superannuation tax treatment has led to the selling off of some assets, particularly rental housing, as people sought to take advantage of the opportunity to add funds to their superannuation accounts and claim them back later tax-free. People were allowed to transfer up to $1 million into their superannuation accounts before 30 June 2007, after which an annual maximum of $150 000 of after-tax contributions could be made. The effect of this change in the rules was enormous. In the June quarter of 2007, $22.4 billion was transferred to superannuation accounts by individuals, compared to $7.4 billion in the June quarter of 2006. June 2007 was the first time in Australia that member contributions to superannuation exceeded employer contributions (APRA 2007).

There has been some criticism of the tax reform of the Howard government, much of it focused on the apparent generosity of the taxation cuts and income transfers to families. Even the Treasury Secretary, Ken Henry, cautioned the government about giving tax cuts in 2007 and beyond – at a time when consumer spending was considered to be running too high (Henry 2007). The role of fiscal policy is usually to dampen spending in times of economic boom. Instead, the Howard government's fourth term was characterised by income tax cuts and higher levels of government spending. However, it should be remembered that during the fourth term, strong economic growth led to a huge increase in tax receipts. The tax cuts were largely returning the unexpected tax take. Tax reform also addresses the problem of 'bracket creep', whereby higher nominal incomes push people into higher income tax brackets and they end up paying higher rates of tax, yet possibly have less real take-home pay than they did before they received their pay increases. Further, some evidence may be emerging that the money from the tax cuts of 2006 and 2007 may not all have been spent, but instead people are putting the funds into savings and mortgages.

Monetary policy

The control of aggregate demand and spending in the economy has increasingly fallen to the Reserve Bank of Australia (RBA), which implements monetary policy to control inflation. In the early 1990s, the RBA was given independence from the government in its use of monetary policy, an independence that has been demonstrated numerous times, the most notable of which was increasing the rate of interest during the election campaign in November 2007. The RBA uses monetary policy to target interest rates, which should in turn affect investment and consumer spending, and also the exchange rate and therefore exports and international income and investment flows.

Probably the most notable use of monetary policy under Howard's fourth term of government has been the rise in interest rates. The official cash rate, upon which other interest rates such as mortgage rates, personal loans and credit cards are based, was increased six times between 2004 and 2007, although by a relatively modest total rise of 1.5 per cent over the period (RBA 2007b). Prior to the rate rises, interest rates were at record lows, which the RBA indicated were expansionary, and would be increased over time. Such action is a normal application of monetary policy to contain inflation at a time of strong economic growth and in an economy nearing maximum capacity. The rate rises were not due to any economic weakness, as was perceived to exist in the high interest rate period of 1988–90, but were due to the strength of the economy, with the general perception that the Australian economy was in danger of overheating and cuts to aggregate demand were required.

However, much attention was drawn to the rate rises, as Howard's 2004 election campaign claimed that only the coalition could be trusted to keep interest rates low. Given the Howard government's previous claims, the rate rises gave the ALP considerable ammunition during the 2007 election campaign. Further, the huge increases in housing prices during the fourth term of the Howard government meant that small rate rises translated into significantly larger interest rate repayments for borrowers. With housing affordability at an all-time low due to very strong demand pushing up prices, together with shortages in rental accommodation, higher interest rates increased the burden for the 30 per cent of Australians with a mortgage and further reduced the ability of potential first home owners to enter the market.

These developments highlight one of the major problems with monetary policy. It is often accused of being a 'blunt instrument'. To contain inflation and reduce total spending, it affects some sectors of the economy and some groups of people more than others. It is effective in slowing down the rate of economic growth and spending, but those on higher incomes, those with savings earning interest, and those who have made windfall gains in the value of their assets due to the housing boom, increase their spending under higher interest rates. It is the marginal borrowers and lower income earners who are dealt the hardest blow. Similar unequal effects and burdens result from the appreciation of the exchange rate that higher interest rates cause. A higher exchange rate can significantly reduce export income for the agriculture, manufacturing and services sectors, as these sectors face substantial competition in international markets. However, it is likely that, given the current thirst for minerals and energy of China and India, mining sector products will be largely price-inelastic – that is, demand will still be strong even if the higher exchange rate means that the relative price of minerals and energy is higher.

International trade and the balance of payments

For decades Australia has operated with a current account deficit and a financial account surplus in its balance of payments. A current account deficit is normal for a small, developed economy with insufficient savings to fund the borrowing and investment activity of a healthy and growing economy. Much of the money borrowed for business investment and private expenditure is sourced from overseas, with the outflow of interest repayments on these borrowings always giving Australia a current account deficit in the balance of payments. Further, the sum of dividends and interest paid on overseas portfolio investment in Australia is also measured as a negative item (outflow of funds) in the current account; therefore the more profitable investment is in Australia, the greater the outflow of funds in the current account.

Between 2002 and 2007, the balance of trade component of the current account (the difference between export earnings and expenditure on imports) fell from a surplus of just over $1 billion in 2002 to a deficit of $12 billion, having reached a $22.6 billion deficit in 2005. Over the same period, the total deficit of the current account increased from $18.7 billion in 2002 to over $59 billion in 2007 (ABS 2007e). The biggest increase in the trade deficit occurred during the third term of the Howard government, largely because of huge expenditures on imports of machinery and equipment due to the mining boom, and due to the severe drought of 2002–03 that significantly reduced agricultural exports.

During Howard's fourth term, the balance of trade deficit fell by over $10 billion, with falls in agricultural exports in 2006 due to another severe drought more than offset by the huge increase in the export of minerals and energy. In this period, it was the large increase in the outflow of interest repayments and dividends that was the main factor in the growing current account deficit. The deficit reflected an increase in private sector borrowing, and the fact that Australia was seen as an excellent place for overseas investors – awash with cash – to put their investment funds. Between 2004 and 2007, the deficit in this net income component of the current account increased from $24.2 billion to $46.7 billion (ABS 2007e). Given that the factors underlying the growing current account deficit reflect economic strength rather than weakness, the deficit does not signal a growing problem with foreign indebtedness or structural problems with the economy.

Significant trade policy initiatives during Howard's fourth term were the free trade agreements signed with a number of countries. The one that received most attention is the US–Australia Free Trade Agreement which was signed in 2004 and took effect in 2005. It was widely condemned by many academics at the time (see, for example, Weiss et al. 2004), but what evidence there is after three years does not suggest much harm to Australia. Australian exports to the US during 2005–06 grew by 9.4 per cent, and imports grew even faster, by 12.9 per cent. The trade deficit with the US, which has persisted for decades and is structural, widened from $12 billion to $14.3 billion. However, these aggregate figures mask the advantages which have flown to Australia given the mining boom and the need for imported machinery and equipment. The US is the major producer of the heavy machinery used by the mining sector and, since mining companies no longer have to pay tariffs on this machinery from the US, they are better off. This cost saving has been greatly assisted by the appreciation of the Australian dollar against the US dollar.

The strength of the Australian dollar is always a two-edged sword. On the one hand, it helps to keep inflation down through reduced import prices, but on the other hand, it reduces Australia's export income, particularly for farmers experiencing years of drought, and also for the manufacturing and services sectors, who compete with many other countries on international markets. By early November 2007, the Australian dollar had reached around $US0.94 due in large part to falling interest rates in the US and rising interest rates in Australia.

Living standards and income distribution

During periods of strong economic growth, living standards generally rise, as unemployment falls and disposable incomes grow. However, the benefits of higher incomes and profits are not necessarily distributed evenly throughout society, and during a time of growth the income disparity between high- and low-income earners can widen: the rich get richer and the poor get richer but not by as much. Therefore the fourth term of the Howard government presents an interesting time to examine income distribution.

To measure changes in income distribution, the ABS uses 'equivalised disposable household income', which is disposable household income adjusted using an equivalence scale. Disposable income includes payments from all sources (including social security payments) minus income tax and minus the Medicare levy. For a sole-person household it is equal to disposable household income. For a household comprising more than one person, it is an indicator of the disposable household income that would need to be received by a sole-person household to enjoy the same level of economic well-being as the household in question.

According to the ABS, the real average equivalised disposable household income in 2005–06 was $644 per week, which was 10 per cent higher than in 2003–04, at $585 per week. However, when analysing income distribution, the average level does not indicate which income groups are becoming better off. When looking at the incomes of those households that are considered to have the lowest levels of economic well-being, the ABS looks at those people with household income between the bottom 10 per cent and bottom 30 per cent of incomes. In this category, incomes grew by 8 per cent, or $24 per week, between 2003–04 and 2005–06, which is the same percentage as for middle-income people, but lower than the 13 per cent growth in incomes for high-income earners. Table 8.2 provides some internationally recognised measures of income inequality based on measures of equivalised disposable household income.

The P20/P50 ratio is the ratio of the earnings of the lowest quintile of income recipients (the bottom 20 per cent) to median earnings. The ABS classification of 'low incomes' excludes the bottom 10 per cent due to

Table 8.2   Selected income distribution indicators: equivalised disposable household income

	1995–96	2000–01	2005–06
Ratio of incomes at top of selected income percentiles (P)			
P20/P50 ratio	0.61	0.59	0.60
P80/P50 ratio	1.57	1.56	1.54
P80/P20 ratio	2.58	2.63	2.55
Percentage share of total income received by persons according to income category			
Low income[a]	11.0	10.5	10.6
Middle income[b]	17.7	17.6	17.6
High income[c]	37.3	38.5	38.5
Gini coefficient	0.296	0.311	0.307

a Persons in the second and third income deciles
b Persons in the middle-income quintile
c Persons in the highest-income quintile

SOURCE ABS 2007c.

difficulties with unreported income. The P80/P20 ratio is the ratio of the highest 20 per cent of income recipients to that of the lowest 20 per cent of income recipients and so on. The Gini coefficient is a summary measure of inequality whereby the lower its value the higher the degree of inequality.

It appears that there has been no significant change in income inequality from the mid-1990s to 2005–06. This situation may seem at odds with the observed earnings inequality arising from labour markets where demand and wages for those with higher skills and training have grown at a faster rate than for those with lower skills (Lewis & Mahony 2007). The reason for unchanged distribution of income is the relative generosity of the Howard government with respect to welfare payments. Pensions (but not unemployment benefits) are index-linked to male average weekly ordinary time earnings and therefore grow with the general strength of the labour market. The continuing growth in employment, and reduction in unemployment, has meant many more people have moved from the unemployment benefit to paid work. Perhaps not so welcome is the observed movement of people from unemployment benefits to the more generous sole-parent and disability pensions (Lewis 2007). The Howard government has significantly increased payments to families, a move which has also benefited the low and middle-income earners. Therefore during the Howard government's terms, there is likely to have been an increase in *earnings* inequality (for example, increasing wage differentials), but not in overall *income* inequality, which includes transfer payments and other benefits.

Conclusion

The fourth term of the Howard government was a period of strong economic growth, unprecedented jobs growth and the lowest rate of unemployment in over 30 years. Equally noteworthy has been the capacity of the Australian economy to adjust to economic shocks without reductions in economic growth or rises in unemployment. Growth continued during the 2006–07 slowdown of the US economy, during the long drought, major stock market adjustments and oil price increases. The obvious resilience of the economy to both external and internal shocks is, however, not a result of the actions of Howard's government alone, but has its foundations in economic policy changes since the 1980s.

While the fourth term saw the continuation of policies from previous terms, and from previous Labor governments, there were some distinguishing policies including a renewed focus on labour market reform, taxation reform, and an increase in government spending and benefit payments. Commonwealth government debt was completely repaid during the fourth term, with the government becoming a net saver, and large yearly budget surpluses became the entrenched expectation from the public. In some areas, the Howard government has moved the economic policy of both major political parties further to the right of the political spectrum, with the ALP having promised the same taxation cuts and continued budget surpluses when in government. Yet, given the growth in income transfers to low- and middle-income earners, Howard has not moved government as far to the right as many of his supporters, including those in his own party, might like.

Note

1   This measure of the unemployment rate is the international standard definition used by the ABS and is not to be confused with the number of people receiving unemployment benefits, data collected by Centrelink.

References

ABS (Australian Bureau of Statistics) (2007a) *Labour Force, Australia, Detailed – Electronic Delivery*, cat. no. 6291.0.55.001, at <www.abs.gov.au>.
—— (2007b) *Australian National Accounts: National Income, Expenditure and Product*, cat. no. 5206.0, Canberra.
—— (2007c) *Household Income and Income Distribution*, cat no. 6523.0, Canberra.
—— (2007d) *Migration, Australia*, cat. no. 3412.0, Canberra.
—— (2007e) *Balance of Payments and International Investment Position, Australia*, cat. no. 5302.0, Canberra.
APRA (Australian Prudential Regulation Authority) (2007) *Statistics: Quarterly Superannuation Performance June 2007*, at <www.apra.gov.au/Statistics/upload/Quarterly-Superannuation-Performance-June-2007.pdf>.
ATO (Australian Taxation Office) (2007) Individual income tax rates, Residents, at <www.ato.gov.au/individuals/content.asp?doc=/content/12333.htm&mnu=5464&mfp=001/002
Australian Government (2004) Budget 2003–04, Budget Speech, at <www.budget.gov.au/2003-04/speech/html/speech.htm>.
Australian Treasury (1998) *1998–99 Commonwealth Budget*, Appendix 1 Public debt interest in 1998–99, at <www.budget.gov.au/1998-99/>.
—— (2007) *2007–08 Budget Overview*, Appendix G – Historical budget and net debt data, at <www.ato.gov.au/budget/2007-08/overview/html/overview_40.htm>.
Costello, P (Treasurer) (2004) Discussion during Budget night, May 2004, Transcript of interview with Ross Stevenson and John Burns, 3AW, 1 April, at <www.treasurer.gov.au/tsr/content/transcripts/2005/033.asp?pf=1>.
—— (2007) Interview statement, Australian Broadcasting Commission, Rudd unveils $2.3b education tax refund, 19 October, at <www.abc.net.au/news/stories/2007/10/19/2064412.htm>.
Daly, A (2005) Taxation policy. In C Aulich & R Wettenhall (eds) *Howard's Second and Third Governments: Australian Commonwealth Administration 1998–2004*, UNSW Press, Sydney: 208–23.
DEST (Department of Education, Science and Training) (2007) *Higher Education Endowment Fund*, at <www.heef.dest.gov.au>.
Future Fund (2007) About the Future Fund, at <www.futurefund.gov.au>.
Hartcher, P & Coorey, P (2007) Let the good times roll: PM, *Sydney Morning Herald*, 17 October.
Henry, K (2007) Secretary's speech to staff, 17 March, at <www.treasury.gov.au>.
Hilmer, F, Rayner, M & Taperell, G (1993) *National Competition Policy*, Report by the independent committee of inquiry, AGPS, Canberra.
Lewis, PET (2007) *The Impact of Minimum Wages: Some considerations for the Australian Fair Pay Commission in its second decision on the minimum wage*, Report to the Australian Fair Pay Commission.
Lewis, P & Mahony, G (2007) Aspirations for a knowledge economy - Lessons in the evolution of skills and structural change from Singapore, Ireland and Australia. In C Ammi (ed.) *Innovative Technology and Globalization,* Cambridge Scholars Press, Singapore: 247–77.
Lim, G, Chua, M, Chin, L & Tsiaplias, S (2007) Outlook for the Australian economy, Speech given at the Public Economics Forum, Melbourne Institute of Applied Economic and Social Research, Hyatt Hotel, Melbourne, Victoria.

RBA (Reserve Bank of Australia) (2007a) Statistics: Measure of Consumer Price Inflation, Table G01, at <www.rba.gov.au/Statistics/Bulletin/G01hist.xls>.
—— (2007b) Statistics: Cash rate target – Reserve Bank of Australia monetary policy changes, at <www.rba.gov.au/Statistics/cashrate_target.html>.
Weiss, L, Thurbon, E & Mathews, J (2004) *How to Kill a Country: Australia's Devastating Trade Deal with the United States*, Allen & Unwin, Sydney.

9
Rural policy issues

Linda Courtenay Botterill

The two previous books in this series which looked at the Howard government (Singleton 2000; Aulich & Wettenhall 2005) did not include a discussion of rural policy, an area of government activity that tends to attract little public scrutiny outside the rural policy community. However, during the fourth Howard government two high-profile matters drew attention to rural policy: the ongoing severe drought in much of the country and the involvement of AWB Limited in the 'oil-for-food' scandal. The 2002–07 drought was not the first severe drought in recent years but it was the first which had a major impact in urban areas. Increasing concern about the low levels of water in important urban water storages and the imposition of increasingly tough water restrictions in major cities moved the drought from a rural policy issue to a national policy concern. One of the consequences of this was the rise to prominence of water policy at commonwealth level. Interestingly, water policy has been handled independently of drought policy, possible reasons for which are discussed below (further discussion of water policy is included in chapter 12).

The involvement of AWB Limited in providing kickbacks to Saddam Hussein's regime in Iraq similarly moved the issue of the operation of the export monopoly for wheat from the confines of rural policy debate to nightly news stories in urban areas. In addition to this renewed urban interest in rural policy, the role of rural policy settings in sustaining the National Party as a force in Australian politics makes the inclusion of a discussion of rural

A drought?! But that only happens in the country!

Courtesy of Peter Nicholson, *The Australian*, 7 November 2006

policy issues in the present volume particularly timely. Although the term 'rural' can be interpreted broadly to include non-metropolitan and non-farm communities, it is used more narrowly in this chapter to cover agricultural industry policy and related policies aimed at farmers. The privatisation of Telstra, for example, which was of considerable concern outside metropolitan areas, is not addressed in this chapter but is covered in chapter 4.

As this is the first discussion of rural policy under the Howard government in this series, this chapter commences with a brief background section on agricultural policy-making in Australia. This is followed by an examination of the two major policy issues of the period 2004–07, the drought and the oil-for-food scandal, with the final section examining the role of rural policy in sustaining the National Party as a separate voice within the federal coalition.

Background

Historically, rural policy in Australia has developed incrementally with little change in direction when there has been a change of government. Policy development can be broadly divided into three phases: the pre-1960s approach based on government intervention and 'stabilisation'; the breakdown of the policy consensus and the development of more economically based policy; and, since the election of the first Howard government, a settling down and some re-emergence of agrarian tendencies.

In the 1930s and 1940s low farm incomes were of particular concern to governments and a 'bewildering array' (Throsby 1972: 13) of stabilisation schemes was introduced to support farm incomes through intervention in the prices of agricultural products. In the 1950s the focus of rural policy was on increasing production although the policy instruments employed to achieve this goal were largely unchanged from earlier schemes and remained focused on providing income security for farmers and stable prices for consumers. From the 1960s agricultural economists began to question the policy direction and advocate more free-market approaches to rural policy. The change of government in 1972 provided an opportunity for these alternative views to be heard. The cosy relationship between farm lobby groups and National Party ministers was broken and a more economically rational basis to policy emerged. The first step in this was the 1974 rural policy green paper (Harris et al. 1974) which expressed a preference for market-based approaches to resource allocation in agriculture with government intervention 'partly to improve the manner in which the market operates and partly to compensate some for its, at times, harsh consequences' (Harris et al. 1974: 195). The green paper was followed by the inclusion of agricultural policy in the ambit of the new Industries Assistance Commission. The latter was particularly important in motivating farm groups to be more professional in their policy advocacy and was an important trigger for the formation of the National Farmers' Federation (NFF) in 1979. By 1980 the agricultural policy community had undergone a significant metamorphosis with the emergence of a strong neo-liberal focus to NFF policies and a similar shift in the policies being developed by relevant government agencies (Botterill 2005). The election of the Hawke government in 1983 with its agenda of deregulation and internationalisation of the Australian economy saw a continued unwinding of agricultural support programs.

The incoming Howard government in 1996 inherited rural policy settings based on productivity improvement and the facilitation of structural adjustment in the farm sector. Although a number of the programs developed by its predecessors were dismantled, they were replaced with similar schemes with common objectives. Several generous packages were assembled to facilitate the adjustment process, such as the nearly $2 billion allocated to assist dairy farmers following deregulation of that industry, but the policy remained focused on supporting farmers through change rather than attempting to mask or reverse structural adjustment. Rural policy throughout the period was developed in an archetypal closed policy community made up of the Department of Agriculture, Fisheries and Forestry, the Australian Bureau of Agricultural and Resource Economics and the NFF, along with the NFF's commodity councils. Even when policy was apparently aimed at non-industry issues, such as the development of welfare programs for farmers, there is little evidence that advocates from outside the policy community, such as welfare lobby groups, were involved in the policy development process.

As has been the tradition with coalition governments in Australia, the agriculture portfolio under all four Howard governments was held by a member of the National Party. In the fourth term this was Warren Truss, who became the longest serving agriculture minister in 40 years, and, from July 2005, Peter McGauran. Although the policy direction was largely consistent with earlier approaches, there is evidence that agrarian sentiment began re-emerging and that agricultural policy was developed without reference to broader government economic policy direction. The increasing generosity of drought relief is a particular example of policy which, while rhetorically consistent with earlier positions, in implementation appeared to be drifting away from the direction evident across the rest of economic policy, for example in the differential treatment given to farmers in receipt of welfare.

The two big issues: drought and wheat

The two major policy issues which attracted public attention during the fourth Howard government were the ongoing severe drought and the oil-for-food scandal which culminated in the Cole Inquiry and foreshadowed changes to the export monopoly arrangements for wheat.

The latest severe drought to impact on agricultural production began in 2002. During 2007 there were hopeful signs that it was coming to an end with the breakdown of the 2006 El Niño event and above-average rainfall across southern Australia between January and April 2007, and near-average rainfall across much of the Murray-Darling Basin (Bureau of Meteorology 2007). By September, these hopes appeared to have been dashed with discussions turning to the possibility of large number of farmers leaving the land as the government announced enhanced exit grants in drought-affected areas (Howard 2007a). In April 2007, the government announced that it was delivering in excess of $2 million per day in drought assistance to farmers in the form of both business support and welfare payments (McGauran 2007a) and by September the total drought relief committed by the federal government was in excess of $3.5 billion (Morris & Crowe 2007). This support was provided within the framework of the National Drought Policy (NDP) which had been agreed by commonwealth and state ministers in 1992, following the removal of drought from the natural disaster relief arrangements.

The NDP is a good example of the continuity of rural policy from the previous Labor government through all four Howard administrations. The policy is based on the principle that drought is a normal part of the Australian farmer's operating environment and should be managed like any other risk facing the farm business. The policy is aimed at developing self-reliance and risk management skills and was intended to move away from ad hoc crisis responses to drought. While the rhetoric and overall policy principles of the NDP remained in evidence during the 2002–07 drought, the implementation of the policy increasingly gave the impression that the policy was a farm support program rather than a program of self-reliance. The origins of this shift are in the original drought policy itself – that is, the development of the concept of 'exceptional circumstances'. When the policy was agreed in 1992, it included the important caveat that occasionally circumstances occur of such severity that even the best risk manager cannot be expected to cope. In these 'exceptional circumstances', it was agreed that increased government support was warranted. In 1994 a welfare payment was added to the support available to farmers during exceptional circumstances drought and this has had the effect of making an exceptional circumstances declaration much more attractive (for further detail about the NDP and its evolution, see Botterill 2003). Since the NDP came into effect, there has been ongoing debate about how 'exceptional circumstances' are to be defined and this has resulted in the increased politicisation of the program. Each definition brings with it different winners and losers and the more generous the program becomes in terms of opening eligibility to more farmers, the less consistent it is with the objective of self-reliance and risk management. The incentives built into the program are such that demonstrating the severity of the drought becomes more important than managing an emerging dry spell. The result is that the program increasingly resembles the ad hoc disaster response that the NDP set out to avoid.

The clearest example of the increasing generosity of drought relief was the announcement by Minister Truss in May 2005 of changes to the means test for the welfare component, the exceptional circumstances relief payment (ECRP). Until this time, the level of the ECRP and its eligibility criteria were equivalent to the tests applying to other welfare recipients in the community. Truss's announcement in May 2005 signalled a clear break with this equitable treatment by exempting $10 000 of off-farm income from the income test for the payment (Truss 2005). This exemption was doubled to $20 000 in September 2007 (Howard 2007a). Farmers in receipt of this payment were also not subject to any mutual obligation requirements further differentiating their treatment from that of other welfare recipients.

A further indication that drought policy was moving away from its original intention was the failure to make the linkage with water policy when the National Water Initiative was developed during the fourth term of the Howard government. Drought policy remained quarantined in the agriculture portfolio while water policy proceeded at high levels through the Council of Australian Governments. There appeared to be no strong policy rationale for this different treatment, especially when there is the very real possibility that drought relief programs could be inconsistent with the objectives of national water policy.

The other major rural policy issue that was important was the high-profile involvement of AWB Limited in the oil-for-food scandal. The privatisation of the former statutory Australian Wheat Board[1] was effected by the first Howard government following several years of deliberation by the grains industry over the board's future. The privatised AWB Limited was listed on the Australian Stock Exchange in August 2001.

There were two notable features of the privatisation. First, the process was almost entirely driven by industry. Consideration of the future structure of the Australian Wheat Board was undertaken largely through a tripartite working group comprising the Department of Primary Industries and Energy, the Grains Council of Australia and the Australian Wheat Board itself. Government representatives were little more than observers in this process and there was no clearly defined government position on the direction the restructure debate should follow (Aulich & Botterill 2007). In effect, AWB Ltd became an industry-owned company (Wettenhall & Thynne 2005: 276). Second, the privatised AWB Limited effectively inherited the export monopoly (the so-called 'single desk') arrangements from its predecessor through arrangements that allowed it to veto any applications from competitors to export wheat in bulk.

Although these elements made the privatisation stand out from other government divestments, the public spotlight did not turn to AWB Limited until it was revealed that the company was one of the biggest offenders in bypassing sanctions against Saddam Hussein's regime in Iraq. The extent of

AWB Limited's involvement in the oil-for-food scandal was initially revealed by the US Independent Inquiry Committee (IIC) lead by Paul Volcker and then investigated in more detail by the *Inquiry into Certain Australian Companies in relation to the UN Oil-for-Food Programme* (the Cole Inquiry) which was set up by the Australian government in November 2005.

An oil-for-food program for Iraq was first proposed in 1991 (Meyer & Califano 2006: 2) but it took until April 1996 before the Iraqi government agreed to the terms of its operation. The program was developed to alleviate the negative humanitarian impact of sanctions that had been initiated following Iraq's invasion of Kuwait in 1990. The oil-for-food program allowed Iraq to sell oil but the proceeds of such sales were only to be applied to the purchase of specified humanitarian goods. This was achieved through the mechanism of an escrow account into which Iraq deposited the proceeds of oil sales and from which approved humanitarian imports were financed. As Meyer and Califano have argued so persuasively, the oil-for-food program was troubled from the outset with corruption of the program's operation extending to the head of the UN Office of the Iraq Program who was receiving oil allocations from the Iraqi government (Meyer & Califano 2006: 201). Paul Volcker, chairman of the IIC, described Saddam Hussein's manipulation of the program as 'gaming' (Meyer & Califano 2006: xix). This gaming consisted of providing oil allocations to individuals and then, more blatantly as the program progressed, seeking 'surcharge' payments and 'after sales fees' as well as manipulating charges for transporting goods once they arrived in Iraq. These latter tactics were designed to enable the Iraqi regime to access for other purposes the hard currency that the oil-for-food program was attempting to quarantine for humanitarian purchases.

The Australian Wheat Board was the first western grain trader to take advantage of the program (Australian Wheat Board 1996) and made its first shipment in December 1996. From July 1999, AWB Limited's trade with Iraq involved elements of Saddam Hussein's gaming of the program. The first technique for bypassing the sanctions regime was the imposition of a transportation fee, initially $12 per tonne on wheat shipments, to be paid through a Jordanian-based but Iraqi-controlled company, Alia for Transportation and General Trade. These payments were included explicitly in contracts forwarded for UN approval in July and October 1999 and the UN failed to pick up that they were inconsistent with the terms of the agreement with Iraq for the operation of the oil-for-food program. After October 1999 the payments were built into the wheat price and it is clear from evidence before the Cole Inquiry that the officers who set up the mechanism were aware that the inland transport fee was a means for Iraq to bypass the escrow account. The second mechanism introduced in November 2000 was the imposition of a 10 per cent 'after sales service fee' which was also built into the wheat price and was therefore not evident in the documentation sent to the UN for approval. The Cole Inquiry uncovered two other issues relating to the operation of the oil-for-food program which similarly reflected badly on AWB Limited (for a more detailed commentary on AWB Limited's activities in Iraq and the findings of the Cole Inquiry see Botterill 2007).

Substantial concerns with the operation of the program came to light in 2003 following the fall of Saddam Hussein's regime and the IIC was established by UN Secretary-General Kofi Annan in April 2004 to investigate. According to Meyer and Califano:

> The IIC's investigation was unprecedented. There has never been an investigation of similar breadth and intensity into the internal workings of the UN, the related activities of its member states, and the conduct of thousands of private company contractors that participated in the Oil-for-Food Program. (Meyer & Califano 2006: 244)

As part of its investigation, the IIC visited Australia and sought information from AWB Limited about its involvement in the oil-for-food program. It emerged during the subsequent Cole Inquiry that AWB Limited was less than transparent in its dealings with the IIC, withholding documents from investigators, particularly those relating to an internal AWB Limited investigation into problems with the company's dealings with Iraq. AWB Limited employed a series of stalling tactics including seeking a confidentiality agreement from the IIC, seeking prior notice of which AWB Limited officers the IIC wished to interview as well as provision of questions to be asked in advance, and refusal to have interviews recorded. Commissioner Cole described AWB Limited's response to the IIC as a 'strategy of "passive co-operation", providing only what was specifically asked for and ... negotiating to restrict the documents sought' (Cole 2006, vol. 1: 235).

The involvement of AWB Limited as the single biggest offender under the oil-for-food program gained public attention in Australia. By the time of the offences, AWB Limited was a private company, yet it still effectively held a monopoly on the export of wheat, an arrangement that was overseen by a commonwealth agency, the Wheat Export Authority (WEA). Although the WEA's powers were very limited, public debate focused on whether the authority should have uncovered the so-called kickbacks to the Iraqi regime and whether the government and ministers knew, or should have known, about the illicit payments prior to their revelation in 2003. A series of cables to the Department of Foreign Affairs and Trade (DFAT) which came to light during the Cole Inquiry indicated that general concerns were being raised about AWB Limited's operations in Iraq from January 2000, and questions of ministerial cover-up were raised by the opposition. However, the Cole Inquiry uncovered no evidence that the government was aware of the payments. It did find that the officers within AWB Limited involved in the various schemes went to considerable lengths to cover their tracks, both within AWB Limited itself and also by withholding information from the WEA and DFAT, including manipulating correspondence with government agencies to give the impression that DFAT approval had been obtained for payment of transport fees. AWB Limited assured the government in writing (Cole Inquiry Exhibits 2006: Exhibit 0085 Exh.0001.0087) that its behaviour was beyond reproach, advising Minister Downer in a letter in June 2004 that: 'All AWB's contracts were passed through the good offices of DFAT for on forwarding to the United Nations (UN) as required under UN guidelines and particularly UN Security Council Resolution 986.' It also advised that: 'Wheat was delivered to Iraq by AWB for distribution to all governorates of Iraq in accordance with the Distribution Plan for the relevant phase of the OFF program as approved by the UN.'

In terms of rural policy, the real fallout from the oil-for-food scandal was the scrutiny of AWB Limited's operation of the single desk for wheat. Following the government's receipt of the Cole Inquiry Report, the Prime Minister announced that the veto power which effectively gave AWB Limited the wheat export monopoly would be transferred to the Minister for Agriculture, Fisheries and Forestry and that a review of wheat marketing arrangements would be undertaken involving extensive grower consultation (Howard 2006). On 12 January 2007, the government announced the composition of a Wheat Export Marketing Consultation Committee to consult with growers and report to government on their views on future export marketing arrangements for wheat (McGauran & Vaile 2007). The committee reported at the end of March and on 22 May the government announced that growers had been given until 1 March 2008 'to establish their own company, separate from AWB Limited, to manage the single desk' (McGauran 2007b). Until that time, the veto power would remain with the minister and AWB Limited would manage and market the 2007–08 export wheat crop. The export of wheat in bags and containers was effectively deregulated, although the quality of shipments would require certification.

The Minister for Agriculture, Fisheries and Forestry stated that if growers did not have a company in place by 1 March 2008, 'the Government reserves the right to introduce its own wheat marketing arrangements' (McGauran 2007b). In a hint of the differences within the coalition over the wheat export monopoly, the Prime Minister expressed this sentiment somewhat more strongly, telling the Parliament that:

> If growers are not able to establish the new entity by 1 March next year, the government will propose other marketing arrangements for wheat exports. Let me make this clear to the House. The options available would include further deregulation of the wheat export market. (Howard 2007b: 1)

This decision deferred the politically contentious question of the future of the export monopoly until after the 2007 election; however, it raises some interesting questions about the nature of rural policy development. In an era of deregulation and competition policy, the future of an important monopoly was left in the hands of graingrowers, with little scope for broader national interest considerations associated with the arrangement to be included. There were also some intra-industry differences emerging, with the process of developing the new company structure being run by a Wheat Export Marketing Alliance comprising WA Farmers Federation, NSW Farmers, the Victorian Farmers Federation, and AgForce Queensland. While the latter two bodies are members of the Grains Council of Australia (GCA), GCA itself took a hands-off position, indicating only that it would 'provide help to this group when required' (GCA 2007). A key question for growers will be raising the capital necessary to finance the pool – the government ruled out providing funding and it seems unlikely that the non-grower shareholders of AWB Limited will be keen to finance the demerger (Heard 2007). The Wheat Export Marketing Alliance presented a business plan to the government in 2007, in which it called for further public funding to put the plan into effect. There was no public response from the government to the plan before the election was called.

Rural policy in the coalition relationship

In January 2006 National Party Senator Julian McGauran defected from his party to join the Liberals, reportedly noting that 'there is no longer any real distinguishing policy or philosophical difference between the Nationals and Liberals' and that 'the Liberals now represented the bush better' than the

Nationals (Dodson & Murphy 2006). Drought policy and support for the wheat single desk are the only real remaining areas of policy differentiation between the two parties, the first because it attracts little interest outside the agriculture portfolio where it is managed by a National Party minister and the second because it is subject to more deep-seated ideological differences. During the fourth Howard government both of these issues attracted interest from outside the National Party's constituency. As a result, debate extended beyond the confines of the narrow agricultural policy community, opening up the possibility of the injection of new ideas and policy objectives into the debate. On the issue of drought response, the policy community succeeded in protecting its interests through the seemingly illogical division of drought and water policy, with the latter being added to the COAG agenda, while the former remained with the Minister for Agriculture, Fisheries and Forestry, operating largely out of the public gaze.

The future of the single desk for wheat was not dealt with so neatly. While the National Party remained staunchly in support of the export monopoly, many Liberals, including some with large farmer constituencies themselves, were increasingly outspoken about the issue. The difference has been described as 'a jihad issue for some in the Liberal Party, and an icon issue for the Nationals' (Grattan 2006a). The most notable opponent of the export monopoly was Wilson Tuckey who consistently criticised the wheat marketing arrangements, making clear in the restructuring debates of 1997 and 1998 his hostility to the granting of an effective monopoly to a private company. He was not alone. Treasurer Peter Costello was reportedly opposed to the single desk (Grattan 2006b) and in May 2007 Liberal Senator Judith Adams was considering bringing forward a private member's bill to increase competition in export wheat marketing. Liberal backbencher Peter Slipper described the single desk as 'outdated, a relic of agrarian socialism' (Slipper 2006: 127).

These differences of opinion are arguably important to the National Party. As Warhurst notes, 'The logic of a Coalition rather than an amalgamation is strengthened when the Nationals look different' (Warhurst 2006: 15). The party does not have a monopoly on the rural conservative vote (Verrall et al. 1985: 9), particularly under the socially conservative Howard. In the fourth Howard government, the Liberals held 25 of the 44 seats that the Australian Electoral Commission classifies as 'rural' as against 12 held by the Nationals, four held by Labor and three by independents. It can be argued that in order to maintain a profile the Nationals need to retain a clear identity. It is worth noting that within the ranks of the National Party there were a few outspoken members who had in the past criticised the coalition's policy direction, members such as Ron Boswell, Bob Katter (now an independent) and De-Anne Kelly. More recently Senator Barnaby Joyce has taken a similar position, threatening to cross the floor over the privatisation of Telstra. In welcoming the single desk decision in May 2007, Joyce indicated his strong support for the retention of the export monopoly:

> If we fail in achieving a new single desk by next March there will be a return of the deregulation forces, more organised and stronger than before ... We will be at a strategic disadvantage if we lose the single desk. A deregulated market will ultimately result in one thing: less money for the majority of wheat farmers and less money for the nation. (Joyce 2007)

As indicated earlier, the Prime Minister signalled that this opposition to full deregulation of the wheat industry was not shared across the coalition.

Policy continuity

Overall, rural policy under the Howard government continued the trend of incremental policy development that has characterised the process since the 1970s. The underpinning principles of facilitating rather than impeding structural adjustment and moving away from regulated marketing continued. In 2005 the government appointed an Agriculture and Food Policy Reference Group, chaired by NFF President Peter Corish, to 'review policies and develop recommendations for improving the profitability, competitiveness and sustainability of the Australian agriculture and food sector over the next ten to fifteen years' (AFPRG 2006: 34). Both the Corish Report and the government's response continued the language of self-reliance and productivity improvement. The report identified the following 'Foundations for success' for agriculture:

- A stronger emphasis on *innovation* in production and marketing, underpinned by leading edge research and development, is fundamental to longer term business success.
- Sound macroeconomic and microeconomic policies, supported by substantial ongoing investment in infrastructure, will be vital to a low cost, *globally competitive* sector.
- A *whole of chain*, paddock to plate approach is needed to service consumer requirements efficiently and effectively.

- Policies must focus on achieving greater *self-reliance* of business operators.
- The *regulatory burden* facing businesses must be reduced.
- Relevant information must be *communicated* in a clearer, more timely, accessible and accurate manner.
- A *partnership approach* between businesses and governments will bring the best longer term improvements to the sector's viability and sustainability.
- A genuinely *cooperative and consistent* approach by governments — Australian, state and territory — is essential for policies and programs affecting the sector. (AFPRG 2006: 2, emphasis in original)

None of these principles is particularly new nor signals a change in direction for rural policy. The government's response agreed with the broad themes of the report and foreshadowed a comprehensive rural policy statement to be released in 2007, covering 'the Government's policy and programme direction in a holistic way' and including 'outcomes of current evaluations of key portfolio funding programmes' (DAFF 2006: 2). The statement 'Future Harvest' was released in May 2007 and was largely a catalogue of existing farm programs, some of which had been around for well over a decade.

Like much rural policy, the Corish Report and the government's response received almost no media attention at the time of their release and policy developments such as the increases in welfare payments to drought-affected farmers were subjected to little if any public scrutiny. As Wahlquist has observed:

> Most city people gain their understanding of rural Australia from the media: newspapers, television and radio. But most members of the media reflect their country: they are overwhelmingly city people, with little understanding of country life. The problem is exacerbated by the lack of specialist rural reporters in most metropolitan media. (Wahlquist 2003: 69)

Much of the reporting that does occur reflects an underlying sympathy for farmers based on stereotypical imagery and a generally unacknowledged agrarian sentiment. An analysis undertaken in September 2005 of reporting on rural issues revealed that only around 1 per cent of the items examined was even slightly critical of farmers (Botterill 2006: 27–28). The sector does not attract particularly large sums of government spending so it fails to attract the attention of commentators to the extent that, for example, health or education programs might. Even announcements such as the $2 million per day being spent on drought relief received little reporting.

The lack of general interest and debate about rural policy issues is apparently reflected within government as rural policies are developed largely without reference to broader government policy direction. The two major issues discussed in this chapter which arose during the fourth Howard government illustrate this point. The privatisation of the Australian Wheat Board was undertaken through a process which left the decision for the final structure largely in the hands of graingrowers. There was little active government intervention in the process and the government did not have a preferred position with respect to the privatisation model beyond broad principles relating to industry self-determination (Aulich & Botterill 2007). The retention of the export monopoly by the privatised entity was inconsistent with the principles set out in the Hilmer Inquiry into National Competition Policy which had devoted a chapter to the problem of privatising monopolies (Hilmer et al. 1993). When the *Wheat Marketing Act 1989* was reviewed under the National Competition Policy in 2000, convention was again ignored with the review being undertaken, not by the Productivity Commission as is often the case, but by an appointed committee including a former president of the Grains Council of Australia (Irving et al. 2000). The National Competition Council (NCC) found that 'the Commonwealth Government had not met its [competition principles agreement] clause 4 and 5 obligations arising from the Wheat Marketing Act' (NCC 2003: 1.8).

As discussed, in the area of drought policy, the welfare component of the exceptional circumstances program delivered income support to farmers on more generous terms than welfare payments to other disadvantaged members of the Australian community. Apart from the additional $20 000 per annum which could be earned by farmers before their payments were reduced, there were no mutual obligation commitments attached to the receipt of the exceptional circumstance relief payment. The lack of recognition that this payment was in fact a welfare payment was evident in the 2004 Senate Poverty Inquiry which made no reference to the welfare programs in the agriculture portfolio when calling for a whole-of-government approach to poverty alleviation (SCARC 2004: 420). None of the 95 recommendations made by the inquiry committee related to farm incomes.

Cockfield noted in 1997 that '[d]espite what the parties would claim, recent rural policy is characterised more by conformity than change associated with a change of government' (Cockfield 1997: 158). This trend continued from 1996 to 2007. Areas of disagreement between the government and the opposition on rural policy were largely matters of detail and rhetoric rather than direction. On sensitive issues such as the export arrangements for wheat, the opposition has remained silent, limiting its attacks during the Cole Inquiry to the government and whether or not it was aware of AWB's kickbacks to Iraq. John Howard managed the difficulties in the coalition relationship over rural policy by avoiding a possibly awkward debate over the wheat single desk in the lead-up to the 2007 election while leaving open the option for further deregulation.

Note

1   In order to avoid confusion between the statutory authority and the privatised entity, this chapter applies the following usage. When referring to the pre-1999 statutory authority, the terms 'the Australian Wheat Board' or 'the Wheat Board' have been employed. For the post-1999 situation 'AWB Limited' is used.

References

AFPRG (Agriculture and Food Policy Reference Group) (2006) *Creating our Future: Agriculture and Food Policy for the Next Generation*, Report to the Minister for Agriculture, Fisheries and Forestry, Canberra.
Aulich, C & Botterill, L (2007) A very peculiar privatisation: The end of the statutory Australian Wheat Board. Paper presented at the Australasian Political Studies Association Conference, Monash University, 24–26 September.
Aulich, C & Wettenhall, R (eds) (2005) *Howard's Second and Third Governments: Australian Commonwealth Administration 1998–2004*, UNSW Press, Sydney.
Australian Wheat Board (1996) AWB off the mark in Iraq (AWB Grain Statement), 22 May.
Botterill, L (2003) Uncertain climate: The recent history of drought policy in Australia, *Australian Journal of Politics and History*, 49(1): 61–74.
—— (2005) Policy change and network termination: The role of farm groups in agricultural policy making in Australia, *Australian Journal of Political Science*, 40(2): 1–13.
—— (2006) Soap operas, cenotaphs and sacred cows: Countrymindedness and rural policy debate in Australia, *Public Policy*, 1(1): 23–36.
—— (2007) Doing it for the growers in Iraq?: The AWB, Oil-for-Food and the Cole Inquiry, *Australian Journal of Public Administration*, 66(1): 4–12.
Bureau of Meteorology (2007) Short term relief but long term drought persists (Drought statement), 3 May, at <www.bom.gov.au/announcements/media_releases/climate/drought/20070503.shtml>
Cockfield, G (1997) Rural policy: More of the same? In S Prasser & G Starr (eds) *Policy and Change: The Howard Mandate*, Hale & Iremonger, Sydney: 158–71.
Cole, T (2006) *Report of the Inquiry into Certain Australian Companies in relation to the UN Oil-For-Food Programme*, Commonwealth of Australia, Canberra.
Cole Inquiry Exhibits (Inquiry into certain Australian companies in relation to the UN oil-for-food programme) (2006) Exhibits, <//203.94.171.34/offi/exhibits.htm>.
DAFF (Department of Agriculture, Fisheries and Forestry) (2006) *Australian Government*

Response to the Agriculture and Food Policy Reference Group report, Creating our Future: Agriculture and Food Policy for the Next Generation, Department of Agriculture, Fisheries and Forestry, at <www.daffa.gov.au/__data/assets/pdf_file/0005/56363/corish-response.pdf>.

Dodson, L & Murphy, D (2006) Senator's defection rocks the coalition, *Sydney Morning Herald*, 24 January.

GCA (Grains Council of Australia) (2007) Government listens to GCA on new wheat marketing policy (News release), 23 May.

Grattan, M (2006a) Monopoly's a dangerous game, *Sun-Herald*, 19 February.

—— (2006b) Now, look who's stalking, *Age*, 27 October.

Harris, SF, Crawford, JG, Gruen, FH & Honan, ND (1974) *The Principles of Rural Policy in Australia: A Discussion Paper* (Report to the Prime Minister by a Working Group), AGPS, Canberra.

Heard, G (2007) Desk decision: Race against time, *Farm Online* at <www.farmonline.com.au/news_daily.asp?ag_id=42831>.

Hilmer, FG, Rayner, MR & Taperell, GQ (1993) *National Competition Policy*, Report by the independent committee of inquiry, AGPS, Canberra.

Howard, J (Prime Minister) (2006) Joint press conference with the M Vaile, Deputy Prime Minister and Minister for Transport and Regional Services, Parliament House, Canberra, 5 December.

—— (2007a) Australian government strengthens drought support (Prime Minister of Australia Media release), 25 September.

—— (2007b) Questions without notice: Wheat, *Com. Parl. Debs HoR*, 22 May.

Irving, M, Arney, J & Lindner, B (2000) *National Competition Policy Review of the Wheat Marketing Act 1989*, NCP-WMA Review Committee, Canberra.

Joyce, B (2007) Joyce welcomes single desk decision (Media release), 23 May.

McGauran, P (Minister for Agriculture, Fisheries and Forestry) (2007a) Drought assistance hits all-time high (Media release by Federal Minister for Agriculture, Fisheries and Forestry DAFF07/044PM), 15 April.

—— (2007b) Interests of wheat growers prevail (Media release by Federal Minister for Agriculture, Fisheries and Forestry DAFF07/064PM), 22 May.

McGauran, P & Vaile, M (2007) Consultation on wheat export marketing arrangements (Joint statement by Australian Federal Minister for Agriculture, Fisheries and Forestry and Australian Minister for Transport and Regional Services DAFF003/07PM), 15 April.

Meyer, JA & Califano, MG (2006) *Good Intentions Corrupted: The Oil-for-Food Scandal and the Threat to the UN*, Public Affairs, New York.

Morris, S & Crowe, D (2007) Drought rescue bill tops $3.5 billion, *Australian Financial Review*, 26 September.

NCC (National Competition Council) (2003) *Assessment of governments' progress in implementing the National Competition Policy and related reforms: 2003* – vol. 2: *Legislation review and reform*, AusInfo, Canberra.

SCARC (Senate Community Affairs References Committee) (2004) *A Hand Up Not a Hand Out: Renewing the Fight Against Poverty*, Report on poverty and financial hardship, Department of the Senate, Canberra.

Singleton, G (ed.) (2000) *The Howard Government: Australian Commonwealth Administration 1996–98*, UNSW Press, Sydney.

Slipper, P (2006) *Com. Parl. Debs HoR*, 13 February.

Throsby, CD (1972) Background to agricultural policy. In CD Throsby (ed.) *Agricultural*

Policy: Selected Readings, Penguin Books, Ringwood, Vic.: 13–22.

Truss, W (Minister for Agriculture, Fisheries and Forestry) (2005) More support for drought affected farmers (Media release by the Federal Minister for Agriculture, Fisheries and Forestry DAFF05/152WT), 30 May.

Verrall, D, Ward, I & Hay, P (1985) Community, country, party: Roots of rural conservatism. In BJ Costar & D Woodward (eds) *Country to National: Australian rural politics and beyond*, Allen & Unwin, Sydney: 8–22.

Wahlquist, A (2003) Media representations and public perceptions of drought. In LC Botterill & M Fisher (eds) *Beyond Drought: People, Policy and Perspectives*, CSIRO Publishing, Melbourne: 67–86.

Warhurst, J (2006) Little reason for Nats to continue in separate role, *Canberra Times*, 3 February.

Wettenhall, R & Thynne, I (2005) Ownership and management in the public sphere: Issues and concerns, *Asia Pacific Journal of Public Administration*, 27(2): 263–90.

10
Industrial relations and the labour market

Phil Lewis

The industrial relations legislation known as Work Choices was no doubt a major turning point for the Howard government's popularity with the electorate. Howard underestimated the reaction to the legislation and acted too late: when he tried to make it more palatable by adding a series of 'fairness tests' the electoral damage had been done. Furthermore, the industrial relations laws after these later amendments were of little use to employers seeking to make the changes to pay and conditions which they considered necessary. So the result was an industrial relations system which did not meet employers' needs but was still very unpopular with many employees. The question will no doubt be asked for some time as to why a prime minister regarded as politically astute could have made a political miscalculation of such magnitude.

It is common among commentators, union leaders and politicians to portray the industrial relations changes under the Howard government as a major break from the past, whereas it will be argued here that it makes more sense to regard them as a part of a continuum of labour market reform first begun by the Hawke Labor government in 1983. In order to appreciate this, it is necessary to describe the changing nature of the Australian labour market which is the subject of the next section. This will provide a basis for a discussion of the perceived need for industrial relations reform in the third section. The coalition's changes to industrial relations law and the response of the ALP will be discussed in following sections. The chapter will conclude with discussion of the likely impacts of the respective policies on industrial relations and economic performance.

The changing Australian labour market

To put the necessity of successive industrial relations reform in perspective consider the unemployment rate over time in Australia (figure 10.1). The historical average for the unemployment rate until the mid-1970s was about 2 per cent but it rose almost continuously until the early 1980s. The so-called 'oil shocks' of the 1970s demanded significant structural adjustment which was hindered by excessive regulation, including trade protection, plus a lack of labour market flexibility, particularly downward wage rigidity and inappropriate macroeconomic policy (Lewis 2002). The impact of the Prices and Incomes Accord in reducing real wages can be seen in the early 1980s and the impact of the huge rise in interest rates in the early 1990s is also evident (for further discussion on the Accord, see Singleton 1990). The subsequent fall in the unemployment rate was due to a combination

Figure 10.1   Unemployment rate, 1960–2007, per cent

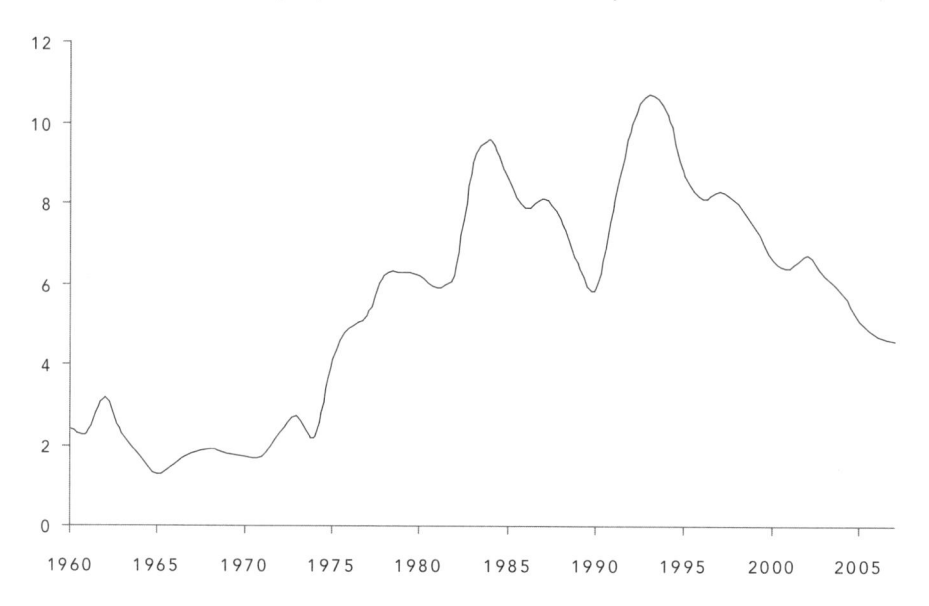

SOURCE ABS 1960–2002, 2003–07.

of factors including increased global demand, better macroeconomic management and reduced regulation of the economy, including the labour market (Lewis 2002).

One of the major factors in the fall in the unemployment rate since the mid-1980s is the fall in real unit labour costs (RULC) over the same period. RULC is the cost of employing labour adjusted for inflation and labour productivity, expressed as an index. RULC can fall due to wages rising slower than inflation or rising by less than the growth in productivity.

The very high level of RULC in the early 1980s (figure 10.2) was associated with the very high levels of unemployment at that time. The success of the Accord in breaking the nexus between wages and prices, especially through the ending of full indexation, was particularly important in reducing RULC and unemployment (Lewis & Spiers 1990). The continuing fall in RULC through the 1990s and 2000s was due to microeconomic reform, including labour market deregulation, by successive ALP and coalition governments. More recently, mainly because of the commodities boom, producer prices have been rising at a faster rate than labour costs.

Figure 10.2   Real unit labour costs, 1984–2006

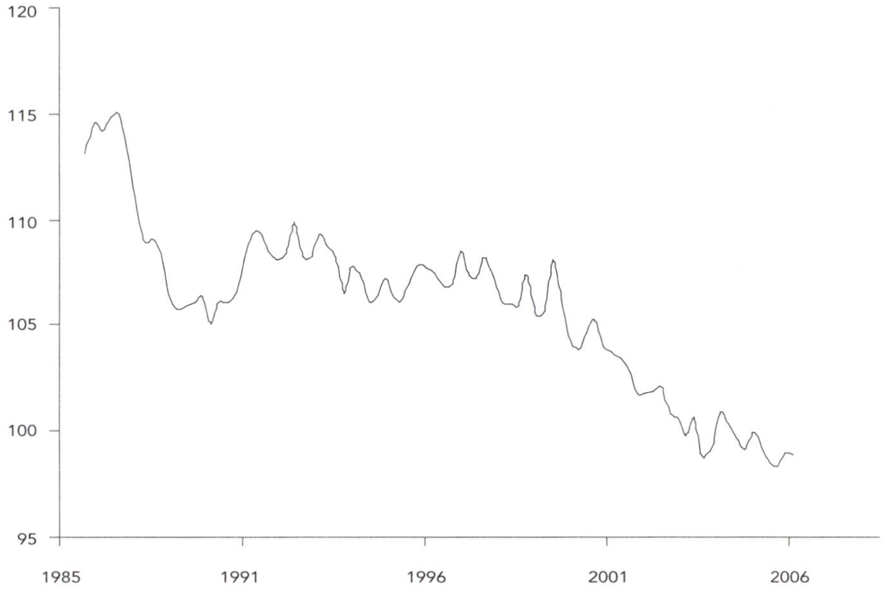

SOURCE ABS 1984–2006.

The Australian economy has undergone significant structural change over the past three decades, the pace of which accelerated in the late 1980s and 1990s following the implementation of broad-ranging microeconomic reform policies. These changes have continued in the 2000s. While policy has changed, industries have also embraced new technologies and have become increasingly involved in the global economy.

There have been important changes in labour demand (Lewis et al. 2006). The demand for full-time workers, particularly males, has not kept pace with supply. The growth in part-time work has been an important source of jobs growth. There has been a substitution of females, particularly part-time females, for full-time males. For certain groups, the changes in demand have been especially noticeable. For instance, a full-time job for anyone 15–20 years old is now an exception rather than the rule and the chance that youths who are in part-time jobs are students is over 80 per cent (Lewis & McLean 1998). Another major feature of the changing Australian labour market is the growth in casual employment. The growth of casual work was an important phenomenon in the 1980s and 1990s but since 2000 the proportion of the workforce that is casual has reached a plateau of about 27 per cent (Lewis et al. 2006). The above developments suggest that many of the considerations which may once have been relevant, such as what are 'normal' working hours, have lost their relevance in today's labour market.

Much of the changing composition of employment can be attributed to changing industry mix. In 1975 services accounted for just over 50 per cent of all jobs, but by 2007 the service sector accounted for over 70 per cent of all jobs (ABS 2003–07). By contrast, manufacturing's share of total employment almost halved over the same period to about 11 per cent in 2007. There were similar reductions in the relative shares of jobs in the 'industrial' services such as electricity, gas and water. For brevity the change in distribution of jobs by occupation is not given here but the picture that emerges when combined with the industry distribution is that a 'typical' Australian worker today is a 'white-collar' employee in the service sector (Lewis et al. 2006).

Changes in industry composition have combined with technological change to systematically alter the demand for skills, with technological change the dominant influence (Kelly & Lewis 2003, 2006). It has allowed for, or even driven, a restructuring of occupations within industries. A combination of structural and technological change has significantly influenced the demand for labour with respect to part-time employment, gender and skills. Less skilled workers are more vulnerable, as are younger and older workers (Lewis 2002). More generic and general skills rather than firm-specific skills are required. There is also evidence of growing wage dispersion (Lewis et al. 2006). The overall outcome is a more highly skilled workforce and a more efficient economy.

According to the OECD (2003: 1):

> Dogged pursuit of structural reforms across a very broad front, and prudent macroeconomic policies firmly set in a medium-term framework, have combined to make the Australian economy one of the best performers in the OECD, and also one notably resilient to shocks, both internal and external. Incomes growth has remained brisk, employment is expanding, inflation is under control, and public finances are healthy. All the indicators are that the continuing effects of previous reforms will continue to help the economy to combat shocks in the immediate future. In order to meet the longer-term objective of raising living standards towards the highest in the OECD, further reforms to labour, product and financial markets and to social policies will be needed, that will encourage more people to join the labour force, remain in it, and steadily raise their productivity.

For most Australians the labour market and its education and training system have facilitated the adjustment of labour supply to meet those changes in demand. The increased participation of women and students in the workforce has generated the greatly increased demand for part-time workers and those with interactive skills. In addition the education system has significantly increased the average cognitive and education levels (Lewis & McLean 1998). Labour supply has, generally, adjusted well to labour demand due to structural and technological change. Poor labour market outcomes are not experienced by the large majority of Australians but by specific groups of people who are disadvantaged and are fairly easily identifiable (Dockery & Webster 2001). The total number of disadvantaged is, however, quite large, perhaps as high as 1.3 million, and is a major challenge for labour market reform including minimum wages, welfare-to-work legislation, more flexible working arrangements and unfair dismissal (Lewis 2007).

Another important change in the Australian labour market is the decline in union density from over 50 per cent in the 1970s to 20 per cent in 2006. In the private sector union density is below 15 per with over 90 per cent of businesses having no union members employed at all (ABS 2006). As a consequence, union power has significantly diminished, especially as employment has shifted from the public sector to the private sector. Union membership is being seen as less relevant for employees generally and, in particular, for casual employees and for those in the service sector where the growth of part-time, female and youth employment has been greatest.

Industrial relations reform

Australia had, for most of the 20th century, a system of wage determination, and of industrial relations more generally, that had only one or two counterparts in the rest of the industrialised world. This system underwent considerable change in the 1980s and 1990s and this continued under the coalition administration. A major distinguishing feature of the Australian system was the role played by a range of arbitration and conciliation tribunals, the dominant institution being the Australian Industrial Relations Commission (AIRC), although it formerly had other names. These tribunals set the minimum rates of pay and the conditions of work of employees as outlined in awards. Awards came about as a result of submissions made by unions and by employers, on which the tribunals arbitrated. In the early 1980s compulsory arbitration was the dominant form of wage determination; however, by 2005 only about 20 per cent of Australian workers relied on awards for their pay determination. It should be noted that the conditions and rates of pay of some awards were, in fact, reached, not through arbitration, but through bargaining between unions and employers. The role of industrial tribunals was simply to ratify these bargains. Such awards became known as 'sweetheart' or 'consent' awards. With these exceptions, wage determination was highly centralised. When a tribunal made a decision it affected all firms and workers in the occupation or industry covered by that award.

In the period 1983–87, regular adjustments were made to all award wages – that is, every award wage was increased by the same proportion or dollar amount. In 1987, in what some observers described at the time as the most significant National Wage Decision since the system's inception, the AIRC ruled that the wage increases granted would not automatically be applied to every award. Instead, firms and employees would have to justify them through what was termed the 'structural efficiency principle'. Other wage decisions of a similar nature followed and finally, in its 1991 decision, the AIRC encouraged workers and their employers to bargain directly with each other at the enterprise level. This introduction of 'enterprise bargaining' was perhaps the most significant change to industrial relations in Australia's history.

Enterprise bargaining was given a further stimulus by the 1993 Industrial Relations Act which came into force in 1994. By 2006 half of all employees in the federal jurisdiction were covered by enterprise agreements. In some states more dramatic changes occurred. In Western Australia and Victoria legislation permitted workplace agreements which are completely outside the award system. The Howard government's 2006 amendments to the Workplace Relations Act were intended, among other things, to further facilitate the spread of enterprise bargaining. The effects of industrial relations reform can be seen as a systematic undermining of awards as a means of determining wages. Enterprise bargaining replaced awards for most workers who were able to bargain for better pay and conditions. The Howard reforms, had they been implemented as first proposed, would have effectively got rid of awards for the remainder of workers without strong bargaining power.

People increasingly were having their pay determined through less regulated bargaining. What are the advantages of less regulated bargaining? First, it is argued that it leads to greater labour market flexibility. It is conventional to distinguish between numerical flexibility and functional flexibility. Numerical flexibility refers to how easily the quantity of labour inputs can be varied, whereas functional flexibility refers to how easily the tasks performed by workers can be altered. Labour market inflexibility and compliance costs are proportionately higher for small firms (Cabalu et al. 1996).

Supporters of less regulated labour markets argue that numerical flexibility is best achieved by relative wage adjustments. In industries and occupations where demand, relative to available supply at existing wages, is high, then wages should increase relative to those elsewhere, and vice versa. As employers and employees respond to the signals and incentives given by these wage changes, demand and supply adjust and numerical flexibility will be secured.

Setting minimum award wages for the various occupations and industries, and imposing the same minimums on all firms within an industry, it is argued, severely impedes such adjustment. Further, because any relative wage changes that occur tend to be cancelled out through flow-on effects – that is, by workers in other industries receiving similar increases – it follows that adjustment is further impeded.

Functional flexibility can take many forms, but an important one is the gain which would accrue if firms are given more control over arrangements of working hours. Most awards set down the hours during which standard hourly rates of pay apply and the premium (or penalty) that has to be paid for hours outside this. These penalties may constrain firms, particularly where demand reaches peaks outside standard hours. Extending the range of hours over which standard pay rates apply and, more generally, abolishing limits on working arrangements again leads to greater flexibility. Imposing blanket conditions across firms impedes functional flexibility.

Several other advantages are claimed for labour market flexibility. It is argued that it enables workers to identify with the enterprise and its performance because improved work practices should lead to increases in pay. It should also encourage dispute resolution in the workplace. The previously highly regulated labour market may have impeded the development of good industrial relations in enterprises because the parties may have come to believe that disputes would ultimately be arbitrated.

Enterprise and individual bargaining brings with it some disadvantages which have to be weighed against its benefits. These are concerned with equity. The system of compulsory arbitration acted to protect workers in weak bargaining positions and these are, of course, likely to be lower paid workers. The evidence shows that the relative pay of low-paid workers is higher in Australia than in most industrialised countries (Lewis 2006). Increased labour market flexibility would be expected to cause a decline in the position of low-paid workers. This is recognised by governments in many countries, including Australia, with what are called 'safety-net' increases in pay for those unable to conclude enterprise bargains. Safety-net increases should always tend to be of a lesser amount than bargained pay increases. Critics of individual contracts extend the argument that the ability of individuals is far less than that of workers as a whole to bargain for wages and conditions.

It is generally recognised that Australia's previous regime of centralised wage bargaining and one of its major planks, indexation, were major reasons for perpetuation of inflation in the 1970s and early 1980s. Indeed the very success of the Prices and Incomes Accord to reduce inflation was to act as a circuit breaker in the centralised system, reducing real wages by 10 per cent below what would have been expected under a strict indexation regime (Lewis & Spiers 1990).

A major feature of the more decentralised wage bargaining system, begun under the Hawke–Keating governments and continued under the coalition, is the decoupling of wages and prices through automatic indexing of wages to inflation, removing a mechanism for the direct transmission of prices to wages and, in turn, wages to prices. For much of the period of centralised wage determination, there was some form of regular indexation of wages to the CPI. In wage bargaining today this does not generally occur.

THE WORKPLACE RELATIONS AMENDMENT (WORK CHOICES) ACT 2005

The coalition's stance on industrial relations can be traced back to the ill-fated *Fightback!* proposals of John Hewson (Hewson & Fischer 1991). One of John Howard's major achievement has been to introduce almost all the essential elements of *Fightback!* during his period in office. These include the introduction of a broad-based goods and services tax (GST) and a toughening of eligibility rules for welfare recipients as well as industrial relations reform. Australian Workplace Agreements (AWAs) were introduced by Peter Reith, the then Minister for Employment, Workplace Relations and Small Business, in 1996 but by 2005 less than 5 per cent of employees were on AWAs. In 2005 the government announced plans (subsequently introduced in Work Choices) for significant changes to the workplace relations system, including:

- the creation of a national workplace relations system for Australia;
- increasing the capacity of employers, employees and unions to make agreements;
- modernising the role of awards and the AIRC;
- reforming the setting of minimum wage and conditions;
- the establishment of the Australian Fair Pay Commission (AFPC) to replace the AIRC for the purpose of setting minimum wages and conditions;
- unfair dismissal protection removed for workplaces of 100 or fewer workers or for 'operational reasons';
- Australian Workplace Agreements (AWAs) no longer subject to the 'no disadvantage test' and can override other types of agreement;
- secret ballots before strikes;
- union rights of entry prohibited from agreements.

Work Choices refers to the substantial amendments made to the *Workplace Relations Act 1996* by the *Workplace Relations Amendment (Work Choices) Act 2005*, the bulk of which commenced on 27 March 2006. Work Choices shifted the constitutional basis for federal industrial relations law from the traditional conciliation and arbitration power to the corporations power. By using the corporations power to this extent for the first time, the Howard government was able to legislate directly for minimum conditions of employment for all employees (as long as they are employed by a constitutional corporation).

Any power of the states and territories over industrial relations was essentially limited to small firms, state employees and those under 18 years of age who come under child protection legislation which is the states' jurisdiction. The Australian Fair Pay and Conditions Standard required employers to provide only five minimum conditions, including a minimum rate of pay, maximum ordinary hours of work, annual leave, personal leave, and parental leave.

Although awards had not been abolished, the federal award system would wither away, as new awards were not able to be arbitrated. The only way in which a 'new' award could be made was as a result of the award rationalisation process, which was largely subject to ministerial direction, rather than as a decision of an independent arbitral body. Awards provided only residual protections, with the emphasis firmly on the making of individual and collective agreements between employers and employees, with no approval mechanisms and no comparison to otherwise applicable award conditions. Once an agreement was lodged, the award that would have otherwise applied to the relevant employee became no longer applicable for that employee, and an employee could never return to coverage by that award. The only obligation of the employer was to ensure that that the five minimum conditions were provided.

Unfortunately, and somewhat unusually, for John Howard, the industrial relations proposals lacked the thoroughness and preparation that had gone into reforms such as the GST and welfare. For instance, the GST was only introduced after much research and economic analysis by Treasury, sounding out of media response and public opinion – there was to be no repeat of John Hewson's infamous performance with the birthday cake! Welfare reform arose from the McClure committee's report which resulted from extensive consultation and research input from academics. By contrast, in May 2005 Howard released only a broad outline of his industrial relations proposals, despite the likelihood that something similar to Work Choices must have been on the drawing board since Peter Reith's plans were unveiled in 1996. Perhaps the opportunities provided by a Senate majority clouded Howard's judgment. There was a strong ideological consideration also at work, not just concern about the performance of the economy. Howard and some of his ministers had a long history of contempt for aspects of union activity. For instance, as a young lawyer Peter Costello played a pivotal role in the (in)famous Dollar Sweets case in 1985 (Wood 2000); the perceived threat posed by union leaders in a prospective Labor government became a major element in the coalition's advertising before the 2007 elections.

The need for industrial relations reform was taken as an act of faith with no reasoned analysis of the benefits to the economy such as more jobs, higher productivity or lower unemployment. Perhaps most telling was the obvious discomfort displayed by the Prime Minister when quizzed in the media about whether anyone would be worse off under his proposals. Regulation of markets always benefits some parties to the detriment of others. For instance, regulation of shopping hours benefits small retailers at the expense of large retailers and consumers. When regulation is removed, those who benefited from the regulation (rent seekers) are worse off but hopefully everyone else benefits. Under the industrial reforms proposed by Howard, workers who could not command market wages and conditions would see their pay and conditions worsen. The onus is on those supporting deregulation to demonstrate the benefits of deregulation to the economy as a whole. Apparently, the government had no stomach for economic analysis!

The proposals themselves were also subject to criticisms, both for their content and for the haste in which the legislation was introduced (see chapter 5). One commentator noted that at 762 pages, large slabs of the legislation were:

> Virtually unintelligible to all but the most persistent and expert reader, while the haste with which the legislation was rushed through parliament has meant that areas of uncertainty as to the meaning or effect of certain changes have been overlooked or left unresolved. (Stewart 2006: 25)

The lack of reasoned argument and detail made Howard a perfect target for Labor, the ACTU and much of the media – because the exact proposals were unknown, the broad outline was open to many interpretations and misinterpretations. It could be argued, however, that the whole process was a very clever way of testing the market before launching the final proposals. For perhaps the first time in Howard's term of office, the business community was getting worried by the government's failure to sell its industrial relations message.

It did not take long for Work Choices to have an impact at least in the media. Four days after the Work Choices act came in, the Cowra abattoir served notice to sack 29 employees for 'operational reasons' and invited them to apply for 20 jobs on lower pay. The then Minister for Workplace Relations, Kevin Andrews, was forced to step in, as he did frequently during the next 10 months to put political pressure on employers to withdraw many of the more extreme proposals to worsen pay and conditions. In a desperate attempt to stem the tide of adverse public opinion, Howard replaced Andrews with the

Courtesy of Peter Nicholson, *The Australian*, 7 July 2005

more popular Joe Hockey but the damage had been done and the electoral cost of the new industrial relations laws was already evident.

In the face of almost daily adverse reports of unpopular impacts of Work Choices, the government was forced to announce a new 'fairness test' to apply to all new AWAs after 7 May 2007 under *The Workplace Relations Amendment (A Stronger Safety Net) Act 2007*. The fairness test required the newly strengthened Workplace Authority, previously the Employment Advocate, to vet all agreements and to be satisfied that employees get fair compensation for modifying or removing protected award conditions such as penalty rates, overtime payments, breaks and leave loadings. The fairness test applied only to employees earning less than $75 000 per year and related only to the conditions that would be covered by the award (if any) relevant to that job.

The role of the Workplace Ombudsman, previously known as the Office of Workplace Services, was clarified with respect to investigating and prosecuting employers who break the law. The Workplace Ombudsman provided additional protection for employees and had a greater role in ensuring that employers complied with their legal obligations by: investigating alleged breaches, undertaking compliance audits and prosecuting employers who broke the law.

Of the 1.13 million employees registered between March 2006 and June 2007, 399 000 or 35 per cent were on AWAs and 32 per cent of these were in retail, accommodation and food services. Whereas AWAs had been most prevalent among mainly professional workers, they were now most prevalent among those in low-skilled, low-paid employment.

THE AUSTRALIAN FAIR PAY COMMISSION

The objective of wage determinations of the Australian Fair Pay Commission (AFPC) and matters to which it is to have regard are set out in section 23 of the Workplace Relations Act:

> the objective of the AFPC in performing its wage-setting function is to promote the economic prosperity of the people of Australia, having regard to the following:
>
> - the capacity for the unemployed and low paid to obtain and remain in employment;
> - employment and competitiveness across the economy;
> - providing a safety net for the low paid;
> - providing minimum wages for junior employees, employees to whom training arrangements apply, and employees with disabilities that ensure that these employees are competitive in the labour market.

The AFPC has wide powers to determine its own procedures including:

- the timing and frequency of wage reviews;
- the scope of particular wage reviews;
- the manner in which wage reviews are to be conducted;
- when wage-setting decisions are to come into effect.

For the purposes of performing its wage-setting function, the AFPC may inform itself in any way it thinks appropriate, including by:

- undertaking or commissioning research; or
- consulting with any other person, body or organisation; or
- monitoring and evaluating the impact of its wage-setting decisions.

The AFPC, in its first decision, handed down a two-tiered increase with an immediate adjustment to the minimum wage of $27.36, with a lesser increase for awards above $700 per week. Since it covered a period of 18 months after the previous safety-net adjustment, on an annual basis the adjustment could be seen as equivalent to an annual increase of $18.24. Employers were taken by surprise in regard to its size. In its second decision in July 2007, the AFPC increased the standard Federal Minimum Wage and all pay scales up to $700 a week by $10.26 per week and all pay scales paying $700 a week and above by $5.32 per week. Both increases applied from the first pay date on or after 1 October 2007. Taken together, the Commission's 2006 and 2007 increases delivered an additional $37.62 per week to Australia's lowest paid workers. The increases were of the same order of magnitude as the increases that had become the norm during the period of safety-net adjustment undertaken by the AIRC.

What was also of note was that the increases for the lowest paid over the period since the last safety-net adjustment were, in percentage terms, almost identical to the movement in the CPI over the same period. For employers the result had an ominous look of having been based on an underlying, but unstated, concept of wage indexation. The concern therefore was that the process of wage adjustment being introduced, despite the gloss of its being economically based, was in reality a continuation of centralised wage fixation under a different name. No principles were introduced that would provide an upper limit on the level of increase. Indeed no principles at all were introduced, and the appearance of a system of ad hoc decision-making based on the personal views of the five commissioners was the essence of the new system (Lewis 2007). Nevertheless, at a time when average earnings were rising at a faster rate than inflation, the safety-net rises represented a fall in the relative minimum wage. Such decline would have increased the demand for low-paid workers but nowhere was this stated by the AFPC as one of its aims.

Labor's response

It was up to Kim Beazley, the then Leader of the Opposition, to lead the charge against the government. For someone with aspirations to the prime ministership this promised to be a golden opportunity. For virtually the first time in Howard's fourth term, here was an issue on which there was a clear distinction between the ALP and the coalition – and the government's proposals were clearly unpopular with the majority of voters. Beazley, however, was not up to the task and just over a year after attacking Howard's 'extreme industrial relations legislation' in parliament in November 2005, he was voted out of the ALP leadership and replaced by Kevin Rudd.

Work Choices was overwhelmingly supported by employers, and the retreat by Howard in response to the public backlash was almost universally condemned by business groups. Perhaps not surprisingly, Work Choices was vigorously attacked by the unions. They and the ALP had obviously struck a chord with the general public, if we are to believe opinion polls, and the ACTU put massive resources into a campaign against Work Choices. Workplace industrial relations was shaping up to be one of the defining issues in the upcoming federal election.

With this in mind it was important for the ALP and Kevin Rudd to come up with an alternative which would wind back many of the most feared parts of Work Choices. Yet it was also important that Rudd did not give the impression that the ALP was simply a puppet of the union movement and 'roll back' Australian industrial relations to a largely discredited inflexible system which had existed under the old AIRC. Rudd also had a problem of not wanting to get offside with business, and sought to project himself as a moderate, economic manager and friend of business.

Rudd's 'Fair Work Australia' tellingly was launched on a public holiday, ANZAC Day 2007. As was becoming fairly common in the election campaign, the proposals lacked detail. Fair Work Australia received, apart from comments about the appalling name, much discussion in the media, stage-managed support from the ACTU (particularly Greg Combet, the ACTU Secretary) and almost unanimous condemnation by business leaders. The key feature of the proposals was the abolition of the Australian Fair Pay Commission, the Office of the Employment Advocate, the Office of Workplace Services and the Industrial Relations Commission, and with their functions coming together under a Fair Work Commission (Fair Work Australia). Many of the 'unfair' dismissal provisions removed under Work Choices would also be returned. However, Rudd's proposals would mean a significant diminution of union rights.

The proposals came under fire from several quarters including legal experts who considered them to be a breach of the 1956 High Court case which ruled that industrial relations bodies that made awards and orders could not have the power to exercise them. The Rudd proposals had the potential to create one of the greatest upheavals in Australian industrial relations history with little assessment of any gains to efficiency.

Perhaps the most telling thing about Rudd's proposals was that only one side, the unions, was consulted. This inevitably gave rise to the opinion that Fair Work Australia would simply be a source of jobs for Labor mates, union-friendly ex-commissioners and union hacks. The final proposals were announced in August 2007, along with a suggested timetable for implementation in 2008, if Labor were elected. The main points were:

- enterprise bargaining and awards to be the main bases of wage determination;
- AWAs abolished and existing AWAs phased out by 2012;
- individuals earning over $100 000 can negotiate employment contacts without reference to awards;
- safety-net minimum conditions expanded from five to ten;
- secondary boycotts to remain outlawed;
- no pattern bargaining;
- restrictions to union officials' right of entry to workplaces to remain;
- unfair dismissal claims can be made after 12 months employment in firms with fewer than 15 employees and after 6 months in firms with 15 or more employees.

These proposals represented a significant deregulation of the labour market compared to pre-Howard days and have angered many union leaders. Although the proposals leave much of Work Choices essentially intact, they received almost unanimous condemnation by business leaders. The major fears of business related to the tightening of unfair dismissals legislation and the scrapping of AWAs. It was argued that the ALP proposals would increase the costs of employing labour, reduce labour market flexibility and leave open the door for a future ALP government to reduce flexibility further under the influence of unions.

Of most concern from business's perspective and from many economists was that Labor's proposals threatened to reverse the trend to greater labour market flexibility pursued first by Hawke and Keating and continued under the coalition. There was now general acceptance that the freeing-up of the labour market had been a major factor in the success of the Australian economy. Differences between the two main parties are not necessarily due to significant differences in structures, but there could be major consequences depending on who is put into key positions in the Work Fair institutions.

Conclusion

Howard did not do a good job in selling his industrial relations reform. He left himself wide open to attack by the ACTU by announcing his proposals before the legislation was ready. When they were released, he failed to explain why they were necessary and what benefits they would achieve. One of the unintended consequences of the government's failure was that it noticeably improved the quality of the research and lobbying material produced by the employers' organisations, particularly in submissions to the AFPC. Faced with the government's inability to state the case for reform, they were forced to do it themselves.

By contrast, the ACTU campaign was marked by the poor quality of and the paucity of reasoned argument in its materials, but there was no doubt that it had been effective in creating opposition to the industrial relations reforms among the majority of voters. The reforms were not radical or a major departure from the path of reform begun by Hawke and Keating. They recognised that improving the well-being of Australians, including through the ability of government to provide for the least fortunate, relies on economic growth which can be achieved only by enhancing competitiveness and productivity. Labour market regulation prevents businesses from organising labour and capital in different ways in order to achieve competitiveness and productivity – Howard and Rudd both knew this. Howard failed to get this over to the electorate while Rudd chose to ignore it or to avoid the inevitable clash with his union backers.

The fundamental principle underlying the argument for labour market deregulation relates to the employment decisions of firms. Employers hire people at a wage to do work for which the worker can add to the profit of the business. Employees make decisions on what they are willing to accept in terms of remuneration, hours of work and conditions. It can be expected that normally the labour market results in employment outcomes that meet the needs of both employers and employees. Hence the growth in the number of workers on AWAs to over one million. Care must be taken in framing restrictions on flexibility in the labour market such that employment opportunities are not lost. There is a perception among businesses that if Labor's workplace proposals are introduced as proposed, restrictions on business, and therefore costs, will increase significantly.

References

ABS (Australian Bureau of Statistics) (1984–2006) *Australia's National Accounts*, cat. no. 5206.0.
—— (2006) *Employee Earnings, Benefits and Trade Union Membership*, cat. no. 6310.0.
—— (2003–07) *Labour Force*, cat. no. 6202.0.
—— (1960–2002) *Labour Force*, cat. no. 6203.0.
Cabalu, H, Doss, N & Dawkins, P (1996) *Employers' Compliance Costs*, Discussion Paper 96/10, Centre for Labour Market Research, Curtin University of Technology, Perth.
Dockery, A M & Webster, E (2002) Long-term unemployment and work deprived individuals: Issues and policies, *Australian Journal of Labour Economics*, 5(2): 175–94.
Hewson, J & Fischer, T (1991) *Fightback!* Liberal and National Parties, Canberra.
Kelly, R & Lewis, PET (2003) The new economy and the demand for skills, *Australian Journal of Labour Economics*, 6(1): 135–52.
—— (2006) Measurement of skill and skill change. In Brown, P, Liu, S & Sharma, D (eds) *Contributions to Probability and Statistics: Applications and Challenges*, World Scientific, Singapore: 17–27.
Lewis, PET (2002) What do we know about job creation?, *Australian Journal of Labour Economics*, 5(2): 279–88.
—— (2006) *Minimum Wages and Employment*, Report to the Australian Fair Pay Commission, at <www.fairpay.gov.au/NR/rdonlyres/24E4540F-4CC4-44F4-9361-2396D6AC2 883/0/Minimumwagesandemployment_CLMR.pdf>.
—— (2007) *The Impact of Minimum Wages: Some Considerations for the Australian Fair Pay Commission in its Second Decision on the Minimum Wage*, Report to the Australian Fair Pay Commission, at <www.fairpay.gov.au/NR/rdonlyres/A445ED73-B2F2-4738-86F5-B9B7757F6 244/0/Employers_First_Submission_2007.pdf>.
Lewis, P, Garnett, A, Hawtrey, K & Treadgold, M (2006) *Issues, Indicators and Ideas: A Guide to the Australian Economy*, 4th edn, Pearson Education, Sydney.
Lewis, PET & Mclean, B (1998) The youth labour market in Australia, *Australian Journal of Labour Economics*, 2(2): 157–72.
Lewis, PET & Spiers, DJ (1990) Six years of the Accord – an assessment, *Journal of Industrial Relations,* 32(1): 53–68.
OECD (Organisation for Economic Cooperation and Development) (2003) *Economic Survey – Australia*, at <www.oecd.org/dataoecd/5/5/2496702.pdf>.
Singleton, G (1990) *The Accord and the Australian Labour Movement*, Melbourne University Press, Melbourne.
Stewart, A (2006) WorkChoices in overview: Big bang or slow burn, *The Economics and Labour Relations Review*, 16(2), at < www.austlii.edu.au/au/journals/ELRRev/2006/3.html>.
Wood, S (2000) The death of Dollar Sweets, Paper presented to the 21st conference of the HR Nicholls Society, Melbourne.

In the name of failure: A generational revolution in Indigenous affairs

Will Sanders

In April 2004, towards the end of its third term, the Howard government announced its intention to abolish the Aboriginal and Torres Strait Islander Commission (ATSIC), the statutory centerpiece of commonwealth Indigenous affairs administration over the previous 15 years. In so doing Prime Minister Howard and his Minister for Immigration and Multicultural and Indigenous Affairs, Senator Amanda Vanstone, referred to ATSIC as an 'experiment in separate … elected representation, for Indigenous people' which had been a 'failure' and which would not be replaced. Instead a group of 'distinguished Indigenous people' would be appointed to 'advise' the government and ATSIC's former programs would be 'mainstreamed' to line government departments, though there would still be 'a major policy role' for the Minister for Indigenous Affairs (Howard & Vanstone 2004).

This chapter will focus on the way in which the idea of past policy failure has become the driving motif of Australian Indigenous affairs during the period of the fourth Howard government and on how, in the name of failure, the government has argued repeatedly for significant organisational and policy change. The first section documents, in chronological style, this constant linking of the idea of failure with arguments for change. The second section asks, in a more analytic style, what sort of change is now occurring in Australian Indigenous affairs? I argue that the change is best thought of as a generational revolution, which combines a major disowning of the work of the previous generation in Indigenous affairs with a significant ideological swing to the right. I suggest that this generational revolution has taken some seven or eight years to build and can be related to two major dimensions of Australian Indigenous affairs policy: its highly morally charged nature and its highly cross-cultural nature. I also suggest that a similar generational revolution, drawing on the same moral and cross-cultural dynamics but moving in the opposite ideological direction, occurred in Australian Indigenous affairs between 1967 and 1976.

The identification of two generational revolutions in Australian Indigenous affairs in the last 40 years could perhaps encourage governments of all ideological persuasions to be a little more cautious about abandoning established approaches in Indigenous affairs in the name of failure, and striking out so self-assuredly on supposedly new, more enlightened, more informed paths.

Failure and change

In February 2005, in an address to the National Press Club as the continuing Minister for Immigration and Multicultural and Indigenous Affairs in the new, fourth Howard government, Senator Amanda Vanstone identified as a 'brutal reality' that: 'for all the dollars spent – over decades – and for all the goodwill, we are a long way from seeing all first Australians enjoy the opportunities the rest of us take for granted' (Vanstone 2005a: 1). This condemnation of an inadequate past was returned to several times as Minister Vanstone went on 'happily' to outline a 'quiet revolution' that was 'already underway' in Indigenous affairs, even though the legislation to abolish ATSIC was still, at that time, yet to finally pass the Senate.[1] The minister identified two 'key aspects to this change', both of which, in pointing the way forward, also condemned the past. The first was 'genuinely giving Indigenous Australians a voice', which she argued ATSIC had not done. The second was 'realising that the way we work, the way we organise ourselves as governments, has been a large part of the problem' (Vanstone 2005a: 1–2). Expanding on this last, Vanstone outlined the recent establishment of a network of regional Indigenous Co-ordination Centres, through which Indigenous communities could 'deal with the Australian Government as a whole', and an Office of Indigenous Policy Co-ordination within her department in Canberra. She also pointed to a secretaries group which was meeting monthly in Canberra, through which 'some of our best public servants' were 'turning their minds to the issue'. And there was a parallel ministerial taskforce meeting regularly, both with the secretaries group and with the foreshadowed Indigenous advisory body, the National Indigenous Council (NIC). All this, Minister Vanstone said, was 'unprecedented', required 'dramatic change' and was thus 'a quiet revolution' (Vanstone 2005a: 6–8).[2]

By the end of 2005, in a speech entitled 'Beyond Conspicuous Compassion', Minister Vanstone was adding a cutting moral dimension to her arguments about past failure and emerging change. She defined conspicuous compassion as 'a culture of ostentatious caring which is about feeling good, not doing good' and argued that, for those who were 'comfortable indulging' in it, the new 'environment will be challenging' (Vanstone 2005b: 1). This moral condemnation of established interests in Indigenous affairs which might resist the failure and change analysis was an interesting addition to ministerial rhetoric.

In early 2006, a major reorganisation of ministerial responsibilities saw Indigenous affairs relocated alongside families and community services under a new cabinet minister, Mal Brough. The new minister's policy focus and rhetoric, perhaps unsurprisingly, began to reflect this new grouping of portfolio responsibilities. In his first major speech in late April 2006 Minister Brough focused on the family as 'the most important element of our society', the 'fundamental building block' through which children are instilled with 'values and principles' and prepared for the 'challenges of the future'. Most Australian families, he argued, are 'strong', and, with government assistance, this leads to strong communities. However a 'small percentage' of Australian children, he argued, do not 'receive the necessary support, nutrition, education and life skills from their parents or carers despite the provision of considerable financial and practical support from the Federal Government'. He went on to describe 'dysfunctional families' in which alcohol, drug abuse and gambling are prevalent and the cash provided by the welfare system is used for these purposes, rather than in caring for the children. The minister suggested that many in his audience would be 'familiar' with such 'circumstances' and would have 'devoted much thought to how to address these challenges'. He then referred to two other public figures who shared this familiarity and concern: NIC Chair Sue Gordon, and Cape York Aboriginal leader Noel Pearson. Dysfunctional families were thus seen as a particular problem in Aboriginal communities, though the minister insisted that this was 'not a problem unique to Aboriginal communities'. Voluntary family income management arrangements had helped overcome some of these problems, although he noted that the voluntary arrangements were not always taken up. He argued that it was 'time to take the tough decisions and move to a system that requires certain welfare recipients to have part of their payments directed specifically to the benefit of their children' (Brough 2006a: 1–2). The minister believed that such families could be identified, that the technology was available, and that it was 'reasonable' for 30 per cent of welfare payments to be directed in this way. He believed that the proposal 'would have a dramatic and positive impact on some indigenous communities' but that it could also have a 'positive impact … more widely'. He concluded that April 2006 speech by noting that these thoughts were his 'own' and had been inspired by 'visiting distressed Aboriginal communities', but that they were 'not government policy' (Brough 2006a: 3).

While the word failure was not directly used, Minister Brough's sentiments about the past were clear and so too was his linking of these sentiments to an argument for future policy and organisational change. Three days before giving this speech, he had announced that $3m would be directed to the Cape York Institute (CYI), headed by Noel Pearson, to 'map out a new direction for Indigenous people receiving welfare' (Brough 2006b).

Less than a month later sexual abuse of Indigenous children erupted into national attention on the ABC's *Lateline* program through the revelations of a central Australian crown prosecutor, Nanette Rogers, of some horrific cases in which she had been professionally involved (*Lateline* 2006a). The minister's response was to label the current situation a 'disgrace' and to call for the state and territory governments to meet with the commonwealth in a summit to develop a 'National Plan for Action Against Indigenous Violence and Child Abuse' (Brough 2006c). On 21 June, in the lead-up to that summit, further allegations of sexual abuse of Indigenous children relating to the Northern Territory Aboriginal community of Mutitjulu, adjacent to Uluru, were aired on the ABC (*Lateline* 2006b). In light of this development, Northern Territory Chief Minister Clare Martin announced an inquiry into child abuse in all the territory's Aboriginal communities, in addition to a taskforce which was then being set up between the Northern Territory's family and community service administration and police (Martin 2006).

Following this outbreak of public debate over sexual abuse of Aboriginal children, the idea of past failure in relation to child welfare was now widely accepted. All that remained, in this policy area at least, was for the minister to develop ideas for change. However, in other policy areas the diagnosis of past failure was not yet quite so clear.

During August 2006 a raft of amendments to the *Aboriginal Land Rights (Northern Territory) Act 1976* was passed through the commonwealth parliament. Some of the amendments had been agreed to by the land councils, after protracted negotiations, and were uncontroversial. Others relating to township leasing were of more recent and contested origins, but were defended by the minister as offering more 'choice and opportunity' to Aboriginal people than past land rights arrangements in relation to 'home ownership and business development on Aboriginal land' (Brough 2006d).[3] Then in September/October 2006, Brough began an effort to reform the permit system that had operated on Aboriginal land under this act.[4] The minister's argument for change, under the heading 'Permit system no protection for the vulnerable', began from the idea that the permit system of the last '30 years' had 'contributed to dysfunction and exploitation' and done 'more harm than good' (Brough 2006e).

In December 2006, in his second major policy speech, Brough began with some brief comments which again suggested past failure. These can perhaps be selectively quoted as follows:

> Australia ... is a proud, strong and supportive nation ... [But] Sadly, too many Indigenous Australians are not leading independent lives. They are not sharing the opportunities and choices. The standard of health and low life expectancy are unacceptable. Too many are trapped in an intergenerational cycle, a welfare trap that needs to be broken.

He went on to talk of 'families' in Indigenous communities he had visited 'crying out for help', and of the 'sense of urgency' that was behind his 'promoting and introducing fundamental reforms' (Brough 2006f: 2–3).

Three months later, the failure and change analysis was directed more specifically at the Community Housing and Infrastructure Program (CHIP), which the commonwealth Department of Family and Community Services had inherited from ATSIC in 2004.[5] The 'overall conclusion' of a review of the program conducted by PriceWaterhouseCoopers was that:

> The housing needs of Indigenous Australians in remote areas have not been well served and the interests and expectations of taxpayers have not been met. ... CHIP in its current form contributes to policy confusion, complex administration and poor outcomes and accountability of government funded housing, infrastructure and municipal services. The Community Housing and Infrastructure Program should be abolished. (PWC 2007: 16)

Brough's view, made clear when he released the report, was as follows:

> CHIP, previously managed by ATSIC, has clearly failed to deliver and needs urgent reform ... While billions of dollars have been

> invested in Indigenous housing, there is little to show for it
> ... We've been chasing our tail and not seeing any significant progress in overcoming the Indigenous housing problem in remote Australia particularly ... The review of CHIP ... found current Indigenous housing arrangements flawed and unsustainable. It provides a sober analysis of the situation and a radical way forward. (Brough 2007a)

This report had outlined a 'new strategic framework' which essentially involved combining Indigenous community housing with public housing and providing assistance for home ownership, including in remote areas on community title land (PWC 2007: 23). The minister's response was that these, 'along with other views', would be 'considered by the government in exploring future directions in Indigenous housing' (Brough 2007a). But as the Nicholson cartoon reminds us, Prime Minister Howard had already, two years earlier, clearly expressed his enthusiasm for increasing home ownership among Indigenous people as the preferred way forward (see also Sanders 2005).

Over the next couple of months, these future directions in Indigenous housing began to emerge through a number of funding packages specific to

Courtesy of Peter Nicholson, *The Australian*, 7 April 2005

particular places. In the hope of encouraging home ownership, many of these packages which Brough announced tied housing funding commitments to land tenure change. This led to a degree of controversy and, in the case of the Alice Springs town camps, to rejection of a funding package (Brough 2007b, 2007c; Tilmouth 2007). Some packages, like the ones for the Tiwi Islands off Darwin and for Noel Pearson's home community of Hope Vale in Cape York, ranged into areas like education, sport and welfare reform, but all had housing and land issues at their core (Brough 2007d, 2007e).

Amid all this activity on housing and land packages, on 30 April 2007 NT Chief Minister Clare Martin announced that she had received an 'advance copy' of the report of the Inquiry into the Protection of Aboriginal Children from Sexual Abuse and that it would be made public 'as soon as it is printed' (Martin 2007a). In the event it was 15 June, over six weeks on, before Martin could announce that she had been given the 'final report'; she would table it in the Legislative Assembly in the next week. Martin foreshadowed a 'full response to the report in the August Sittings of Parliament', but immediately committed her government to 'implementing the key action areas of this report' and 'tackling this deeply disturbing issue'. She listed nine specific areas of action, including three areas of legislative change (Martin 2007b; BIPAC 2007).

It is not clear when the commonwealth first gained access to the NT board of inquiry findings. But on 19 June Brough announced that he had received the separate Welfare Reform Project Report from the Cape York Institute (CYI) which he had funded just over a year earlier. He expressed his agreement with that institute about the 'absolute priority' of the 'welfare of children' and of 'dealing with the causes of child neglect and abuse'. He also noted that the communities 'want changes', and thanked both the communities and the institute for their involvement in a 'high quality report which is ambitious and wide ranging' (Brough 2007f; CYI 2007). Noel Pearson and CYI seemed to have done something in their inquiry process which, in Minister Brough's and Prime Minister Howard's judgment, Clare Martin and the NT government had not; for the commonwealth response to the NT inquiry was very different.

On 21 June 2007, Howard and Brough held a joint press conference which the Prime Minister opened thus:

> Mr Brough and I have called this news conference to announce a number of measures to deal with what we can only describe as a national emergency in relation to the abuse of children in

indigenous communities in the Northern Territory. Anybody who's read or examined the report prepared by Pat Anderson and Rex Wild entitled *Little Children Are Sacred* will be sickened and horrified by the level of abuse. They will be deeply disturbed at the widespread nature of that abuse and they will be looking for the responsible assumption of authority by a government to deal with the problem. We are unhappy with the response of the Northern Territory Government. (Howard 2007a)

Howard detailed this unhappiness with the NT government and then announced eleven specific intervention measures. These measures were repeated in summary form in a media release by Minister Brough, as follows:

- Introducing widespread alcohol restrictions on Northern Territory Aboriginal land;
- Introducing welfare reforms to stem the flow of cash going towards substance abuse and to ensure funds meant to be for children's welfare are used for that purpose;
- Enforcing school attendance by linking income support and family assistance payments to school attendance for all people living on Aboriginal land and providing meals for children at school at parents' cost;
- Introducing compulsory health checks for all Aboriginal children to identify and treat health problems and any effects of abuse;
- Acquiring townships prescribed by the Australian Government through five year leases including payment of just terms compensation;
- As part of the immediate emergency response, increasing policing levels in prescribed communities, including requesting secondments from other jurisdictions to supplement NT resources, funded by the Australian Government;
- Requiring intensified on ground clean up and repair of communities to make them safer and healthier by marshalling local workforces through work-for-the-dole;
- Improving housing and reforming community living arrangements in prescribed communities including the introduction of market based rents and normal tenancy arrangements;
- Banning the possession of X-rated pornography and introducing audits of all publicly funded computers to identify illegal material;

- Scrapping the permit system for common areas, road corridors and airstrips for prescribed communities on Aboriginal land; and
- Improving governance by appointing managers of all government business in prescribed communities. (Brough 2007g)

While the word failure was not to the fore in these announcements of intervention and institutional change, the sentiment of arguing for change on the basis of past failure clearly was. In an interview with Prime Minister Howard that night on *Lateline*, the word 'failure' did indeed appear. In response to a question which asked whether this was 'one of the significant acts' of his 'time', the Prime Minister replied:

> Certainly in the social area, yes, because there has been a complete breakdown of these communities and this represents a cumulative failure of the policy approach over a long period of time. We are certainly suspending certain approaches and certain practices in the name of saving the children, because the past approach has failed. (*Lateline* 2007)

Four weeks later, Brough combined forces with the Minister for Employment and Workplace Relations, Joe Hockey, to announce a twelfth intervention measure – the replacement of Community Development Employment Projects (CDEP) in the NT with 'real jobs, training and mainstream employment'. CDEP provided part-time, base-rate employment to 8000 Indigenous people in the NT. But the aim of this intervention measure was to move just 2000 into 'real work', while the rest would do 'training' or 'work for the dole' (Brough & Hockey 2007). These numbers were a source of immediate criticism of this intervention measure (Altman 2007).

In early August five bills were passed through the commonwealth parliament to enact these changes. The first focused on welfare reform and essentially did three things:

- it introduced a general nationwide scheme making income support for children conditional on school attendance and providing for income management in cases of parental neglect;
- it introduced a specific income management scheme for the prescribed areas in the Northern Territory, where all residents would have half their income support payments managed for an initial period of 12 months, renewable for up to five years;

- it introduced a scheme for Cape York which recognised a new body established under Queensland state law which would have some power to direct management of a person's income support from Centrelink.

The second and third bills were directed specifically to the Northern Territory and overrode in quite specific detail certain aspects of the existing commonwealth *Northern Territory (Self-Government) Act 1978*, *Aboriginal Land Rights (Northern Territory) Act 1976* and *Racial Discrimination Act 1975*. The fourth and fifth were appropriations bills, allocating an additional $587 million during financial year 2007–08 to the 'Northern Territory National Emergency Response'. In introducing the bills specific to the Northern Territory, Brough began his second reading speech on 7 August as follows:

> When confronted with a failed society where basic standards of law and order and behaviour have broken down and where women and children are unsafe, how should we respond? Do we respond with more of what we have done in the past? Or do we radically change direction with an intervention strategy matched to the magnitude of the problem. (Brough 2007h: 7)

Courtesy of Peter Nicholson, *The Australian*, 7 August 2007

Here again we see a classic statement of the past failure and fundamental change argument which in Indigenous affairs had become the driving motif of the fourth Howard government. Nicholson's view that day was that 'rough justice' was being replaced by 'Brough justice'. On Friday 10 August a one-day Senate committee inquiry was held into these five bills and a report prepared over the weekend (SCLCA 2007). The legislation was then passed through the Senate unchanged.

Over the next three months, the intervention in the NT continued to attract public attention, much of which was supportive but some of which was very critical. One notable example of the latter was the Charles Perkins Oration given at the University of Sydney on 23 October by Marian Scrymgour, one of two Indigenous ministers in the NT government. Scrymgour condemned the intervention as 'a black kids' Tampa' and 'a vicious new McCarthyism' in which Minister Brough 'launched attacks on anyone who has raised doubts'. She referred to the Howard government's 'assault on Aboriginal Territorians' and condemned 'its motivation; ... its operations; ... and its moral basis'. To the idea that the government was 'saving the children', she said it was 'doing nothing of the kind' (Scrymgour 2007). This provoked Minister Brough to call for Scrymgour to be sacked, and others to fall in behind these two protagonists in some fairly unusual combinations. Scrymgour apologised for some of her more provocative words, but not the general tenor of her speech. The Howard government's failure and change analysis was leading to high emotions and political stakes a month out from the November election.[6]

A generational revolution

This second, more analytic section of the chapter asks: what sort of change have we been observing in Australian Indigenous affairs under the fourth Howard government? At the outset it is important to emphasise two aspects of the foregoing arguments about failure and change. First: the past being denigrated in these arguments is a period of about 30 or 40 years, or about the length of an average working career spent in Indigenous affairs. Second: many of these arguments have a highly moral tone, with words like 'compassion', 'disgrace', 'disturbing' and 'shame' often to the fore. What seems to be going on here, as much as an argument for change, is a moral denigration of the previous generation of people working in Indigenous affairs.

Building on these two observations, I suggest that Indigenous affairs is an, if not the, moral cause célèbre of Australian nationhood. It is one of the primary ways in which settler Australians, in particular, try to demonstrate their moral adequacy, or superiority, both to each other and to the world. I also suggest that this struggle for moral ascendancy has had both temporal and ideological aspects. Succeeding generations of settler Australians characteristically have believed themselves to be better at dealing with Indigenous issues than earlier generations, and so too have competing ideological groupings within Australian society at any one time. This has led to some interesting alliances and dynamics.

Noel Pearson's columns in the *Weekend Australian* also comment on this moral dimension of Indigenous affairs. In late 2006 he noted the moral importance of 'indigenous policy' to Australia and the way in which it could generate 'goodwill across the community, from the cities and the regions' and 'across the political spectrum'. However, he also wondered 'why has this goodwill not translated into reform' (Pearson 2006). Four months later, on the eve of the 40th anniversary of the famous 1967 Aborigines constitutional alteration referendum, he answered his own question by suggesting that, in Indigenous affairs, Australia is 'still divided into two ideological tribes':

> One tribe comprising most indigenous leaders and possibly most indigenous people (but by no means an overwhelming majority) and their progressive supporters holds the view that the absence or insufficient realisation of rights is the core of the indigenous predicament in this country. The other tribe comprises most non-progressive, non-indigenous Australians and their conservative political leaders (including substantial numbers in the Labor Party) who hold the view that it is the absence of responsibilities that lies at the core of our people's malaise. (Pearson 2007a)

Pearson sees these two ideological tribes as 'insistent and deafly opposed camps', which helps explain why Indigenous policy debate is 'still at such a juvenile stage' in Australia. He sees the rights-oriented progressives, or the liberal left, as having generally dominated debate in Australian Indigenous affairs over the years since the 1967 referendum and the more responsibility-oriented conservatives as having risen to prominence in more recent times. Pearson himself has been a major critic of the liberal left over the last eight years and clearly supports the rise of an approach focused more on behavioural responsibilities (Pearson 2007b). But he is also critical of the conservatives for their denial of Indigenous-specific rights and sees himself as trying to enunciate a more sophisticated 'radical centre' in Australian Indigenous affairs which advocates 'a synthesis of the rights and responsibilities paradigms' (Pearson 2007a).

This analysis, while very general and schematic, is quite helpful. It suggests that there has been a generational swing in Australian Indigenous affairs policy debates in recent years back from the dominance of the liberal left towards some greater influence for the once-dominant, directive or protective right. It also suggests how this is a very emotive, tribal and ideological swing, which individuals like Pearson have great trouble transcending.

While this generational left–right swing analysis is helpful, I suggest another generational dynamic is operating. In introducing their 2006 book on developments and debates in Australian Indigenous studies Cowlishaw, Kowal and Lea wondered whether they might have discerned a 30-year cycle in Australian Indigenous affairs, from 1910 to 1940, then 1970 to 2000. Having identified this idea, however, they discarded it as obviating 'responsibility to analyse the history that has brought us to this point' in the early 2000s (Cowlishaw et al. 2006: 1). While historical details need to be understood, the idea of a rough 30-year, or generational, cycle in Australian Indigenous affairs does have some credibility, and it can be related to the cross-cultural dimension of Indigenous affairs.

Indigenous affairs is about developing relationships between a large-scale industrial society and a number of much smaller scale hunter-gatherer societies. While all these societies, or cultures, are clearly changing, and to some extent possibly even merging through interaction, there is still a very clear sense in which Indigenous affairs is deeply cross-cultural. There are still today modern hunter-gatherers whose life practices are very substantially different, and to some extent autonomous, from those of the encapsulating industrial society, particularly in remote areas of Australia (Altman 1987; Tonkinson 2007). Because of this cross-cultural dimension, settler government programs to ameliorate the circumstances and opportunities of Indigenous people seldom, if ever, work as intended. Things happen, through these government programs interacting with Indigenous agency, and through which Indigenous people may hopefully derive some benefit. But the results of government intervention are always a long way from program design (see Folds 2001). There is, in short, an iron law of cross-cultural unintended consequences and unrealised expectations in Indigenous affairs.

One further consequence of this cross-cultural dimension is that it is very easy for participants in Indigenous affairs to begin to lose faith in what they are doing through government programs. Indeed I would argue that the cross-cultural nature of Indigenous affairs combines with its highly morally charged nature to produce a particular, characteristic policy dynamic, in which periods of pursuing a particular philosophical and organisational approach to Indigenous issues with some confidence and conviction alternate with periods of greater policy questioning and self-doubt. What Cowlishaw and colleagues were identifying in their dating of the rough 30-year cycles of Australian Indigenous affairs were these recurring periods of rising self-doubt, the current one being correctly dated to the year 2000.

In that year Pearson published *Our Right to Take Responsibility*, his critique of the way in which Aboriginal people had gained access to social security incomes in the previous 30 years in remote areas of Australia like Cape York, and the way in which, when combined with access to alcohol, this was rendering the communities of Cape York 'severely dysfunctional' and 'clearly unsuccessful' (Pearson 2000: 15). Also in that year a senior academic anthropologist, Professor Peter Sutton, delivered the Inaugural Berndt Foundation Lecture at the University of Western Australia (subsequently published as 'The politics of suffering: Indigenous policy in Australia since the 1970s'). Sutton argued that there were not 'enough signs of improvement' in Indigenous circumstances to 'allow for any further complacency about the correctness of existing approaches':

> The contrast between progressivist public rhetoric about empowerment and self-determination on the one hand, and the raw evidence of a disastrous failure in major aspects of Australian Aboriginal affairs policy since the early 1970s, is now frightening. Policy revision must now go back to bedrock questions, with all bets off, if it is to respond meaningfully to this crisis. (Sutton 2001: 125)

This style of argument marked a turning point in Indigenous affairs policy, the beginnings of a period of collective self-doubt. In the previous 20 years, when things were not working as well as expected, the predominant form of analysis would be to suggest that the existing policy approach, variously labelled self-determination or self-management, was not being well implemented. The predominant proposed remedy would be for participants in Indigenous affairs to try harder genuinely to implement the existing policy philosophy through existing, or partly reformed, policy institutions. Now however, another form of analysis was beginning to take hold in the public rhetoric: the failure, crisis and fundamental change form of analysis.

After Pearson and Sutton had given this other form of analysis some public prominence, others began to join in. In March 2002, the Northern Territory's first Indigenous minister within the new Martin Labor government, John Ah Kit, declared in a ministerial speech that:

> Aboriginal Territorians are facing a stark crisis. To say anything else would be to lie – and I believe that now is the time for the truth to be told. We cannot – indeed must not – continue to guild the lily about what is happening on our communities ... The simple fact is that it is almost impossible to find a functional Aboriginal community anywhere in the Northern Territory. (Ah Kit 2002: 2)

With such analyses coming from both prominent Indigenous leaders and respected academics, it was not long, as we have seen above, before the Howard government joined in. From there, it was but a series of repeated rhetorical steps to the events of June–August 2007, which can I think rightly be seen as the climax of a generational revolution in Australian Indigenous affairs. Along the way, during the term of the fourth Howard government, the institutional innovations and policy ideas of the previous generation of participants in this difficult cross-cultural and highly morally charged area of Australian public policy were summarily dismissed and discarded, in the name of failure, and a new institutional architecture and policy rhetoric for the next generation's efforts began to be built.

Consistently with this cycles explanation, I believe there was another generational revolution in Australian Indigenous affairs running from the mid-1960s to 1976, drawing on the same basic moral and cross-cultural dynamics but involving an opposite ideological swing from right to left. In this previous period of rising collective self-doubt, the existing objects of negative assessment that were said to have 'failed' were a policy of 'assimilation' and established state and territory native welfare organisations which restrictively managed Aboriginal people on areas of land known as reserves. In the 1960s this restrictive management was increasingly seen as unjust and untenable, as having failed. Restrictions on Aboriginal people, like limited access to alcohol and social security payments, began to be changed and lifted. The entry of the commonwealth into Indigenous affairs on a national scale, rather than just in the territories, was seen as one of the primary ways in which Indigenous affairs might be very significantly, even fundamentally reformed in this earlier generational revolution. Hence, the importance to that generational revolution of the 1967 referendum, in which the commonwealth extended its powers to legislate in regard to 'the Aboriginal race in any state'. Thereafter, the commonwealth could encourage and cajole significant reform in the states knowing that it had a clear new legislative power.

In the Northern Territory, this previous emerging revolution took the form of a battle between the new commonwealth Office of Aboriginal

Affairs and the old Darwin-based Welfare Branch within the Northern Territory Administration of the Department of Territories. It was the new commonwealth Minister for Aboriginal Affairs and also Social Security, WC Wentworth, who in 1968 directed that there be a move away from the predominant existing practice of paying a large portion of the social security entitlements of Aboriginal people in remote areas to third parties on their behalf and towards direct payment to entitled individuals. The Welfare Branch resisted this move, but was disparaged by the new players as a self-serving, morally complacent established interest. As a consequence of such resistance, the Welfare Branch was abolished in 1972 and incorporated into the new commonwealth Department of Aboriginal Affairs which grew out of the previous office.

My contention is thus that there have been two generational revolutions in Australian Indigenous affairs within the last 40 years, both of which, in the name of failure, have similarly disparaged and discarded the work of a previous generation of participants, even as they have also moved in opposite ideological directions.[7] If this analysis is accepted, it should invite considerably more critical thinking about the nature of change in Australian Indigenous affairs under the fourth Howard government. More fundamentally it could also invite the question, are generational revolutions as good as it gets in Indigenous affairs policy-making? Or can governments, by being aware of the moral and cross-cultural dimensions of Indigenous affairs and the way in which they tend to produce generational revolutions, possibly move beyond such revolutions?

Notes

1   The legislation to abolish ATSIC was referred to a Select Committee of the Senate in June 2004 which did not report until March 2005 (SCAIA 2005). This did not, however, stop the third Howard government from immediately removing the vast bulk of ATSIC's funding and pushing ahead administratively with its proposed changes to Indigenous affairs arrangements from 1 July 2004 (see Gray & Sanders 2006).
2   Rowse (2006: 168) notes that Senator Ellison used the terminology of a 'quiet revolution' to describe changes in Indigenous affairs in debates in the commonwealth parliament in December 2004.
3   See also OIPC (2005).
4   The system has required intending visitors to Aboriginal land in the NT to apply for permission stating the purpose and duration of their visit. Permission is granted by traditional owners via the land councils.
5   This program funded the provision of 'community rental' housing for Indigenous people which, after construction, was vested in Indigenous community housing organisations for ongoing management.

6   The other aspect of Indigenous affairs which was causing controversy in the lead-up to the election was reconciliation and constitutional recognition. On 11 October, in an address to the Sydney Institute, Howard committed himself, if re-elected, to a referendum to recognise the 'special status' of Indigenous Australians as 'the first peoples of our nation' in the preamble to the constitution (Howard 2007b). While this was seen as Howard now recognising the importance of symbolism to reconciliation, controversy erupted over whether there should be more substantive change in the body of the constitution. Another paper would be required to explore the Howard government's changing approach to reconciliation during its later years. Suffice to say here that back in 2005 Howard had already expressed some new understanding of the importance of symbolism, and even rights, to reconciliation (Howard 2005).
7   Doubters of the idea that the period 1967 to 1976 involved a similar generational revolution could read Paul Hasluck's account (1988) of his involvement in Indigenous affairs from the 1925 to 1965. His penultimate chapter entitled 'Ring in the new: Pull the plug on the old' reflects on the years after 1965 in which he clearly felt disparaged and discarded as an embodiment of past policy failure.

References

Ah Kit, J (Minister Assisting the Chief Minister on Indigenous Affairs) (2002) Ministerial statement, 7 March.

Altman, J C (1987) *Hunter-Gatherers Today: An Aboriginal Economy in North Australia*, Australian Institute of Aboriginal Studies, Canberra.

—— (2007) Scrapping CDEP is just plain dumb, Topical Issues Paper 7/2007, Australian National University, Centre for Aboriginal Economic Policy Research, at <www.anu.edu.au/caepr>

BIPAC (Board of Inquiry into the Protection of Aboriginal Children from Sexual Abuse: Rex Wild & Pat Anderson, Inquiry Co-chairs) (2007) *Ampe Akelyernemane Meke Mekarke: Little Children are Sacred*, Northern Territory Government, Darwin.

Brough, M (Minister for Families, Community Services and Indigenous Affairs) (2006a) Speech – Social innovations dialogue, 29 April.

—— (2006b) Brough backs Indigenous Study (Media release), 26 April.

—— (2006c) National plan for action against Indigenous violence and child abuse (Media release), 18 May.

—— (2006d) Northern Territory Indigenous people now free to choose (Media release), 17 August.

—— (2006e) Permit system no protection for the vulnerable (Media release), Minister for Families, Community Services and Indigenous Affairs, 5 October.

—— (2006f) Blueprint for action in Indigenous affairs, University of Canberra, National Institute of Governance, Indigenous Affairs Governance Series, 5 December.

—— (2007a) Review recommends major reform of Indigenous housing (Media release), 8 March.

—— (2007b) Major Howard government investment in Alice Springs Indigenous accommodation (Media release), 13 March.

—— (2007c) Minister disappointed by decision on Alice Springs town camps (Media release), 23 May.

—— (2007d) Breakthrough agreement on Aboriginal land in the NT (Media release), 3 May.

—— (2007e) Brighter future for Hope Vale (Media release), 11 May.

—— (2007f) Government receives Cape York Institute report (Media release), 19 June.
—— (2007g) National emergency response to protect Aboriginal children in the NT (Media release), 21 June.
—— (2007h) Second reading speech, *Com. Parl. Debs HoR,* 7 August.
Brough, M & Hockey, J (2007) Jobs and training for Indigenous people in the NT (Joint media release*),* 23 July.
Cowlishaw, G, Kowal, E & Lea, T (2006) Introduction: Double binds. In T Lea, E Kowal & G Cowlishaw (eds), *Moving Anthropology: Critical Indigenous Studies*, Charles Darwin University Press, Darwin: 1–15.
CYI (Cape York Institute For Policy & Leadership) (2007) *From Hand Out to Hand Up: Cape York Welfare Reform Project*, Cairns.
Folds, R (2001) *Crossed Purposes: The Pintupi and Australia's Indigenous Policy*, UNSW Press, Sydney.
Gray, W & Sanders, W (2006) *Views from the Top of the 'Quiet Revolution': Secretarial Perspectives on the New Arrangements in Indigenous Affairs*, Discussion Paper No. 282, Centre for Aboriginal Economic Policy Research, ANU, Canberra.
Hasluck, P (1988) *Shades of Darkness: Aboriginal Affairs, 1925–1965*, Melbourne University Press, Melbourne.
Howard, J (Prime Minister) (2005) Transcript: Address at the National Reconciliation Planning Workshop, Old Parliament House, Canberra, 30 May.
—— (2007a) Interview Transcript: Joint press conference with the Hon Mal Brough, Minister for Families, Community Services and Indigenous Affairs, 21 June.
—— (2007b) Transcript: Address to the Sydney Institute, Wentworth Hotel, Sydney, 11 October.
Howard, J & Vanstone, A (2004) Transcript of the Prime Minister, Joint press conference with Senator Amanda Vanstone, Parliament House, Canberra, 15 April.
Lateline (2006a) Crown prosecutor speaks out about abuse in Central Australia, 15 May.
—— (2006b) Sexual abuse reported in Indigenous community, 21 June.
—— (2007) Tony Jones talks to Prime Minister Howard, 21 June.
Martin, C (Northern Territory Chief Minister) (2006) Chief Minister orders inquiry into child sex abuse (Media release), 22 June.
—— (2007a) Inquiry report (Media release), 30 April.
—— (2007b) Inquiry report (Media release), 15 June.
OIPC (Office of Indigenous Policy Coordination) (2005) *The Northern Territory Land Rights Act: Unlocking the Potential – Making it Easier to Own a Home and Develop Business*, Dept of Immigration and Multicultural and Indigenous Services, Canberra.
Pearson, N (2000) *Our Right to Take Responsibility*, Noel Pearson and Associates, Cairns.
—— (2006) Labor's ideas mature, *Weekend Australian*, 9–10 December.
—— (2007a) Hunt for the radical centre, *Weekend Australian*, 21–22 April.
—— (2007b) Leftist policies pave kids' road to hell, *Weekend Australian*, 21–22 July.
PWC (PriceWaterhouseCoopers) (2007) *Living in the Sunburnt Country – Indigenous Housing: Findings of the Review of the Community Housing and Infrastructure Programme*, Department of Families, Community Services and Indigenous Affairs, Canberra.
Rowse, T (2006) The politics of being 'practical': Howard's fourth term challenge. In T Lea, E Kowal & G Cowlishaw (eds), *Moving Anthropology: Critical Indigenous Studies*, Charles Darwin University Press, Darwin: 167–84.
Sanders, W (2005) *Housing Tenure and Indigenous Australians in Remote and Settled Areas*, Discussion Paper No. 275, Centre for Aboriginal Economic Policy Research,

Australian National University, Canberra.
SCAIA (Select Committee on the Administration of Indigenous Affairs) (2005) *After ATSIC – Life in the Mainstream?* Department of the Senate, Canberra.
SCLCA (Standing Committee on Legal and Constitutional Affairs) (2007) *Social Security and Other Legislation Amendment (Welfare Payment Reform) Bill 2007 and four related bills concerning the Northern Territory National Emergency Response*, Department of the Senate, Canberra.
Scrymgour, M (2007) Whose national emergency? Caboolture and Kirribili? Or Milikapiti and Mutitjulu?, Charles Perkins Oration, University of Sydney, 23 October.
Sutton, P (2001) The politics of suffering: Indigenous policy in Australia since the 1970s, *Anthropological Forum*, 11(2): 125–73.
Tilmouth, W (2007) Saying no to $60 million. In J Altman & M Hinkson (eds) *Coercive Reconciliation: Stabilise, Normalise, Exit Aboriginal Australia*, Arena Publications, Melbourne: 231–38.
Tonkinson, R (2007) Aboriginal 'difference' and 'autonomy' then and now: Four decades of change in Western Desert society, *Anthropological Forum*, 17 (1): 41–60.
Vanstone, A (Minister for Immigration and Multicultural and Indigenous Affairs) (2005a) Address to the National Press Club, 23 February.
—— (2005b) Beyond conspicuous compassion: Indigenous Australians deserve more than good intentions, Address to Australia and New Zealand School of Government, Australian National University, Canberra, 7 December.

12
Discovering the environment

Jenny Stewart and Carolyn Hendriks

This chapter will use the concept of agenda to trace the Howard government's political management of environmental issues. This management kept green groups on the defensive, and pushed conflict away from the national arena. The price of this skilful agenda management, however, was that the government was ill-equipped, in policy terms, to address the massive, intertwined issues of energy, climate change and water, and the challenges they posed to the nation's resource-based economy.

Despite the growing certainty of climate scientists that global warming was the consequence of human activity, the Howard government remained sceptical. In the *realpolitik* of international responses to climate change, Australia was adamant in its refusal to ratify the Kyoto Protocol. Ratification, the Prime Minister firmly believed, would harm Australia's economic interests (Howard 2002).

Nevertheless, during the Howard era, public action on environmental issues became increasingly part of the institutional policy agenda. The policy work was not obviously visible, but formed part of the day-to-day business of government, involving action at the federal level (such as through the Australian Greenhouse Office) and in a variety of intergovernmental contexts.

In developing these themes, we first provide a brief background to environmental policy in Australia, and then trace the approach taken by the Howard government since it first came to power. We argue that, by the end of 2006, a combination of biophysical and political factors on both the domestic and international fronts saw environmental issues such as water and climate change become much more prominent on the public agenda. With a strengthening opposition party and a pending election, the Howard government decided to 'discover' the environment and to green its agenda.

Context

ENVIRONMENTAL POLICY IN AUSTRALIA

While the commonwealth's role in environmental matters has grown considerably since the 1980s, much of the policy work has been done by the states, especially in the areas of land and water use, urban and regional planning and waste management. Because species, air, water and carbon do not respect political boundaries, co-operative intergovernmental relations clearly lie at the heart of successful environmental policy and administration. While a number of important national strategies were articulated through the Council of Australian Governments (COAG) during the 1990s, genuine progress proved hard to achieve. Interstate conflict over water management in the Murray-Darling Basin was one of the prime examples (Connell 2007). Other policy fields where co-ordinated responses were needed (such as waste management and packaging regulation) also suffered from the inevitable delays of federalism (Institute for Sustainable Futures 2004).

Whatever the formal distribution of powers, commonwealth involvement in environmental questions is as much politically as administratively determined. In the early 1980s, the assertion of federal power was significant in saving the Franklin River from being dammed, and in an earlier period, federal intervention saved Fraser Island from sand mining. During the Hawke era (1983–91), environmental issues were prominent on the policy agenda, reflecting a period of pronounced and sustained public interest (Economou 1999).

The Keating period, however, saw something of a retraction, and a desire to move some environmental questions back to the states. The Intergovernmental Agreement on the Environment, signed by Keating, the state premiers and the Australian Local Government Association in 1992, established common values and principles for policy-making, but specifically acknowledged the separate (although complementary and often overlapping) spheres of the commonwealth and the states.

When Howard came to power in 1996, he inherited and extended this approach. Under his leadership the commonwealth's role focused on international environmental relations, the management of Antarctica, and the determination of national heritage and environmental impact assessment (where its own activities were involved). But it is important to appreciate that, at the time, the political realities did not favour strong environmental engagement by either major party. For both the ALP and the coalition, issues such as forest management that led to conflict between key interests were 'no-win' political situations, particularly when problems spilled over into the federal arena. From a coalition perspective, to favour the green cause risked losing business support as well as potentially antagonising the Howard 'battlers', while from a Labor perspective, there could be costs in union support as well as votes.

Towards the end of the 1990s, there was a growing realisation, affecting politics and business as well as the wider community, that environmental conservation was only part of a much more complex and deep-seated set of problems that went to the heart of Australia's traditional political economy. Australia could, in a sense, hide behind its relatively small population. But per capita, it was undeniable that Australians were among the most environmentally profligate of any of the world's inhabitants, in terms of water use, energy use and waste production. ABS data shows that between 1974–75 and 1995–96, household energy use increased by 46 per cent in the aggregate, and also increased per capita (ABS 1998). Water use and waste production showed the same pattern (ABS 2006).

The broader pattern of the economy, however, did not encourage a move towards environmental modernisation where economic growth and environmental conservation are mutually supportive (Mol 1996). Australia had long since ceased to ride on the sheep's back. But riding in the coal truck and the liquefied natural gas (LNG) carrier meant that Australia was not only an exporter of energy to other countries (notably China), but a very energy-intensive economy in terms of its manufacturing base. Water intensity was increasing, too, as agriculture moved away from the broad-acre farming of the first half of the 20th century and into water-intensive crops such as cotton, vines and horticulture. Whichever political party held power, the task of making real environmental improvement while managing the interests (and realities) of economic growth in Australia would prove particularly daunting and difficult.

AGENDA MANAGEMENT

We use the concepts of policy agenda and of agenda management to explore the Howard government's relationship with environmental issues. The distinction offered by Cobb and Elder (1972) between the institutional (formal) agenda and public (informal) agenda is particularly relevant here. The institutional policy agenda refers to the list of subjects or problems on which government and relevant policy actors are focusing their attention (Howlett & Ramesh 2003: 132). It differs from the public agenda which represents those issues discussed and debated in the broader public domain. Both agenda types change over time and issues move from one to the other, in response to different pressures, ideas, priorities and norms (Cobb, Ross & Ross 1976). But agendas can also be skilfully managed, particularly the public agenda.

Agenda management techniques range from symbolism, tokenism, diversion, postponement, co-option of dissenting groups, discrediting opponents, manipulating or restricting information, redefining the problem, shifting the blame, or making the issue disappear (see Harding 1985). In the following sections we discuss some of the Howard government's key environmental polices over the 1996–2006 decade including its response to biodiversity and conservation, water and climate change. Together these initiatives represent a series of ongoing exercises in management of both the institutional and public agenda. By the beginning of 2007, after a decade in government and with the combination of a worsening drought and pending election, the Howard government was forced to address the severity of environmental issues and the long-term bio-physical, financial and social problems they posed.

Policy case studies

ENVIRONMENT PROTECTION & BIODIVERSITY CONSERVATION ACT 1999

All environmental policy represents a compromise between the needs and interests of economic development, and those of the environment. In this context, the *Environment Protection and Biodiversity Conservation Act 1999* (EPBC Act), which came into operation in 2000, represents the most enigmatic of the Howard era legislative changes. The key objectives of the new legislation were to ensure that actions affecting 'matters of national environmental significance' were subject to permission and control and would engender the ecologically sustainable use of natural resources (McGrath 2005). The protection of biological diversity was also a significant component of the act.

Academic opinion remains divided on the extent to which the EPBC Act represented an advance or a retrenchment of public capacity in relation to key areas of environmental decision-making (see for example Scanlon & Dyson 2001; Gumley 2005; McGrath 2006). It was the mode of operation of the act that attracted the most contention. Some commentators saw the pattern of commonwealth–state relations implied by the act as undermining the exercise of commonwealth power, largely because the act provided for the development and use of bilateral agreements between the two levels of government (Gumley 2005). In the lead-up to the passage of the act, these arrangements were seen as 'handing back' powers to the states (see Stewart 2000). Others saw these agreements as being of limited impact, and pointed to the fact that proponents of developments that were 'triggered' by the act had to apply directly to the minister for approval to proceed, representing a considerable centralisation of power (Scanlon & Dyson 2001: 17). In practice, it was the lack of resources provided to the department to implement key provisions of the act that was of most concern (see for example Chapple 2001).

The extent of 'traffic' under the act proved to be considerable – over 1900 decisions on development proposals were made in the first six years of operation (Macintosh 2006). That almost all the requests to proceed were approved suggested that the act itself was not exercising a decisive influence. Nevertheless, there was a potential for the legislation to extend its reach where conservation-minded individuals were prepared to take action. One celebrated case, where a farmer cleared land in an internationally protected area without applying for approval first, and was subsequently prosecuted and fined for his actions, suggested that the EPBC might be able to reach where state government land-clearing policies had not.

The Howard government itself clearly saw a danger to its own interests in these developments, because in 2006 it pushed a number of significant amendments to the act through the parliament. These amendments were designed to restore 'certainty' for developers, in part by restricting the involvement of third parties in the approvals process.

With the appointment of Senator Ian Campbell as environment minister in 2005, the government began to see political possibilities for itself in the act, especially in relation to the approval of new wind farms. Wind farms that could affect wildlife were 'controlled actions' in the terms of the EPBC. Prior to 2005, the commonwealth had approved ten such applications, but Senator Campbell refused on what were generally considered to be skimpy environmental grounds a proposal to build a wind farm in a politically sensitive electorate where there was considerable opposition to the development (ABC 2006a).

This mode of activity – institutional and incremental, low-key and quasi-legalistic – undoubtedly suited a government that wished to move slowly, while keeping its political options open. It was probably at the bureaucratic level that the lack of genuine political support for key provisions of the act became most apparent. The Australian National Audit Office (ANAO) found that the Department of the Environment and Water Resources was failing to implement the biodiversity elements of the act by not keeping up to date its list of threatened species. Neither had the department met a commitment made in 2000 to have recovery plans implemented for 583 endangered species by 2004 (ANAO 2007). The government's answer – to allow the minister to prioritise assessments – was, as the Australian Conservation Foundation noted, no answer at all (ACF 2006).

The proposal by Tasmanian company Gunn's to build a pulp mill in the Tamar Valley came at a particularly inopportune time for the coalition. Minister Malcolm Turnbull, required to give his approval under the terms of the EPBC Act, was caught between the politics of the Tasmanian electorate (solidly pro-mill) and the need to force Gunn's to adopt a more environmentally responsible approach to its investment.

NATURAL HERITAGE TRUST

Viewed as a piece of political management, the Natural Heritage Trust (NHT) was undoubtedly one of the Howard government's master-strokes (Crowley 2001). As announced prior to the 1996 election, a portion of the funds from the first-tranche sale of Telstra were to be ear-marked for a trust, expenditure from which would be used to improve the environment.

In setting up the trust, the coalition killed several birds with one stone. It established its green credentials with an unprecedented volume of funding, while at the same time, in spending most of the money in rural and regional Australia, helping to neutralise opposition 'in the bush' to the sale of Telstra.

The trust allocated funds, and generated matching funds, for investing in the 'conservation, sustainable use and repair of Australia's environmental, agricultural and natural resources into the twenty-first century' (Crowley 2001: 255). From the outset, however, the administration of the NHT proved controversial. The opposition claimed there was political bias in the allocation of funds. The Auditor-General found this claim unproven, but did express the view that more should be done to enhance the geographic reach of the program, to improve the level of expertise on assessment panels, and to clarify ministerial priorities in decision-making (ANAO 1998).

Evaluations of the NHT proved problematic. Hassall and Associates (2003), undertaking an evaluation of the first two years of the program, found that while much good had been done, data limitations and the diversity of the projects that had been undertaken complicated the evaluation task.

In the early years of the trust's operation, the enormous sums of money available seemed to overwhelm the administrative infrastructure that was supposed to manage them. Relations with state governments, who were supposed to match commonwealth funding for many projects, became quite tetchy. With the second injection of funds from 2001–02, the financial accountabilities and project management side of the trust's operations were clarified and made more transparent. From 2003–04, regional NHT programs were co-delivered with the National Action Plan for Salinity and Water Quality (NAP), for which funding had commenced in 2000–01 (NRMMC 2005).

Whatever their outcomes, the large sums expended by the trust represented a steady flow of resources to regional and rural Australia. The NHT's initial five-year budget was for $1.3 billion but with subsequent extensions and additions, the total volume of funds to 2007–08 was estimated at close to $3 billion (NHT 2005). Between 1996–97 and 2001–02, just under $1.5 billion in funding was approved by the Natural Heritage Trust Ministerial Board (NHT 2002).

Although the NHT continued to arouse criticism from a number of sources throughout its years of operation, in political terms it served the government well. It was highly popular among recipients, as well as enabling the government to weaken the conservation movement by driving a wedge between local and state-based conservation groups (who were directly involved with, and largely supported the policy) and national-level organisations such as the Australian Conservation Foundation, who opposed it (Crowley 2001: 265).

REGIONAL FOREST AGREEMENTS

In 2004, John Howard pronounced himself well-pleased with the Tasmanian Regional Forest Agreement (RFA). It had, he observed, brought 'stability and balance' to the logging industry (Whinnett 2004). By this stage, there were ten of these agreements, covering forestry operations on public land in five states. In an era of steady centralisation, the RFAs were remarkable for the fact that, once signed, they effectively dealt the commonwealth out of forestry management, leaving the states to pursue their own priorities. Moreover, as the commonwealth's EPBC Act did not apply to forestry operations, there was no opportunity for ongoing impact assessment of major new operations (Walker 2004).

The RFAs have been extensively studied as forms of governance (see Stewart & Jones 2003; Mercer 2000; Lane 1999). While the verdict on their political efficacy has been favourable, assessment of their performance in ensuring sustainable forest management has been much more equivocal.

Most agreements were the subject of annual reports for the first five years, with reviews at five-year intervals thereafter. Not surprisingly, there was a divergence of views on the extent to which goals had been achieved. In Victoria, annual reports recorded modest progress against milestones. The verdict of Victorian environmentalists, however, was scathing. Implementation of the basic sustainability requirements of the agreements had been compromised. For example, the main instrument for regulating logging, the Victorian Forestry Controls, had not been updated to reflect the requirements of the RFA. Walker (2004: 61) concluded that 'Victoria's forests are not managed in an open, accountable and transparent manner'.

Similarly, the Tasmanian RFA attracted widespread criticism from environmentalists (ABC 1999). In New South Wales, on the other hand, environmental criticism was much less apparent, perhaps reflecting the 'greener' starting point for the RFA process in that state (Stewart & Jones 2003).

Despite (or perhaps because of) the environmental movement's opposition to the RFA, the management of Tasmania's forests continued to offer political opportunities to the coalition. In the lead-up to the 2004 election, Howard was able completely to wrong-foot Labor leader Mark Latham, who had decided to court the green vote, by strongly endorsing the RFA.

The political importance (to both parties) of winning seats in Tasmania underpinned the continuing durability of the RFA in that state over the next three years. For both sides of politics, the basic political purpose of the RFAs was to keep forest politics out of the federal sphere, and in this endeavour the agreements had succeeded admirably, despite continuing concerns about their environmental effectiveness.

WATER MANAGEMENT AND THE CRISIS IN THE MURRAY-DARLING BASIN

Water management is a good example of a policy issue that, for much of the Howard government's first three terms, remained on the institutional, rather than the public agenda. This accorded well with the government's general preference for keeping environmental matters away from the spotlight, until events (in this case an unprecedented drought) necessitated a more active response.

Major problems had long been apparent in the management of the Murray-Darling basin, the catchment encompassing the major irrigated production areas of much of south-eastern Australia. When it first came to office, the Howard government inherited the commonwealth's role in the complex intergovernmental machinery that had been put together to cap water extractions from the river system through negotiated agreements between participating states (Queensland, New South Wales, Victoria and South Australia) and the ACT.

The intergovernmental apparatus took the form of a ministerial council (comprising state, territory and commonwealth ministers), and the Murray-Darling Basin Commission, an administrative, implementing and research body that reported to the council. By 1996, the commission (founded in its current form by the Hawke government in 1992) itself formed part of a complex network of intergovernmental relations that reflected initiatives in natural resource management including salinity, water quality improvement and total catchment management (MDBC 2001).

In the years that followed, the Howard government funded many water-oriented initiatives (such as riparian tree-planting) through the Natural Heritage Trust (see discussion above). It also contributed (from 2003) to the COAG-sponsored Living Murray initiative, and from 2000 to a major intergovernmental action plan, the National Salinity Action Plan (co-delivered with Natural Heritage Trust projects) to counter salinity and to improve water quality (Kemp 2004).

Meanwhile, despite this activity, the river systems and the wildlife associated with them continued to deteriorate. Environmentalists and many water scientists called for more co-ordinated action. For example, in 2002 the Wentworth Group of Concerned Scientists put forward several submissions to COAG (*Blueprint for a Living Continent, Blueprint for a National Water Plan*) calling on governments to take action on the management of Australia's water resources. The Wentworth Group proposed a combination of water rights and market allocation to ensure that Australia's use of urban and agricultural water better reflect our dry climatic conditions (see Wentworth Group 2002, 2003; Lowe 2004: 46).

A further major effort came in 2004 with the announcement of a $2 billion National Water Initiative (NWI). Initially conceived as a ten-year plan, the

NWI was aimed at improving water management in rural and urban Australia, and featured ambitious plans for the introduction of water trading. Part of the initiative involved the establishment of an independent statutory body, the National Water Commission, to assist with implementation (NWI 2004).

The extreme drought of 2001–05, coming as it did on the back of less-severe but still extensive droughts during the 1990s, ravaged the system still further, and caused unprecedented damage to production in the basin. But it was not only rural Australia that was affected. As the drought worsened, water restrictions were imposed in the major cities of Brisbane, Sydney, Melbourne, Adelaide and Canberra, as well as in many other smaller coastal towns. The drought had come to suburban Australia, and in doing so, began to dominate the public agenda.

The water crisis that intensified during 2006 presented the government with both a challenge and an opportunity. The challenge was to craft a program that would highlight the government's credibility as a sound environmental manager. The opportunity was to seize the initiative, in the lead-up to an election, from state governments that could be portrayed as recalcitrant or, worse, complicit in the poor management of the precious water resource.

Howard moved quickly to seize the high ground. In early November 2006, he called a crisis meeting with premiers from the Murray-Darling basin to assess the scale and severity of the drought. Following the meeting the Prime Minister announced that the NWI would be accelerated and that water trading between the states could commence in early 2007 (Brissenden 2006).

Then in January 2007 Howard announced his National Plan for Water Security – a $10 billion investment over the next ten years in water management in the Murray-Darling basin (over $9 billion), the Great Artisan Basin and Northern Australia (less than $1 billion) (Howard 2007). This was soon followed by the appointment of high-profile Liberal Malcolm Turnbull to a new portfolio of Environment and Water Resources. The plan was bold: under it, the commonwealth would seek to take control of water management from the states, with the aim of (ultimately) putting an end to overextraction of water from the river system. To achieve its goals, the plan offered irrigators generous payouts and subsidies.

Howard's water plan can be interpreted as a strategic move in an election year — an attempt to trump the new opposition leader's popularity with the electorate. As one commentator noted: 'its scale and radicalism goes far beyond anything Labor had dared propose' (*SMH* 2007).

The plan soon met with criticism from diverse groups: water authorities, farmers and some states. Initially concerns were voiced over the lack of consultation, detail, planning, and institutional consideration. These concerns were not alleviated when Treasury Secretary Ken Henry was reported to have said at a departmental meeting in March that the Treasury had had little input into the water plan (ABC 2007). Green groups also criticised the plan on the grounds that the Howard government continued to deny the role of climate change in water management (Peters 2007).

After a relatively short period of negotiation, the premiers of Queensland, New South Wales and South Australia announced that they were prepared to hand over to the commonwealth their powers over water. Victoria's Premier, on the other hand, announced that his state would do no such thing. Among 44 closely argued concerns, Premier Bracks' central objection was that the water plan 'holds no guarantee to ensure the security of Victoria water rights and the integrity of our irrigation systems, which we believe are being well managed' (Topsfield et al. 2007). In an effort to ensure that Victoria did not end up compensating for the mismanagement of water in other jurisdictions, Bracks put forward his own plan (Topsfield et al. 2007). When John Brumby, also a strong critic of the Howard plan, took over from the retiring Bracks in August 2007, it appeared that Howard's water revolution would have to be adjudicated in the High Court before it could be implemented (Marris 2007a).

Had the water plan backfired? Yes and no. Its weaknesses, in terms of a lack of detailed planning and consultation, had been exposed. But in being seen to take control of an important environmental issue, Howard had not only showed himself to be a strong leader, he had taken control of the public agenda by leaving the opposition leader with very little room to manoeuvre, and by casting blame for much of the crisis onto state Labor premiers and their associated special interests.

ENERGY AND THE RISING CONCERN OVER CLIMATE CHANGE

Climate change is another policy area where the Howard government's agenda management has shifted from the institutional to the public realm, resulting in a considerable policy back-flip. Not long after it was elected, the Howard government participated in negotiations on reducing global greenhouse emissions within the context of the United Nation's Framework Convention on Climate Change (UNFCCC), where Australia in the early 1990s had been a leader (McDonald 2005).

At the first meeting of the UNFCCC after Howard came into power, the government argued against uniform legally binding targets in favour of a system of *differentiated* emission targets that would account for population and economic growth (Pearse 2007: 73). Australia also demanded special consideration for its high population growth, dependence on primary industries, and reliance on fossil fuel for transport and exports (Papadakis 2002: 267). Though this position represented a continuation from the Keating government, the new coalition government was far more willing to sacrifice diplomatic relations and international obligations for the protection of national interests (McDonald 2005: 222–23).

On the domestic front in 1997 the Prime Minister announced the 'Safeguarding the Future' package which offered some financial and institutional greenhouse initiatives. A key component of the package was financial support for the renewables industry as well as the Mandatory Renewable Energy Target (MRET) which required electricity producers to source 2 per cent of their energy from renewables (Howard 1997). Initiatives were also directed at the transport and industry sectors, for example to improve energy efficiency. A new agency was also created – the Australian Greenhouse Office (AGO) – to administer climate change policy.

At the UNFCC meeting in December 1997 in Kyoto, Japan, then federal Minister for the Environment Robert Hill pulled off an extraordinary diplomatic feat. Hill managed to secure an emissions target for Australia of an 8 per cent *increase* over 1990s levels, while other nations on average were required to *decrease* their emissions by approximately 5.2 per cent (McDonald 2005: 227). In addition, Hill managed to push through a special clause that excluded land clearing from emissions calculations, effectively ensuring that Australia did not have to account for extensive deforestation since 1990.

Having negotiated significant concessions, it was anticipated in the international community that Australia would ratify Kyoto. But despite Hill's efforts, Cabinet support for Kyoto waned considerably between 1997 and 2002 (see McDonald 2005; Pearse 2007). Then on World Environment Day, 5 June 2002, Howard announced that Australia would not be ratifying the Kyoto Protocol. According to one Liberal insider:

> This decision [was] made unilaterally by the PM not by his cabinet …[his] announcement was made before any recommendation by the Australian parliament's Joint Committee on Treaties, and before the completion of the National Interest Assessment by the Department of Foreign Affairs and Trade. (Pearse 2007: 77)

Why did Australia refuse to ratify an international agreement that it had negotiated so hard to water down? This question is a puzzle to many (Christoff

2005; Hamilton 2007; McDonald 2005; Papadakis 2002). The government's own justification rested on two arguments: first, that Kyoto was limited because it did not include commitments from developing countries and the United States; and second, that Kyoto would cost Australia jobs and damage the economy (Howard 2002).

Whatever the rationale, the refusal to ratify Kyoto was, from a political management perspective, undoubtedly a mistake. From this point onwards, the government appeared to be in denial on climate change, despite the fact that in the institutional sphere it continued to bring forward initiatives to assist industry to reduce emissions. In 1999, for example, the government had announced a Greenhouse Gas Abatement Program (GGAP) as part of its Measures for a Better Environment (the successor of the Safeguarding the Future package). The GGAP initiative was valued at $400 million over four years aimed at funding carbon dioxide emission reduction programs of the largest polluters (Pearse 2007). After re-election in 2004 the Howard government released its Energy White Paper (EWP), *Securing Our Energy Future*, which committed around $700 million to climate change. Over 75 per cent of these funds were directed into clean coal technologies through the Low Emission Technology Demonstration Fund (DPM&C 2007).

Though it abandoned Kyoto, the Howard government continued to work on the international scene. On 18 May 2004, Australia and the US signed a Joint Statement on Environmental Cooperation to further strengthen the relationship between the two countries on environment issues. Then in July 2006 Howard announced while in Laos an international agreement between Australia, China, India, Japan, Republic of Korea and the USA which he described as 'significantly better than the Kyoto Protocol on reducing greenhouse gas emissions' (ABC 2006b). The six nations, representing 45 per cent of the global population and 49 per cent of global energy use and green house gases, formed an Asia Pacific Partnership on Clean Development and Climate (AP6).

These (largely symbolic) initiatives enabled the government to appear to be doing something about climate change. From this point onwards however, they effectively lost control of the agenda, as a revitalised opposition under Kevin Rudd began to make headway on the issue. At the same time, international efforts continued to raise awareness of the potential implications of a warmer planet. For example, in September 2006 Al Gore's movie *An Inconvenient Truth* was released in Australia and served to popularise the climate change issue. A new report from the International Panel on Climate Change (IPCC) added further scientific weight to the growing consensus about the reality and seriousness of human-induced climate change. By the end of 2006, Howard's attempts to downplay the seriousness of climate change were no longer appropriate and his policies began to shift. On 10 December 2006, the Prime Minister announced a taskgroup on emissions trading (ABC 2006c), followed in February 2007 with the release of an issues paper on Emissions Trading (Taskforce 2007).

In election year 2007, climate change became a first-order issue. Several opinion polls revealed the growing public concern over global warming and related government policies (Hartcher 2006; Lowy Institute 2007; ABC 2006d). The business community were also making more noise about the federal government's climate change policy, calling for a national emissions trading scheme (ABRCC 2006; BCA 2007). The economic costs of not acting on climate change were also gaining more attention, due in large part to the British report by Sir Nicholas Stern (Stern 2007).

All this was not good news for the Howard government in an election year. It responded by ramping up its climate change activities and by June 2007 it had announced that it was committed to an emission trading scheme. The proposed scheme (which would be established 'no later than 2012') would be administered by the Department of Prime Minister and Cabinet and based

Courtesy of Peter Nicholson, *The Australian*, 2 September 2006

on a 'cap and trade' emissions system (DPM&C 2007). But criticisms of the scheme were voiced from both the business community and green groups for the lack of detail in the government's trading proposal, especially with respect to the targets (the cap) (ACF 2007; Marris 2007b).

By mid-July 2007 climate change was a central theme of Howard's department, with the release of *Australia's Climate Change Policy – Our Economy, Our Environment, Our Future*. Other initiatives were also announced in July 2007 including a five-year $336.1 million program for schools to install solar hot water systems and rainwater tanks, and $252.2 million over five years for solar hot water rebates of $1000 for households and for further development of nuclear power options.

The issue of nuclear power deserves particular mention here because Howard strategically introduced it onto the political agenda on the back of the climate change debate. Nuclear energy was a source of frustration to the other parties; it had plagued Labor since its Three Mines Policy, and confused the Greens' public message. At the same time, nuclear power was undoubtedly a low carbon-emission technology. While ever-mindful of the political sensitivities involved, the Prime Minister nevertheless commissioned a report from former Telstra boss and nuclear physicist Ziggy Switkowski, which found in favour of promoting use of Australia's uranium resources though processing and nuclear energy (UMPNERT 2006). In April 2006 Australia signed an agreement to supply uranium to China, and in August 2007 it entered into similar negotiations with India – a controversial move given India's refusal to sign the international Nuclear Non-proliferation Treaty.

Howard's greatest climate change moment was undoubtedly the Sydney declaration of September 2007, when the Prime Minister made the most of his position as leader of the nation hosting the annual APEC (Asia Pacific Economic Cooperation) conference, to showcase a major statement on climate change. By placing climate change at the centre of a new, post-Kyoto agenda, the government hoped to leave Labor little room to manoeuvre in the run-up to the 2007 election. But by this stage, it was Labor, not the government, that was perceived as 'owning' climate change as an issue.

John Howard and the political management of the environment

Looking back on ten years of Howard government environmental policies, what conclusions can we draw? The major 'upfront' priorities of the first three Howard governments were clearly not environmental. Nevertheless, unprecedented sums were spent in rural and regional Australia in the name of environmental improvement (see chapter 9 for further details).

In defusing opposition to the sale of Telstra, the government had shown itself to be a master of agenda management. At the same time, this very tactic meant that it was difficult for it to claim any credit for its actions, because so much of the activity it funded took place in widely dispersed and often fragmented contexts that were difficult both to manage and to evaluate.

But this dispersion was also strategically useful. Throughout its first three terms, the government operated at a distance from environmental groups. As it proved in amending the EPBC Act in 2006, and in its continuing opposition to the ratification of the Kyoto Protocol, its primary loyalties were to those seen as generators of economic growth. In moving environmental issues off the public agenda, it marginalised much of the environmental movement, restricting its political opportunities and its funding, and forcing it from the national stage (see Hamilton & Maddison 2007).

Only where the stakes were much less high did the government attempt to promote its environmental credentials. Throughout its first three terms and well into its fourth, it took a delicious pleasure in playing a noisy upfront role (on the side of the whales) in the convoluted politics and tortuous negotiations of the International Whaling Commission.

Apart from agenda factors, there were important political reasons for the government's luke-warm approach to environmental questions. Howard himself was not known to have green sympathies, and the overwhelming identification of the green vote with the left of politics meant that, as a conservative Liberal, he saw little political advantage in cultivating it.

Environmental issues were undoubtedly connected in the Prime Minister's mind with the culture wars, and he had successfully identified his government with anti-elitist policies. Australians wanted to feel relaxed and comfortable – they did not want to be hectored about their shortcomings. The electoral support for One Nation evident in the 1996 and 1998 elections reinforced the Prime Minister's desire to distance his government from leftist environmental priorities.

The coalition with the National Party was important in refocusing the coalition's concern on regional issues, which after 1998 became an important part of the strategy to combat One Nation. The National Party had two leaders during the first three Howard governments – Tim Fischer, leader until 1999, was known to be a passionate advocate for regional Australia, and an enthusiastic annual bushwalker, but not an environmentalist. His successor

John Anderson, leader until 2005 and Minister for Transport and Regional Services during that time, was an even stronger proponent of 'the bush'.

Howard's environment minister from 1996 until 2001, Robert Hill, provided an additional impetus towards the kinds of policies the coalition pursued in office. An intelligent politician, Hill realised that progress on environmental issues could still be made by renovating the Intergovernmental Agreement on the Environment (the original version of which dated from 1992) – a process that eventually produced the *Environment Protection and Biodiversity Conservation Act 1999*. This act could be seen as federalism of convenience. John Howard would unabashedly use federal power to quash territory government policies of which he did not approve, and when the issue was one dear to his heart (as in labour market reform), he did not hesitate to use the commonwealth's corporations power as a base for remaking the industrial order.

In his fourth term in office, Howard's piecemeal and cautious approach to environmental policy attracted increasing criticism. In particular a central value in the coalition's approach to environmental matters, namely that environmental policy is detrimental to the economy, was coming under closer public and corporate scrutiny. Concerns were not only coming from the usual academics and scientists, left-leaning think tanks and international bodies (UNAA 2007), but also from many of Howard's own, including 2007 Australian of the Year Tim Flannery, the business community and the medical profession (ABRCC 2006; AMA 2005; Peatling 2007).

What is significant here is that many criticisms were being voiced by those whose interests the coalition sought to represent and protect, such as the corporate and private sector. To frame environmental matters as something for 'radical lefties' was now too simplistic. A new generation of green thinking was emerging as environmental risks shaped the broader context in which businesses and governments now operate.

As we have seen, by 2007 the government had accepted that it had to 'assume political responsibility' for tackling the immensity of environmental issues facing the nation (Kelly 2007). Nevertheless, the Prime Minister's political brilliance could not paper over deep-seated problems in the institutional and governance capacities of the Australian federation in relation to environmental issues. Economic management was the government's self-professed forte, and it had shown, in relation to industrial relations, that it was not only willing, but eager to centralise power in the pursuit of its goals. But these skills were insufficient to enable the government effectively to address the complex questions of intergovernmental co-operation, regional adjustment and resource management needed to resolve the problems of the Murray-Darling basin.

The impasse over Gunn's proposal to build a pulp mill in Tasmania's Tamar Valley recalled the fate of an earlier, failed proposal, dating from the 1980s, to build a similar mill at Wesley Vale, further to the west. The capacity to make well thought-out, inclusive and carefully bargained decisions in relation to new industrial developments had scarcely moved since the earlier period. For a country heavily dependent upon resource-based industries for its prosperity, ecological modernisation continued to seem a long way off.

References

ABC (Australian Broadcasting Corporation) (1999) Regional Forest Agreement legislation, *ABC Radio National Earthbeat,* 13 February, at <www.abc.net.au/rn/science/earth/stories/s18955.htm>.
—— (2006a) Campbell defends wind farm review, *ABC Newsonline,* 4 August, at <www.abc.net.au/news/stories/2006/08/04/1706721.htm >.
—— (2006b) Climate change deal better than Kyoto: Howard, *ABC Newsonline,* 28 July, at <www.abc.net.au/news/newsitems/200507/s1425101.htm>.
—— (2006c) Taskforce to report on emissions trading, *ABC Newsonline,* 10 December, at <www.abc.net.au/news/newsitems/200612/s1808157.htm>.
—— (2006d) Voters urge more action on climate change: Poll, *ABC Newsonline,* 2 November, at <www.abc.net.au/news/newsitems/200611/s1779238.htm>.
—— (2007) Treasury not consulted on water plan: Ken Henry, *The World Today – ABC Radio National,* Transcript from 4 April, at <www.abc.net.au/worldtoday/content/2007/s1889779.htm>.
ABRCC (Australian Business Roundtable on Climate Change) (2006) *The Business Case for Early Action,* at <www.businessroundtable.com.au/pdf/F078-RT-WS.pdf>.
ABS (Australian Bureau of Statistics) (1998) Use of resources: household energy use, *Australian Social Trends,* cat. no. 4102, ABS, Canberra.
—— (2006) *Australia's Environmental — Issues and Trends,* cat. no. 4613.0, ABS, Canberra.
ACF (Australian Conservation Foundation) (2006) Submission to the Parliamentary Inquiry into the Environment and Heritage Legislation Amendment Bill (No. 1) 2006, *ACF online,* at <www/acfonline.org.au/uploads/res/res_epbcsub.pdf>.
—— (2007) Cap-and-trade needs a cap, *ACF online,* at <www.acfonline.org.au/articles/news.asp?news_id=1328>.
AMA (Australian Medical Association) (2005) New report shows climate change threatens human health (Media release), 22 September, at <www.ama.com.au/web.nsf/doc/WEEN-6GFAZM>.
ANAO (Australian National Audit Office) (1998) *Preliminary Inquiries into the Natural Heritage Trust,* Report No. 42 1997–98, ANAO, Canberra.
—— (2007) *The Conservation and Protection of National Threatened Species and Ecological Communities,* Report No. 31 2006–07, ANAO, Canberra.
BCA (Business Council of Australia) (2007) *Strategic Framework for Emissions Reduction,* at <www.bca.com.au/Content.aspx?ContentID=101042>.

Brissenden, M (2006) Leader's summit warned of huge scale of drought crisis, *7.30 Report*, 7 November, Australian Broadcasting Corporation.
Chapple, S (2001) The EPBC act: One year later, *Environmental and Planning Law Journal*, 18(6): 523–39.
Christoff, P (2005) Policy autism or double-edged dismissiveness? Australia's climate change policy under the Howard government. *Global Change, Peace and Security* 17(1): 29–44.
Cobb, R. & Elder, C (1972) *Participation in American Politics: The Dynamics of Agenda-building*, Allyn & Bacon, Boston.
Cobb, R, Ross, J & Ross, M (1976) Agenda-building as a comparative political process, *American Political Science Review*, 70: 126–38.
Connell, D (2007) *Water Politics in the Murray-Darling Basin*, Federation Press, Sydney.
Crowley, K (2001) Effective environmental federalism? Australia's Natural Heritage Trust, *Journal of Environmental Policy and Planning*, 3(4): 255–72.
DPM&C (Department of Prime Minister and Cabinet) (2007) *Australia's Climate Change Policy – Our Economy, Our Environment, Our Future*, at <www.pmc.gov.au/publications/climate_policy/index.cfm>.
Economou, N (1999) Backwards into the future: National policy making, devolution and the rise and fall of the environment. In K Walker & K Crowley (eds) *Australian Environmental Policy: Issues in Decline and Devolution*, Sydney, UNSW Press: 65–80.
Gumley, W (2005) The current fragmentation of the legal framework in Australia is a major handicap to more efficient biodiversity conservation, *Law Institute Journal*, 79(7): 58–61.
Hamilton, C (2007) *Scorcher: The Dirty Politics of Climate Change*, Black Inc. Agenda, Melbourne.
Hamilton, C & Maddison, S (2007) (eds) *Silencing Dissent*, Allen & Unwin, Sydney.
Harding, A (1985) Unemployment policy: A case study in agenda management, *Australian Journal of Public Administration*, 44(3): 224–46.
Hartcher, P (2006) Canberra, 'Take note: Climate change is what terrifies us', *Sydney Morning Herald*, 3 October.
Hassall and Associates (2003) *Evaluation of the NHT Phase 1 Facilitator, Coordinator and Community Support Networks*, Hassall and Associates, Sydney, at <www.nht.gov.au/publications/books/network-evaluation.html>.
Howard, J (Prime Minister) (1997) *Safeguarding the Future: Australia's Response to Climate Change*, Policy Statement at Parliament House, 20 November.
—— (2002) *Com. Parl. Debs HoR*, 5 June 2002.
—— (2007) *A National Plan for Water Security,* at <www.pm.gov.au/docs/national_plan_water_security.rtf>.
Howlett, M & M Ramesh (2003) *Studying Public Policy: Policy Cycles and Policy Subsystems*, Oxford University Press, Don Mills, Ontario.
Institute for Sustainable Futures (2004) *Review of the National Packaging Covenant*, Paper Prepared for the Nature Conservation Council of NSW, University of Technology, Sydney.
Kelly, P (2007) Climate change a mainstream issue, *Australian,* 28 February.
Kemp, D (2004) Howard government's record $2.4 billion for Australia's environment (Media Release), 1 May, at <www.environment.gov.au/minister/env/2004/mr11may04.html>.
Lane, M (1999) Regional Forest Agreements: resolving resource conflicts or managing

resource politics? *Australian Geographical Studies,* 37(2): 142–53.

Lowe, I (2004) *A Big Fix: Radical Solutions for Australia's Environmental Crisis*, Black Inc, Melbourne.

Lowy Institute (2007) *Lowy Institute Poll 2007: Australia and the World – Public Opinion and Public Policy,* Sydney.

Macintosh, A (2006) *The EPBC Act: An Ongoing Failure,* The Australia Institute, Canberra.

McDonald, M (2005) Fair weather friends? Ethics and Australia's approach to global climate change, *Australian Journal of Politics and History*, 51(2): 216–34.

McGrath, C (2005) Key concepts of the Environment Protection and Biodiversity Conservation Act 1999 (Cth), *Environmental and Planning Law Journal,* 22(1): 20–39.

—— (2006) Review of the EPBC Act, Paper prepared for the 2006 Australian State of the Environment Committee, Department of the Environment and Heritage, Canberra at <www.environment.gov.au/soe/2006/publications/emerging/epbc-act/index.html>.

Marris, S (2007a) PM hopes Brumby will reverse water, *Australian,* 30 July.

—— (2007b) Carbon trading details stay under wraps – climate wars, *Australian*, 18 July.

Mercer, D (2000) *A Question of Balance: Natural Resource Conflict Issues in Australia*, Federation Press, Sydney.

MDBC (Murray-Darling Basin Commission) (2001) *Basin Salinity Management Strategy 2001–2015,* MDBC, Canberra.

Mol, A P J (1996) Ecological modernisation and institutional reflexivity: Environmental reform in the late modern age, *Environmental Politics*, 5: 302–23.

NHT (Natural Heritage Trust) (2002) *Annual Report 2001–02*, NHT, Canberra.

—— (2005) *Annual Report 2004–05*, NHT, Canberra.

NRMMC (Natural Resource Management Ministerial Council) (2005) *National Action Plan for Salinity and Water Quality; Natural Heritage Trust Regional Programs Report*, Department of Agriculture, Fisheries and Forestry, Canberra.

NWI (National Water Initiative) (2004) *Intergovernmental Agreement on a National Water Initiative Between the Commonwealth of Australia and the Governments of New South Wales, Victoria, Queensland, South Australia, the Australian Capital Territory and the Northern Territory*, at <http://svc044.wic032p.server-web.com/nwi/docs/iga_national_water_initiative.pdf>.

Papadakis, E (2002) Global environmental diplomacy: Australia's stances on global warming, *Australian Journal of International Affairs*, 56 (2): 265–77.

Pearse, G (2007) *High and Dry: John Howard, Climate Change and the Selling of Australia's Future*, Viking, Melbourne.

Peatling, S (2007) Flannery berates Howard on climate, *Sydney Morning Herald*, 27 January.

Peters, D (2007) Plan starts taking root – but climate change not addressed, Greens warn, *Courier Mail*, 26 January.

Scanlon, J & Dyson, M (2001) Will practice hinder principle? Implementing the EPBC Act, *Environmental and Planning Law Journal*, 79(7): 14–22.

Stern, N (2007) *The Economics of Climate Change: The Stern Review*, Cambridge University Press, Cambridge.

Stewart, J (2000) The Howard government and federalism: The end of an era? In G Singleton (ed.) *The Howard Government: Australian Commonwealth Administration 1996–98*, UNSW Press, Sydney: 151–61.

Stewart, J & Jones G (2003) *Renegotiating the Environment: the Power of Politics*, Federation Press, Sydney.

SMH (*Sydney Morning Herald*) (2007) The water plan John Howard had to have, 26 January.
Taskforce (on Emissions Trading) (2007), *Issues Paper,* at <www.industry.gov.au/assets/documents/itrinternet/emissions_trading_issues_paper20070207150633.pdf>.
Topsfield J, Grattan, M & Ker, P (2007) Bracks to PM: My water plan is better, *Age,* 21 February.
UMPNERT (Uranium, Processing and Nuclear Energy Review Taskforce) (2006) *Uranium Mining, Processing and Nuclear Energy – Opportunities for Australia,* Report to the Prime Minister by the Uranium, Processing and Nuclear Energy Review Taskforce, Canberra.
UNAA (United Nations Association of Australia) (2007) *Australia and the United Nations,* United Nations Association of Australia, at <www.unaa.org.au/pdf/UNAA1/220Report1/220Card1/2202007.pdf>.
Walker, A (2004) Forest reform in Victoria: Towards ecologically sustainable forest management or mere greenwash? *Alternative Law Journal,* 29(2): 58–64.
Wentworth Group (of Concerned Scientists) (2002) *Blueprint for a Living Continent,* at <www.wentworthgroup.org/docs/blueprint_for_a_living_contintent.pdf>.
—— (2003) *Blueprint for a National Water Plan,* at <www.wentworthgroup.org/docs/blueprint_national_water_plan.pdf>.
Whinnett, E (2004) Howard happy with RFA, *Mercury* (Hobart), 14 February.

13
From multiculturalism to citizenship

Heba Batainah and Mary Walsh

This chapter examines the key issues that resulted in the passing of the *Australian Citizenship Act 2007* and the establishment of a citizenship test that now applies to those seeking to become Australian citizens. Underpinning the new act and the accompanying test was the Howard government's desire to establish a mainstream Australian national identity based on common, shared values bounded by the concept of 'citizenship' rather than 'multiculturalism'. The Howard government sought to create social cohesion through an emphasis on the value and understanding of citizenship and the period under review marks an official shift away from multiculturalism as an outcome of immigration policy to a new focus on citizenship. By early 2007 this shift in emphasis was reflected in the change of name of the Department of Immigration and Multicultural Affairs (DIMA) to the Department of Immigration and Citizenship (DIAC). However, the transition has not been without its tensions, or its critics. Tensions developed between the need for the immigration of skilled workers to fuel economic growth and prosperity, the need for Australia to fulfil its humanitarian obligations and the deepening concern by senior Howard ministers that citizenship needed to be made more difficult, perhaps more 'precious' than previously. This has led to ferocious debate about what constitutes an Australian identity and the values of Australian society. This chapter traces the incremental policy shift from multiculturalism to citizenship and maps the key events, debates and tensions which arose along this new policy trajectory.

The incremental policy shift

During the Howard years, successive governments have shown concern, even antipathy, towards policies which favoured multiculturalism as a concept around which an emerging, diverse Australian society could be organised. Events such as *Tampa*, 11 September 2001 and the Bali bombings in 2002 were used to garner bipartisan support for the previous Howard governments to implement border protection and anti-terrorist measures targeted largely at external aggressors (see chapter 14 for further discussion of the anti-terrorism laws). These events came to provide the justification for Howard's rejection of 'multiculturalism', a term which he had reluctantly accepted in 1999 (see Galligan & Roberts 2004), in favour of 'social cohesion' as a weapon against terror. This shift was managed incrementally, focusing on one or a few issues at a time rather than exposing the entire broad policy to public scrutiny and debate.

During the fourth term events such as the Madrid bombings in early 2004, the London bombings in 2005, the Cronulla 'race' riots, and the numerous controversies leading to the resignation of Australia's Mufti, Sheik Taj Al-Din al-Hilali in 2007, fuelled the debate on citizenship and national identity and gave further impetus to the Howard government to unapologetically diverge from policies that favoured and fostered 'Australian multiculturalism', to those that emphasised shared values and a single Australian identity. Indeed, one significant focus of the fourth Howard term seemed to be on internal ethnic politics, especially as Howard's insistence on 'shared values' came to be viewed by many as largely a denial of and an attack on Australia's diversity and a specific assault on Muslim and Arab-Australians (see Humphries 2006; Wong 2006; and Batainah 2007). The media's two-year focus on 'ethnic' gang rapes which occurred in 2000 amid fears associated with 'home-grown terrorism' informed the government's position on institutionalising a preferred national identity. It seemed that the Howard government's sentiments towards multiculturalism in its many guises were in clear denial of Australia's ethnic and cultural diversity. Jayasuriya's (2003: 1) explanation of the contested nature of an Australian multiculturalism seems apt here since it also inadvertently explains the Howard government's two-pronged attack on Australian multiculturalism:

> The problematic nature of multiculturalism as a contested notion
> of public policy arises from two alternative ways of conceptualising
> multiculturalism as it has been understood in Australian society:
> as a philosophy of migrant settlement catering to the needs
> of newcomers through public policies designed to help their
> integration into the socio cultural structures of Australian society;
> the other views normative multiculturalism as a constitutive
> principle of the Australian nation, one which is central to how we
> regard ourselves as being Australian in a multicultural nation.

In November 2006, it was reported that the Howard government was looking for alternative words to 'multiculturalism' (Hart 2006), a term deemed to be too vague in that it attempted to mean 'different things to different people' (Howard 2006d). When the term 'multiculturalism' was officially dropped from the name of the federal portfolio in January 2007 and replaced with the word 'citizenship', it became clear that the policies associated with multiculturalism were to be replaced also, leaving the future of policies under multiculturalism and general ethnic relations in Australia uncertain and at the same time alienating various multicultural councils around Australia. Indeed, multiculturalism became a project sponsored primarily by state governments when the Council for Multicultural Australia, a federal initiative designed to promote 'community harmony and the benefits of cultural diversity for all Australians' ended with the completion of its second 3-year term on 30 June 2006.

However, Howard (2007) denied that the new Department of Immigration and Citizenship meant that multiculturalism was defunct:

> The desired progression is that an immigrant becomes an
> Australian, as simple as that. I think the title of the new department
> expresses the desire and the aspiration, and that is that people
> who come to this country, who immigrate, immigrants, become
> Australians. That's what the Australian people want.

Lopez (2007), author of *The Origins of Multiculturalism in Australian Politics*, agreed with Howard, suggesting that history had proven multiculturalism to be resilient, and that a change in name did not necessarily mean a change in nature. However, the resilience of Australian multiculturalism in the face of an incremental policy shift was already under threat in 2002 when Neville Roach (ABC 2002), former head of the Council for Multicultural Australia, resigned, stating that the federal government's policy stance on asylum-seekers was legalistic, inflexible and 'against Australian multiculturalism'. At face value the change in name from DIMA to DIAC appears insignificant in that 'multicultural affairs' remains a key program within the department. However, the promotion of the benefits of multiculturalism was no longer federal policy and potential citizens are now screened specifically for 'cultural suitability' (such as English proficiency and a demonstrated understanding of Australian values), despite assurances by Howard (2006d) that '[w]e will retain a non-discriminatory immigration policy'. This gradual rejection of multiculturalism by the Howard government was partly built on the belief that ethnic minorities received too many concessions from government and that there was a need for 'white' Australia to reassert itself and to place 'greater emphasis on the things that unite us rather than the things that make us different' (Howard 2006d).

Howard's approach to national unity was reinforced by changes to immigration conditions whereby potential citizens would now have four years to prepare for a language and citizenship test. However, not all ministers believed that national unity could be achieved even by this measure; Immigration Minister Kevin Andrews indicated that some, especially Sudanese immigrants, were incapable of integrating with Australian society, citing a dossier on issues such as Sudanese gang-related violence as evidence (*Age* 2007b). Queensland Premier Anna Bligh (in Caldwell 2007) rebutted Andrews' 'deep South'-style racist remarks, using police statistics to argue that members of the Queensland Sudanese community were 'law-abiding' as they were underrepresented in crime figures. The vilification of certain ethnic groups harks back to the debate centring on the cultural dimensions of 11 September, the Lebanese gang-rapes during the early 2000s, the Pakistani gang-rapes in 2002 and later the reprisal attacks following the Cronulla riots in 2005. These incidents were used to generalise criminal attributes of specific ethnicities, particularly Muslims, and these generalisations have informed the debate on values (for treatment of Arabs and Muslims in Australia see Poynting et al. 2004 and Poynting & Noble 2004). Concerns about 'problematic immigrants' resulted in a reduction in the approval of African immigrants and Arabic applicants for visas have been subjected to more questioning than any other ethnic group for reasons of 'national security' (ABC 2007a). Further, Australian citizens with Muslim backgrounds have been subjected to numerous raids by the Australian Security Intelligence Organisation (ASIO) without charges being laid. While Howard (ABC 2005a) denied the raids were anti-Muslim, Dr Ameer Ali (who was hand-picked by Howard to head the Muslim Advisory Group, a group often labelled as a 'rubber stamp' for government policy) disagreed publicly.

Sometime later, the 14-member Muslim Advisory Group was 'gagged' by the DIMA and subsequently abolished (Duffy 2006).

Multiculturalism was blamed for its inherent separatism and indirectly for tolerating what was deemed to be racially motivated criminal actions, leading to the idea that immigrants *should* integrate, but that people from specific cultural or religious backgrounds *could not* integrate and therefore should 'clear off' (see Brendan Nelson's comments on Muslims and Australian values in Grattan 2005; also Lawrence 2006: 27–38). Howard (2006a) expressed his desire for immigrants to integrate:

> We want them to learn about our history and heritage. And we expect each unique individual who joins our national journey to enrich it with their loyalty and their patriotism ... Keeping our balance means we reform and evolve so as to remain a prosperous, secure and united nation. It also means we retain these cherished values, beliefs and customs that have served us so well in the past. ... Within limits, all Australians have the right to express their culture and beliefs and to participate in our national life.

Over the past 11½ years, the Howard governments have steadily dismantled multiculturalism in Australia in a bid to revert to an integrationist immigration policy. This dismantling has taken shape initially by targeting the term 'multiculturalism' as divisive and by suggesting that an Australian 'culture' as such should be the glue that holds Australian society together. This approach cemented the notion that Australian society needed to be based on a set of shared, common values under the umbrella of an imagined national identity designed to circumvent possible terror threats, particularly from 'home-grown terrorists'.

Imagining the national identity

The shift from a focus on multiculturalism to one on citizenship marked the basis for a new framework for Australian society (see Jupp, Nieuwenhuysen & Dawson 2007). This approach attempted to overcome perceived inadequacies of both assimilationist strategies, which overemphasised conformity, and multiculturalism, which 'exaggerated the maintenance of diversity' (Galligan & Roberts 2004: 73). Indeed, in his Australia Day speech in 2006, Howard (2006e) claimed that 'Australia had now successfully rebalanced national identity and ethnic diversity'. However, Howard created further division when he also claimed that Australian values were based upon 'a mix of

Judeo-Christian ethics, the spirit of the Enlightenment and British political institutions and culture'. He argued that Australia's identity was based on Anglo-Celtic Christianity and the ANZAC spirit, insisting that not only new immigrants, but also current citizens with immigrant backgrounds, should learn to speak English and integrate (Howard 2006a). In September 2006, on talkback radio Howard (2006b) refined those views stating that:

> Fully integrating means accepting Australian values, it means learning as rapidly as you can the English language if you don't already speak it ... And it means understanding that in certain areas, such as the equality of men and women ... people who come from societies where women are treated in an inferior fashion have got to learn very quickly that is not the case in Australia.

Later in the year, Andrew Robb (2006), then Parliamentary Secretary to the Minister for Immigration and Multicultural Affairs, delivered a speech at the Australian National University where he pointed out that some Australians believed that multiculturalism was a doctrine that put allegiance to original culture ahead of national loyalty. The address noted that this was the first time that an alternative doctrine had been articulated by government as part of the wider debate on Australian values (see Phillips & Smith 2000; Dyrenfurth 2007). Robb (in Heywood 2006) claimed that shared values were the core of what bound Australians together:

> A shared identity is not about imposing uniformity. It is about a strong identification with a set of core values, whilst permitting a large measure of personal freedom and 'give and take'... A community of separate cultures fosters a rights mentality, rather than a responsibilities mentality. It works against quick and effective integration.

Members of the Ethnic Communities' Council of Victoria disagreed with Robb that Australia had one overriding culture and argued instead that Australia was a multicultural society with people united around democracy, the rule of law and a shared homeland. Van Vliet (2006), executive officer of the Ethnic Communities' Council of Victoria Statewide Resources Centre, claimed Robb's analysis was problematic because it rejected multicultural reality, with only 30 per cent of Australians having an Anglo-Celtic background, down from 97 per cent in the first part of the 20th century. He suggested that the government was trying to travel back in time to 1950s:

> The problem with trying to define Australian values or culture
> beyond democracy and the rule of law is that they are not
> necessarily agreed values. Pluralism, or the right to hold different
> values beyond the acceptance of democracy and the rule of law,
> is arguably one of the most important values in a multicultural
> society and effectively rejects a detailed list of agreed values.
> Multiculturalism could also be considered a quintessential
> Australian value, as recently argued by former governor-general Sir
> William Deane. (van Vliet 2006)

Earlier federal government funding of the compulsory 'Values for Australian Schooling' program had introduced prescribed values to school children (Nelson 2005). An editorial in *The Age* (2005) asked 'whose Australia and whose values are they talking about' when it was revealed that myths such as 'Simpson and his donkey' were used as the epitome of Australian values. On a Sydney radio station, Howard claimed that the new emphasis on Australian values 'is not designed to keep anybody out. It's designed to include everybody, integrate everybody into the national fabric' (Howard 2006c). However, former Liberal Prime Minister Malcolm Fraser questioned whether the Howard government was creating fear by raising the issue of citizenship and suggested the forthcoming election might turn into a referendum for Muslim immigration. He asked, 'Is this the politics of race? Is the government using code to say that Muslims are different and that they don't fit in?' (Fraser 2006). The values were later prescribed in the DIAC publication *Living in Australia* (2007).

Those who would not or could not embrace Australian values were increasingly accused of being 'unAustralian', described by Hugh Mackay (2007: 141) as the 'ugliest word in the language'. Indeed, a debate has raged in the last few years over who and what is an Australian and certainly who is and what behaviours are 'unAustralian'. This discussion was brought into focus with the Howard government's reaction to the Cronulla riots that took place on 11 December 2005. An estimated 5000 people converged on a beach in Cronulla, Sydney after disputes between lifesavers and beach users erupted the weekend before (*SMH* 2006a). It was reported that 'more than a dozen arrests have been made after several people of Middle Eastern appearance were abused and assaulted by members of the crowd' (ABC 2005b; see also Collins 2007). While the riots may have exposed the levels of racism and ethnic tensions building in Australia, the Howard government's response was largely to deny any such tensions and to explicitly focus on the 'criminality' of the riots and the 'revenge' attacks that followed.

234 • Policy Issues

Courtesy of Peter Nicholson, *The Australian*, 25 August 2005

Howard repeatedly suggested that he did not 'care' about people's backgrounds and that the Australian people also did not care where people had come from. At the same time the Howard government clearly marked those citizens with primarily Muslim backgrounds as not wishing to integrate and insisted that they must assume Australian values. Almost a year after the Cronulla riots, the controversy surrounding Australian values continued and *The Australian* (2006) noted that:

> John Howard has singled out Muslim migrants for refusing to embrace Australian values and urged them to fully integrate by treating women as equals and learning to speak English. The call for a shift in attitude among some Muslims infuriated community leaders last night, and comes as *The Australian* can reveal the Prime Minister's own Islamic advisers have already accused Mr Howard and senior ministers of fuelling hatred and mistrust by using 'inflammatory and derogatory' language.

Immigration

While it has been said that 'the Howard years were marked by "benign neglect" in immigration and multicultural policy, with all controversy and most resources concentrating on asylum' (Jupp 2005: 174), immigration issues mired the Howard government's reputation following its re-election in 2004. Despite voicing the desire to limit immigration from cultures deemed to have values that were seen as incommensurate with the prescribed 'Australian values', a significant increase in immigration occurred during the period of review, driven by economic demands and the need for a constant supply of skilled workers to fuel economic growth. *The Age* (2007a) reported that the Howard government had doubled the size of the migration program and tripled the number of skilled migrants with employers urging the government to increase the skilled migrant program by 20 000 in each of the next two years, after the unemployment rate hit a 32-year low at 4.5 per cent. Figures in 1997–98 indicated that total migrant intake was 67 000, with family intake at 31 310 and skilled intake 34 670. In 2006–07 total migrant intake was 144,000 with family intake 46 000 and skilled intake 97 500 (*Age* 2007a). However, measures introduced by the Australian Citizenship Act 2007 made permanent residence harder to achieve and the deterrents were put in place to ensure that fewer asylum-seekers gained permanent residence.

In fact, the Howard government adopted an unwavering position on asylum-seekers and refugees, even in the face of international criticism and numerous 'mistakes' by the immigration department. Historically, Australia's intake of refugees and asylum-seekers has been modest in comparison to the other immigrant-receiving countries (Crock & Saul 2002). More recently UNHCR statistics indicate that Australia has experienced a large drop in asylum claims and processes, especially in comparison to other industrialised countries (UNHCR 2004). While the Howard government has claimed the decrease as a success due to Australia's strict immigration control, in reality, these UNHCR figures have not included persons who have arrived offshore or who have been processed on Manus Island, Papua New Guinea, or Nauru since 11 September 2001 (UNHCR 2004). Following the re-election of the Howard government in 2004, numerous changes and fine-tuning of the immigration policy transformed the status of the Howard government's attitude towards immigration from one of 'benign neglect' to one of active, targeted policy.

The adoption of an active, targeted immigration policy resulted in various actions that caused controversies for the fourth Howard government, specifically: breaching UN Conventions on the detention of asylum-seekers and refugees; confusion and problems associated with public servants exercising regulatory authority in relation to people suspected of being in Australia illegally (see APSC 2006); the detention or deportation of those incapable of protecting themselves, particularly the mentally ill and children; and illegal detention of citizens and lawful non-citizens. While the extent of illegal detention is still to be revealed, investigations of 201 people who were detained in accordance with the policy reveal that '[t]en of the 20 people covered in these reports were Australian citizens at the time of their detention, four were permanent residents, four were temporary visa holders, and two were unlawful non-citizens' (Commonwealth Ombudsman 2006).

Media reports (Topsfield 2007) indicate that then Minister for Immigration Senator Vanstone was dismissed from her position as a result of the Comrie Report, which placed blame for the numerous mistakes in treating citizens as illegal non-citizens (such as Cornelia Rau and Vivien Alvarez Solon) on the culture and systemic problems within the then Department of Immigration and Multicultural Affairs. Despite the embarrassment faced by the government, these issues remained shrouded during the lead-up to the 2007 election, with a *Lateline* (ABC 2007b) report suggesting that yet another person, Tony Tran, had been illegally detained. According to then Shadow Minister for Immigration, Tony Burke, the Minister, Kevin Andrews, had refused access to departmental information concerning Tran, who was allegedly detained illegally for five and a half years while his Australian-born son was allegedly deported to a South Korean orphanage. Burke suggested that Andrews was the only minister to subvert the convention on departmental access during the caretaker period (for further discussion of these immigration cases and their accountability consequences see chapters 2 and 7).

On 10 August 2006 the Migration Amendment (Designated Unauthorised Arrivals) Bill 2006 (Senate Bills List) was passed by the Australian House of Representatives but was withdrawn by the Prime Minister before it was voted on in the Senate (ABC 2006b). The controversial bill was designed to ensure that all asylum-seekers who arrive on mainland Australia would be sent to the 'offshore' processing islands mentioned above. This controversial bill would have resulted in Australia breaching its obligations under the UN Refugee Convention (RCOA 2006) and thus Australia would have no obligation to process asylum-seekers or take in any refugees. Senator Hurley (2006), Labor's citizenship spokesperson, explained how such bills, while targeting 'refugees', actually marginalise and alienate current Australian citizens: 'I cannot talk about a multicultural community without talking about the Migration Amendment (Designated Unauthorised Arrivals) Bill 2006, which should be seen as an insult to the many existing and established Australian refugee and migrant communities.'

It is clear that successive Howard governments have reneged on Australia's international obligations (Pickering 2005; Dauvergne 2005) as the treatment of refugees and asylum-seekers has had far-reaching consequences for both Australia's international reputation and for its dealing with its direct neighbours and Australia's local 'multicultural' population. Indeed, policies targeting non-citizens have informed the national conversation on ethnicity and identity in Australia for much of the Howard fourth term. The Howard policies in the areas of immigration and security have consistently denied the dynamic nature of a multi-ethnic, Australian society in pursuing an integrationist agenda, which has been contested in many quarters.

Australian citizenship: much more than a ceremony

In September 2006, the Howard government released a discussion paper, *Australian Citizenship: Much more than a Ceremony*, which sought public consultation on the merits of introducing a formal citizenship test. When the discussion paper was released, the public was slow to respond. Very little was actually said in the public arena before late November. It could be argued that the timing of the release, with its response period shortly before Christmas, was aimed at restricting the possibility of significant discussion. However, this was a sleeper issue and legislation was generated quickly and passed through parliament with seemingly widespread support from the Australian community.

Parliamentary Secretary Andrew Robb explained in the foreword that 'Australia has successfully combined people into one family with one overriding culture, based on a set of common values' (DIMA 2006: 5). Australian values identified in the paper included respect for freedom, the dignity of the individual, democracy, the rule of law, equality for men and women, a fair go, mutual respect and compassion for those in need. The discussion paper outlined the requirements of citizenship testing in the United Kingdom, the United States, Canada and the Netherlands, all of which already had in place formal testing arrangements for citizenship, as part of the government's justification for the need for a citizenship test in Australia.

As the title of the discussion paper suggested the Howard government understood citizenship as more than just the citizenship ceremony, with Australian citizenship described 'a privilege, not a right' (DIMA 2006: 5).

Citizenship was linked to the Australian national identity, giving Australians a common rallying point. The Howard government expressed a strong preference for those people coming to Australia to participate in Australian life to the fullest extent as Australian citizens. It argued that immigrants should develop a level of English language proficiency sufficient to communicate with other Australians and contribute to Australian society, through employment and education. It was also deemed important that immigrants understand the Australian way of life and demonstrate a commitment to Australian values. In the paper, it was argued that a formal citizenship test would facilitate these goals and prevent what Andrew Robb feared was a processes of giving away Australian citizenship like 'confetti' (*SMH* 2006b).

Various groups in the community responded to the discussion paper and the subsequent legislative changes to citizenship law and policy. The Migration Institute of Australia (MIA) did not support the introduction of a formal citizenship test because it believed that becoming an Australian citizen should be a process that is accessible to all regardless of age, origins, culture or education. It saw the new proposed arrangements as providing disincentives to becoming a citizen. The MIA argued that there was no evidence that those who possessed proficiency in English at a basic level ensured would necessarily become good Australian citizens. While the MIA considered a broad knowledge of Australian history, political institutions and legal system desirable for citizens, it did not endorse any formal testing of knowledge about Australia as part of the citizenship test (MIA 2006: 3). On the issue of the importance of demonstrated commitment to the Australian way of life and Australian values for those who intend to settle permanently or spend extended time in Australia, the MIA was concerned that it might be difficult to actually articulate a single set of values. It suggested that Australian lifestyles and values vary between cities, between city and country and between states. It argued that shared lifestyle and values were located in the democratic political institutions, the legal system and rights and liberties, and advocated the current Australian citizenship pledge as an adequate indication of loyalty to Australia.

The test was greeted with concerns from some members of Howard's own party, in particular Liberal MP Petro Georgiou (in Nicolaides 2007). Georgiou declared that the proposed test would have prevented his own father from ever becoming an Australian citizen and being able to contribute to Australia in his unique way. In addition, concerns were raised that the new citizenship regime particularly targeted the Muslim community (see ABC 2006a; Megalogenis 2006; Steketee 2006). However, these claims were rejected by both Andrew Robb and John Howard and, in an article published in *The Australian*, they were reported as saying 'there is no evidence the new rules will be used unfairly or not applied to everyone who seeks citizenship, regardless of their country of origin, cultural background or religious beliefs'. They also suggested that Australia needed to examine overseas experience and invest in social cohesion upfront rather than pay later. They claimed that feedback on the government discussion paper showed overwhelming public support for the new initiatives, with 95 per cent of respondents agreeing that basic English language skills should be compulsory and 93 per cent believing that an understanding of Australian values was crucial for migrants to make the most of opportunities in Australia (*Australian* 2006).

However, the Ethnic Communities' Council of Victoria (ECCV 2006) responded to the government's citizenship paper and accused the government of being discriminatory and breaching Australia's human rights obligations. The ECCV claimed that those most affected would be immigrants from the Middle East and parts of Africa, who came to Australia as refugees without formal education in any languages (see also FECCA 2007). The seemingly simple requirements of an English test and knowledge of Australian culture and values were seen as paradoxical because the Citizenship Act already required English language skills and knowledge of the responsibilities of citizens; the new requirements appeared to be designed to raise further the threshold for eligibility. Moreover, Howard's urging of immigrants from non-English speaking backgrounds to integrate and learn English puzzled many who witnessed cuts in government spending on English language training for immigrants from 1999. On 1 December 2006 the Labor Party suggested that the Howard government focus on teaching migrants to speak English rather than testing their proficiency in English. The Labor immigration spokesperson Senator Hurley was critical of the government cutting almost $11 million from English language programs for migrants and accused the Howard government of downgrading multiculturalism and failing in migrant settlement and integration programs (Peake 2006; Heywood 2006). It was largely due to this kind of criticism that the federal budget in 2007 included increased spending on English language training and humanitarian settlement assistance (ECCV 2007).

In March 2007, the Australian Citizenship Bill was passed by parliament with the *Australian Citizenship Act 2007* coming into effect from 1 July 2007. The first citizenship test commenced 1 October 2007 and comprised 20 randomly selected questions from a possible 200 drawn from *Becoming an Australian Citizen* (Australian Government 2007). The key aspects of the test included knowledge of Australia, commitment to Australian values and knowledge of English. The citizenship test was complemented by an internet-based test for English language skills and an interview. The legislation required migrants to reside in Australia for four years before becoming eligible for Australian citizenship, doubling the previous provisions of two years. The exemption age for passing a basic English test increased from 50 to 60. Minister for Immigration and Citizenship Kevin Andrews believed that increasing the time limit to four years before migrants could apply for citizenship would allow them to develop a better understanding of Australian values. He understood citizenship not just as an event (the ceremony), but a process where migrants came to know and understand Australian values. The legislation also provided ASIO with authority to veto an application for citizenship if a direct or indirect risk was perceived, while also making it simpler for those who may have renounced their citizenship to regain it.

Conclusion

The demise of 'multiculturalism' and its replacement by 'citizenship' was a key change during the term of Howard's fourth government. The introduction of the *Australian Citizenship Act 2007* and with it the citizenship test signalled the formal end of multicultural policy in Australia. This move was seen as denying access to those deemed to be too different from the perceived mainstream Australian. The importance of citizenship law and policy marked a shift away from multiculturalism with its central tenet of acceptance and respect for different cultures as the means of social cohesion, to the tight control of immigration and the adherence to a common set of Australian values, loosely termed 'citizenship'. With the application of the citizenship test and the difficulties faced by refugees seeking asylum in Australia, it is easy to conclude that the Howard government has positioned Australia with a more insular focus in our global world – an 'Australia first' policy focus. The legacy of the Howard years is still to be determined but it may well be that the mechanisms it put in place to strengthen the cohesion of the Australian community prove to be mechanisms for social divisiveness. The Howard government argued for social cohesion via acceptance of a common set of values rather than by the acceptance of the values of those from different cultures. What makes Australia's situation unique is that Howard brought to this understanding of citizenship his own brand of what it is to be an Australian and a particular sense of what constitutes Australian identity (see

Johnson 2007). Howard was able to blend a certain pride in Australian national identity with the development of an understanding of common 'Australian' values, without basing the concept of citizenship upon greater citizen involvement in political decision-making. Given the shift experienced in Australian politics in the 2007 election, it remains to be seen whether a Rudd Labor government will reverse this trend or continue to follow the new Howard doctrine of citizenship.

References

ABC (2002) Roach resigns in protest over immigration policy, *7.30 Report*, ABC Program Transcript, at <www.abc.net.au/7.30/content/2002/s464949.htm>
—— (2005a) PM denies raids anti-Muslim, *ABC Online*, 9 November.
—— (2005b) Mob mentality shameful: Police commissioner, *ABC Online*, 11 December.
—— (2006a) Citizenship test under consideration, *ABC Online*, 28 April
—— (2006b) Howard disappointed by immigration bill scrapping, *ABC Online*, 14 August.
—— (2007a) Immigration widens checks for visas for Arabs, *ABC Online*, 17 July.
—— (2007b) Tony Jones discusses the Tran case with Labor's immigration spokesman Tony Burke, *ABC Lateline*, 13 November.
Age (2005) Chasing the donkey vote on values, 26 August.
—— (2007a) Bracks to urge migrant boost, 26 April.
—— (2007b) Andrews unbowed, Sudanese tensions brew, 11 October.
APSC (Australian Public Service Commission) (2006) *State of the Service Report 2005–06*, APSC, Canberra.
Australian (2006) New citizenship test is a wise investment, 13 December.
Batainah, H (2007) Democratic iterations, political membership and the (non)citizen 'other' in Australia, Unpublished paper, University of Canberra.
Caldwell, A (2007) Bligh rebuts Minister's 'racist' comments on Sudanese, *ABC Online*, 5 October.
Collins, J (2007) The landmark of Cronulla. In J Jupp & J Nieuwenhuysen with E Dawson (2007) *Social Cohesion in Australia*, Cambridge University Press, Melbourne: 61–79.
Commonwealth Ombudsman (2006) Ombudsman releases three reports on immigration detention (Media release), 6 December.
Crock, ME & Saul, B (2002) *Future Seekers: Refugees and the Law in Australia*, Federation Press, Sydney.
Dauvergne, C (2005). *Humanitarianism, Identity, and Nation: Migration Laws of Australia and Canada*, UBC Press, Vancouver.
DIAC (Department of Immigration and Citizenship) (2007) *Living in Australia*, DIAC, Canberra.
DIMA (Department of Immigration and Multicultural Affairs) (2006) *Australian Citizenship: Much more than a Ceremony*, Discussion paper, Consideration of the merits of introducing a formal citizenship test, September.
—— (2007) *Becoming an Australian Citizen*.
Duffy, C (2006) Govt's Muslim advisory group finishes twelve-month term, *AM*, ABC Local Radio, 8 November, at <www.abc.net.au/am/content/2006/s1783707.htm>.

Dyrenfurth, N (2007) John Howard's hegemony of values: The politics of 'mateship' in the Howard decade, *Australian Journal of Political Science*, 42(2): 211–30.
ECCV (Ethnic Communities' Council of Victoria) (2006) ECCV rejects Robb's comments (Media release), 27 November.
—— (2007) English and settlement funding welcome: But $123 million citizenship test a waste (Media release), 9 May.
FECCA (Federation of Ethnic Communities' Councils of Australia) (2007) Supporting people from culturally and linguistically diverse backgrounds to be part of Australian society: Migration, citizenship and cultural relations policy statement, at <www.fecca.org.au/Policies/2007/policies_2007003.pdf>.
Fraser, M (2006) Armour of mateship to protect our nation, *Daily Telegraph*, 14 December.
Galligan, R & Roberts, W (2004) *Australian Citizenship*, Melbourne University Press, Melbourne.
Grattan, M (2005) Accept Australian values or get out, *Age*, 25 August.
Hart, C (2006) Multiculturalism is a dirty word, *Australian*, 4 November.
Heywood, L (2006) National identity gets a makeover, *Courier Mail*, 28 November.
Howard, J (Prime Minister) (2006a) A sense of balance: The Australian achievement in 2006, Australia Day Address to the National Press Club, 12 January, at <www.australianpolitics.com/news/2006/01/06-01-25_howard.shtml>.
—— (2006b) PM tells Muslims to learn English, *Australian*, 1 September.
—— (2006c) All the same, only different – Election 2007, *Australian*, 16 December.
—— (2006d) PM defends citizenship tests, ABC *PM*, Interview with Chris Uhlmann, 12 December.
—— (2006e) Howard claims victory in national culture wars, *Age*, 26 January.
—— (2007) PM shuffles frontbench and revamps portfolios, *ABC News Online*, 23 January.
Humphries, D (2006) Live here and be Australian, Howard declares, *Sydney Morning Herald*, 25 February.
Hurley, A (2006) *Com. Parl. Debs S*, 16 June.
Jayasuriya, DL (2003) *Australian Multiculturalism Past, Present, and Future*, Crawley School of Social Work and Social Policy, University of Western Australia, at <www.socialwork.arts.uwa.edu.au/__data/page/33070/diversity.pdf >.
Johnson, C (2007) John Howard's 'values' and Australian identity, *Australian Journal of Political Science*, 42(2): 195–209.
Jupp, J (2005) Immigration and multiculturalism. In C Aulich & R Wettenhall (eds) *Howard's Second and Third Governments: Australian Commonwealth Administration 1998–2004*, UNSW Press, Sydney: 173–88.
Jupp, J & Nieuwenhuysen, J with Dawson, E (2007) *Social Cohesion in Australia*, Cambridge University Press, Cambridge.
Lawrence, C (2006) *Fear and Politics*, Scribe Publications, Melbourne.
Lopez, M (2007) Multicultural Spirit Lives on, *Australian*, 25 January.
Mackay, H (2007) *Advance Australia ... Where? How We've Changed, Why We've Changed and What Will Happen Next*, Hachette, Sydney, Australia.
Megalogenis, G (2006) Our kind of people, *Australian*, 23 September.
MIA (Migration Institute of Australia) (2006) Australian citizenship: Much more than a ceremony, Consideration of the merits of introducing a formal citizenship test, Submission to the Department of Immigration and Multicultural Affairs.
Nelson, B (Minister for Education, Science and Technology) (2005) Brendan Nelson addresses Islamic schools on Australian values, Interview with Samantha Hawley on *The World Today* (ABC radio), 24 August.

Nicolaides, H (2007) Enforcing the Anglo world view, *Age*, 14 August.
Peake, R (2006) ALP wants migrants to be taught English as a priority, *Canberra Times*, 1 December.
Phillips, T & Smith, P (2000) What is 'Australian'? Knowledge and attitudes among a gallery of contemporary Australians, *Australian Journal of Political Science*, 35(2): 203–24.
Pickering, S (2005) *Refugees and State Crime* (Monograph series no. 21), University of Sydney Institute of Criminology, Federation Press, Sydney.
Poynting, S, Noble, G, Tabar, P & Collins, J (2004) *Bin Laden in the Suburbs: Criminalising the Arab Other*, Institute of Criminology, Sydney.
Poynting , S & Noble, G (2004) *Living with Racism: The Experience and Reporting by Arab and Muslim Australians of Discrimination, Abuse and Violence since September 11, 2001*, Human Rights and Equal Opportunity Commission and Centre for Cultural Research, University of Sydney.
RCOA (Refugee Council of Australia) (2006) RCOA backs Senate Committee's rejection of Immigration Bill, 14 June, at <www.refugeecouncil.org.au/docs/releases/2006/0606141/220RCOA_urges1/220rejection1/220of1/220migration1/220bill.pdf>.
Robb, A (2006) The importance of a shared national identity, Address to the Transformations Conference at the Australian National University, Canberra, 27 November.
Steketee, M (2006) Pledges on paper are all about marks on the ballots, *Australian*, 14 December.
SMH (Sydney Morning Herald) (2006a) Told to learn, denied the right, 9 September.
—— (2006b) 'Fair go' for immigrants, 17 September
Topsfield, J (2007) PM dumps Vanstone from cabinet, *Age*, 24 January.
UNHCR Statistical Yearbook (2004) at <www.unhcr.org/statistics/STATISTICS/44e96c842.pdf >.
van Vliet, P (2006) Diversity is a fact, not a doctrine, *Age*, 29 November.
Wong, P (2006) Values and politics (Public lecture), Adelaide University, 26 October.

14
Searching for the national interest

Daniel Baldino

In contrast to the 'khaki' election of 2001, foreign policy did not feature as a significant issue during the 2004 election. Nonetheless, in facing the world stage, the Howard government promised not to sacrifice Australian interests in dealing with ongoing security threats from state and non-state actors. The government claimed a 'realistic' and 'pragmatic' approach to security problems. In broad terms, it maintained its focus on preserving national sovereignty and a military preponderance in a world still coming to terms with the costs and consequences of 11 September 2001 (hereafter referred to in the American style as 9/11). While the Howard government planned to fight terrorism in many stages, it continued to shift focus from multilateralism to the primacy of the US alliance. The UN was discounted as largely irrelevant, international law was treated with deep suspicion and interest in Asia remained primarily economic. An assertive Australian outlook was also closely connected to an intensified nationalism that stressed the preservation of distinctive Australian 'values'.

In a Lowy Institute speech in March 2005, Howard (2005a) articulated the benefits of a 'big Australia' that should not be underestimated. The government's diplomatic energy tended to place greater weight on the primacy of state sovereignty in the global environment, with traditional state-to-state relations being regarded as the basic building block of coalition diplomacy. Demonstrative of this stance, Howard indicated a strong willingness to achieve a closer relationship simultaneously with China and the United States. He argued that Australia did not believe there was anything inevitable about escalating strategic competition between the two great powers.

Howard's optimism in managing China's rise was offset with a more gloomy analysis regarding the pressures of globalisation and, in particular, the changing nature of conflict in dealing with transnational terrorism. He defended his government's defence procurement record despite projects being plagued by long delays and spiralling costs. He rejected any retreat in war-torn Iraq and Afghanistan. He advocated the broader strategic shift toward a 'forward defence' that moved defence operations beyond regional emergencies. In an attempt to kill off coinciding criticisms from opponents that the government was too eager to participate in US military operations across the globe, he set about distancing himself from the 'deputy sheriff' tag. Instead, Howard asserted that he preferred the label 'honest broker' to describe Australia's unique role as a western power and key American ally with substantial, if sometimes strained, Asian ties (see Keating 2005).

In July 2007, the Prime Minister again reinforced his promise to help build a democratic Iraq and continue to fight the war on terrorism. Howard reminded his audience not to forget the essential lessons of 9/11 – that failed states could swiftly become breeding grounds for global terror. He discarded claims that his government was neglecting Asia by pointing out that ignoring threats further afield would only invite problems to materialise closer to home (Walters 2007). In short, the best defence would be a strong offence. Howard's call to arms to fight a manifest 'evil' also witnessed the sharp expansion of executive power in the areas of law enforcement and intelligence, including the introduction of a series of controversial anti-terrorism bills, in order to help root out potential domestic terrorist perils. Doing little to alleviate a heightened sense of public fear about 'foreign' influences, he had previously warned that mosques and Muslim schools would be monitored to guarantee that the 'virtues of terrorism' were not being preached within the Islamic community (Grattan 2005).

High-flying presentations citing the pre-eminence of patriotic Australian characteristics and the US as an unwavering guarantor of Australian safety became a major component of the war on terror. Nonetheless, Howard's understandings can be criticised for offering a very narrow formulation of the national interest. Pivotally, he tended to overrely on or oversell militarised solutions to meet complex, often political, problems. Thomson (2005), who compared Australia's modest contribution to the US-led campaigns in Iraq and Afghanistan with that of other countries, even raised the question of whether Australia was 'pulling its weight' on the world stage. Further, other important foreign policy goals were forgotten and sidelined. Perhaps one of the most important changes heralded by 9/11 was the talking up of bilateral obligations and a use of war-like gestures that dislodged debate on 'non-traditional' security matters such as human rights, foreign aid, international law and climate change. For example, notwithstanding Howard's usually astute sense of popular opinion, his political radar appeared to misread the public mood shift on climate change, with procrastination resting on 'our own independent assessment' of the national interest (Dodson & Gordon 2005) (see chapter 12 for further discussion on climate change).

After more than a decade in power, Howard's pragmatism displayed an increasing inclination towards inflexibility in considering alternative courses of action. In his attempts to manage a global environment that was shifting at an unanticipated velocity, a mischaracterisation of threats and the consolidation of a hawkish mindset to protect both territorial and cultural integrity led to adverse and highly disproportionate policy responses. The character of the government's flawed interpretation of the lessons of 9/11 not only entailed serious implications for Australia's middle power recognition but failed to give sufficient weight to the longer term difficulties which a political myopia could produce.

Home-grown terrorism

Howard's declarations of cultural assertiveness and attempts to twist public opinion in the war against terror demonstrated an acute sensitivity to immediate electoral considerations. Keen to remove constraints of accountability and to marginalise dissent, he displayed a readiness to capitalise on a national mood that was stricken by bouts of rising insecurity and uncertainty.

Given a post-9/11 environment, it had become clear to governments all around the world that they had a primary responsibility to sponsor the development of law that would protect their citizens from terrorism. The Howard government was not alone in hardening national methods on policing and intelligence at all levels of government to better identify and reduce vulnerabilities to their citizens. Managing the problem of individual radicalisation was underlined by Paul O'Sullivan, Director-General of the Australian Security Intelligence Organisation (ASIO), who advised policy-makers in 2007 that there were still small and loose networks of extremists in Australia preparing for acts of indiscriminate violence (O'Sullivan 2007).

The Howard government repeatedly touted that Islamic fundamentalism was the greatest threat facing Australia. Giving credence to this claim, the federal government passed more than 41 terrorism-related laws after 9/11 (Williams & Lynch 2006). Yet despite the government's determination to create a more mobile, intelligence-driven operational response and adapt law to deal with terrorism, many commentators urged the government to proceed carefully. For example, David Wright-Neville (2005) argued that rapid movements in law-making were highly divisive and potentially counter-productive and queried whether the domestic threat was being exaggerated by the Howard team for political ends.

Others suggested that the result of the 2004 Australian election had been a catalyst for the wholesale abandonment of parliamentary convention in security affairs. The government's sincerity in ensuring greater community building and proper parliamentary appraisal was quickly brought into question when it moved to suppress public information and ensure fewer opportunities for scrutiny of its statements and papers in the Senate (see chapter 5 for further details of Senate activities during the fourth period).

Warnings not to overreact to terrorism related not only to issues covered by particular bills but also to limitations made to law-making procedures. In 2006, for example, when a government-appointed committee identified the need for redrafting what were described as 'convoluted and elastic draft terror laws', Howard responded by offhandedly disregarding its recommendations (Nicholson 2006). Application of the anti-terror laws in the case of Gold Coast doctor Mohamed Haneef further exposed shortfalls in counter-terrorism arrangements that made them appear politically motivated and lacking safeguards against manipulation by authorities (Neighbour 2007).

After initially agreeing to consider options for harmonising state and territory legislative provisions after the London bombings, some premiers and chief ministers expressed concerns over Howard's resistance to finding the right balance between human rights and the need to protect citizens from terrorism (Banhman 2005). Further, a more inclusive, open approach to security protection was mooted as indispensable in fostering wider public trust in intelligence and policing. Some commentators had distanced themselves from supplementary legislation, arguing that no cogent case had been made to support the extension of ASIO and police powers. Former Prime Minister Malcolm Fraser argued that the laws simply pandered to 'conservative elements in Australian society' (Fraser 2005). Part of the problem was that the lack of public consultation and parliamentary debate threatened to alienate core sections of the moderate Muslim community and reinforce anti-Muslim sentiment (Kerbaj 2007).

In October 2005, a 107-page copy of a draft-in-confidence version of the Anti-Terrorism Bill (No. 2) was posted on the internet by ACT Chief Minister Jon Stanhope. Stanhope refused to remove the confidential document, despite complaints from the Prime Minister's office. Stanhope stated that he had released the draft to ensure that an exceedingly centralised process was 'reasonably adaptive' to both the requirements of liberal democracy and national security. He declared that 'law of this significance made in this haste can't be good law' (cited in McKenzie 2005). Stanhope's rationale for a rigorous process of review, and his belief that the government's actions were overshadowing the importance of identifying the possible root causes of Muslim estrangement, was dismissed by Howard as being 'soft' on terrorism (Bonner 2005).

On 2 November, Howard announced that the government would immediately recall the Senate to introduce an amendment to the criminal code to stop a 'specific' terrorist act. Citing operational matters, Howard stated that he would not provide any detailed advice on the nature or timing of the planned threat. As a result, the Senate Legal and Constitutional Legislation Committee had only one day to consider the merits of the amendment and conduct public hearings. Defence Minister Senator Hill acknowledged that a hampered inquiry was 'obviously not as good as a long inquiry' but claimed that time was 'of the essence in this matter' (cited in Dodson 2005) and the bill was eventually passed. Legal expert Andrew Lynch (2006) expressed unease at the circumstances surrounding this hurriedly presented bill, arguing the adequacy of existing laws to allow pre-emptive action and citing inconsistencies in the bill. These inconsistencies included disparities between Howard's early statements on fixing 'operational offences' and the draft laws that were eventually tabled by the Attorney-General.

Second-rate justice

Howard's unwillingness to adapt to new facts could make him a very hard-eyed customer. In the wake of the atrocities of 9/11, a number of individuals suspected of involvement with terrorist organisations or associated activities were apprehended. After he was captured by Northern Alliance forces in Afghanistan in December 2001, David Hicks was sold to the American military for a $1000 bounty and transferred to a prison camp in Guantanamo Bay, Cuba. For much of his detention, Hicks was held in a concrete solitary confinement cell waiting trial by an arbitrarily constructed military commission

(Lasry 2006). Recasting legal conventions, the Bush administration decreed that al-Qaeda and Taliban members would not be accorded prisoner-of-war status. Under the newly invented category of 'unlawful enemy combatant', none of the usual protections of due process would apply – suspects would not even have the right to examine the evidence against them.

As other governments, including those of Britain and France, moved promptly to retrieve their citizens from US custody, Howard steadfastly defended Hicks' prolonged detention without trial and the independence and impartiality of the military system. He claimed that the Australian government intended to do 'whatever is necessary' to defend against potential terrorists and other enemies. Howard's singular focus, however, exposed a willingness to sit on the wrong side of longstanding democratic traditions and international obligations. The rolling situation of confusion and uncertainty within the legal black hole of Guantanamo served to transform Hicks into a figure of national sympathy (Grattan 2007). Other observers added that not only had Hicks been mistreated but that being a poor international actor was not in Australia's long-term strategic interests. Australia had a vested interest in, and remained heavily dependent on, the protections offered in a law-based world: 'As a middle-sized nation in a volatile region, we must recognise the need for a viable international legal framework and prevent despoiling it in a way that will prevent us having access to it in the future' (Hovell 2005).

At the very least, Guantanamo Bay became a symbol of abuse of executive power, and was roundly criticised. Hicks' defence council Major Michael Mori argued that his client should be tried in a normal court of law; German Chancellor Angela Merkel called for the closure of the facility at Guantanamo as quickly as possible; British Attorney-General Lord Goldsmith stated that the cumbersome military commission process was neither fair nor independent; even in his first weeks as US Defense Secretary, Robert Gates had argued (unsuccessfully) that the detention facility had become tainted, with the trials hampering the broader war effort to win 'hearts and minds' (Shanker & Sanger 2007).

Acting with a calculated firmness, Howard declared that Australia would make up its 'own mind about these things'. He maintained that the US president had a 'right' to put Hicks before the military commission – an experimental system that the White House had refused to condone for its own citizens. In June 2006, with the Australian government seemingly caught by surprise with the decision, the US Supreme Court ruled that the military commissions were illegal as they violated international law (McGarry 2005). Howard stated that he had been wrongly advised but remained unapologetic, referring to 'the crimes that he [Hicks] committed' and that he did not want Hicks to return to Australia (Grattan 2006). He reinforced the point that the Australian government had no qualms with the application of retrospective law, or apparently, with the dismissal of fundamental elements of due process and the conditions under which Hicks was incarcerated.

In March 2007 Hicks appeared before the US military's faintly revamped commission system. Although the validity of the second commission remained in doubt, a concern reinforced after the presiding judge removed two of the defendant's three lawyers, Hicks pleaded guilty to the charge of providing material support for terrorism. He was sentenced to a seven-year jail term with all but nine months suspended and agreed not to talk about his experiences for a year. A senior US official within the Office of Military Commissions described the case as 'very ordinary', concluding that ' for people wanting to see the worst of the worst, this was not going to be it' (Stewart 2007).

Alliance pressure

A critical factor in Howard's preparedness to stand by the Guantanamo process was based on a tradition of 'mateship' with great and powerful friends as well as a willingness to pay an insurance premium to the Bush administration in the event of any future crisis on Australian soil. Yet the government did not seem to fully grasp the nature of, or make preparations for, intra-alliance differences and the need to sometimes reassert Australian national interests in a the highly asymmetrical alliance context.

Set the task of adapting to a post-9/11 world, the crafting of foreign and defence policy had pinpointed the priority of the US relationship. The government's 'followership', which eagerly implicated itself in US global and regional strategy, gave full expression to the notion that Australia and the US had automatically identical interests. Despite critics such as former US President Jimmy Carter describing the Bush administration as the 'worst in history' for its impact around the world, the Australian government made little attempt to generate a more independent alliance role. The Bush administration's ideas of empire found a sympathetic, steadfast junior ally.

For more than 50 years, ANZUS has been seen as a vital cog of Australian security planning. How to successfully maintain a durable, credible and healthy alliance while managing limited resources, sometimes conflicting diplomatic demands and a shifting balance of global power has produced a considerable test for Australian decision-makers. As Paul Dibb (2003: 5–6)

Courtesy of Peter Nicholson, *The Australian*, 8 December 2006

succinctly pointed out, the tragic events of 9/11 upset established defence positions – initial participants had always assumed that ANZUS would be about an ultimate 'security blanket' protecting Australia. In the wake of the terrorist attacks, Australia was expected to take on bigger strategic burdens by adapting to an expeditionary warfare for crisis management and peacekeeping. Howard's gamble shifted Australian troops from the immediate region to a more dangerous, open-ended global engagement, although he deliberately avoided local counter-insurgency skirmishes in Iraq. With the cut and thrust of politics no longer able to offer a relaxed and comfortable interpretation of events, he emphasised that a premature departure from the Middle East would embolden militant groups and be detrimental to Australian interests. Such a stark appraisal appeared at odds with US National Intelligence Estimate reports revealing not only that Iraq had become a training ground to provide militants with battlefield experience but also that the invasion had given a strong tactical boost to al-Qaeda by allowing it to regroup and regenerate (Elliott 2007).

In contrast to the government's culture of compliance in dealing with the state of US–Australia relations, the US agenda was prepared to bruise feelings in order to create the conditions for a renewed American century. Deputy Secretary of State Richard Armitage, in particular, made much of the suspension of ANZUS obligations that had characterised the US–New Zealand relationship during the 1980s (Kerin 2004). US Ambassador Tom Schieffer – who apparently had not yet read the 800-odd word text of the ANZUS treaty – even dabbled in pre-election debate by warning the then Labor leader Mark Latham of 'very series consequences' if he did not repeal his drive for a troop pull-out from Iraq (Barker 2004).

Australia's voice on the world stage also had to contend with the lingering picture that Australia was a US outpost in the region. Howard's drive to make Australia more reliant on US power, in part, served to strain public support for the alliance. According to a detailed opinion poll conducted by the Lowy Institute in 2005 (with the direction of its main findings reinforced by a similar poll by the United States Centre at the University of Sydney in 2007), Australians expressed more positive views towards France, Japan and China than the US. Sixty-eight per cent believed that the Australian government took 'too much notice' of the US in setting foreign policy. Further, only 58 per cent had 'positive' feelings towards the US (Gordon 2005). While ANZUS itself was interpreted as being either very important or fairly important by 70 per cent of the respondents, the think-tank's executive director Allan Gyngell (2006–07: 115) observed that deepened scepticism had uncertain implications for the future of the alliance as the Australian public viewed the US 'with a mixture of dependency, respect, disenchantment and in some cases resentment'.

Howard's habit of blind loyalty towards the current US administration was highlighted in February 2007, when presidential hopeful Senator Barack Obama had introduced legislation that attempted to set a withdrawal plan for US combat troops in Iraq. In a very undiplomatic fashion, Howard warned that al-Qaeda would be 'praying as many times as possible' for an Obama victory (Carney 2007). Obama retorted by stating that, given Howard's sabre-rattling and insistence that military defeat in the region would be catastrophic for western civilisation, the Prime Minister's next step should be to significantly increase the actual deployment of Australian forces in the Gulf sandpit. Some added that Howard's reliance on the advantages of a personal chemistry with Bush was badly overstated. ANZUS was not an exclusive political marriage between two people or parties but rather an adaptable historic relationship between two nations (Lewis 2007).

Trouble in Asia

Howard's distaste for multilateral coalitions displayed a reluctance to offer up new vision of the future. Operating with a business-like demeanour, his search for a maximum output from a minimum input within Asia neglected the possibilities for regional institution-building to deliver a more purposeful engagement.

Howard's general approach to the Asian region tended to concentrate on direct commercial benefits. He personally engaged with the conclusion of an A$45 billion gas export deal with China, and he supported Australia's ongoing negotiations towards a free trade agreement with China. He favoured building on common interests rather than being overwhelmed by differences in relations with China and cited China's ambitions for peaceful global integration and its 'constructive approach' to a range of security matters (Megalogenis & Warren 2007).

Closer to home, in November 2006 (after some tricky manoeuvring to mend a rift fuelled by the granting of asylum to a group of West Papuans), Australia signed a wide-ranging security pact with Indonesia. Unsurprisingly, the Howard government's diplomacy was firmly entrenched in the promise not to intervene in Indonesia's internal affairs or undermine its territorial integrity over restive provinces, including West Papua. The agreement also put in motion a framework for bilateral nuclear co-operation and the Australian export of uranium for Jakarta's civil nuclear power program (Kingsbury 2006). Notwithstanding some measure of bilateral harmony, the reality was that Howard's efforts to balance Australia's history and geographic location remained bonded to an anachronistic view of the region. In contrast to his approach to China and Indonesia, the Prime Minister's attitude to multilateralism was considerably less constructive and forward-looking than that of other members of his own coalition, including the Foreign Minister. In an Asia-Link speech, Downer (2005) had contrasted the United Kingdom's belated entry into the European Union with Australia's involvement in development of regionalism in Asia where Australia is 'in at the start'.

The Prime Minister was not so upbeat. A meeting of ASEAN governments had made adherence to a code of conduct – requiring signatories to refrain from interfering in each other's affairs and settle disputes peacefully – a precondition for attending the East Asian Summit to be held in Kuala Lumpur in December 2005. Howard's refusal to sign the Treaty of Amity and Cooperation (TAC) at the 2004 ASEAN Summit in Vientiane because it was not 'appropriate' reflected a serious blind-spot: a belief that Australia did not need to actively participate in a multilateral world nor did Australia have to adapt to keep pace with regional linkages and restore regional legitimacy (Kelly 2005).

Australia was the only potential invitee that had not signed; China, India, Japan, New Zealand, South Korea and Russia had done so. Howard downplayed the importance of the TAC, arguing that the non-aggression pact would undermine existing alliance duties, even if other active US allies, such as Japan, had no problem in signing. Howard's stance also appeared linked to concern that the TAC would preclude his provocative stance that Australia had a right to unilateral pre-emptive strikes on terrorist cells in regional countries. Finally, the TAC was judged as corrupting the government's (highly selective) capacity to cast a spotlight on human rights violations. Nonetheless, while predicting that 'we are not knocking on doors begging admission – we don't need to do that', Howard's lecturing jeopardised Australia's place in a dynamic region and our ability to lend influence in addressing shared challenges (cited in Walters 2005).

While Downer appeared more cool-headed, even offering to discuss with ASEAN the concerns Australia had with the conditions and criteria of the TAC, former Liberal leader John Hewson described Howard's refusal to consider the symbolic weight of the treaty as 'churlish' (cited in Barnes 2005). Howard's dogged mantra of 'being ourselves in the region' brought historical and cultural rivalries to the fore and reinforced Australia's image problems in the region. Howard did attempt to bridge Australia's growing diplomatic isolation during a trip to China, but Beijing's interest in Australia's presence at the summit appeared to be waning. The best he could allege was that encouraging remarks had been made in a private conversation with Chinese officials. Problematically, Howard failed to sell the security merits of regional groupings to Australian audiences at home.

In July 2005, the Foreign Minister announced that the government had acceded to the treaty, after extensive consultations had resolved Australia's longstanding issues regarding its compatibility with Australia's bilateral and multilateral treaties and the UN Charter. The price of admission having been duly paid, Australia was invited to the inaugural East Asian Summit (EAS) and the preceding preparatory meeting of foreign ministers in December 2005. The Prime Minister's approach to the summit was manifested in doorstop interviews in Kuala Lumpur. He stated that APEC was the 'premier body' because it included the United States, conceding that 'it doesn't mean that other groupings are unimportant' (Howard 2005b).

Asked about a free trade bloc of 16 countries, and unlike Downer's welcome for the concept, the Prime Minister said that it was 'far, far too early to be talking about that' (Howard 2005b). The EAS Chairman, Malaysia's Prime Minister Abdullah Badawi, not unexpectedly responded by arguing that although Australia may be on Asia's doorstep it was not geographically part of East Asia and should not expect to become an integral part of a future regional community (Levett 2005). Howard replied by publicly welcoming his comment! Malaysia's former Deputy Prime Minister Anwar Ibrahim reflected that Australia was still regarded with underlying suspicion. He argued that many relationships remained decidedly shallow and vulnerable to erratic shifts in public opinion. Interactions continued to be exposed to a self-induced stereotype that Australians had 'not changed considerably from their old racist white supremacy, or racist policies' (cited in Perry 2007).

Fretting on the Pacific

After finally acknowledging that something might have to be done to address the plight of nations across the South Pacific, good fortune and diplomatic progress for Australia had occurred despite, not because of, the Prime Minister. The government failed to set the stage for a more inclusive conception of human development and security. Developments within the domestic sphere as well as the international realm also tested claims that Australia was a dominant shaper and mover.

The ramifications of the collapse of Afghanistan and the impact of 9/11 profoundly jolted Australia's relations with countries in the Pacific. Following years of inattention, the 'Howard doctrine' had reinterpreted Australia's role as an active, metropolitan regional leader to combat the risk of failed states in a region of tiny and impoverished island nations that included Timor, Tonga, Papua New Guinea, the Solomon Islands and Fiji. Howard mounted a case for a more interventionist style by accepting the argument that unstable states would create wider security headaches. Foreign assistance and the careful deployment of combat soldiers would be used to help mitigate the domestic conditions that acted as a breeding ground for criminal activity and the recruitment of terrorist cells.

Rejecting claims that his government aspired to be the region's sheriff, Howard promoted the line that Australia had a special responsibility, both altruistic and strategic, to intercede and actively work to help restore law and order and prevent the potential breakdown of the state. Commentators such as Peter Hartcher (2006) suggested that Australia had acquired an 'accidental empire'. Sharply preoccupied with making economic growth and the somewhat elusive concept of 'good governance' a complete policy antidote in dealing with separate predicaments in different countries, the government set about reversing a low-profile role in favour of a more direct state-building task. That would involve the setting of strict demands on aid delivery and other 'best practice' criteria, conditions that would potentially override notions of self-determination in targeted countries.

Howard's efforts to reassert Australian influence through the conduit of 'enhanced regionalism' had to wrestle with a number of intricate issues. Questions were raised regarding the heavy reliance on Australian public servants in delivering a technocratic project to remodel bureaucratic institutions. Part of this reform formula included the repair of a neo-liberal governance model that hoped economic 'trickle-down' would act as a sort of self-stabilising mechanism to meet various Pacific challenges. Some argued for more diplomatic fine-tuning and a less paternalistic mix in confronting problems at all levels, citing a stronger need to build mutual respect with affected communities and appreciate the fine-print of national contexts or local circumstances, including the impact of existing urban–rural disparities (Kilby 2007).

Despite the elevation of its regional assistance program as a template to which the rest of the world could refer in the future, progress remained sluggish and diplomacy remained deadlocked with a collection of Pacific states. A string of policy squabbles served to strain the basis for ally-friendly regional nation-building between Australia and its neighbours. Such predicaments included the Julian Moti affair, Howard's refusal to sign the Kyoto Protocol (particularly unpopular among low-lying island nations), the carving up of revenue from oil fields in the Timor Sea, the Australian Wheat Board's scandal under the oil-for-food program and the government's rejection of a scheme that would open up Australia's labour markets and provide temporary visas for unskilled and low-skilled guest workers from the region.

Howard did not demonstrate that he was taking the concerns of the Pacific community seriously. Resentment had been stoked at the Pacific Forum meeting in 2005, for example, where a tense showdown continued between Howard and other leaders over efforts to tackle conditions of poverty and other problems within large sections of the Pacific island area. PNG's Sir Michael Somare was one of the most vigorous proponents for a seasonal guest-worker scheme. He argued that special visas would recognise fundamental dilemmas such as PNG's underutilised human capital and poor employment prospects. Howard sidestepped the proposal for the establishment of any type of pilot program, refusing to give attention to the topic of labour migration. Observers argued not only that Australia had missed a golden opportunity to foster goodwill and dampen hostility but (as World Bank President Bob Zoellick pointed out) such initiatives should be viewed as an important component in contributing to meaningful poverty reduction; they would provide concrete steps to reduce the future likelihood of economic collapse and growing social dysfunction (Hartcher 2007).

The 2006 White Paper on Australian aid had called for an urgent marshalling of resources to deal with intra-state inequalities. Howard reconfirmed an 'unstinting commitment' to the internationally agreed Millennium Development Goals for reducing global-order concerns such as chronic poverty and hunger. There remained a question mark over the government's support for global community perspectives, however, due to disparities between declared policy and the actuality of the country's aid budget. In practice, the government set itself to contribute to a minimum net amount of 0.7 per cent of gross national income to tackle world poverty, but funding shortfalls resulted in expenditure reaching only around half of the longstanding international target (Elks & Hannan 2007). Even though it had found itself confronted by an avalanche of good economic news, Australia ranked 15th of 22 of the world's richest nations in the relative share of its aid burden to address personal and political insecurities in vulnerable countries (Costello 2007).

Critical openings for action on poverty were squandered. Australia's development contribution became merged within a policy direction that swung sharply from multilateral programs to bilateral agreements with individual governments, including special payments to Nauru to ensure maintenance of a detention facility and the offshore processing of asylum-seekers. The implementing of the Pacific Solution led to the emergence of 'phoney' and 'fig-leaf' aid. A former head of AusAID's Nauru program went so far as to label aid delivery to the debt-ridden island as an 'unmitigated bribe' (cited in Jopson 2007). Beyond Nauru, the government's clout in seeking to do more for poorer countries was tarnished by a deceptive re-branding of foreign assistance (used to artificially inflate budget figures) that incorporated items such as writing off Iraqi wheat debt, the inclusion of payments for temporary protection visa holders in Australia and the costs incurred for legal fees during the Cole Inquiry. Not-for-profit activist group AidWatch found that almost a third of the entire aid budget, or around A$1 billion, was being spent on official programs in which no new money to target poverty had flowed into the countries nominated as recipients (Jopson 2007).

Conclusion

A significant drawback to Howard's role as a war leader was that, rather than exploring alternative ideas and fully capitalising on favourable circumstances, genuine leadership opportunities were eschewed or badly undermined and mishandled. A preoccupation with military force and retaliatory muscle, combined with a stubborn refusal to accommodate those different from him, made diplomatic relations more complicated than they needed to be. Problematically, his favoured rhetoric on the war of terrorism remained terribly lopsided. His hard-line approach unnecessarily undercut the search for a more balanced, expanded notion of security that gave sustained and serious consideration to areas such as human, legal, economic and environmental security.

While witnessing some major re-alignments, including a willingness to exploit links with China, Howard constructed a core policy framework for dealing with a post-9/11 world that lacked an innovative long-term vision. The Howard government seemed to be engaging with a dynamic regional or international context through a rear-view mirror. Howard's Lowy Institute speech included a sentence which he may have regarded as defining his approach to foreign policy: 'We have learned that, if we make the right choices, Australians can shape our environment and our destiny, not simply be takers of trends set elsewhere' (Howard, 2005a). Whatever judgments may be made about Howard in other fields, his government's approach to foreign and security policy is likely to be seen in historical perspective as characteristically that of 'takers of trends set elsewhere'.

References

Banhman, C (2005) Beware alarmist rubbish, says Beattie, *Sydney Morning Herald*, 7 November.
Barker, G (2004) US alliance comes at a price, *Australian Financial Review*, 19 February.
Barnes, G (2005) Australia to remain outside if it refuses to sign treaty, *Manila Times*, 7 December.
Bonner, R (2005), Australian leader puts nation on terror alert, *International Herald Tribune*, 2 November.
Carney, S (2007) Man of spiel, *Age*, 13 February.
Costello, T (2007) We are winning the war on poverty but our government can do more, *Age*, 2 August.
Dibb, P (2003) Australia's alliance with America, *Melbourne Asia Policy Papers*, 1(1): 1–16.
Dodson, L (2005) Surprise ploy turns spotlight on a tightly guarded secret, *Sydney Morning Herald*, 18 October.
Dodson, L & Gordon, J (2005) Howard defiant on Kyoto rejection, *Age*, 5 September.

Downer, A (Minister for Foreign Affairs) (2005) Australia's engagement with Asia, Speech at Asia-Link Chairman's Dinner, Melbourne, 1 December.
Elliott, G (2007) Downer's denial won't change the terrible facts, *Australian*, 19 July.
Elks, S & Hannan, E (2007) Aussies are mean with foreign aid, says Geldof, *Herald Sun*, 20 November.
Fraser, M (2005) Laws for a secret state without any safeguards, *Sydney Morning Herald*, 20 October.
Gordon, M (2005) US influence disturbs Australians, *Age*, 29 March.
Grattan, M (2005) Accept Australian values or get out, *Age*, 25 August.
—— (2006) Shelling out false justice, *Sunday Age*, 2 July.
—— (2007) Hicks case backfires for Howard, *Age*, 2 February.
Gyngell, A (2006–07) Paradise revisited, *Griffith Review*, 14, Summer.
Hartcher, P (2006) Messy times ahead for this ragtag empire, *Age*, 30 June.
—— (2007) Open your gates to migrants: Bank chief, *Sydney Morning Herald*, 2 August.
Howard, J (2005a) Australia in the world, Speech at the Lowy Institute for International Policy, Sydney, 31 March.
—— (2005b) Transcript of doorstop interview, Regent Hotel, Kuala Lumpur, 14 December.
Hovell, D (2005) International law must not be 'foreign' to Australians, *Age*, 19 June.
Jopson, D (2007) Phantom aid never leaves out shores, *Age*, 28 May.
Keating, P (2005) Howard: Our Asian recalcitrant, *Age*, 4 April
Kerbaj, R (2007) Fear keeps Muslims silent on terrorism, *Australian*, 28 May.
Kelly, P (2005) Howard taught a lesson in Asia, *Australian*, 27 April.
Kerin, J (2004) US warns Labor on future of ANZUS pact, *Australian*, 11 June.
Kilby, P (2007) The Australian aid program: Dealing with poverty?, *Australian Journal of International Affairs*, 61(1): 114–29.
Kingsbury, D (2006) Pleasing Indonesia, *Age*, 9 November.
Lasry, L (2006) Ruling a substantial victory, *Canberra Times*, 1 July.
Levett, C (2005) Malaysia delivers a short, important face slap, *Sydney Morning Herald*, 15 December.
Lewis, S (2007) Howard overplays his US hand, *Australian*, 13 February.
Lynch, A (2006) Legislating with urgency: The enactment of *The Anti-Terrorism Act [No. 1] 2005*, *Melbourne University Law Review*, 30(3): 747–81.
McGarry, A (2005) US court ruling buoys Hicks supporters, *Australian*, 2 February.
McKenzie, N (2005) Stanhope flags doubts on hasty terrorism bill, at <www.abc.net.au/news/newsitems/200510/s1483482.htm>.
Megalogenis, G & Warren, M (2007) Chinese ties in new era after gas deal, *Australian*, 7 September.
Neighbour, S (2007) Guilty until proven innocent, *Australian*, 19 July.
Nicholson, B (2006) Rights 'breached' by terror laws, *Age*, 16 June.
O'Sullivan, P (2007) Extremists can turn violent fast, *Australian*, 28 February.
Perry, K (2007) Australia perceived as racist, former Malaysian PM says, at <www.abc.net.au/lateline/content/2007/s1863771.htm>.
Shanker, T & Sanger, D (2007) New to job, Gates argued for closing Guantanamo, *New York Times*, 23 March.
Stewart, C (2007) Hicks was never dangerous, says US, *Australian*, 28 April.
Thomson, M (2005) Punching above our weight? Australia as a middle power, *Strategic Insight*, No. 18, Australian Strategic Policy Institute, Canberra.
Walters, P (2005) Downer hopeful of invite to ASEAN, *Australian*, 13 April.
—— (2007) Defence battle-lines drawn, *Australian*, 6 July.

Williams, G & Lynch, A (2006) Fix-it later legislation no way to govern, *Australian*, 28 December.
Wright-Neville, D (2005) Fear and loathing: Australia and counter-terrorism, ARI no.156, Institute for Strategic and International Relations (Real Instituto Elcano de Estudios Internacionales y Estratégicos), at <http://www.realinstitutoelcano.org/analisis/871/Wright-Neville871.pdf.>

PART III

John Howard, Prime Minister

15 Staying on

David Adams

On a number of occasions in John Howard's fourth term as Prime Minister he might have followed his hero Sir Robert Menzies and left office undefeated, on his own terms and with a high degree of approbation. He could have done it upon completing 'The Howard Decade', which was assessed, evaluated, praised and criticised in articles, books, speeches and conferences in March 2006. He could have done it in the latter, even late, stages of the fourth term to allow Peter Costello to succeed him and to lead the government into the 2007 election. But he stayed on. This led his biographers to suggest (in August 2007) that his best years were behind him and that he 'had made the one mistake in politics that he wouldn't be around to learn from – misjudging his optimal retirement date' (Errington & Van Onselen 2007: 402). Opinions varied as to why he stayed so long. Was it egomania? Or vanity? An inability to give up power? Or, more prosaically, his belief that he was more likely than Costello to keep the coalition in office? No doubt his motives were mixed, but if one of them was maximising the government's chances of securing another term, it is not surprising that Costello did not share in this assessment. Costello said that a fifth term was 'a very difficult thing to win' and there would have been more chance of doing so if there had been 'a fresh f ace on the Coalition' (ABC 2007b). But Howard wanted (part of) one more term before handing over to Costello.

John Howard's fourth term was not his best, not just because it ended in defeat but because on a number of issues his political skills were not of the order they had been during his previous terms. This was demonstrated in small ways such as his comments about Senator Obama and the war in Iraq, as described in chapter 14. The 'extraordinary intervention' into the Mersey hospital was hard to defend on the basis of policy rationality, even if the political rationality was starkly evident (for details, see chapter 6). Howard's faltering skills showed in more substantial ways as he fumbled the leadership succession and lost control of two issues which, like the leadership messiness, were to damage him in the 2007 election: Work Choices and climate change.

Policy impact: incremental? radical? populist?

Phil Lewis (in chapter 10) is sympathetic to Howard's industrial relations reforms but argues that he did a poor job in selling them. The proposals 'lacked the thoroughness and preparedness that had gone into reforms such as the GST and welfare'. Perhaps, says Lewis, Howard's judgment had been clouded by having a Senate majority but another potent factor was the contempt that Howard and some ministers had towards aspects of union activity. The need for industrial relations reform was 'taken as an act of faith with no reasoned analysis of the benefits to the economy'. This had allowed the Labor Party and the ACTU scope to attack the proposed reforms. And the first minister charged with selling the legislation, the doleful Kevin Andrews, was not a public relations asset. He was faced with a skilful advocate from the ACTU, Greg Combet, who wrote of Work Choices 'smashing institutions', the 'gutting' of industrial relations tribunals and 'a full frontal assault' being made on unions and collective bargaining (Combet 2005). After the election Joe Hockey, the minister who took over from Kevin Andrews in 2007, conceded that Work Choices had gone 'too deep' (*Age* 2007) and Tony Abbott reflected on the 'poor politics' of the way Work Choices was 'sprung' on the electorate after the Senate majority had been secured (Abbott 2007).

If Work Choices went too deep and too far, the opposite was the case with policies on climate change. The very fact that chapter 12 in this volume is titled 'Discovering the environment' suggests that the government was slow in recognising the public sentiments that had formed round issues concerned with climate change and global warming. As Stewart and Hendriks argue in that chapter, the government's 'piecemeal and cautious approach to environmental policy attracted increasing criticism'. Again, ideology is part of the story. Stewart and Hendriks write that 'the overwhelming identification of the green vote with the left of politics, meant that, as a conservative Liberal, he saw little political advantage in cultivating it' (see pp. 221, 222). As Baldino notes, Howard's 'political radar appeared to misread the public mood' (p. 246).

Although the politics of Work Choices and climate change differed in many ways, the authors of the chapters dealing with these issues have identified essentially incremental approaches to policy change. They are not alone. Linda Botterill's discussion of rural policy in chapter 9 notes the history of incremental policy-making in the sector and ends by suggesting that partisan disagreements are largely matters of detail and rhetoric rather than direction. Chris Aulich identifies the 'subtle, incremental use' of particular privatisation technologies, although he notes the government's underlying 'strong ideological commitment to private over public enterprise' (p.58). Garnett and Lewis's discussion of the economy suggests that 'the economic reform process carried out during Howard's term in government can be thought of as a mix of new policy together with a continuation of the reform processes' which began under previous Labor governments. They conclude that 'Howard has not moved government as far to the right as his supporters, including those in his own party, might like' (pp. 136, 149). So the story of the Howard years is one of a good deal of continuity and incrementalism. Howard's biographers have made the same point:

> After ten years of stirring both vitriolic criticism and ungainly praise, John Howard simply hadn't made the difference his more ideological supporters had hoped he would, other than keeping Labor away from the treasury benches. For all the angst from the welfare lobby, income inequality has been stable. For all the government's talk about income tax cuts, average rates are the same as they were before the introduction of the GST. If we judge Howard by his own standards as a reformer, there isn't a good deal to show for his lengthy period of office. (Errington & Van Onselen 2007: 390)

While John Howard might find this a rather niggardly assessment he was happy to proclaim that his approach had indeed been incremental:

> Incremental reform usually gets a bad press, especially from editorial writers accustomed to dispensing advice in 800 words or less. But incremental or piecemeal reform is in fact the kind of reform that liberals and conservatives invariably are most

> comfortable with. Indeed, as Karl Popper taught us half a century ago, it is often the most rational approach especially if the alternative is utopian social engineering. (Howard 2005)

But other observers saw something more than incrementalism. Howard was 'a radical prime minister' who 'fundamentally changed' the taxation system, turned industrial relations on its head, sold Telstra, engaged in massive spending on middle-class welfare, was responsible for the liberation of East Timor, forcefully intervened in the affairs of neighbours such as Papua New Guinea and the Solomon Islands, and involved Australia in 'the unpopular inferno of Iraq and what promises to be an endless operation in Afghanistan' (Daley 2007b). Michael Gordon said that even 'the Howard haters would agree he is a leader who has left big footprints' (Gordon 2007). And some contributors to this volume also explore areas where change has been more than incremental; the total effect of a number of incremental changes can sometimes be substantial and can be seen in relation to reconstructing the public sector into a more centrally managed organisation (see chapters 2 and 3), federalism (chapter 6), Indigenous affairs (chapter 11), the shift from multiculturalism to citizenship (chapter 13). Aulich (chapter 4) argues that the actions of the four Howard governments have, albeit in increments, had the substantial outcome of developing a two-tiered state where public services are 'residual' (p. 71).

So judgments about Howard's policy impact have varied. Thus his comment – as he announced the date of the 2007 election – that 'love me or loathe me, the Australian people know where I stand and what I believe in' (Howard 2007b) is less than straightforward. Indeed a common theme of commentary about Howard is that people did not know what he stood for or believed in. In 1998 a commentator said that 'even after all this time on the political stage, nobody really knows him' (Walsh 1998). Eight years later George Megalogenis asked 'but who is John Howard and what does he really stand for?'(Megalogenis 2006: 172), and he wrote of the 'puzzle of Howard' (Megalogenis 2006: 195). He remained elusive even to his biographers. They begin their book by saying:

> There are many John Howards. There is the ordinary bloke who enjoys spending time with his family and watching the cricket. There is the strong-willed man of principle whom his supporters like to imagine. There is the rat-cunning opportunist feared and loathed by his opponents. Then there are all the gradations in between. John Howard's extraordinary success as a politician has

come about because he is all of these things and many more. (Errington & Van Onselen 2007: vii)

And in two later parts of the book they say:

> At various times, Howard can be a liberal, a conservative or a radical. The precise mix depends on the demands of the economy and electoral politics and on the cajoling from the various wings of his party at any one time. (Errington & Van Onselen 2007: 217)

> Depending on the audience and the issue of the day, we might have seen the ideologue or the pragmatist, the conservative or the reformer (Errington & Van Onselen 2007: 281).

Here was a protean politician: liberal, conservative, radical, ideologue, pragmatist, reformer. And one who was constantly alert to electoral politics, party cajoling and the sensitivities of his various audiences. The comedians John Clarke and Bryan Dawe had a similar take on the Prime Minister's intermittent populism. Here is Clarke, as the prime minister, defending the government's intervention in the Northern Territory, discussed in chapter 11:

> **Clarke**: It's degrading, it's unhygienic Bryan. People should not be living like this.
>
> **Dawe**: And how long has this been going on?
>
> **Clarke**: In its current form?
>
> **Dawe**: Yeah.
>
> **Clarke**: About 11 years Bryan.
>
> **Dawe**: Well, that's terrible.
>
> **Clarke**: It's shocking Bryan, we've got to do something about it.
>
> **Dawe**: Why hasn't something been done about this beforehand?
>
> **Clarke**: Well, we had the Ashes last season, Bryan. We've got the global heating of the icebergs, warmation thing.
>
> **Dawe**: Global warming?
>
> **Clarke**: Pardon?
>
> **Dawe**: Global warming?
>
> **Clarke**: Yes indeed. (Clarke & Dawe 2007)

And this excerpt begins with the decision not to privatise the Snowy Hydro Scheme (see chapter 4) and moves on to the environment (see chapter 12):

Clarke: We were asked to listen to the people and we listened to the people.

Dawe: People power.

Clarke: People power, Bryan! Very, very important. Victory for people power.

Dawe: And will you be listening to people on other issues as well?

Clarke: Well, I listen to these bloody – to people all the time, Bryan.

Dawe: Well, the GST, they didn't want that?

Clarke: Well, you don't ask turkeys whether they want an early Christmas, do you, Bryan? Let's be sensible.

Dawe: Well, they didn't want the sale of Telstra either.

Clarke: Well, of course they didn't, Bryan – they owned it.

Dawe: Yes, well, they didn't want to go to war in Iraq.

Clarke: Well, they would have, if our argument had made any sense at all.

Dawe: OK, and now you've announced an inquiry into nuclear power.

Clarke: We have, Bryan. A very, very important inquiry.

Dawe: And this is an independent inquiry?

Clarke: Open and very independent – fiercely independent inquiry, yes.

Dawe: What is it called?

Clarke: It's called 'How Can we Best Introduce Nuclear Power Right Across the Country by Tuesday?'

Dawe: And who's running it?

Clarke: Good point, Bryan. Good point. This is run by people who want it introduced by Monday. (Clarke & Dawe 2006)

The Roman poet Horace aimed to 'tell the truth, laughing' – Clarke and Dawe have followed in his footsteps. They are the great caricaturists of the Howard years, along with Australia's excellent crop of cartoonists like Nicholson whose drawings enrich this volume.

Prime ministerial governance

Because politicians emphasise different things to different audiences it is dangerous to read into any particular utterances what they really stand for. But by going on the record they are indicating that what they say is something they are prepared to defend. So we should not dismiss as mere flattery the comments that Howard made at the dinner to mark the 50th anniversary of the magazine *Quadrant.* He singled out three people for praise:

> Reagan, the man who gave America back her confidence and optimism in the wake of a decade of setbacks and who began to talk openly and candidly about an 'evil empire' – the sort of talk that sends diplomats the world over into panicked meltdown;
>
> Thatcher, the Iron Lady who as well as anyone grasped and articulated the essential connection of personal, political and economic freedom;
>
> Pope John Paul II – a man of enormous courage and dignity whose words of faith and hope inspired millions behind the Iron Curtain to dream again of a Europe whole and free. (Howard 2006)

Here are the people with whom Howard wished to associate himself, people espousing the virtues of optimism, plain-speaking, freedom, courage, dignity, faith and hope. This is perhaps a sketch for a self-portrait. Interestingly two of these three people were among the leaders discussed by Graham Little in his book *Strong Leadership* (1988), a development of an earlier work *Political Ensembles* (1985). Judith Brett and James Walter (and his co-author Paul Strangio) have both drawn on Little's work in their analyses of Howard. Brett wrote that the strong leader's message is: 'Leave it to me, I'm in charge'. 'His peacetime purpose is to provide the safe shield behind which people can get on with their lives.' Strong leaders are 'emotionally organised for survival in a difficult world. They thrive on competition and stress the virtues of independence, individual responsibility, hard work and tough decisions' (Brett 2007a: 12–13). And Walter and Strangio (2007: 21) say that 'writing long before Howard's accession, Little captures the essence of his style': hard-working, driven, controlling and moralistic. Strong leaders 'see the world as threatening and believe that order can only be maintained by strength'. This description of strong leaders provides a helpful view of Howard. But it is a partial one. Some of the characteristics of the strong leader outlined by Little fit Howard poorly. He was not 'admired for his aloofness'. He was not a man of anger rather than amiability. He was hardly 'daunting'. And he had some of the features of a second type of leader described by Little: the group leader.

> The group leader must always be easy to talk to and more available than not. The leader should listen to complaints and offer help and encouragement; at the very least he would not raise an eyebrow at having been asked however humble the petitioner. …[he must know] what the membership is thinking. (Little 1985: 146–47).

Howard was a hybrid. (Little also distinguished the inspiring leader who is marked by charisma – this was not Howard.)

Within his government he was undoubtedly a leader of strength. He was said to have Imperial (Hartcher 2007b) or Bonapartist (Wanna 2005) tendencies. For Brian Toohey he was The Lone Ranger.

> Power has been concentrated in the hands of the prime minister, a post that doesn't even rate a mention in the Constitution. The traditional position of a prime minister as *primus inter pares* has been rendered obsolete; certainly no minister believes that Howard is merely first among equals in the exercise of power. (Toohey 2007: 26)

Mungo MacCallum suggested that 'the office of the prime minister, once regarded as no more than the first among equals', had been turned into an unaccountable commissariat ruling by absolute fiat (MacCallum 2004: 2). This mention of first among equals and *primus inter pares* is a red-herring. Even the formulator of the phrase (in the 19th century) said that the position of prime minister was 'one of exceptional and peculiar authority' (Hennessy 1996: 83). But did Howard push the office beyond 'exceptional authority' into something over-mighty? Paul Kelly was more measured than some other observers. He also stressed the incremental. While describing Australian government as being 'prime ministerial governance' he said: 'The paradox in Prime Ministerial Governance from Whitlam to Howard lies in its powerful continuity. Each succeeding Prime Minister builds upon his predecessor's legacy. There are no legacies that have been dismantled' (Kelly 2006: 7). And he went on to say that it is:

misleading to exaggerate Howard's break from the past. He must be seen within that current of powerful continuity that constitutes Prime Ministerial Governance. Howard is no more preoccupied by executive authority than Fraser; no more hostile to the Senate than Keating; no more reliant upon ministerial staff than Hawke. (Kelly 2006: 8)

So, for Kelly, Howard was continuing what his predecessors had set in train. The institutional logic of what Howard and other prime ministers have done is clear and they were well explained by Howard himself:

[I]f things go wrong, the prime minister is always to blame. I accept ultimate responsibility for the decisions of the government and I take ultimate responsibilities for the political misjudgments of the government and I suppose occasionally if I get something right I'm entitled to get some of the credit. (Channel Ten 2007)

All prime ministers want to maximise the credit and to minimise the blame. To that end they will want to control as much as they can. They will want a strong prime ministerial office; they will want a public service that is 'responsive'

Howard eyes the history books
Courtesy of Peter Nicholson, *The Australian*, 20 August 2005

(although this is not always a straightforward concept); they will want people they trust in key political and administrative posts. The key dynamic for not just prime ministers but chief executives everywhere has been well captured by Terry Moe writing about American presidents. He notes the president's desire to achieve 'leadership in a system largely beyond his control' (Moe 1993: 367). Australian prime ministers have more control over the political system than American presidents (see Kelly 2006 and also Walter & Strangio 2007), but there is still a great deal that is beyond their control. And this can frustrate them. As Michelle Grattan noted in the battle over water (see chapters 6 and 12):

> John Howard always strives to be in control, whether of the policy agenda or the tactics of a particular political skirmish. In his takeover bid for the Murray-Darling Basin, the Prime Minister has found himself at the mercy of other players, and he's hated it. (Grattan 2007)

No prime minister, chief executive or president likes being at the mercy of other players, but with Howard there was a particular (more personal) twist. Here is Matt Price:

> Howard bristles with energy and never allows himself the luxury of feeling overly comfortable in the top job. This constant political paranoia – a sense of always expecting the unexpected – is born of bitter experience and has served Howard well. 'That's right, I've always been like that', he told me in 2003. 'Somebody said to me this morning something complimentary, and I just looked around and said, there's always an Exocet coming over the horizon … you can never tell in politics'. (Price 2006: 60)

And here – invoking a concern for self-protection that perhaps falls only a little short of political paranoia – is Ann Tiernan's view in her book on ministerial staff:

> Perhaps because of Howard's experiences of treachery and betrayal during his tenacious climb to Australia's top job, a key concern has been to surround himself with personally loyal appointees; people who had proven themselves during his years in the political wilderness. Competence and the ability to gain the trust of a prime minister who does not trust easily are criteria for entry to Howard's advisory network. His preference for dealing with people with whom he has had long associations and/or familial

> connections is well documented and clearly evident, especially within his prime minister's office ... From the beginning of his prime ministership, Howard has asserted his right to work with people he knows and feels comfortable with, and who share his political philosophy. (Tiernan 2007: 123–24)

Accusations were also made about Howard's approach to the public service, exemplified by the famous 'night of the long knives' (Kelly 2007) when six departmental heads were removed in 1996 and by the appointment of a bruiser, Max Moore-Wilton, to head the Department of the Prime Minister and Cabinet (DPM&C). Geoffrey Barker wrote that under Howard the service had 'been remade to ensure its compliance with the government's political agenda. With honourable (and often modest exceptions), the fearless mandarins of the past have been largely replaced by cautious transient managers, some of whom are open government allies' (Barker 2007: 147). Barker had the grace to note that the government did 'little that was not started by earlier, and usually Labor governments' and he records the view of Richard Mulgan, an eminent scholar in the field, that 'politicisation of the APS, in the sense of appointments to suit the preferences of the government of the day, has been gradually increasing over recent decades' (Barker 2007: 127). The staunchest defender of the continued professionalism of the public service was Peter Shergold, the successor to Moore-Wilton as the Secretary of DPM&C. He said he could attest that the Prime Minister had 'never sought to determine the content or arguments of the departmental advice, still less to prevent information being conveyed to him', and that neither he or his secretarial colleagues 'have been politicised in the sense of withholding information from or tailoring advice to the known preferences of our ministers' (Shergold 2004: 10).

Turning to public appointments more generally, a former Howard chief of staff thought ideological or partisan affinity had been important:

> John Howard is more like a Labor politician than any other leader of Australia's political conservatives, all the way back to 1901. Mr Howard is very much like the tribal political leaders who have traditionally prevailed in the ALP. Qualified supporters get government funded positions; qualified opponents do not. This is in marked contrast to the governments headed by the two long-term Liberal Party prime ministers – Robert Menzies and Malcolm Fraser. When I worked with John Howard two decades ago, I recall him commenting that to be a Liberal Party supporter during the Fraser years was all but a disqualification from government

preferment. That certainly cannot be said of the Howard Government. (Henderson 2006: 2)

In an earlier essay on Howard I compared him to Sir Robert Peel (Adams 2000). Here is another point of comparison. When it came to making governmental appointments Peel's advice was that 'you cannot conciliate your enemies, therefore give everything to the most zealous of your friends' (Hurd 2007: 322). John Howard would concur. As Tiernan notes:

> The Howard cabinet devotes more time to government appointments than any of its predecessors. A former cabinet minister confirmed that the prime minister's staff are deeply engaged in vetting government appointments. Taken together with control of ministerial staff appointments through the government staff committee, this gives Howard significant authority. The emergence of a staffing apparatus to support this explicitly political activity is a further organisational expression of prime ministerial power. (Tiernan 2007: 135)

Power and control

Those who see an imperial or Bonapartist prime ministership are partly right. But the mechanisms of control used by John Howard seemed to be equally grounded in defensiveness. Trouble was to be prevented, and when it occurred it was to be contained. Patrick Weller's comment that 'controlled' is a good description of Howard's cabinet could be extended to the government in general (Weller 2007: 176). Arthur Sinodinos gave an interview on his retirement as Howard's Chief of Staff which reinforces these points (Hartcher 2007a). He outlined a number of lessons about how John Howard governed. Most of them indicate that he was constantly on the alert for an Exocet – and they reveal the hybrid traits of the strong and group leader. Sinodinos said that Howard approached every day as if it could be his last. 'We always took the view that you always act as if you're in opposition and your back's to the wall – and you fight accordingly.' Howard 'never took being in power for granted'. And he was always happy to fight:

> The Prime Minister is always at his best when he has a cause to fight for. It always brought out the best in him – in terms of his fighting skills, his advocacy skills, it really brought out the passion in him. And when he's out there on the hustings fighting for what he believes in, the public responds very well. (Hartcher 2007a)

There was a desire to shape the political agenda. The Prime Minister and his staff spent a lot of time monitoring the media and developing 'lines' to promote. 'Because if you leave a vacuum it will be filled by others – keep the initiative.' Unity was strength. Brian Loughnane, the federal director of the Liberal Party, worked closely with the coalition's parliamentary leadership to maintain the unity of the government's political message. Howard was careful never to appear arrogant or complacent – 'not to be seen to cock a snook at the electorate. They want you to earn their vote'. Howard had developed a 'sophisticated radar system' to warn of impending political problems. This involved polling but there was also a concern to talk to people with gripes. 'He hates cheer squads (Hartcher 2007a).' You need radar if you are expecting Exocets.

Sinodinos was also interviewed by Howard's biographers. He told them that 'Howard's approach [was] all tied back to getting into government and staying in government' (Errington & Van Onselen 2007: 398). This quotation was seized on by an interviewer to make the case that Howard was a partisan opportunist. The Prime Minister's rebuttal was straightforward:

> **Kerry O'Brien**: … would you agree that description sounds more like political self-interest, like hanging onto power for power's sake rather than governing in the national interest?
>
> **John Howard**: Kerry, it's the responsibility of a Prime Minister to try and keep his party in government.
>
> **Kerry O'Brien**: At any cost?
>
> **John Howard**: No, not at any cost and I would reject any suggestion that it's been at any cost. If I'd run the country into deficit as Mr Keating did, it would have been at any cost. But I haven't run the country into deficit. It's still healthily in surplus. But hello, it is the responsibility of a political leader to get his party into power and when it's there to try to keep holding onto power. I haven't struck a Prime Minister yet who set out to get voted out of office. (ABC 2007a)

'But, hello!' If you are not in office, your opponents are. And that is what John Howard wanted to prevent. He was tribal. We should remember that Rod Tiffen has called Howard the Geoffrey Boycott of Australian politics (Tiffen 2006). Boycott did not like being dismissed; he wanted to bat forever and he was obsessed with the game to the point of monomania. And like Boycott, Howard was the subject of regular criticism, some of it from his team-mates. Relations with the Deputy Leader of his party were often fraught. Peter

Costello wanted to be prime minister. Unfortunately for him Howard wanted it more. In 2006 it was reported (Milne 2006) that as far back as 1994, when they were in opposition, an undertaking had been entered into which would see Howard give way to Costello after only a term or two in office. This undertaking had (obviously) not been honoured. There was a flurry of comment about this alleged arrangement. The most sensible view of the matter came from Mrs Howard when she told Errington and Van Onselen:

> You talk about a whole lot of things when you're trying to convince people to do things but you don't go back and honour every single one of those unless you have made a firm commitment about it and John wasn't into making firm commitments. (Errington & Van Onselen 2007: 384)

This comment showed cant-free commonsense about some fairly speculative discussions being conducted when the Liberals were out of office. Mrs Howard knows about political quasi-promises. The interviews that Costello gave Errington and Van Onselen attracted even more attention than Mrs Howard's *realpolitik*. He talked of the lack of dinner invitations to Kirribilli House; he criticised Howard's record as Treasurer in the Fraser government and, most significantly, he expressed his concerns about Howard's penchant for public spending. Errington and Van Onselen write:

> The fiscal price that Howard has been prepared to pay for winning elections has been a source of tension between prime minister and treasurer. Massaging public opinion has been expensive for the Howard government. In considering the future, Costello questions the fiscal responsibility of some of the government's spending patterns. 'I have to foot the bill and that worries me,' Costello says, 'and then I start thinking about not just footing the bill today but if we keep building in all these things, footing the bill in five, and ten and fifteen years and you know I do worry about the sustainability of all these things.' Clearly, the purpose of Costello's Future Fund was not only to lock the proceeds of budget surpluses away from a future Labor government, but to keep them away from Howard as well. Plenty of money has been spent, but often only as a bandage between elections, rarely as part of a considered plan. Howard claimed to have governed for all Australians, but his willingness to indulge favoured constituencies who threatened to park their votes elsewhere was more typical. (Errington & Van Onselen 2007: 388–89)

And this typicality continued into the 2007 election when Howard made so many promises of substantial new public expenditure that Kevin Rudd could climb onto the high horse of fiscal rectitude to say 'loud and clear that this sort of reckless spending must stop' (Rudd 2007). Howard's claim, noted earlier, that 'the Australian people know where I stand and what I believe in' looked even shakier towards the end of an election campaign in which he threw 'vast sums of money at almost all issues and all areas identified as problematic for the party. Never has so much been offered to so many' (Waterford 2007b). But while this largesse was being dispensed, the electorate was also being told that 'steady, reliable, safe economic management is the bedrock of good government' (Howard 2007a). What Howard stood for and believed in, beyond trying – as he said to Kerry O'Brien – to 'keep holding onto power', was not as clear as he had suggested.

A question of character

This is a book which focuses on policy and administration but no history of the Howard governments would be complete without drawing attention to some of the divergent views of the character of the man at its centre. Janet Albrechtsen, in a column saying it was time for him to hand over to Peter Costello, said:

> John Howard has been the finest prime minister Australia has had ... He rebuilt a political philosophy of individual responsibility for a new generation. His legacy is profound. From workplace reform to welfare to indigenous politics, to our sense of national identity, Howard has changed the nation in a way very few leaders ever do. Each step rankled his opponents as they clung to old orthodoxies. Yet Howard, through sheer dint of character and intellectual fortitude, prevailed. (Albrechtsen 2007)

It was character and intellectual fortitude that his enemies were unwilling to acknowledge. Those enemies were sometimes called 'Howard haters'. But hatred is not the most accurate emotional description; there seemed more disdain, indignation, anger, distaste and contempt than hatred. For example, David Marr thought Howard was dishonest:

> We've watched Howard spin, block, prevaricate, sidestep, confound and just keep talking come what may through any crisis. Words grind out of him unstoppably. He has a genius for ambiguity

we've almost come to applaud, and most of the time he keeps himself just this side of deceit. But he also lies without shame. Howard invented the breakable or non-core promise – the first was to maintain ABC funding – five years before those children weren't thrown overboard. The truth is we've known he was a liar from the start. (Marr 2007: 5)

MacCallum thought he was an unscrupulous, manipulative fear-monger:

> the electorate has consistently fallen for the oldest trick of all, the naked appeal to those most basic of emotions, fear and greed. Howard may have lacked vision, integrity, even normal human decency, but he learned how to push those buttons, connecting them to everything from refugees to mortgage rates; and, his ambition having been honed by years of failure into an almost megalomaniac desire to hang on to his hard-won position, he showed less and less scruple about the way he manipulated public opinion at every level. (MacCallum 2004: 3)

Manne disliked:

> the incapacity to admit error, as with Iraq; the poll-driven opportunism on questions like global warming and Hicks; the mania for control; the unwillingness to engage opponents in honest debate; the fondness for repetition and cliché; the mock modesty; the moral complacency; above all, the thinly disguised ruthlessness when engaged in a hunt. (Manne 2007: 15)

David Williamson echoed a number of these accusations. The coalition had 'abandoned any moral dimension in its quest to retain power' (Williamson 2007b). Williamson looked forward to Howard's defeat and a return to simple decency. He argued that people with the 'remnants of a conscience' found it 'hard to stomach' Howard; his period in office had involved 'shameless exploitation of fear and hysteria', 'moral sleaze', 'blatant and immoral pork barrelling', 'constant and unrelenting grovelling to George Bush' and a 'deathbed conversion to climate change and reconciliation-lite' (Williamson 2007a).

Howard's biographers were waspish about the critics:

> Humanities academics, the arts community, public broadcasters and the Fairfax broadsheets could hardly have shared a world view more different from that of John Howard. This group tolerated Keating because he supplemented the economic

liberalism they hated with attention and funding for their various obsessions. Howard, in studied contrast, rejected the triumvirate of reconciliation, multiculturalism and republicanism. It turned out to be very convenient for Australia's intellectuals to have the sum of all their fears bound up in one political leader. (Errington & Van Onselen 2007: 259)

Jack Waterford, himself a frequent critic of Howard, was pithier. His preferred word was 'Pharisees', 'thanking the Lord they are not like other people' (Waterford 2007a). Part of Howard's appeal to those who were not humanities academics, members of the arts community, public broadcasters and Fairfax journalists was said to be that he actually was like other people. Judith Brett noted his persona as 'a reassuringly suburban Australian everyman' (Brett 2007b: 10). Michelle Grattan noted his 'awesome ordinariness' (Wainwright & Stevens 2004), an ordinariness that Matt Price suggested was 'entirely unconfected' (Price 2002). Norman Abjorensen wrote that:

> The very ordinariness of Howard provides him with a rapport with the average Australian in a way that few if any of his immediate predecessors had. Keating had fled middle Australia, Hawke was an Edna Everage-like superstar, Fraser was remote, Whitlam was Olympian, McMahon was simply inept, Gorton a privileged larrikin, Holt a socialite, and Menzies was too conscious of his own superiority. Chifley was the last man of the people. Howard has never left his heartland, a fact that drives his critics to distraction. It is worth remembering that when he was Treasurer in the Fraser government his home phone number was listed in the telephone book, an act as courageous as it was rare. That in itself speaks volumes about the man and his perception of the electorate. (Abjorensen 2006)

The dictionary suggests that rapport involves 'harmonious accord, close and harmonious relation'; being in 'sympathy', in 'harmony'. The election result of 2007 suggested any days of harmonious accord were past. If Howard thought he was en rapport with the populace, the loss of office and his seat would have disabused him of that. But even as they rejected him electorally, were people still reasonably favourably disposed towards him? They had not thought kindly of Paul Keating when they rejected him in an equally emphatic fashion in 1996. Keating went out of office with a net approval rating of minus 18 (38 per cent satisfied; 56 dissatisfied). When it was Howard's turn to leave office he had a net approval rating of plus six (51 per cent satisfied; 45 dissatisfied). As figure 15.1 shows, his journey to November 2007 was moderately bumpy:

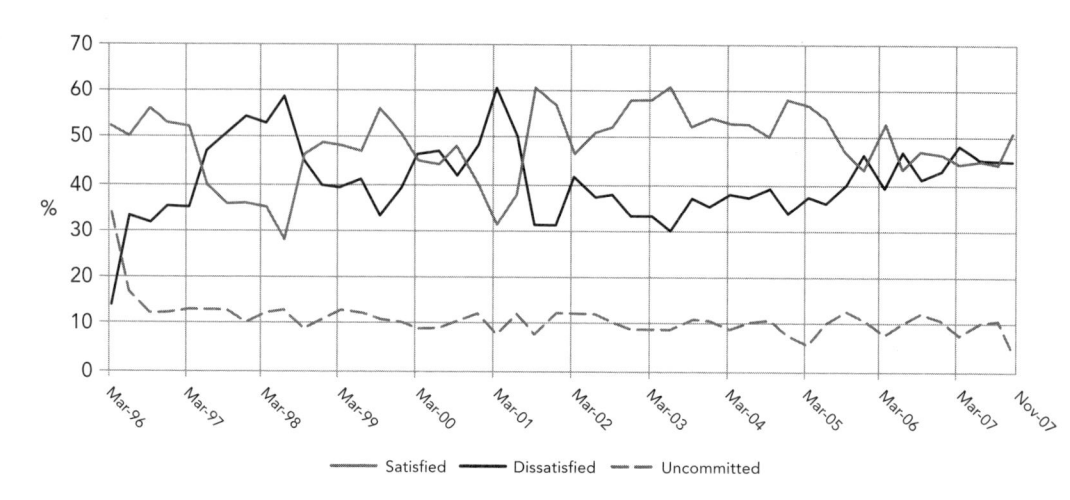

Figure 15.1   Satisfaction with the Prime Minister

——— Satisfied   ——— Dissatisfied   – – – Uncommitted

SOURCE based on Newspoll data 1996–2007.

a honeymoon in 1996; spells of dissatisfaction until early 2001; the golden, or at least glistering, years from 2001 to the second half of the fourth term; a decline and then a short final boost. Note the spike in approval in March 2006, the tenth anniversary of his election as Prime Minister. This would have been a good time to have left.

Overall, the judgment is one of modest approval or, as David Burchell suggested, 'benign toleration' (Burchell 2007). How was the fourth-term John Howard regarded on particular measures? As he reached the end of his time in office *Newspoll* reported on the public's perceptions of his personality and character.

The results in table 15.1 suggest a view of Howard as a competent leader. But the last two measures indicate rapport was missing. And roughly the same proportion of people found him arrogant as found him likeable. The former is a little problematic. Howard's persona was far from standard notions of arrogance (Keating regularly scored above 80 during his prime ministership), so perhaps it reflected his modest rating for being 'in touch with voters' (54 per cent) and also perceptions about his unwillingness to relinquish office. This refusal to move on is a form of arrogance, although hubris might be closer. And hubris leads to nemesis.

Turning from character to capacity, *Newspoll* also asked a series of questions about which leader was better able to handle a range of public

Table 15.1   Perceptions of Howard

Characteristic as leader	% agreeing
Experienced	95
Decisive and strong	84
Understands the major issues	76
Has a vision for Australia	75
Cares for people	68
Arrogant	62
Likeable	61
In touch with voters	54
Trustworthy	52

SOURCE Newspoll 2007.

issues. The answers to these questions foreshadow a second general judgment about who was the preferred prime minister. Table 15.2 presents the data for Howard compared to Beazley in November 2006 and to Rudd in November 2007.

The economy was Howard's strength, particularly against Beazley. National security also favoured him. But on social issues both Labor leaders outscored him, Rudd by very substantial margins. By the end of his fourth

Table 15.2   Which leader is more capable of handling issues?

	Nov 2006 Howard % agreeing	Nov 2006 Beazley % agreeing	Nov 2007 Howard % agreeing	Nov 2007 Rudd % agreeing
The economy	59	20	55	33
National security	55	25	47	34
Education	40	40	30	55
Health	37	42	30	53

SOURCE Newspoll 2006–07.

Figure 15.2 Who would be the better prime minister?

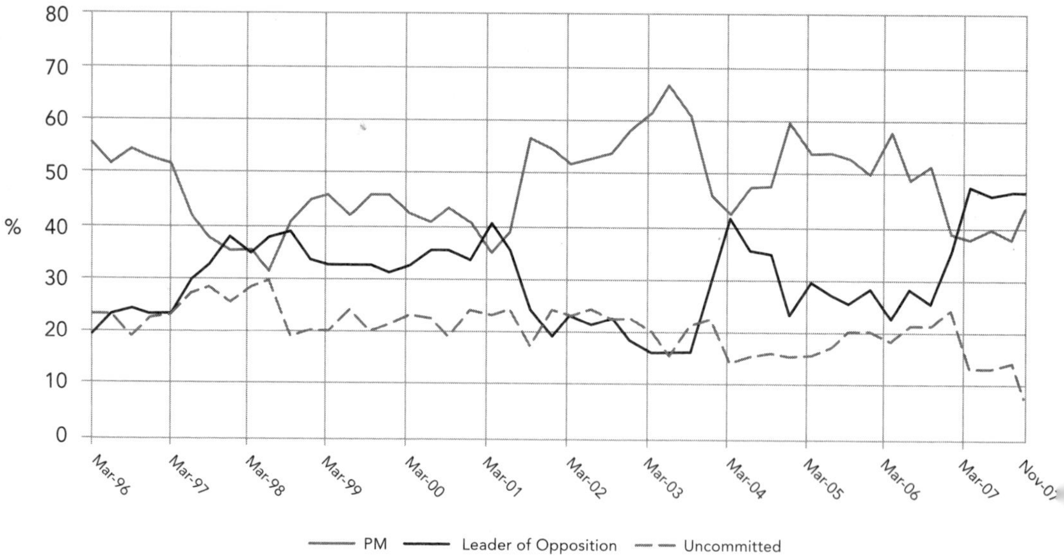

——— PM   ——— Leader of Opposition   – – Uncommitted

SOURCE based on Newspoll data 1996–2007.

term the ability to handle the economy was not enough to make Howard a preferred prime minister to Rudd.

Figure 15.2 shows the public's preference between John Howard and the four leaders of the opposition he faced. There were moments in the election years of 1998 (Beazley), 2001 (Beazley) and 2004 (Latham) when it was a near-run thing, but it was only when Rudd replaced Beazley that Howard was consistently challenged (the Crean years were a happy time for Howard). From February 2007 through to the election Rudd was *always* the preferred prime minister. Howard had met his electoral match. (Again, there was a spike in March 2006, reinforcing the point about this being a propitious time to retire).

By the end of his final term in office Howard was still held in fair public regard but no longer was he Australia's preferred prime minister. That was made official on 24 November 2007. From a personal point of view he had stayed too long. The extent of the electoral defeat suggests this may also have been the case from a party and government point of view but no one knows what would have happened if Peter Costello had taken over the leadership. It did not happen. And there is little evidence to suggest a change to Costello would have given the government a fifth term. In May 2007 a survey reported in the *Bulletin* found that, while a majority of people felt Howard should have retired, only 17 per cent believed that Costello would be a better prime minister (Daley 2007a). Retirement would have been better for John Howard, but it might not have been any better for his party. In September, with his time running out, Howard said 'the Australian people, in the end, always get it right' (*CT* 2007). This was a statement of hope. That hope was to be dashed, but his analysis may have been correct.

References

Abbott, T (2007) Opposition, too, has promises to keep, *Sydney Morning Herald*, 5 December.
ABC (Australian Broadcasting Corporation) (2007a) *7.30 Report*, 19 July, at <www.abc.net.au/7.30/content/2007/s1983192.htm>.
—— (2007b) Virginia Trioli talks to the former Treasurer Peter Costello, *Lateline*, 30 November, at <www.abc.net.au/lateline/content/2007/s2106788.htm>.
Abjorensen, N (2006) Common touch: The rise and rise of John Howard, *Canberra Times*, 2 March.
Adams, D (2000) John Howard: Never great, always adequate. In G Singleton (ed.) *The Howard Government: Australian Commonwealth Administration 1996–1998*, UNSW Press, Sydney: 1–25.
Age (2007) We went too deep on Work Choices: Hockey, 28 November.
Albrechtsen, J (2007) Pass baton to Costello, *Janet Albrechtsen's blog*, 6 September, at <http://blogs.theaustralian.news.com.au/janetalbrechtsen/index.php>.
Barker, G (2007) The public service. In C Hamilton & S Maddison (eds) *Silencing Dissent*, Allen & Unwin, Sydney: 124–147.
Brett, J (2007a) The nation reviewed, *The Monthly*, 21, March: 10–14.
—— (2007b) The nation reviewed, *The Monthly*, 25, July: 10–13.
Burchell, D (2007) His Master's Voice: The corruption of public debate under Howard (review), *Australian,* 9 June.
Channel Ten (2007) Interview with Prime Minister, John Howard, *Meet the Press*, broadcast 24 June, at <http://legacy.ten.com.au/library/documents/MTP1/2202406.doc>.
Clarke, J & Dawe, B (2006) Clarke and Dawe wrap up the week in politics, *7.30 Report*, 8 June, Australian Broadcasting Corporation, at <www.abc.net.au/7.30/content/2006/s1658886.htm>.
—— (2007) Invading Indigenous communities, *7.30 Report*, 5 July, Australian Broadcasting Corporation, at <www.abc.net.au/7.30/content/2007/s1971168.htm>.
Combet, G (2005) Economic challenges & WorkChoices: The wrong strategy, Speech to the National Press Club, delivered at the Progressive Essays Dinner, Evatt Foundation, Sydney, 2 November, at <http://evatt.labor.net.au/publications/papers/152.html>.
CT (Canberra Times) (2007) Howard admits: We're in trouble, 5 September.
Daley, P (2007a) Not happy, John, *The Bulletin*, 29 May, at <http://thebulletinelection.ninemsn.com.au/not_happy_john.htm> .
—— (2007b) The wizard of Oz, *The Bulletin*, 22 November, at <http://thebulletinelection.ninemsn.com.au/the_wizard_of_oz.htm>.

Errington, W & Van Onselen, P (2007) *John Winston Howard*, Melbourne University Press, Melbourne.
Gordon, M (2007) Howard the not-so-great, *Age*, 21 November.
Grattan, M (2007) PM enters troubled waters, *Age*, 23 February.
Hartcher, P (2007a) Secret of power, from PM's lieutenant, *Sydney Morning Herald*, 4 May, at <www.smh.com.au/news/national/the-power-behind-the-pm/2007/05/04/1177788405108.html>.
—— (2007b) The Howard imperium, *Sydney Morning Herald*, news blog, posted 22 May, at <http://blogs.smh.com.au/newsblog/archives/peter_hartcher/013439.html>.
Henderson, G (2006) John Howard: 10 years on, speech to the New South Wales Fabian Society, 22 March, at <www.fabian.org.au/1048.asp>.
Hennessy, P (1996) *The Hidden Wiring: Unearthing the British Constitution*, Indigo, London.
Howard, J (Prime Minister) (2005) Reflections on Australian federalism, Address to the Menzies Research Centre, Melbourne, 11 April, at <www.pm.gov.au/media/Speech/2005/speech1320.cfm>.
—— (2006) Address to the *Quadrant* magazine 50th anniversary dinner, Sydney, 3 October, at <http://pandora.nla.gov.au/pan/10052/20061221-0000/www.pm.gov.au/news/speeches/speech2165.html>.
—— (2007a) Australia rising to a better future, Address to the Millennium Forum, Sydney, 20 August, at <http://pandora.nla.gov.au/pan/10052/20070823-1732/www.pm.gov.au/media/Speech/2007/Speech24507.html>.
—— (2007b) Australia's choice, 14 October, at <www.liberal.org.au/info/features/november24-australiaschoice.php>.
Hurd, D (2007) *Robert Peel: A Biography*, Weidenfeld & Nicolson, London.
Kelly, P (2006) Re-thinking Australian governance: The Howard legacy (Cunningham Lecture 2005), *Australian Journal of Public Administration*, 65(1): 7–24.
—— (2007) Steady as she goes, *Australian* (blog), 5 December, at <http://theaustralian.news.com.au/paulkelly/index.php/theaustralian/comments/>.
Little, G (1985) *Political Ensembles*, Oxford University Press, Melbourne.
—— (1988) *Strong Leadership: Thatcher, Reagan and an Eminent Person*, Oxford University Press, Melbourne.
MacCallum, M (2004) *Run, Johnny, Run*, Duffy & Snellgrove, Sydney.
Manne, R (2007) The nation reviewed: Comment, *The Monthly*, April: 12–15.
Marr, D (2007) His master's voice: The corruption of public debate under Howard, *Quarterly Essay*, 26.
Megalogenis, G (2006) *The Longest Decade*, Scribe, Melbourne.
Milne, G (2006) Secret pact, *Sunday Mail*, 9 July.
Moe, TM (1993) Presidents, institutions and theory. In GC Edwards III, JH Kessel & BA Rockman (eds) *Researching the Presidency: Vital Questions, New Approaches*, University of Pittsburgh Press, Pittsburgh: 337–85.
Price, M (2002) So ordinary, this man's extraordinary, *Australian*, 14 December.
—— (2006) Getting personal. In N Cater (ed.) *The Howard Factor*, Melbourne University Press & The Australian, Melbourne: 55–63.
Rudd, K (2007) Federal Labor campaign launch, *ALP*, 14 November.
Shergold, P (2004) 'Lackies, careerists and political stooges'? *Australian Journal of Public Administration*, 63(4): 3–13.
Tiernan, A (2007) *Power without Responsibility: Ministerial Staffers in Australian Governments from Whitlam to Howard*, UNSW Press, Sydney.
Tiffen, R (2006) The Geoffrey Boycott of Australian politics, Paper delivered to a symposium:

A Decade of Howard Government, 23 February. Published in *Australian Review of Public Affairs*, at <www.australianreview.net/digest/2006/02/tiffen.html>.

Toohey, B (2007) The Lone Ranger: John Howard's concentration of power, *The Monthly*, 22, April: 24–30.

Wainwright, R & Stephens, T (2004) Canterbury tales, *Sydney Morning Herald*, 18 September.

Walsh, K-A (1998) Running hard, *The Bulletin*, 7 October.

Walter, J & Strangio, P (2007) *No, Prime Minister: Reclaiming Politics from Leaders*, UNSW Press, Sydney.

Wanna, J (2005) The arch-conductor orchestrates big government, *Canberra Times*, 3 May.

Waterford, J (2007a) Howard set to defeat himself, *Canberra Times*, 25 July.

—— (2007b) Tired tactics leave Howard's message lost in translation, *Canberra Times*, 17 November.

Weller, P (2007) *Cabinet Government in Australia, 1901–2006: Practice, Principles, Performance*, UNSW Press, Sydney.

Williamson, D (2007a) Time to end John's party, *Crikey*, 19 November, at <www.crikey.com.au/Email/Preview/DailyEmailPreview.aspx?pid=983f40c0-1732-422d-b6fe-33fd0a1b7c3e&source=cmailer>.

—— (2007b) Decent bloke, to give Don's party a happier ending, *Sydney Morning Herald*, 26 November, at <www.smh.com.au/articles/2007/11/25/1195975868444.html>.

Index

Abbott, Tony 109, 264
  defence of Howard government 115, 117–18, 127–29
  Minister for Health 101–2, 103–4, 117
ABC 41
  Lateline program 190, 195, 236, 275
Abetz, Senator Eric 85
Aboriginal and Torres Strait Islander Commission (ATSIC) 40–41, 187, 188
Aboriginal Australians *see* Indigenous Australians
Aboriginal land 190–91, 193
Aboriginal Land Rights (Northern Territory) Act 1976 190–91, 196
abortion drug RU486 85–86, 117
Access Card 87
access to government information 128
accountability 26, 116, 122, 123, 124–27
  see also inquiries; Senate
  access to government information 128
  Rudd government agenda 27–28
  'State of the Service' report 16
accrual-based accounting 22
Acts of Parliament *see* legislation
ACTU 183, 185, 264
Adams, Senator Judith 162
Administrative Appeals Tribunal 41
advertising 42, 178
affordability of housing 144–45
Afghanistan 245–46, 248
African immigrants 230, 239
'agencificationists' 44
AgForce Queensland 161
agriculture 152–68
  see also wheat marketing

exports 146
irrigation and water 66, 208, 214–15, 216
land clearing 210
Agriculture and Food Policy Reference Group 163–64
Ah Kit, John 200–201
AidWatch 257
AIRC 174, 177, 183
Ali, Dr Ameer 230
Allison, Senator Lyn 81, 86
ALP *see* Australian Labor Party
al-Qaeda 249, 251, 252
Alvarez, Vivian 25
Ameer Ali, Dr 230
ANAO *see* Australian National Audit Office
Anderson, John 222
Andren, Peter 66
Andrews, Kevin
  Minister for Immigration 123, 230, 236, 240
  Minister for Workplace Relations 179–80, 264
Anglo-Celtic background 232
Annan, Kofi 159
annual reports *see* reporting
Anwar Ibrahim 255
ANZUS alliance 250–52
APEC 220, 254
apolitical public service 26–27, 42, 273
appointments 27, 42, 273–74
APS *see* Australian Public Service
Arab Australians *see* Muslim Australians
Armitage, Richard 252
ASEAN 253–55
Asia 136, 218, 220, 245, 253–55
Asia Pacific Partnership on Clean Development and Climate (AP6) 218
ASIO 41, 230, 247

power to veto citizenship application 240
'aspirational (conservative) nationalism' 95–96, 103–4, 109
asset sales 143
see also Telstra sale
government 59–67
assimilation policy 201
asylum seekers/refugees and border protection 229–30, 235–337
offshore processing 87, 235, 236, 257
from West Papua 253
ATSIC 40–41, 187, 188
Auditor-General *see* Australian National Audit Office
Australian Broadcasting Corporation *see* ABC
Australian Bureau of Agricultural and Resource Economics 155
Australian Capital Territory 87, 248
Australian citizenship *see* citizenship
Australian Citizenship: Much more than a Ceremony 237–40
Australian Citizenship Act 2007 239–40
Australian Commission for Law Enforcement Integrity 40
Australian Communications and Media Authority 40
Australian Conservation Foundation 211, 212
Australian Constitution *see* constitution
Australian Consumer and Competition Commission 64
Australian Council of Trade Unions (ACTU) 183, 185, 264
Australian Defence Force 40
Australian Democrats 75, 80–81, 86
legislative amendments in committee of whole moved by 77
Australian dollar 146–47
Australian Fair Pay and Conditions Standard 178
Australian Fair Pay Commission 53, 177, 181–82, 183
Australian Federal Police 41
Australian Greenhouse Office 217
Australian Healthcare Agreement 101, 103–4
Australian history, teaching of 99
Australian identity 228, 231–34, 238–39
see also values
Australian Industrial Relations Commission (AIRC) 174, 177, 183
Australian Labor Party (ALP) 38
see also commonwealth–state relations; elections (2007); Hawke government; Keating government; Rudd, Kevin
environmental policy 208, 220
immigration 236, 239
industrial relations 97, 182–84
public's preference between Howard and leaders of opposition 280–82
rural policy 165–66
rural seats held by 162
Australian Labor Party (ALP) and privatisation 7, 58–59
Medibank Private 63
Snowy Hydro Scheme 66
Telstra 60, 61
Australian Labor Party (ALP) senators 75, 83, 85
legislative amendments moved in committee of whole by 77
questions asked in question time 77–78
Australian Local Government Association 207
Australian Medical Association 103
Australian National Audit Office (Auditor-General) 43
reports and findings 22, 24, 211–12
Australian Public Service 13–30, 42, 235
see also departments
public servants before Senate estimates committees 85, 89–90
senior appointments 27, 273
Australian Public Service Commission 16, 27
Australian Research Council 38
Australian Reward Investment Alliance 40

Australian Security Intelligence
  Organisation *see* ASIO
Australian Technical Colleges 100
Australian Trade Commission 38
Australian values *see* values
Australian Wheat Board (AWB Ltd)
  25–26, 40, 157–61, 165
  see also Cole Inquiry
  Senate estimates questions on 85
Australian Workplace Agreements
  (AWAs) 177, 181, 185
  see also Work Choices
  fairness test 180
  Labor election promise 184
*Australia's Climate Change Policy – Our
  Economy, Our Environment, Our
  Future* 220
Australia's Right to Know report 128
award system, industrial 174–76, 178

baby bonus 142
Badawi, Abdullah 255
balance of payments 145–46
Bartlett, Senator Andrew 80
Beazley, Kim 182–83, 281, 282
Becoming an Australian Citizen 239–40
'Better Super' 142–43
bills *see* legislation
biodiversity conservation 209–11
Bishop, Julie 99, 100, 101
Bligh, Anna 230
board template 35, 37, 53
border protection *see* asylum seekers
Boycott, Geoffrey 275
bracket creep 143–44
Bracks, Steve 216
Brett, Judith 5, 269, 279
Britain *see* United Kingdom
Brough, Mal 189–97
Brumby, John 216
budget *see* finance
Building and Construction Industry
  Commission 39–40
building industry 108–9
Bulletin survey (May 2007) 283
Burke, Tony 236
Bush Administration 249–52, 278
business community 179, 183, 208,
  219–20

cabinet 17, 274
Cabinet Implementation Unit 17
Campbell, Senator Ian 210–11
Canada 42, 129, 237
Cancer Australia 40
Cape York 193, 196, 200
Cape York Institute 190, 193
capital gains, tax treatment of 143
Carr, Bob 109
cash accounting 22
casual employment 172, 173–74
Catholic Services Australia 69
CDEP 195
centralisation 3, 8, 15–20, 44
Centrelink 19–20, 37
*Challenging Ethical Issues in
  Contemporary Research on
  Human Beings* 117
character 277–83
charities 68–69
Chifley, Ben 66
child care 70
children 142
  Indigenous 189–97
Child Support Agency 37
China 245, 253
  East Asia Summit 254
  environmental cooperation 218
  minerals and energy exports to 136,
    145, 208, 220, 253
CHIP 191–92
citizenship 227–43
  Hicks, David 248–50
Civil Unions Act (ACT) 87
Clarke, John 267–69
clean coal technologies 218
climate change 108, 216–20
cloning 86–87
COAG *see* Council of Australian
  Governments
coal 208
  clean technologies 218
coalition dissent 85–88, 90
  Medibank Private sale 63–64
  rural policy 161–63
  Telstra sale 59, 60, 87
Cole Inquiry 26, 85, 158–60, 166

legal fees 257
Prime Minister before 125
collective (enterprise) bargaining 174–76, 184
Colson, Senator Mal 60
Combet, Greg 264
'commissions' 53
Commonwealth Authorities and Companies (CAC) Act 1997 32–33, 36, 40
number of bodies under 41, 54
Commonwealth of Australian Constitution *see* constitution
Commonwealth Ombudsman 41
reports on immigration matters 25
Commonwealth Scientific and Industrial Research Organisation (CSIRO) 42
commonwealth–state relations 38, 95–113
see also Council of Australian Governments; Murray-Darling Basin
environmental policy 207–8, 210, 211, 212–13, 222–23
Indigenous affairs 6, 193–97
terrorism laws 107–8, 248
Community Development Employment Projects 195
Community Housing and Infrastructure Program 191–92
companies, government-owned 32–33, 36, 40, 55
see also privatisation
company income tax 139
competition policy 107, 108, 136–37, 165
competitive tendering 68
computing (IT) outsourcing 68
Comrie Report 236
conscience votes 86–87, 90
conservatism *see* political culture/philosophy
conservative ('aspirational') nationalism 95–96, 103–4, 109
'conspicuous compassion' 189
constitution
'aboriginal race' power 201
corporations power 98, 101, 177–78

external affairs power 40
health power 101
industrial relations power 97
Joyce's view of senator's role under 88
rivers power restriction 104
construction industry 39–40, 108–9
Consumer Price Index *see* inflation
contracting out (outsourcing) 67–69
Corish Report 163–64
corporate governance and Uhrig Report 18, 34–39, 54–56
corporate services, outsourcing of 68
corporations power 98, 101, 177–78
corporatisation of Snowy Hydro Scheme 64–65
Costello, Treasurer Peter 109, 142, 178
GST and 106–7
Howard and 61, 107, 263, 275–76, 277, 282–83
Medibank Private sale 64
wheat marketing arrangements 162
Council for Multicultural Australia 229–30
Council for the Australian Federation 109–10
Council of Australian Governments (COAG) 107–8, 207
National Water Initiative 39, 104–5, 157, 214–15
Snowy Hydro Scheme reform and corporatisation 64–65
'councils' 53
counter-terrorism *see* terrorism
Cowra abattoir 179
CPI *see* inflation
Crean, Simon 60, 282
Cronulla riots 233–34
cross-agency programs *see* whole-of-government strategy
cross-cultural dimension of Indigenous affairs 199–202
CSIRO 42
culture 227–34, 237–40
teaching of Australian history 99
culture wars 221
culture within public service 18, 21–22
Department of Immigration and Multicultural Affairs 24–25, 236

current account deficit 145–46
curricula 99, 100

Dawe, Bryan 267–69
debate in Senate, limiting of 79–82
debt levels 61, 140
decision-making 117, 118, 125
   public sector 22–23
   Rudd government accountability agenda 27–28
defence and national security 244–60, 281
   see also asylum seekers; Iraq; terrorism
   administration of military justice 40
   procurement 5, 245
Defence Force 40
Defence Materiel Organisation 5
deforestation 217
democratic theory 119–22
Democrats *see* Australian Democrats
Department of Aboriginal Affairs 202
Department of Agriculture, Fisheries and Forestry 155
Department of Family and Community Services 191
Department of Finance and Administration (DoFA) 22, 23, 34, 36
   List of Australian Government Bodies 33–34
   tally of Uhrig-process changes 41
Department of Foreign Affairs and Trade (DFAT) 25–26, 160
Department of Health and Ageing 89, 102
Department of Human Services 20, 37
Department of Immigration and Citizenship (DIAC) 229–30
   Living in Australia 233
Department of Immigration and Multicultural Affairs (DIMA) 24–25, 236
Department of Immigration and Multicultural and Indigenous Affairs 229–30
   Office of Indigenous Policy Co-ordination 188
Department of Primary Industries and Energy 157

Department of Territories, Northern Territory Administration 202
Department of the Environment and Water Resources 211
Department of the Prime Minister and Cabinet (DPM&C) 16–17, 21, 219
   Secretaries 22, 273
   'traffic light' reports to 17–18
Department of the Treasury *see* Treasury
departments 13–30, 32, 51–52, 53
   see also whole-of-government strategy
   heads of 273
detention of David Hicks 248–50
detention of illegal immigrants 25, 235–36
development proposals 210–11, 223
devolution 18–19, 22, 44–45
disability pensions 149
dishonesty *see* honesty
distribution of income 147–49
divestment program (asset sales) 59–67
   see also Telstra sale
dollar 146–47
Downer, Alexander 160, 253, 254–55
downsizing of public service 14
drought 146, 152, 155, 215
drought policy 155–57, 162, 165
dysfunctional families and communities 189–97, 200–201

East Asian Summit 253–54
economy 135–51, 281
   see also labour market; prices
   environmental policy and 208, 210–11, 218, 219–20, 222
   interest rates 42, 126, 144–45, 147
ECRP 156–57
education 40, 99–101, 173, 281
   see also schools and schooling; universities
   student employment 172, 173
elections (1996) 221
elections (1998) 59–60, 221, 282
elections (2001) 60, 244, 282
elections (2004) 282
   foreign policy and national security 244, 247, 252

health policy 40
interests rates 126
Tasmanian Regional Forest Agreement 213
technical colleges promise 100
Telstra sale 60
elections (2007) 1–2, 128–29, 282–83
   climate change 219–20
   Howard's comment on announcing date of 266
   Howard's new public expenditure promises 277
   industrial relations 178, 183–84
   interest rates 126
   Medibank Private sale and 63–64
   Mersey Hospital takeover 6, 102–3
   Rudd Labor opposition pro-federalist stance 110
   tax cuts 142
electricity production 217
   Snowy Hydro Scheme privatisation 64–67, 268
   solar 220
11 September terrorist attacks 245, 246, 251
embryo research 86–87
emissions, greenhouse 216–20
emissions trading 219–20
employment 138–39, 148–49, 170–74, 235
   see also industrial relations
   Indigenous Australians 195
   public sector 14–15, 18, 71
   seasonal guest-worker scheme 256–57
   superannuation policy 142–43
   welfare-to-work policy 68–69, 138
Employment Advocate 39, 183
employment services, value of contracts to 68
endangered species 211
energy see minerals and energy
Energy White Paper 218
English language 232, 238, 239, 240
'enhanced regionalism' 256
enterprise bargaining 174–76, 184
environmental policy 108, 206–26, 268
   see also water
Environment Protection and Biodiversity Conservation Act 1999 (EPBC Act) 209–11, 213, 222
equality/equity 147–49, 176
estimates committees 84–85, 89
ethics 114–31
Ethnic Communities' Council of Victoria 232, 239
'ethnic' gangs 229, 230
   Cronulla riots 233–34
Evans, Harry 80, 85
Evans, Senator Chris 77, 80
exceptional circumstances relief payment 156–57
exchange rates 146–47
executive agencies 32–33, 39, 54
executive level public servants 21
executive management template 35, 37, 53
expenditure *see* finance
exports *see* trade

failed states 245
   combating regional risk 255–56
Fair Pay and Conditions Standard 178
Fair Pay Commission 53, 177, 181–82, 183
Fair Work Australia 183–84
families and communities, dysfunctional 189–97, 200–201
Family First 75
family migration 235
family payments 142, 149
farmers *see* agriculture
federalism *see* commonwealth–state relations
females, in workforce 172, 173, 174
Fielding, Senator Steve 80, 87, 88, 91
   argument against restructuring of Senate committee system 84
Fightback! proposals 177
finance 22, 23, 108, 139–49, 276–77
   see also asset sales; economy; government purchasing; taxation
   aid budget 257
   climate change commitments 218
   cost recovery procedures' returns 70
   drought assistance package 155–56
   education funding 70, 99–101, 233
   health funding 70, 102–4

immigrant programs 239
Natural Heritage Trust finding 211–12
'Northern Territory National Emergency Response' appropriation 196
outsourced contracts, value of 68
public accountability 125–26
Senate estimates hearings 84–85, 89
Snowy Hydro sale fees and other expenditure 67
social welfare expenditure 142
water program commitments 105–6, 215
Financial Management of Accountability (FMA) Act 1997 32–33, 37
number of bodies under 41, 54
fiscal policy *see* finance
Fischer, Tim 221
flagpoles 99
Flannery, Tim 222
foreign development assistance 255–57
foreign exchange rates 146–47
foreign ownership 63, 66, 140
foreign policy 244–60
foreign trade *see* trade
forestry 212–13
deforestation 217
Framework Convention on Climate Change 216–18
Fraser, Malcolm 123, 233, 247
Fraser government 90
government appointments 273–74
Howard as Treasurer 276
freedom of information 128
free trade agreements 146, 253
free trade bloc, ASEAN countries 255
full-time employment 172
functional flexibility 175–76
funding *see* finance
Future Fund 39, 61, 140, 276
'Future Harvest' policy statement 164

gag motions to limit Senate debate 79–80
gangs *see* 'ethnic' gangs
Garrett, Peter 38, 66
gas 208, 253
gay civil unions 87
GDP *see* Gross Domestic Product
generational revolutions in Indigenous affairs 197–202
Georgiou, Petro 238
Germany 249
Gini coefficient 148
global warming (climate change) 108, 216–20
goods and services tax 106–7, 177, 178
Gordon, Sue 189
Gore, Al 218
governance 3–5, 13–131
see also accountability
prime ministerial 3, 269–77
regional forest agreements as forms of 213
South Pacific nations 255–56
governing boards 35, 37, 38, 39, 42
public hospitals 102, 104
Telstra 61
government advertising 42
government asset sales 59–67
see also Telstra sale
government business enterprises 38
government finance *see* finance
government information, access to 128
government inquiries *see* inquiries
government-owned companies 32–33, 36, 40, 55
see also privatisation
government pensions and benefits *see* social welfare policies
government purchasing 5, 245
National Construction Code 108–9
outsourcing 67–69
purchaser-provider arrangements 19–20
government (public) schools 70, 99–100
Governor-General's speech opening 41st Parliament 32
Grains Council of Australia 157, 161, 165
Great Artesian Basin 215
greenhouse gas emissions 216–20
Greenhouse Gate Abatement Program 218
green paper on rural policy (1974) 154
Greens 75, 83, 91, 220

green vote 208, 213, 221
Gross Domestic Product (GDP) 136, 139
    GST revenues as proportion of 106
GST 106–7, 177, 178
Guantanamo Bay, Cuba 248–50
guest-worker scheme 256–57
guillotine motions to limit Senate debate 79–81
Gunn's pulp mill proposal 211, 223

Haneef, Dr Mohamed 41, 123–24, 247
Harradine, Senator Brian 60
Harradine Group 75
Hawke government 57, 128, 154
    see also Keating government
    environmental policy 207, 214
    labour market reform 169, 176
health 70, 89, 281
    Cancer Australia 40
    commonwealth–state relations 6, 101–4
    issues causing Senate dissent 85–87
    Medibank Private 62–64
    medical ethics debate 117
Health Insurance Commission (HIC) 37
Henry, Dr Ken 26–27, 125–26, 143, 216
Hewson, John 177, 178, 254
Hicks, David 248–50
High Court industrial relations decisions 183
    corporations power 98–99, 101, 177–78
higher education 101
Higher Education Contribution Scheme (HECS) 69
Higher Education Endowment Fund 39, 141
Hill, Senator Robert 77, 217, 222, 248
Hilmer Inquiry 136–37, 165
history, teaching of 99
Hobbes, Thomas 120–21
Hockey, Joe 180, 195, 264
'home-grown terrorism' 228, 245, 246–48
home ownership 144–45
    Indigenous 191, 192–93

homosexual civil unions 85
honesty 116, 122–24, 125, 127–29, 277–78
    assumptions made in most commentaries 114–15
    public honour and 117–18
honour 117–18, 124
horizontal (integrated) governance ('joined-up government) 15–22, 44–45
hospitals 6, 101–4
hot water systems, solar 220
household energy use 208
    solar hot water rebate 220
household income 147–49
housing 143, 144–45
    Indigenous 191–93
Howard, Janette 276
Howard, John 8–9, 263–85
    see also coalition dissent
    ATSIC 187
    AWB Limited (Cole inquiry) and wheat marketing 26, 125, 160, 161
    industrial relations 97–99, 178–79
    interest rates 126
    job creation claim 138
    Northern Territory intervention 193–95
    privatisation 58–61, 64, 66–67
    Senate majority statement 76
    Uhrig inquiry 34, 37
    Work Choices 178–80, 183
Howard, John, and environmental policy 221–23
    climate change 217–18, 219, 220
    Tasmanian Regional Forest Agreement (RFA) 213
    water 96, 105, 106, 215–16
Howard, John, and federalism 95–96, 107–8, 109
    education 100
    health 102–4
    industrial relations 97–99
    Murray-Darling management 105, 106
Howard, John, and immigration 229, 230
    citizenship test 239

integration 231, 232, 233, 234
values 228, 231–33, 239
warning to mosques and Muslim school 245
withdrawal of unauthorised arrivals legislation 236
Howard, John, and national interest 244–46, 253–58
Hicks, David 249–50
relations with Bush administration 250, 252, 254, 278
terrorism 245, 246, 251, 252, 255
terrorism legislation 107–8, 247–48
'Howard doctrine' 255–56
human research 86–87
ethics 117
human resource management *see* staff management
Humphrey Review 68
Humphries, Senator Gary 87
Hurley, Senator Annette 236, 239
hydro-electricity 64–67

IDCs 20–21
identity, national 228, 231–34, 238–39
see also values
ideology *see* political culture/philosophy
immigration 24–25, 139, 227–43
see also asylum seekers; Muslim Australians
imports 145–46
income distribution 147–49
income support payments *see* social welfare policies
income tax *see* taxation
An Inconvenient Truth 218
incrementalism 265–66
prime ministerial governance 270–71
Independent Inquiry Committee (IIC) 158, 159
independent MPs 66, 162
independent (private) school funding 70
independent senators 75, 83, 91
Telstra sale 59, 60
indexation 171, 176, 182
baby bonus 142
government pensions 148

India 218, 254
minerals and energy exports to 136, 145, 220
Indigenous Australians 6, 187–205
ATSIC 40–41, 187, 188
John Clarke's take on NT intervention 267
Indigenous Business Australia 41
Indigenous Coordination Centres 188
Indigenous Land Corporation 41
Indonesia 253
industrial development proposals 210–11, 223
industrial relations 39–40, 174–85, 264
advertisements featuring Workplace Authority's Director 42
National Construction Code 108–9
Industrial Relations Act 1993 174
industrial relations legislation 80–81, 84, 97–99
see also Work Choices
Australian Fair Pay Commission objectives under 181
enterprise bargaining 174, 175
Industrial Relations Tribunal (AIRC) 174, 177, 183
Industries Assistance Commission 154
industry, employment by 172
inflation 136, 144–45
see also indexation
1970s and early 1980s 176
Reserve Bank target range 135
information, access to 128
information technology outsourcing 68
infrastructure renewal 8, 137
inquiries 5
see also Cole Inquiry; Senate committees
building and construction industry 40
detention and deportation of Australian citizens 25, 236
National Competition Policy 136–37, 165
sexual abuse of NT Indigenous children 190, 193
Uhrig 18, 34–39, 54–56
Inquiry into the Circumstances of the Immigration Detention of

Cornelia Rau 25
institutional policy agenda 209–23
integrated governance ('joined-up government') 15–22, 44–45
integration of immigrants 231–34, 239
integrity 114–31
    in law enforcement 40
'integrity agencies' 42–43
intelligence services 107, 246
    see also ASIO
interagency collaboration see whole-of-government strategy
interdepartmental committees 20–21
interest rates 126, 144–45, 147
    early 1990s 170
    independence of Reserve Bank in fixing 42
Intergovernmental Agreement on the Environment 207, 222
intergovernmental relations see commonwealth–state relations
international development assistance 255–57
international exchange rates 146–47
international law 249
    see also treaties
International Panel on Climate Change (IPCC) 218–19
international relations 244–60
international trade see trade
International Whaling Commission 221
Investing in Our Schools Program 100–101
Iraq 245–46, 251–52
    see also Australian Wheat Board
irrigation and agricultural water 66, 208, 214–15, 216
Islam see Muslim Australians
IT outsourcing 68

Japan 218, 254
jobs see employment
jobseekers see social welfare policies
Jobs Network 68
joined up (integrated) government 15–22, 44–45
joint teams 21
Joyce, Senator Barnaby 63, 85, 87–88
justice 40, 248–50

Kant, Immanuel 121
Keating government 57, 128, 156, 176
    environmental policy 207, 217
    Keating's approval rating on leaving office 279
    National Competition Policy 136–37
    Senate during 78, 79, 81, 82, 89
Keelty, Commissioner Mick 41
Kirby, Justice Michael 98
Korea 218, 254
Kyoto Protocol 217–18

labour costs 171
labour demand 172–73, 175
labour market 137–39, 148, 169–86
    see also employment; industrial relations
Labour Party see Australian Labor Party
labour shortages 138–39, 235
    public sector 15
land, Aboriginal 190–91, 193
land clearing 210, 217
language 232, 238, 239, 240
Lateline program 190, 195, 236, 275
Latham, Mark 60, 213, 252, 282
law enforcement see police
leadership 269–83
legislation
    see also constitution; industrial relations legislation
    citizenship 237–40
    environmental 209–11, 213, 222
    immigration 81, 236
    Indigenous affairs 188, 190–91, 195–97
    Murray-Darling management 105–6
    Snowy Hydro corporatisation 65
    terrorism 80, 107–8, 246–48
    wheat marketing 165
    whistleblower protection 128
legislation and the Senate 76–77, 79–82, 84, 105
    see also Telstra sale legislation and the Senate
    coalition dissent 85–88, 162
    terrorism 80, 248
legislation covering non-departmental public bodies 32–33, 37, 38, 39–41

number of CAC and FMA bodies 41, 54
liberalism 121
　in Indigenous policy debate 198–202
Liberal Party of Australia 161–62
　see also ministers
　dissent within 60, 86–87, 90, 162, 238
liquefied natural gas (LNG) 208, 253
List of Australian Government Bodies 33–34
Living in Australia 233
Living Murray initiative 214
living standards 147–49
'localism' 96, 103–4, 109
London bombings, Australian legislation passed after 107–8, 247–48
lone parents 138, 149
Loughnane, Brian 275
Low Emission Technology Demonstration Fund 218
low-income earners 147–49, 176, 181, 182
　farmers 154
Lowy Institute 244, 252
lying *see* honesty

McClure committee 178
McGauran, Peter 155
McGauran, Senator Julian 161–62
Machiavelli, N 120
machinery-of-government change 31–56
　citizenship 229–30
　Indigenous affairs 188, 189
Malaysia 255
Mandatory Renewable Energy Target 217
manufacturing industry 172, 208
marginal income tax rates *see* tax rates
market testing 68
Martin, Clare 190, 193
Measures for a Better Environment 218
media 40, 89
　Howard and staff's monitoring 275
media conferences 128
media reporting 125
　'ethnic' gang rapes 228

rural issues 164–65
Medibank Private 62–64
medical profession 222
medical research 86–87
　ethics 117
medicines, patient contributions to 70
Menzies, Sir Robert 263, 273–74
mergers, regulation of 87
Merkel, Angela 249
Mersey Hospital takeover 6, 102–3
microeconomic reform (structural adjustment) 136–37, 171–73
　farm sector 154–55
Middle East 239, 251
　see also Iraq; Muslim Australians
migration *see* immigration
Migration Amendment (Designated Unauthorised Arrivals) Bill 2006 87, 236
Migration Institute of Australia 238
Migration Ombudsman 41
military commissions 249–50
Millennium Development Goals 257
Minchin, Senator Nick 61, 62–63, 65
minerals and energy 146, 216–20
　exports to China 136, 145, 208, 220, 253
　exports to India 136, 145, 220
　household use 208
　nuclear 6, 220, 253
minimum wage *see* industrial relations
ministerial advisers and other staff 26, 27–28, 90
ministerial responsibility 26, 122–24
ministers 35–36, 37, 38, 128
　see also departments
monetary policy 144–45
　see also inflation; interest rates
monopolies 107
　'single desk' export arrangements 157, 160–61, 162, 163, 165
Moore, Senator Claire 86
Moore-Wilton, Max 273
morality 117–18, 121, 125, 129, 278
　in Indigenous policy 189, 197–98, 201
Mori, Major Michael 249
multi-agency forums 21
multiculturalism 228–31, 232, 239

multilateralism 253–55
Murray-Darling Basin 6, 40, 104–6, 213–16, 272
   see also drought
   Howard's explanation of decision to impose commonwealth regime 96, 105
Murray-Darling Basin Authority 40, 105–6
Murray-Darling Basin Commission 6, 104, 105, 214
Muslim Advisory Group 230–31
Muslim Australians 228, 230–31, 233–34, 238–39
   Howard's warning to mosques and schools 245
   terrorism and 247, 248
Mutitjulu 190
mutual obligation 157

Nash, Senator Fiona 86
National Action Plan for Salinity and Water Control 212
National Audit Office see Australian National Audit Office
National Competition Council 165
National Competition Policy 107, 108, 136–37, 165
National Construction Code 108–9
National Drought Policy 156
National Farmers' Federation (NFF) 154, 155, 163
National Health and Medical Research Council 117
national identity 228, 231–34, 238–39
   see also values
National Indigenous Council 41, 189
national interest 244–60
   see also economy
nationalism 95–96, 103–4
   see also values
National Party of Australia 161–63, 221–22
   see also Coalition dissent
   agriculture ministers 154, 155, 156–57, 162
National Party of Australia senators 86
National Plan for Water Security 215–16

National Reform Agenda 108
National Salinity Action Plan 214
national security see defence and national security
National Water Commission 39, 104–5
National Water Initiative 39, 104–5, 157, 214–15
National Welfare Rights Network 69
natural gas 208, 253
Natural Heritage Trust 211–12, 214
Nauru 235, 257
Nelson, Brendan 99
Netherlands 237
new public management 16–18, 44
New South Wales 98, 105, 107
   Cronulla riots 233
   regional forestry agreement (RFA) 213
   Snowy Hydro Scheme 64–66, 67
New South Wales Farmers 161
Newstart Allowance (unemployment benefits) 138, 148, 149
New Zealand 43, 44, 252, 254
NFF 154, 155, 163
9/11 terrorist attacks 245, 246, 251
1967 referendum 201
non-departmental public bodies 31–56
non-government organisations (NGOs) 68–69
non-government school funding 70
Northern Australia 215
Northern Territory Aboriginal people 6, 190–91, 193–97, 200–202, 267
Northern Territory (Self-Government) Act 1978 196
Northern Trust Corporation 140
nuclear power 6, 220, 253
numerical flexibility 175

Obama, Senator Barack 252
occupations 172
   shortages 138–39
OECD 173
Office of Aboriginal Affairs 201–2
Office of Evaluation and Audit (Indigenous Programs) 41
Office of Indigenous Policy Co-ordination 188

Office of the Employment Advocate 39, 183
Office of Workplace Services 39, 183
'officers of parliament' 43
offshore processing of refugees 87, 235, 236, 257
oil-for-food program *see* Australian Wheat Board
Ombudsman 41
    reports on immigration matters 25
    Workplace 180–81
One Nation 75, 221
one-parent families 138, 149
opinion *see* public opinion
orders for production of documents, Senate 82
organisational learning 18
Organisation for Economic Cooperation and Development (OECD) 173
O'Sullivan, Paul 246
Our Right to Take Responsibility 200
outcomes and outputs approach 22, 23
outsourcing 67–69
overseas development assistance 255–57
overseas trade *see* trade
Ozcare 69

P20/P50 ratio 147–48
P90/P10 ratio 148
Pacific Forum meeting (2005) 256
Pacific region 255–57
Pacific solution (offshore processing of refugees) 87, 235, 236, 257
Palmer Inquiry 25
Papua 220
Papua New Guinea (PNG) 235, 256–57
'parallel federalism' 100
Parliament
    see also Senate
    Governor-General's speech opening 32
    'officers of' 43
parliamentary departments 52
Parliamentary Library report on Medibank Private 63
part-time employment 172, 173, 174
patronage appointments 42, 273–74
Patterson, Senator Kay 86–87

pay *see* wages
Payne, Senator Marise 87
Pearson, Noel 189, 190, 193, 198, 200
Peel, Sir Robert 274
pensions and benefits *see* social welfare policies
People's Republic of China *see* China
performance management 22–24
    public schools 99–100
performance pay 23–24
    teachers 100
permit system, NT 191
personnel management *see* staff management
petrol prices 85
Plato 119
Podger, Andrew 27, 101–2
police and law enforcement 107, 246–48
    Australian Commission for Law Enforcement Integrity 40
policy 5–8, 135–260, 264–69
    see also social welfare policies; water
    decision-making for development 22–23
    implementation 17–18
policy agenda management 209–23
political advertising 42
political culture/philosophy 221, 264–69
    conservation ('aspirational') nationalism 95–96, 103–4, 109
    'Howard doctrine' 255–56
    in Indigenous policy debate 198–202
    Mersey Hospital episode 103
    new public management 16–18, 44
    privatisation 58–59
    public integrity 114–31
    small government 14, 58
political parties 75–91
    see also Australian Labor Party; Liberal Party of Australia; National Party of Australia
political patronage in appointments 42, 273–74
politicisation of public service 26–27, 42, 273
Postal Industry Ombudsman 41

poverty 257
Poverty Inquiry 165
prescribed agencies 5, 33, 38
prices 171, 176
    see also inflation
    housing affordability 144–45
    petrol 85
Prices and Income Accord 170, 171, 176
PriceWaterhouseCoopers' review of CHIP 191–92
primary industries see agriculture; minerals and energy
prime ministerial governance 3, 269–77
private child care, funding of 70
private health insurance 62–64, 70
private members' bills 85–86, 162
private school funding 70
private sector, union density in 173–74
privatisation 36, 57–74, 268
    see also Australian Wheat Board
procurement see government purchasing
productivity 137
    rural policy 154–55
project management approach 18
prudence 118
public accountability see accountability
public finance see finance
public hospitals 96, 101–4
public integrity 114–31
'public-interest disclosures' 128
public opinion 119, 128–29
    climate change 219
    Hicks, David 249
    Medibank Private sale 63
    satisfaction with/perception of Howard 279–83
    Snowy Hydro Scheme sale 66
    about United States 252
    Work Choices 183
public policy agenda 207, 209–23
public schooling 70, 99–100
public sector governance 13–74
    see also departments
public sector superannuation 40
    unfunded liabilities 39, 140
public service see Australian Public Service
Public Service Act 1999 33, 37

Public Service Commissioner 16, 27
pulp mills 211, 223
purchasing see government purchasing

Quadrant 50th anniversary dinner, Howard's comments at 269
quangos (non-departmental public bodies) 31–56
Queensland 88, 105, 161, 230
    Cape York 193, 196, 200
    St Vincent de Paul's branch 69
questions and question time, Senate 77–79

Racial Discrimination Act 1975 196
radicalism 266
rainwater tanks 220
Rau, Cornelia 25
real unit labour costs 171
referendum (1967) 201
refugees see asylum seekers
regional forest agreements 212–13
regulatory federalism 107–9
    see also Council of Australian Governments
Reith, Peter 177, 178
religious welfare services 69
remuneration see industrial relations; performance pay
renewable energy 217, 220
    wind farms 210–11
rental housing 143, 145
reporting 22, 23
    by schools 99–100
    'State of the Service' annual report 16
Republic of Korea 218, 254
research and development 141
    medical 86–87, 117
Reserve Bank of Australia 42, 126, 144–45
    inflation target range 135
residential housing see housing
respect 117–18
    for political ethics 128–29
responsible government 122–24
reviews 23
    see also inquiries
    Agriculture and Food Policy

Reference Group (Corish Report) 163–64
statutory authorities against governance templates 36, 38
Robb, Andrew 232, 237, 238, 239
Rogers, Nanette 190
RU486 abortion drug 85–86, 117
Rudd, Kevin 129, 281–82
   Howard's new public expenditure promises 277
   industrial relations proposals 183–84
   pro-federalist stance 110
   tax policy 142
Rudd government 1–2
   accountability agenda 27–28
   Senate and 91
rural and regional Australia 152–68, 211–12, 221–22
   see also agriculture
   telephone services 87
Russia 254

'Safeguarding the Future' package 217, 218
safety-net pay and conditions see industrial relations
St Vincent de Paul 69
same-sex civil unions 87
savings from outsourcing 68
Schieffer, Tom 252
schools and schooling 99–101
   climate change initiatives for 220
   Muslim 245
   private 70
   'Values for Australian Schooling' program 233
Scrymgour, Marian 197
seasonal guest-worker scheme 256–57
Securing Our Energy Future 218
security see defence; terrorism
Senate 75–94, 126–27
   see also Australian Labor Party (ALP) senators; independent senators; National Party of Australia senators
   recall to introduce criminal code amendments relating to terrorism 248
Senate committees 82–85, 87, 89–90, 248
   see also legislation and the Senate
   Indigenous affairs inquiry 197
   military justice inquiry 40
   Poverty Inquiry 165
senior executive service 14, 21
service delivery 17–18
   see also privatisation
   agencies for 19–20, 37
   performance management 22–24
services sector 172, 174
sexual abuse of Indigenous children 190, 193–97
shared values see values
Shergold, Peter 25, 27, 273
shortages of labour see labour shortages
'single desk' (export monopoly) arrangements 157, 160–61, 162, 163, 165
single parents 138, 149
Sinodinos, Arthur 274, 275
sitting hours, Senate 80, 81–82
skills 148, 172–73
   shortages 138–39, 235
small government 14, 58
   see also privatisation
Snowy Hydro Corporatisation Act 1997 65
Snowy Hydro Limited (SHL) 65–66
Snowy Hydro Trading Pty Ltd 64–65
Snowy Mountains Hydro-Electric Authority 65
Snowy Mountains Hydro-Electric Scheme 64–67, 268
social cohesion 227–43
social welfare policies 69, 148–49, 177, 178
   expenditure on 142
   for farmers 154, 155–57, 162, 165
   Indigenous Australians 189–90, 193, 194, 195–96, 202
   Senate bills guillotined and gagged 80
   welfare-to-work programs 68–69, 138
solar hot water systems 220
sole parents 138, 149
Somare, Sir Michael 256
'sourcing' 68

South Australia 105
South Korea 218, 254
South Pacific nations 255–57
staff and advisers, ministerial 26, 27–28, 90
staff management, public sector 14–15
    non-departmental public bodies 33
    performance management 22–24
Stanhope, Jon 248
state-imposed duties 107
Statements of Expectations/Statements of Intent 38
'State of the Service' report 16
state relations see commonwealth–state relations
statutory authorities (corporations, agencies) 18, 32–33
    impact of Uhrig-process changes 34–45, 53, 54, 55, 56
stem cell research 86–87
Stern report 219
structural adjustment see microeconomic reform
'structural efficiency principle' 174
student reports 100
students 70
    employment 172, 173
    university fees 69
St Vincent de Paul 69
Sudanese immigrants 230
superannuation 142–43
    public sector 39, 40, 140
Sutton, Professor Peter 200
Switkowski, Ziggy 220

Taliban 249
Tamar Valley pulp mill 211, 223
Tanner, Lindsay 61
taskforces 20–21, 101–2
Tasmania
    Gunn's pulp mill proposal 211, 223
    Mersey Hospital, Devonport 6, 102–3
    Regional Forest Agreement (RFA) 212, 213
taxation 141–44
    goods and services tax (GST) 106–7, 177, 178
    receipts 139, 143

solar hot water rebates 220
tax rates 141, 142
    bracket creep 143–44
teachers and teaching 99–100
technical colleges 100
technological change 172–73
Telstra sale 59–62, 63, 67, 221
    Future Fund 39, 61, 140, 276
    limits on Senate debate 80, 84
    Natural Heritage Trust funding 211–12
Telstra sale legislation and the Senate 59, 60, 61, 63
    concession made to Senator Joyce 87
    limits on scrutiny 84
terrorism 228, 245, 246–50
    Haneef case 41, 123–24, 247
    in 'Howard doctrine' 255
    Iraq and 245, 251, 252
    legislation 80, 107–8, 246–48
therapeutic cloning 86–87
threatened species 211
Torres Strait Islanders see Indigenous Australians
Torres Strait Regional Authority 41
trade 136, 145–47, 255
    see also wheat marketing
    with China 208, 220, 253
    uranium exports 220, 253
Trade Practices Legislation Amendment Bill (No. 1) 2005 87
trade unions see unions
'traffic light' reports 17–18
Tran, Tony 236
Treasury 90, 178
    Henry, Dr Ken 26–27, 125–26, 143, 216
Treasury Ministers Conference (March 2005) 107
treaties and international agreements
    asylum seekers and refugees 235, 236–37
    climate change 216–18
    free trade 146, 253
    nuclear energy 220, 253
    security 250–52, 253–54
Treaty of Amity and Cooperation (TAC) 253–54
Troeth, Senator Judith 86

Truss, Warren 155, 156–57
trust 119, 129
truth 116, 119–23, 124, 125, 127–29
    see also honesty
Tuckey, Wilson 162
Turnbull, Malcolm 211, 215

Uhrig Report 18, 34–39, 54–56
unanswered Questions on Notice
    78–79
'unAustralian' 233
unauthorised arrivals see asylum seekers
unemployment 138, 148, 149, 170–71
    see also social welfare policies
unfair dismissals 183, 184
unfunded superannuation liabilities 39,
    140
unions 177, 178, 183–84, 208
    ACTU campaign against Work
        Choices 183, 185, 264
    membership 173–74
United Kingdom 44, 237, 249
    appointment process 42
    London bombings, Australian
        legislation passed after 107–8,
        247–48
    Stern report 219
United Nations 244
    AWB Limited and 26, 158–59, 160
    conventions 216–18, 235, 236–37
    UNHCR statistics 235
United Nations Office of the Iraq
    Program 158
United States 245, 248–52, 254, 278
    climate change 218
    economy 136
    free trade agreement with 146
    interest rates 147
    presidential leadership 272
United States dollar 146–47
United States Independent Inquiry
    Committee (IIC) 158, 159
United States National Intelligence
    Estimate reports 251
United States Office of Military
    Commissions 250
United States Supreme Court 249
universities 101
    Higher Education Endowment Fund
        39, 141
    student fees 69
University of Sydney, United States
    Centre 252
uranium 220, 253
user pays 69–70

values 228, 231–35, 240
    identified in citizenship discussion
        paper 237, 238, 239
    teaching 99, 233
'Values for Australian Schooling'
    program 233
Vanstone, Senator Amanda 187, 188–
    89, 236
Vardon, Sue 37
Victoria 43
    industrial relations 97, 175
    regional forestry agreement (RFA)
        213
    Snowy Hydro Scheme 64–66, 67
    water management powers 105–6,
        216
Victorian Ethnic Communities' Council
    232, 239
Victorian Farmers Federation 161
vocational education and training 100,
    108
Volcker, Paul 158

wages and remuneration 148, 173
    see also industrial relations
    indexation 171, 178, 182
    performance pay 23–24, 100
war on terrorism see terrorism
water 208, 212, 213–16
    see also drought; Murray-Darling
        Basin
    National Water Initiative 39, 104–5,
        157, 214–15
    school climate change programs 220
    Snowy Hydro Scheme privatisation
        64–67, 268
water restrictions 152, 215
water rights 214, 216
water trading 215
Weber, Max 118
wedge politics 8–9
welfare see social welfare policies

Welfare Branch 202
Wentworth, WC 202
Wentworth Group of Concerned
    Scientists 214
Wesley Vale, Tas. 223
Western Australia 43, 107, 175
Western Australian Farmers Federation
    161
West Papua 253
Whalan, Jeff 37
whaling 221
Wheat Export Authority 25–26, 159–60
Wheat Export Marketing Alliance 161
Wheat Export Marketing Consultation
    Committee 160
wheat marketing (oil-for-food scandal)
    25–26, 40, 157–61
    see also Cole Inquiry
    export monopoly ('single desk')
        arrangements 157, 160–61, 162,
        163, 165
    Senate estimates questions 85
Wheat Marketing Act 1989 review 165
Wheat Marketing Authority 40
Wheat Marketing Commission 40
whistleblowers 128
white papers
    Australian aid 257
    energy 218
Whitlam, Gough 123
Whitlam government 89, 109
whole-of-government strategy 16–22,
43–44
    Indigenous affairs 188–89
    poverty alleviation 165
wind farms 210–11
women, in workforce 172, 173, 174
work see employment
Work Choices 137–38, 169, 177–81,
    264
    ALP response 182–84
    High Court decision 98–99, 101
    limits on Senate debate 80–81
working hours 175–76, 178
    full-time/part-time 172, 173, 174
Workplace Authority 39, 42, 180
workplace bargaining 174–76, 184
    see also Australian Workplace
        Agreements
Workplace Ombudsman 180–81
workplace relations see industrial
    relations
Workplace Relations Act 1966 177, 181
*Workplace Relations Amendment (A
    Stronger Safety Net) Act 2007*
    180
*Workplace Relations Amendment (Work
    Choices) Act 2005* see Work
    Choices

young people, employment of 172,
    173, 174

Zoellick, Bob 257